SWEET WATER AND BITTER

Siân Rees was born and brought up in Cornwall.
She read Modern History at Oxford, has travelled
widely and now lives in Brighton with her two
sons. Her previous books include the bestselling
The Floating Brothel, *The Shadows of Eliza Lynch*,
and *The Ship Thieves*.

SIÂN REES

Sweet Water and Bitter

The Ships that Stopped the Slave Trade

VINTAGE BOOKS
London

Published by Vintage 2010

2 4 6 8 10 9 7 5 3 1

First published in Great Britain in 2009 by
Chatto & Windus

Vintage
Random House, 20 Vauxhall Bridge Road,
London SW1V 2SA

www.vintage-books.co.uk

Addresses for companies within The Random House Group
Limited can be found at:
www.randomhouse.co.uk/offices.htm

The Random House Group Limited Reg. No. 954009

A CIP catalogue record for this book
is available from the British Library

ISBN 9781845951177

The Random House Group Limited supports the Forest
Stewardship Council (FSC), the leading international forest
certification organisation. All our titles that are printed on
Greenpeace-approved FSC-certified paper carry the FSC logo.
Our paper procurement policy can be found at
www.rbooks.co.uk/environment

Typeset by Palimpsest Book Production Limited,
Grangemouth, Stirlingshire

Printed and bound in Great Britain by
CPI Bookmarque, Croydon CR0 4TD

To procure an eminent good by means that are unlawful is as little conso-
nant to private morality as to public justice. Obtain the concurrence of
other nations, if you can, by application, by remonstrance, by example, by
every peaceable instrument which man can employ to attract the consent
of man. But a nation is not justified in assuming rights that do not belong
to her merely because she means to apply them to a laudable purpose; nor
in setting out upon a moral crusade of converting other nations by acts of
unlawful force. Nor is it to be argued, that because other nations approve
the ultimate purpose, they must therefore submit to every measure which
any one state or its subjects may inconsiderately adopt for its attainment.

Sir William Scott, Admiralty Judge,
Dodson's Admiralty Reports, 1817

Contents

List of Illustrations

Acknowledgements

I am grateful to the National Maritime Museum, the Royal Naval Museum and the Plymouth and West Devon Record Office for allowing me to quote from documents in their possession. Staff at the National Archive have, as always, been informative, helpful and efficient. My thanks also to C. Herbert Gilliland for allowing me to quote from his article '"Some More Wine, Captain Bell?": An Abolitionist Naval Officer and Theodore Canot on the African Coast' (Historic Naval Ships Association, Conference Papers, 2004). Thanks also to my friends Tristan Palmer, Richard Heaton, Nicholas Whitehead and Thomas Whitehead; to Ewelina Krawiec, without whom my London Days would not have been possible; and in particular to my editor, Jenny Uglow.

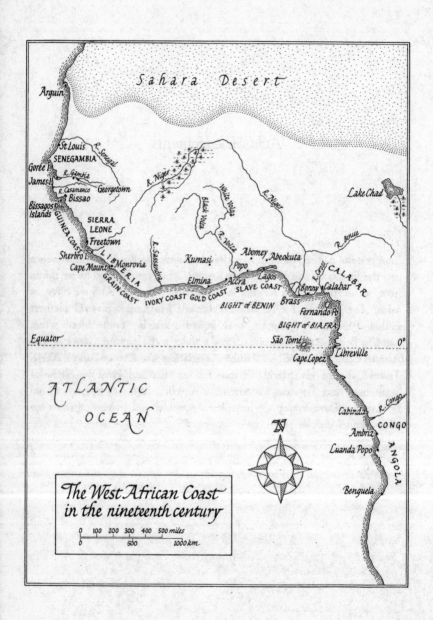

The West African Coast in the nineteenth century

Prologue

In 1817, the radical West African cleric and warrior Usman dan Fodio swept through present-day Nigeria in a maelstrom of jihad and plunder, promising freedom to the slaves who joined his holy army. From the imperial capital of Sokoto, his raiders attacked villages, killed the useless old and sold the rest along the dense, sticky web of slave-trails which bound African to African, family to family, village to village. Some went north across the deserts, some east into the heart of the continent, others south to the sea, sold halter to halter and market to market by traders of a dozen peoples at ceaseless war, sometimes slaving, sometimes enslaved.

One boy caught up in the wars was Ali Eisami, waylaid with a friend in Borno country. Seven men 'seized us', he would remember many years later, 'tied our hands upon our backs, fettered us, put us in the way and then we went til it became day'.[1] He was sold on three times in six months: first to a Hausa; then to a man of the Borgawa people; and lastly to a Yoruba from the west bank of the Niger, who took him to Porto Novo* on the Slave Coast. Here he was chained to a post on the floor of a dim pen which his new owners called a barracoon. More slaves were brought in, speaking different languages and calling on different gods, until there were seven hundred to be roped together and marched to the beach. There they were delivered up to a foreign captain.

*   Ali Eisami knew it as 'Ajashe'.

1

The ship was anchored beyond the breakers, and the slaves went out in great canoes, forty at a time propelled through the tumbling surf by skilled African oarsmen. They were stowed below, naked and ironed one to the next, spoon-fashion on their sides, for there was no room to sit upright. Days passed with no wind and the slave-deck was fetid and awash. They were allowed only briefly on deck, where some walked and others lay, their limbs too cramped to support them, watched by two Hausa who spoke the white men's language. 'All the oldest died of thirst', Ali Eisami said, 'for there was no water. Every morning, they had to take many, and throw them into the water.' At sea at last, with wind in the sails and sharks in their wake, those who were able climbed on deck and 'beheld the sky in the midst of the water'.

As sailors worked calmly around and above them, Eisami strained his eyes towards the horizon, 'saw something far away, like trees', and said to the Hausa overseer, '"I see a forest yonder, far away". Whereupon he said to me, "Show it to me with your finger!" When I had shown it to him, and he had seen the place at which my finger pointed, he ran to one of the white men', and all was suddenly action, with the captain shouting and the sailors running to the 'big big guns with powder and their very large iron'.

'Why do the white men prepare their guns?' Eisami asked, and the Hausa 'said to us, "what you saw were not trees, but a vessel of war is coming towards us." We did not believe it, and said, "We have never seen any one make war in the midst of water," and, after waiting a little, it came.'

The slave-ship fired nine times but the stranger kept her course and fired back. The mainmast fell with a whistle and a crash and there was panic on deck. 'The white men with us', said Eisami, 'ran to the bottom of the vessel and hid themselves.' The other ship rammed her way alongside and shouting men came over the rails with cutlasses in their hands. 'They called all of us', Eisami would remember,

and when we formed a line, and stood up in one place, they counted us, and said, 'Sit down!' So we sat down and they took off all the fetters from our feet, and threw them into the water, and they gave us clothes that we might cover our nakedness, and we also ate food, till we had enough. In the evening, they brought drums, and gave them to us, so that we played till it was morning. We said 'Now our Lord has taken us out of slavery,' and thanked him.

Remasted, with a different officer in command and a different flag flying above, the ship went about to head north through heavy air. Their new destination was Freetown, Sierra Leone, for Eisami had been liberated not by Allah, but by the British Royal Navy.

There is an expectation in our guilt-ridden times that any story involving Britain, Africa and the nineteenth century must be one of wicked imperialism. This is not one of those stories. This is a story of goodwill, force, opportunism and unintended consequences.

On 25 March 1807, with the country hanging on every word of a prolonged and furious debate, the British Parliament passed an Act for the Abolition of the Slave Trade. The last legal British slave-ship left Africa in October of that year, British slavers began to abandon the west coast of Africa and slave-ships ceased to fly the British flag. It was a great achievement. Britain had been the largest transatlantic carrier of slavers in the eighteenth century and the trade's profits had reached virtually every part of British society. Many in Britain had opposed the Abolition Act, partly from self-interest but also because they knew it would not end the slave trade, but merely bar British merchants from taking their share of its profits. Slaving was one of the world's most lucrative businesses and a vast international network fed from it: the shipwrights of Baltimore, Nantes, Cadiz and Liverpool; the manufacturers of 'trade goods' in Manchester; the capitalists of the City of London; seamen of a dozen nationalities and merchants of all degrees: from the richest in New York, Rio, Havana and Paris down to the corner-shop grocers selling cheap sugar in screws of brown paper. These people would not abandon their livelihoods merely because the British Parliament said they must. When the Napoleonic Wars ended in 1815, freeing seamen and ships across the world, a reinvigorated slave trade burst out along the West African coast and soon more slaves were crossing the Atlantic than ever before.

British abolitionists persevered. In 1811, the first step was taken towards internationalising the abolition campaign when the ruler of Portugal was induced to sign a treaty limiting his country's participation in the 'vile traffic'. Other countries soon signed similar agreements, but when they were routinely broken, ignored or abandoned, it became clear they would have to be backed by muscle. In 1819, the Royal Naval 'Preventive Squadron' was created to supply it.

The Royal Navy was the world's most powerful fleet: this was the century that Britain ruled the waves. 'Soon', said the London *Times*, as the first seven ships left for West Africa, 'we shall hear no more of the slave trade.' It was wrong. Like the legislators who authorised the new squadron's activities, the diplomats who dictated its terms of engagement, and the Admiralty which provided its resources, the *Times* had not grasped the challenges it would face. Few had predicted that the Squadron would be resisted with such violence by those who broke the treaties and continued to visit the slaving coasts, or that the Africans who sold them their slaves would show such hostility to abolition. The men of the Squadron had not only to patrol an uncharted three-thousand-mile coast, dogged by fever which killed more efficiently than the slavers' guns; but to persuade, bludgeon or bribe African communities, which had lived from slaving for generations, to abolish it, and to keep away their customers: slave-ships of many nations, better financed, better armed and better manned than they, ruthless in their methods and contemptuous of life. There would be countless attempts to smear their work as a cloak for commercial expansion, and the Squadron as nothing but the brutish tool of imperialism. There would be times when even the British government faltered in its support, and almost gave up. Far from soon hearing nothing of the slave trade, the *Times* was still reporting on the Squadron's attempts to suppress it five decades later.

The 1820s and 1830s were years of action and excitement, with bounty earned and reputations made. Seamen patrolled indefatigably, the Admiralty sent out more and more ships but the Foreign Office struggled to wring meaningful agreements from its diplomatic partners. As each treaty came into force, loopholes were discovered and exploited, and interested lawyers subverted the work of seamen who fought and died to bring slaver-captains to court: detained ships were released under technicalities, rescued slaves were ordered re-embarked and naval officers were sued for damages. The smaller carriers gave up first. The flags of Holland, Denmark and Sweden disappeared during the 1820s, and even France, a tenacious carrier through the 1820s, renounced the trade the following decade. In 1835 and 1839, the first great diplomatic blows were struck against Spain and Portugal, whose ships supplied the rapacious slave-worked plantations of Cuba and Brazil.

Even these, however, were subverted by American and Brazilian ships which took up the trade in their stead.

Frustrated by legal challenges to their aggressive slaver-chasing at sea, a few astute naval officers changed the Squadron's strategy in the 1840s. They were backed by one of Britain's greatest, crustiest, most xenophobic statesmen, Lord Palmerston, who was also one of the country's most determined abolitionists. With his approval, the Squadron's officers began to turn their gaze inland. If treaties with those who took slaves away seemed unworkable, then treaties must be made with those who supplied them. As the nineteenth-century 'opening-up' of Africa began, the envoys of abolition, with Squadron officers at the forefront, found themselves treading the same path as explorers, missionaries and traders. Slave-broking dynasties along the west coast of Africa and their inland suppliers were subjected to the same regime of diplomacy and threat as had been applied to their customers. By the end of the 1860s, even the richest and most powerful of the African slavers had succumbed to force, bribery or persuasion, induced to replace the slave trade with 'legitimate commerce'. Those who refused had been crushed.

The reasons for the deployment of the Preventive Squadron were contentious then, and have remained contentious since. The nineteenth-century historian W.E.H. Lecky, who saw Britain's place in the world very differently to us, famously wrote of the naval campaign as 'among the three or four perfectly virtuous pages . . . in the history of nations'. This view was challenged in 1944 by the Marxist theories of Dr Eric Williams, who insisted that had the capitalists of nineteenth-century Britain not gained more than they lost from abolition, then the slave trade would have continued. During the bicentenary of the Act in 2007, abolition was discussed within the framework of our current obsessions: attribution of responsibility and blame; demand for apology and compensation. This story encompasses many countries, many seas and a vast cast of characters: virtuous and not-so-virtuous naval officers; ruthless slavers, decadent slavers, pathetic slavers dying of fever in lonely compounds; statesmen and colonial officials; reverends and pastors, soldiers and sailors, liberated slaves of a hundred different origins; self-promoters and opportunists, idealists, people of courage and cowards. They illuminate the complexity of the politics behind abolition, and how its realities were experienced by men at the sharp end of the long campaign: those making arduous patrols on a hostile, malarial coast, risking their lives to board ships crewed by armed and violent outcasts, living on hard biscuit and rum from which the cockroaches had to be filtered; longing for home but determined to find enjoyment in the most unpromising of circumstances; inflexibly xenophobic, unthinkingly racist yet dying in their thousands to save individuals with whom they had nothing in common but humanity.

1

Black Bounty

When news that Britain had abolished the slave trade reached the West African coast in 1807, it was met by African slave-brokers with baffled hostility. The British captain Captain Hugh 'Mind-Your-Eye' Crow left Liverpool on 22 July 1807 in the slave-ship *Kitty's Amelia*, guns ready for action in case he fell in with a Frenchman at sea. Reaching the River Bonny* in September, he found a dozen British ships queuing among the mangroves, waiting for slaves. Captain Crow was an old hand in the 'Guinea trade' and a friend of the African middlemen who sold him his slaves. Usually they met him with gifts and finger-cracking bonhomie but this time he found them worried, for there had been reports that the British slavers would soon stop buying. 'My friend King Holiday', Crow recorded, 'repaired on board as soon as we arrived, to inquire if the intelligence were true.'[1] Alas for the shipmasters of Liverpool and the slave-suppliers of West Africa, it was. The damned abolitionists, Crow told his friends, had won their campaign and the slave trade had been outlawed. No British ships had been permitted to fit out for a slave-cargo since May and from January 1808, any Briton found involved in slaving would lose his vessel and be fined £100 for each slave discovered aboard.

The Bonny chiefs were infuriated. Why should a foreign government interfere in a trade sanctioned by custom, religion and profit? King Pepple declared

*In present-day Nigeria.

7

'he would seize all the British ships' at his slave-wharves in revenge and Captain Crow sympathised. It was his 'decided opinion' that 'the traffic in Negroes is permitted by that Providence that rules over all, as a necessary evil and that it ought not to have been done away with to humour the folly or the fancy of a set of people who knew little or nothing about the subject'. King Holiday was more optimistic than King Pepple, for he, like Captain Crow, saw the hand of a greater power in the trade which had brought him so much money. '"We tink trade no stop" he said' – the rendition of his speech was Crow's – '"for all we Jew-Jew man [ju-ju men, or priests] tell we so, for dem say you country no can niber pass God A'mighty".' If God Almighty approved of slaving, then Brother King George in London could not stop it.

'I at length', Captain Crow recalled, 'sailed for the last time from Bonny, where I had, on successive voyages, met with so much kindness and hospitality.' The last four legal British slave-ships ever to leave Africa sailed from the Sierra Leone river in October 1807 with 1,100 Negroes in their holds, escorted by a Royal Naval frigate lest enemy vessels attack on sea-routes made unsafe by war. It was the last time British warships protected slavers. From January, they would be hunting them down instead.

On 1 January 1808, Captain Frederick Parker of the Royal Navy stood outside St George's Church in the flyblown, rudimentary village of Freetown, Sierra Leone. His ship, HMS *Derwent*, was anchored in the river below. It was not an attractive place.

Sailing south-east from the islands of Cape Verde, the men aboard smelt the limes first: that deceptively beautiful scent which wafts from the west coast of Africa before any dim outline of land appears. It grew stronger as the coast took shape, a long fringe of green with mountains rising sheer inland, hazy azure shapes obscured by what sailors called the 'smokes': floating, reddish dust which blows from the deserts and hangs in the air far out to sea. As they passed Cape Sierra Leone and turned upriver, the scent grew stronger but by then its charm had dissipated in the squalor now visible to either side. 'On the right of the town', wrote one visitor, 'was a wood and a swamp; on the left the low bank of the river is frequently overflowed, and a swamp was inevitable; and behind these . . . was a swamp.'[2] Mosquitoes attacked as the sea wind fell off and the crew saw shacks behind the beach, figures squatting on the sand, the smoke from small fires; beasts, dirt, fish bones, fruit skins, manure and flies. 'It was a picture of misery, poverty and meanness', wrote the same disappointed traveller. 'There was no cheering sight, no bustle, no activity, all seemed wretched, naked and disgusting . . . I never knew, nor ever heard mention of so villainous, sickly and miserable an abode, as Sierra Leone.' Few of the *Derwent's* crew were tempted to set foot ashore on a coast whose mortality was legend, but Captain Parker had duty to fulfil.

This small stretch on the edge of a vast and unknown continent was about to become a colony of the British Crown, and forward base of the abolition campaign. That was why Captain Parker was outside the church, wearing dress uniform beneath a biting sun, holding onto his bicorne hat lest the hot harmattan wind blow it away. He was here to represent George III. There was no imperial pomp. Sand whipped and coiled along dirt tracks and through compounds where the chickens ran and goats lifted their heads from rubbish. At ten o'clock, Thomas Ludlam, governor of the Sierra Leone Company, stepped forward and surrendered that company's charter to Captain Parker. Mr Ludlam was an abolitionist of pedigree, a familiar figure on the coast and a fighter for the Negro cause. He supported the British legislation which gave his African home, with this gesture, from private into state control. As the old company flag came down, the Union Jack went up and Mr Ludlam stepped back as governor on behalf of the British Crown. The cannon was fired and answered by a twenty-one-gun salute from the *Derwent* and the party proceeded thankfully to the shade of Fort Thornton for refreshments, their white stockings blotched where the mosquitoes had bitten.

For twenty years, this unpromising strip of mountain, mangrove and malarial coast had been owned by British investors. In 1787, the abolitionist Granville Sharpe had bought 20 square miles from a Temne chief and 411 apprehensive people had disembarked a British ship to pitch their tents beyond the beach.* They were a disparate group: former American slaves who had fought for Britain in the American War of Independence and been promised freedom if they joined the army; black seamen stranded in British cities and the white women they had married; a priest, teachers, surgeons and artisans. Here, surrounded by the operations of the slave trade, they were to establish Granville Town, the world's first settlement for freed slaves. It was a noble experiment but it sank beneath disease, hunger, rain, local hostility and the weight of its own contradictions.

---

* In keeping with the practice of the period, imperial measures are given throughout the book. A close conversion would be: 10 miles = 16 kilometres; 6 feet = 1.8 metres; 10lb = 4.8 kilos.

When Granville Sharpe decided upon this spot to 'repatriate' the 'Poor Blacks', one freed slave living in London had foreseen trouble. 'Is it possible', asked Ottobah Cugoano, biblically, 'that a fountain should send forth both sweet water and bitter?'

The answer was no. This had been slaving country for over three hundred years. Within sight of the tiny, anomalous new settlement were estuaries and creeks where slaves brought from the interior were sold. Over the eastern hills, slave-catching and slave-making tribes formed their caravans or 'coffles' for the long seaward march. On offshore islands to north and south, whole villages lived from servicing ships which called en route to the slaving rivers. Slave-brokers had founded dynasties here, and developed vast commercial networks stretching across the seas to the white empires which consumed their slaves, and down long, complex routes inland to the black empires which supplied them.

To the north, the banks, islands and tributaries of the Sierra Leone, Pongas and Nuñez rivers, interconnected by a dense and mysterious system of waterways, were studded with 'factories', as the slave-broking establishments were known. Some were a few ramshackle huts where a hopeful bachelor had set up a small depot. Others were townships where the counting house handled thousands of pounds, vessels queued at the wharves, hundreds of slaves were penned in the barracoons and the factor lived in luxury. Powerful African middlemen had dominated these rivers for generations, interbreeding with the foreigners who came to buy. Some claimed British blood and nationality, others French, Spanish, American or Portuguese. The Fulani and Mandingo peoples brought their slaves to these middlemen: some in mile-long caravans owned by powerful chiefs; others in twos and threes, brought by petty merchants from communities so saturated in the trade that 'where three men were together', the buyers said, 'and you offered two of them a bribe of salt, you might be sure of the third'.[3]

Further north were the Bissagos archipelago and the sandy labyrinths of the rivers Bissao, Cacheo and Casamanca, where the slave-ships were Portuguese. Further north again were the Gambia and the island of Goree,[4] where Afro-French families sold slaves to work the plantations of the French Caribbean. To the south were the islands of the slow-moving Gallinas estuary,[5] then the scattered villages of Shebar, Sherbro, Cape Mount[6] and Sester. In all these places, slaving had long replaced any other trade, its profits shared by brokers of all colours and all mixtures of colour. For two thousand miles south of Sester, slaving was the main, often the only, commerce. British, Spanish, French, Portuguese, Danish, Swedish, Catalan, Italian and American slave-traders swarmed along the great inward-curving bulge of the Gulf of Guinea and the monotonous, surfbound sweep of beach to the south. Out of sight, beyond the mangroves and the palms, in the interior which no white person knew, the Fulbe and Hausa fought for empire and Allah, with slave-coffles the product of their wars.

In this lonely and exposed position, encircled by hostility and inadequately prepared, Granville Town collapsed. Slave-catchers raided the town and sold their pickings to nearby brokers, and what was worse, several settlers sidled away to work with them. One, Harry Demane, had been lashed to the mast of a slave-ship about to leave the River Thames when Granville Sharpe personally intervened to save him in 1786. He had taken Demane before a London magistrate who forbade his West Indian owner to remove him from Britain, effectively liberating him from slavery, for slavery was not recognised on British soil. When Sharpe heard that even Harry Demane had deserted Granville Town to become a 'dealer in men', he despaired. In 1791, the town was destroyed by local tribes. White slave-traders grudgingly rescued the terrified settlers who fled to islands in the river, but Granville Town was dead.

The colony, and the dream, were resuscitated by the Sierra Leone Company of London, whose directors – stern City men of charity and enterprise – knew that if the settlers were to survive other than by selling each other, they must be given the means to make a legal living. That meant not the dull grind of agriculture, but the greater incentive of commerce. The Company financed and organised a rescue mission to find the settlers and rebuild the town but it was a felicitous influx from a different continent which guaranteed the colony's survival. Some of the American slaves who had fled to British lines and fought their former masters in 1777 had fled onwards to Canada when white Americans won independence and returned the blacks to slavery. The promised land had not materialised north of the border and in January 1792, 1,196 Nova Scotian blacks left for the African 'homeland' which many had never seen. The brave new village of Freetown rose in the ashes of Granville Town. In 1800, Settlers and Nova Scotians were joined by several hundred Maroons, former slaves from Jamaica. By 1807, the population had reached two thousand and the colony looked likely to survive.

Freetown was stronger than Granville Town but bitter waters still flowed all around it. Traders, settlers, artisans and even missionaries came with good intentions, but many were disappointed by hardship and corrupted by poverty, and slipped away to join the slavers. In Freetown, virtue might buy a dirt farm or a small store on the wharf where few ships unloaded. Out on the slaving rivers, vice bought idleness, prestige and wealth and the story of Harry Demane repeated itself time and again. The question discussed over tea at Fort Thornton in January 1808 was this: would the transfer of this troubled colony to the Crown, with all its resources of deterrence and enforcement, make the bitter waters too unpalatable?

The moment seemed propitious. The Napoleonic Wars were being fought across the globe. Crews and ships of the French, Spanish, Portuguese and Dutch slaving fleets had been absorbed into their national navies. Denmark had banned the trade in 1792, and America in 1807, so Danish and American ships were expected to disappear from slaving waters. As for the African suppliers, one travelling British merchant wrote to the *Sierra Leone Gazette* that 'the coastal people' were planning to 'open up trading routes to the interior to bring in cattle, cotton-cloths and camwood'[7] to replace the caravans of slaves. Up the coast, where the British Royal African Corps garrisoned the formerly French island of Goree, a report came that one 'powerful local Chief . . . regret[ted] the abolition himself, as being the means of depriving him of considerable emoluments' but 'intended, as he knew many other natives did, to attend as much as possible to cultivation, particularly cotton'.[8]

An amnesty was offered in the new Crown colony. 'In consequence of the changes', announced Governor Ludlam, 'which have lately taken place . . . all who have been engaged in the slave trade but are now desirous to quit it, [may] return to this Colony at any time within three months of this date without being liable to any prosecution on account of past events.'[9] Some responded. One was Afro-Briton William Savage, born in England to an African father and English mother, who came to Freetown as schoolmaster but was seduced by the trade and slunk away to the bush. Another was Hector Peters of Charleston, who had played French horn for a British regiment during the American War of Independence and had crossed the ocean but also fallen into slaving. A few repentant others arrived from the villages just over the British colonial border. But the larger, longer-established brokers – even the many who claimed British nationality – did not answer Governor Ludlam's call. They waited to see whether Liverpool, New York and Havana would follow London's change of heart.

John Ormond, the largest slaver on the River Pongas, had no intention of renouncing the trade he ran so profitably from Bangalang, his town at the head of the river. 'Mongo John'* was son of a Susu mother and a father who was Liverpudlian, French, Italian or Scottish, depending on who was telling the story. He had learnt English at school in England, educated there in the days when his family's trade was no less respectable than that in sugar or tea. Another Pongas broker claiming British nationality was Samuel Samo. Asked by a merchant captain 'whether he did not intend to become an American on consequence of the Abolition Act', Samo replied 'that he was born an Englishman and would never deny his country for the sake of his interest'.[10] He was nonetheless determined to break its new law. Then there was Sebastian Pearce and his father John – a mulatto,† whose trade was based on the River Nuñez. The Anglophone prince of New Sester, who had learnt his English working aboard British slave-ships, had also resolved to continue and the Curtis brothers – mixed-race, American-born but of British nationality – would carry on trading on the River Pongas. So would the enigmatic, feral Tucker clan in Sherbro, thought to be descended from a Bristol seaman, who processed hundreds, sometimes thousands, of slaves from their wharves and knew no other trade.

Despite the fighting in which Europe and its colonies were embroiled, it was soon clear that the customers would keep coming: the Portuguese from Brazil, the Spanish from Cuba and Puerto Rico, the French, Dutch and Swedish from their Caribbean islands, where slave-worked plantations funded the mother countries' wars. Some Americans and Danes, too, continued to moor at their wharves to bargain for their 'bales', 'mules', 'mahogany logs' or whatever other nod towards deception had been made to the customs officers who authorised their outward voyages. So did a few British. Captain Crow might, with bad grace, have renounced slaving but others had not.

Government, judiciary and navy were feeling their way into a new era. It was clear new resources would have to be deployed to try slavers determined to break the law, to condemn their ships and to rescue any slaves found aboard them. The earliest provisions made to enforce abolition legislation were clumsy and would cause endless unforeseen problems to those

---

* 'Mongo' being a local word for 'chief'.

† The usual term of the time for 'mixed-race'.

attempting to implement them. The illegal slave trade had resources far greater than the British ships and British courts pitted against it. The first colonial officials and naval officers sent to police abolition were to find themselves struggling against an avalanche of entrenched interests and legal uncertainties.

Sierra Leone had been chosen as the logical place of resettlement or transit for 'Recaptives', as slaves rescued from illegal slave-ships were first known. They could live in Freetown and on the little plots of worked land which had begun to spread up the mountain behind. Colonial government and the Anglican Church would teach them the alphabet, the Word of God, the use of the plough, decency in dress and the abolitionist message. The Royal Navy would be responsible for finding them, rescuing them and bringing them in. Many naval men found this abrupt shift in focus unnatural and unwelcome.

During the debates leading up to the Abolition Act, the British slave trade had often been defended as a 'nursery for seamen'. Without it, the argument ran, the country would lose the pool of skilled labour which poured into the navy when required for national defence. There were few warships in 1807 on which no seaman had previously served aboard a slaver: it was simply part of most seamen's past, and, until recently, nobody had thought much about it. There had been some horrible cases of cruelty, which had galvanised the abolitionist campaign, but the treatment of slaves on most slave-ships was not, it was claimed, wilfully cruel: there was no reason for it to be. Some sailors had been shocked at contact with badly run ships while a few had seen plantation life at the end of the voyage and realised the hell to which their human cargo was destined on arrival. Few, however, saw the West Indian colonies beyond the inns and brothels of the ports and of those who had, some nonetheless thought it preferable to what the slaves had come from. One sailor, who visited Africa as a young man, later lived in the Caribbean and still thought slavery a boon. 'To give any idea of the mode of living amongst the blacks of the African coast', he wrote,

> would be a waste of time. Imagination cannot picture people more purely in the state of nature than the poor half starved naked Negro . . . It is a life of continual slavery even in his own country, and should his tribe be invaded, and himself made prisoner, it merely makes his situation about two degrees more dreadful, with all the chance of being

benefited hereafter, for should he be sold again to those who traffic in human flesh . . . and survive the sea voyage, he becomes in the west a slave it is true, but a man, and not a brute; his mind is by degrees enlightened, he has his hut and garden, a doctor if he is ill and food if he is hungry.[11]

The sailors of the last legal British slave-convoy in 1807 had seen 'a caravan of 40 famished slaves' brought into the factory, who, their mulatto overseer explained, were 'mainly pledged for rice'. It was a common practice among the poor. A relative was temporarily handed over in exchange for food, and if payment could not be made within a specified time to redeem the person, he or she became forfeit as a slave. 'A black woman', wrote Captain Hoffman of the Royal Navy escort, 'offered me her son, a boy of about 11 years of age, for a cobb – about four [shillings] and sixpence.'[12] The men who saw such evidence of hunger and the apparent indifference of kith and kin in Africa thought life in America or the West Indies, even as slaves, must be better than this.

Some in the navy went further than even this resignation or indifference. Abolition had never gained universal assent in British society. It had dealt a vicious blow at too many interests: the merchant houses, the shipbrokers, the insurers, the outfitters, suppliers, chandlers, innkeepers and all the others who were paid in slaving dollars in the ports of western England; the manufacturers of the trade goods and the warehouse keepers and retailers who stored them or sold them on; the hundreds of thousands of small investors who had a direct or indirect stake in the wealth of the British West Indies. Many young men in the navy relied indirectly on a slave-worked plantation for their income and connections. Jane Austen, sister of two sailor brothers and goddaughter of a West Indian planter, described their awkward situation in *Mansfield Park*. Sir Thomas Bertram, benefactor to the heroine, Fanny Price, returns from his Antigua plantations to be innocently asked about abolition. The question is received in 'a dead silence'. Without the Bertram plantations, how is the civilisation of life at Mansfield Park to be maintained? And where is Fanny's brother William, a 'poor scrubby midshipman', to find the influence necessary to lift him through the ranks if Sir Thomas's slave-supported income no longer gives him social and financial clout?

Despite its pockets of ambivalence, however, the Royal Navy was the only force which could police the new legislation. For the law-makers who framed the 1807 Act, the slave trade was seaborne – a matter of carrying slaves away from Africa. Nothing was said about the trade in slaves before they arrived at the coast, as almost nothing was known about it. Few Europeans had penetrated the continent to see its operations. 'All Ships and Vessels,' the Act therefore stated, 'Slaves or Natives of Africa, carried, conveyed, or dealt with as Slaves, and all other Goods and Effects that shall or may become forefeited for any Offence committed against this Act, shall and may be seized by any Officer of His Majesty's Customs or Excise, or by the Commanders or Officers of any of His Majesty's Ships or Vessels of War.' No ships could be spared in those years of war solely to hunt down illegal British slavers, nor was any such dedicated anti-slave-trade posse thought necessary. The navy was already busy sniffing out mutineers, pirates, smugglers, blockade-runners and deserters. Now it would add slavers to its list, the additional duty sweetened by the promise of extremely – in fact, unsustainably – generous head-money:

> The Sum of Forty Pounds lawful Money of Great Britain for every Man, or Thirty Pounds of like Money for every Woman, or Ten Pounds of like Money for every Child or Person not above Fourteen Years old, that shall be so taken and condemned, and shall be delivered over in good Health to the proper Officer or Officers, Civil or Military, so appointed as aforesaid to receive, protect, and provide for the same; which Bounties shall be divided amongst the Officers, Seamen, Marines, and Soldiers on Board His Majesty's Ships of War, or hired armed Ships.

On 15 January 1808, HMS *Derwent* left Freetown on the first Royal Naval cruise of the new era. She headed north into the slaving waters of the River Pongas, Senegal and Cape Verde, checking all 'strange sails', exchanging signals, firing a gun in command to heave to, boarding where the other obeyed, chasing where she did not. It was routine war work. They provisioned and wooded in the Pongas but did not sail far enough upstream to find the slavers anchored off Mongo John's wharves. But off Cape Verde, at the northern end of the slaving coast, the man at the masthead shouted 'Sail!' and Captain Parker detained two American schooners, breaking their own country's law by carrying 167 slaves. A 'prize-crew' consisting of a *Derwent* officer and a handful of men went aboard each schooner to navigate them back to Freetown. These Recaptives, released from American holds to stumble up the beaches into Freetown, were the first beneficiaries of the new British legislation. They can have had little idea where they were and less as to why they were there. These people were now the responsibility of Governor Thomas Ludlam but he was almost as bewildered as they.

The Act had left unclear what exactly colonial officials were to do with the Africans being offloaded into their care. Were they to be returned to their old lives? Were they to be provided with new ones and protected from re-enslavement? Where would the money to support them come from? No instructions for their disposal had been given; nor had funds been made available for their maintenance: for housing, medicine, education, regulation, law enforcement and everything else required to run a civil society. The Act had provided for a Vice-Admiralty court to be established in Freetown to try captains of slave-ships, but no judge had yet been appointed to try the angry Americans detained in Governor Ludlam's gaol, or to arrange the auction of their ships if condemned and payment of bounty to the men of the *Derwent*. Until one arrived, Ludlam appointed his old friend, Alexander Smith, formerly storekeeper for the Sierra Leone Company, who brought to his new job negligible knowledge of the courtroom but a great deal of retail expertise.

The 1807 Abolition Act had left many such practical threads hanging, not least the exact status of Recaptives. The language of the Act had been borrowed from traditional naval duty. When a warship captured an enemy at sea in wartime, the enemy ship and her cargo were prize. The legality of the detention, if contested, was determined by an Admiralty court, after which the prize became forfeit to the British Crown, which paid bounty – or 'prize-money' – to the men of the ship that had taken her. When legislators came to frame the new abolitionist duties of detection, emancipation and trial, they had fallen back on the traditional terms of chase, bounty and forfeiture. Suspected slavers had been given enemy status and rescued slaves were the prize. This was to cause many later difficulties.

Clause VII of the Abolition Act, describing 'in what manner such Slaves or natives of Africa shall be hereafter treated and disposed of', had implicitly defined emancipation as the transfer of subjection to the British Crown, with all its habits and agencies of authority, although this change in their status was 'for the Purpose only of divesting and bearing all other Property, Right, Title, or Interest whatever, which before existed, or might afterwards be set up or claimed in or to' them by the slavers from whom they had been rescued; 'in no case should liberated Africans be liable to be sold, disposed of, treated or dealt with as Slaves'. For Governor Ludlam, trying to find out what the Act actually wanted him to do with the 167 blacks camped miserably on the beach, the salient point was that 'His Majesty's officers' were entitled 'to enter and enlist the same, or any of them, into His Majesty's Land or Sea Service, as Soldiers, Seamen, or Marines, or to bind the same, or any of them, whether of full Age or not, as Apprentices, for any Term not exceeding Fourteen Years'.

Ludlam therefore enlisted forty of the 'ablest men' into the colonial militia – the French had been seen cruising off Freetown – and Alexander Smith briskly disposed of the remaining eighteen men, fourteen women and ninety-five children by selling them into 'apprenticeships'. The court charged $20 to any householder or tradesman who would take an 'apprentice' off the colonial government's hands and the men of the *Derwent* were paid their bounty from the money raised. It got the blacks off the beach, housed, fed and clothed them, and it is difficult to see what Ludlam could have otherwise done. Indeed, his solution would have presented itself to most colonial officials. Indentured labour had populated much of the New World, with the blessing of both colonising governments and colonists seeking cheap muscle to work their new land. Moreover, the limited 'freedom' Ludlam had inferred from the Act was that long accepted by other, older British subjects: inhabitants of poorhouses were sold into apprenticeships and the *Derwent* had impressed eight men from merchant ships on her voyage to Africa, their consent deemed unnecessary.

Nobly born the Crown's newest colony might be, but it had been conceived in stained sheets. Governor Ludlam, Alexander Smith, their old company colleagues, the two thousand white, black and mixed-race people with whom they shared Freetown, the Royal Navy and even the legislators of Parliament all brought to the new era the mindset of the old. As law-makers had described the slaves not as victims of trafficking, but as potential prize, so Alexander Smith saw not a court, but an auction-house and store and Ludlam saw not free individuals, but a colonial work-force. It brought trouble. Not nearly as much, however, as the other unprovided-for fact: that the slavers just brought in were not British, but American. British officials had no right to police the citizens of other countries outside British soil, and those who supported the slave trade in Madrid, Lisbon, Paris and Washington knew this. Ships' captains and the

British government were about to find themselves involved in some tedious and costly challenges.

'Nine tenths of the vessels, resorting to this coast for slaves from the Havannah', a later governor of Sierra Leone would explain to the Colonial Office[13] in London,

> are of American build and till the war with America (1812–14), had invariably some of the Citizens of the US on board, under the denomination of Supercargoes, Captains Assistants, Captains of Papers of Pilots, who were in truth part owners of the vessel. No transfer or Bill of sale from the American owner, to the ostensible Spanish one, is ever to be met with among their Papers, and in their Rolls of Equipage, we see men not even deigning to change their English names, attested by the signatures of the officers of His Catholic Majesty [i.e. the King of Spain], as natives of the different Provinces and Colonies of Spain. From the scenes of infamy and perjury which are frequently disclosed in the Vice-Admiralty court of this Colony, the Havannah seems rather a receptacle for the vagabonds and outlaws of Great Britain and North America, than a colony of Spain.[14]

The right of neutrals to engage in seaborne trade in times of war, whether that trade be in slaves or anything else, was already the subject of harsh dispute between Britain and North America. Washington was furious at the Royal Navy's practice during the Napoleonic Wars of detaining and searching American merchantmen to ensure they were not trading with the French and even more so at the impressment of British-born men found aboard them. With the *Derwent*'s detention of two Rhode Island slavers, the untested mechanism of abolition – with Governor Ludlam at its uncomfortably sharp end – was brought up against these old grievances. What, exactly, were the rights or duties of Governor Ludlam and the Royal Navy in enforcing other countries' legislation on those countries' subjects? Did abolition, with its overtones of morality and the ancient but vague idea of 'natural law' ('human rights' had not yet entered the lexicon), have any new bearing on this? America had abolished the slave trade, yes; but did America want to see her ships detained by the British navy and her subjects condemned by a British court for breaking American laws? Resoundingly, that rampantly

Anglophobe ex-colony did not. The capture of a string of American slave-ships brought international tempers to boiling-point.

International law, referred to as the 'law of nations', was a morass of un-codified and developing practice. Governor Ludlam had no qualms about condemning foreign slavers in British courts, but other British officials did. In December 1807, a British privateer took the American slaver *Amedie* off the West Indian island of Tortola. The case went before the British Vice-Admiralty court there, whose judge, unsure of his jurisdiction over foreign vessels, referred it to the Privy Council in London. The matter had to be addressed, for six other American captains had appealed the decisions of other British Admiralty courts and were waiting for their ships to be either condemned, or returned to them with compensation. In 1809, the Master of the Rolls – the third most senior judge in England – came to a very useful conclusion. The slave trade, he said, 'cannot abstractedly speaking, have a legitimate existence'. While Britain had

> no right to control any foreign legislature that may think fit to dissent from this doctrine, and to permit to its own subjects the prosecution of this trade . . . we [i.e. the British] now have a right to affirm that prima facie the trade is illegal and thus to throw on claimants the burden of proof that, in respect of them, by the authority of their own laws, it is otherwise.

As the *Amedie* was American, and America's own law banned slaving, 'there can be no right', the Master ruled, 'to restitution'. It was a blow against the slave trade but it was also a bounty-hunter's charter. Already Britain's declared motives for abolishing the slave trade were derided by other maritime nations who saw their merchant shipping being seized by British officers. The *Amedie* decision only bolstered the belief that the true purpose of abolition was disabling other countries' trade. Humanitarianism had little to do with it, they said; profit and plunder far more.

Governor Ludlam was relieved of his difficulties by the arrival in Freetown of two men who would have to grapple with the problems inherent in the Abolition Act. The first was a ponderous middle-aged barrister called Dr Thorpe, formerly chief judge of Prince Edward's Island, Nova Scotia. In 1808, he was appointed judge of the new Vice-Admiralty court in Freetown and was shocked by what he found. 'A Tradesman' (Alexander Smith), he wrote distastefully to the Colonial Office, 'had nominally presided in this Court, he condemned, he purchased the Cargo and then retailed it, the precedents were erroneous, the officers insufficient and dissatisfied, and the practice indecorous, as there was no Salary every thing was slovenly.'[15]

Judge Thorpe had taken on a difficult office with profoundly inadequate experience. 'I had read Civil Law merely as a Gentleman at College and had a little practice in the Ecclesiastical Court but none in the Admiralty,' he would later write to the Colonial Office, which largely left him to struggle alone. 'Before I left England, I endeavoured as far as I could, without instructions, to learn to what extent Your Lordships' political considerations with respect to America, Sweden, Spain and Portugal would allow me to act against them but was obliged to sail without instructions, documents or assistance of any sort.' As an abolitionist, his sympathy was with the naval effort to hunt down slavers. As a judge, he believed he had to defend the right of foreign nationals to continue the 'foul traffic', if the law of their own countries allowed this and they were trading outside British waters.

The other arrival was the young, febrile and already embittered Thomas Perronet Thompson, come to replace Ludlam as Governor. Both he and Judge Thorpe, unencumbered by experience of Sierra Leone, denounced the disposal of the *Derwent*'s Receptives and swore such methods would not be repeated. One of their first actions was to declare the 'direct or indirect Sale or Purchase' and 'supposed Apprenticeships' of the *Derwent* slaves null and void, in a public reproof to Ludlam and the ex-Company men who had run the new Crown Colony thus far. It was all fine and good in theory but when HMS *Derwent* returned from her next slaver-hunting cruise with another American prize and seventy-eight more 'Liberated Africans', as Governor Thompson rechristened them, there were still no funds from London for their settlement, nor instructions as to how 'political considerations' must govern Judge Thorpe's actions. Some of the children might be enrolled in the just-founded charity school and a few of the more competent adults be given plots of land to farm, but Governor Thompson was embarrassed to find that the only way he could provide for the rest was some version of the system he had said he would never adopt. As many had predicted, but no one seemed able to prevent, a nasty whiff of slavery began to re-emerge.

'Having established extensive connections among the native chieftains', announced Hawkins & Co. of Freetown, 'Brokers and African Agents', in the *Sierra Leone Gazette* of November 1809, they were 'ready to negotiate the redemption of any number of Natives of Africa on the lowest possible terms, for ready money only. Can procure on the shortest notice a couple of prime Negro fellows. Also available', the notice continued unpleasantly, were 'several likely Negro wenches fit for carrying a child or to live with a single gentleman.' Outside the premises of brokers Isaacs & Cohen, sales of 'indentures on prime new Africans' were taking place after slave-ships were brought in by warships and privateers, street-markets in flesh apparently little different to those of Cuba and Rio. A plantation-owner on Liberty Hill was offering $60 for the return of 'three new Negro fellows, named Sambo, Morris and Sadia' who had 'strayed or ran away'. 'To be disposed of by private contract', ran another advertisement that month, 'to religious masters only. The services of a number of Africans lately redeemed and landed . . . also the services of several Negro children who have been for some months in the colony, can say grace before and after meat. Gentlemen in the West Indies supplied with apprentices, on including certificate of their religious principles signed by two ministers.'

Hawkins, Isaacs and Cohen were white. The majority of their customers were black: Settlers, Nova Scotians, Maroons or the few Recaptives who had been given land, needed labour to work it and saw that labour coming up the beach behind them. One, Cato Freeman, placed an advertisement which could have come from any Virginian plantation.

Run Away: a prime negro fellow named Cupid . . . redeemed some months ago from a Swedish guinea-man [i.e. slaver] . . . ran away in consequence of a light whipping given to his wench. Also a well-made Negro wench named Pussey, with her 6-week-old child – calls herself Fatima and says she belongs to the other.[16]

Cupid and Fatima had probably been rescued from the Swedish schooner *Penel*, brought in by a British privateer in 1809: one of those who did not mind whether the prize was a Swedish slaver or a French merchantman, as long as it brought bounty. Sweden had not banned the slave trade and thus the *Penel* sailed legally from St Bartholomew's, a Swedish Caribbean island, commanded by a captain who had been born American but was now a naturalised Swede. In the River Pongas, this man had bought eighteen slaves from Samuel Samo, who had proudly put his Britishness over his 'interest'.

It was this same Britishness which rendered these eighteen slaves eligible for rescue. 'Goods purchased by neutrals', explained Judge Thorpe (Sweden being a neutral in Britain's war with France), 'from British subjects in opposition to the known laws of Great Britain' were 'liable to confiscation as long as they were amenable to British laws, or in other words as long as they were within the reach of a British cruiser'.* The Swede had also bought slaves from brokers who were not British and Judge Thorpe decided, with regret, that there was no legal way to rescue these people. This decision brought him into conflict with the Company men with whom he was already on bad terms, for where he decried their sloppy practice and lax way with indentures, they were outraged by his putting the letter of the law above its spirit. When Thorpe ordered that the unhappy slaves held ineligible for rescue be restored to the Swedish captain, an old Company lawyer appeared in court to 'pray their deliverance'.

'Have any of the slaves', Judge Thorpe asked, 'been sold in this colony or are they natives or inhabitants of this colony?' They had not and were not. 'These', he continued, 'are the only reasons which can exist for interfering with the remaining slaves.' The Company abolitionists did not agree. That night, a posse of interpreters rowed clandestinely out to the *Penel*, anchored in the bay, to 'exhort the slaves to rise and come on shore'. They did not, for whatever reason – fear, mistrust, incomprehension – and the next day a writ of habeas corpus on the slaves was requested. 'This', said Judge Thorpe, 'is a daring and fraudulent attempt to defeat the decision of the court and injure a neutral. I sit here to do justice upon neutrals, not to plunder them.'[17]

Thorpe was correct: he had no right to force British law on Swedish nationals outside British waters. He was not so much defending foreign slavers, however, as defying the men who had brought the writ. They, he thought, represented an old cabal which sought profit from the disposal of newly arrived Negroes. If the slaves left the *Penel*, he knew they would end up in bonded labour on some plantation with the commission on their 'redemption' shared by Hawkins, Cohen, Ludlam, Smith and their friends.

If they were condemnatory of white colonists, Judge Thorpe and Governor Thompson were simply bewildered by the diversity, the ingratitude and the contradictions of the black. 'What African does not see', Thompson lectured from the *Sierra Leone Gazette*, 'that as long as a slave is permitted to breathe

---

* Warships were generally known as 'cruisers' at this time.

in this Colony, neither he nor his children are in safety? What happens to one black man today may happen to another tomorrow . . . you will act the good and brave men; you will defend the Government which defends you; and you will be happy . . .'[18] Judge Thorpe, too, could not grasp that the institution of slavery might go unquestioned even by those rescued from the slave trade. 'Let it not be forgotten,' he said, 'that Slavery is itself not merely the effect, it is also the very cause, of the Slave Trade . . . if Slavery were extinct, the Slave Trade must cease.'[19] Such a statement was incomprehensible to many of those who passed through his court, steeped as they were in an utterly different culture. Thorpe could challenge the whites in their own idiom, cultural and linguistic. The African colonial population was beyond his ken, and largely – the scope of the courtroom was limited – beyond his reach.

Slaving, still endemic across the borders, had been legal in the colony until 1807, however much its founders disapproved. It could not be expected that everyone would immediately renounce it. Charities had begun to find a first footing in Freetown and the villages around, for education and evangelism. The colonial government had established a primary school to give Recaptive children the skills a young colony needed. A school for cadets trained Recaptive boys as officers for a briefly considered African army. Pastors and missionaries made attempts at rehabilitation, to complement the new deterrents of courthouse and navy. The Reverend Jonas Pilot, for example, advertised 'two discourses in the meeting house . . . particularly addressed to the mariners and others formerly engaged in the general Slave Trade and now employed in the new commerce of the colony'.[20] Some of those so 'formerly engaged' had begun to confine their trade to legal merchandise, for fear of punishment if nothing else, but if partners and friends still engaged somehow in the old business, Freetowners, black and white, would not for that reason withhold their company or their credit. It was not easy even for Thorpe and Thompson to disentangle law and culture, or identify the practices they wished to ban.

'Waterloo', a Recaptive who had enlisted in a colonial regiment, set eyes one day on Nancy, a young Recaptive woman.[21] On her arrival in Freetown, Nancy had been sent to live with a 'countrywoman', Peggy Mooney, and Waterloo asked Mooney 'to give [Nancy] to him to be his woman'. Mooney 'gave her to him and she lived with him accordingly as his woman, but was not married to him. She washed for him, cooked for him, had one child for him.' Then she tried to leave him, and return to Peggy's house, and he beat her viciously, then shot her – to frighten, he said, not to kill – and was taken before the magistrates charged with attempted murder. Here, the story of her disposal emerged tangentially. It was not remarked on by witnesses or magistrates as an offence in itself, nor even a practice to be reprobated. The right of Nancy's guardian to determine her future was not questioned any more than that of a British father to dispose of his daughter, or a British husband to assault his wife. To be abolished, slavery had to be defined, and who could define all the variations of exploitation, employment, adoption and kinship in his own country, let alone in this hybrid, uncertain colony?

Judge Thorpe learnt of another young girl, Betsey, living on an outlying farm.[22] Her father had sold her a couple of years ago to a trader collecting slaves just outside the British colony, but destined for sale within it. That trader had offered her for $100 to Mr Francis of Freetown, a black Sierra Leonean so respectable that he held the post of high constable. Francis, unsure of the proprieties, had told the trader 'he could not give him a direct answer till he had seen Mr Ludlam who was Governor for [he] knew that it had been so for some time back that if anybody bought or sold slaves in the Colony they would lose their property'. Governor Ludlam advised him the girl must be 'bound for so many years [as an apprentice] and that a time would be appointed when she must be brought up [i.e. presented to the court].' 'If you live seven years', Ludlam told the little girl, 'you are as free as I am.' Two years later, Judge Thorpe pronounced Betsey 'illegally sold' but no one knew how many others had been bartered about the colony in some muddled concept of abolition, servitude or liberty.

2

Unlawful Force

While Judge Thorpe pondered the uncertainties of abolition within a British colony, other countries were questioning the legality of Britain's attempts to suppress the slave trade at all. The abolitionists of 1807 had hoped the navy's anti-slave-trade patrols would be short-lived, briskly putting down any illegal activity, but there had been no diminution in the number of captives being supplied by the African brokers and taken away by carriers of many nationalities. Worse, those carriers had begun to offer help and protection to their British comrades. While Parliament sought means to prevent this collusion, British naval vessels continued legal, semi-legal and downright illegal bounty-hunting on the West African coasts.

In 1809, rumours reached the British fleet off Spain that two British ships were approaching West Africa from Cartagena de Indios (on the coast of what would become Colombia), sailing under false Spanish colours. Captain Irby of the frigate *Amelia* was ordered to find and detain them. He intercepted the *Galicia* and *Palafox* off Canary and escorted them to Plymouth, where a Vice-Admiralty court ascertained they were the *Queen Charlotte* and the *Mohawk*, owned by a City of London firm. The captain of the *Queen Charlotte* was called before the judges, but spoke little English. The man who did the explaining said he was Don Jorge Madresilva of Spain, and his role in the enterprise was that of 'supercargo', responsible for the purchase, care and disposal of the cargo, but without any authority over the ship herself. 'Supercargoes' would become very familiar to those charged with the

26

suppression of the slave trade. 'Jorge Madresilva' was in fact Englishman George Woodbine and he was in command of the whole enterprise, having left London in the *Queen Charlotte*, organised her nominal transfer to Spanish ownership in Cartagena and hired a man whose nationality matched the new flag to take nominal command.

The international slaving fraternity had swiftly extended its helping hand to British, American and Danish outlaws and Woodbine-Madresilva was not the only one playing this game. A ship with an international crew, calling at ports where merchants and officials were venal and no one disapproved of slaving, could slide easily from one nationality into another. As long as the slavers thus helped did not buy their slaves from a British, American or Danish national (for those slaves were liable to forfeiture under the interpretation of international law reached in the case of the American slave-ship *Amedie*) they sailed with impunity. At Madeira, Funchal and Tenerife, captains bought registration papers which allowed ships leaving Liverpool under British ownership, or New York under American, to re-emerge on the African coast as Spanish or Portuguese – the *Fortune* now *La Fortuna*; the *Catherine*, *La Caterina*. In 1810, the Vice-Admiralty court in Freetown condemned twenty such vessels, to protests from Spain and Portugal that the British had no right to detain, judge or condemn ships flying the Spanish or Portuguese flag, whatever the cause in which it was done.

Shortly after George Woodbine was bailed in 1811 (and went on the run) Henry Brougham stood in the House of Commons. Brougham was an eloquent, persistent and heavyweight lobbyist for abolition of both slave trade and slavery, and he kept a close watch on the execution of the 1807 Act. Brougham wanted an inquiry 'into the measures taken to procure the co-operation of Foreign States in amity with us, in effecting the total abolition of the slave trade', and cited the *Galicia* as only one of several instances recently come to light of Britons evading the 1807 Act with foreign help. Several Spanish slaver-captains, interrogated in Freetown, had declared they had bought their trade goods in England. Naval officers had boarded British ships carrying slave-irons and one British warship on the African coast had press-ganged a carpenter from a British merchantman on which, the man confessed, he had been employed to build a slave-deck. 'A Gentleman recently arrived' from Africa, Brougham said, had reported falling in with a vessel sailing under Spanish colours; from which, on being hailed in the usual manner, a quondam Liverpool captain answered, that he had come from the Havana and intended, after touching at the Isles de Loss [*sic*], to proceed to leeward for slaves, and, in a tone of seeming exultation at the prospect of the resurrection of his favourite commerce, he added, that no less than eighty sail were fitting out for the same destination, when he left Cuba.[1]

If nothing was done to prevent such evasion, Brougham warned, 'the Act of the British Legislature to which it was fondly expected that, in a future age, millions of Africans enjoying the blessings of science and civilisation would look back, as the Magna Charta of their freedom and happiness, will, to every other purpose, remain a dead letter'. Parliament agreed. In May 1811, another Abolition Act was passed, transforming slaving from a misdemeanour into a felony. This was no piece of wordplay. A misdemeanour was punishable by a fine and, as Henry Brougham pointed out, 'one successful [slaving] voyage paid the losses and penalties of three that failed'. A felon, on the other hand, might be transported to Australia, and seven years in convict-irons was a serious deterrent. It was Captain Irby, praised for the detention of George Woodbine's slave-ships, who sailed for the West African coast to make the new Felony Act known to Britons there. He also took with him the first bilateral anti-slave-trade agreement. It was with Portugal, and it had been negotiated by the navy's new partner in the crusade, the Foreign Office.

Portugal had begun exporting African slaves in the fifteenth century, the first European power to do so. Adventurers, and then more stable commercial ventures of other nationalities, had since dislodged the Portuguese from some of their early Gold Coast slave-ports. South of the equator, however, enormous numbers of slaves from the River Congo and the harbours of the long Angolan coast – Cabinda, Ambriz, São Paolo de Loando[2] and Benguela – still fed the great maw of Brazil, the slave-worked jewel in the Portuguese imperial crown, whose plantations required fifteen thousand fresh workers each year.

In 1807, the French invaded Portugal and the Prince Regent (the queen was mad) had fled to Rio de Janeiro, protected by the British Royal Navy. The British minister in Rio was an abolitionist who saw his opportunity in Portugal's new dependence. He induced the Regent to sign the agreement of which Captain Irby now carried a copy. In this, the Regent promised 'to co-operate . . . in adopting the most efficient measures gradually to suppress the slave-trade throughout his dominions; and not to allow his subjects, in the future, to trade in negroes on any part of the coast of Africa which did not belong to Portugal'. Parts 'belonging to Portugal' were, for the time being, accepted as everywhere on the west coast below the equator and a few named ports above in which the Afro-Brazilian slaving fraternity had been settled for generations. It was vague, it was restricted and it came from a country convinced of its own absolute dependence on vast, continual importations of black labour. It nonetheless carried a kick, for it gave the British navy authority over Portuguese shipping. With no Portuguese ships available or willing to police the agreement, British ships would do the job. Perhaps the Regent, although a man of abolitionist sympathy himself, had not realised what he was signing his country up to. Certainly slavers did not at first take the new agreement seriously, for when the *Amelia* reached the Gold Coast in January 1811, waters newly banned to the slavers of Portugal, their ships still swarmed the coast.

Captain Irby fell in with the first Portuguese brig loaded with slaves on New Year's Day 1811 and a prize-crew went aboard to take the vessel and her astonished captain up to Freetown. In the first days of January, the *Amelia* reached the Slave Coast proper: a steaming equatorial stretch between the Volta River and the Niger Delta from which countless Africans had left in chains. On 5 January, the *Amelia* was at Ouidah,[3] a slave-port on the Lagos lagoon. This town of misery and decadence was one of the northern ports where the Portuguese were still allowed to slave, and here the roped lines boarded their ships unmolested, innumerable heads disappearing into the steaming holds, to the sound of drumming of feet and banging on timbers and wailing, as Captain Irby watched and could do nothing. Porto Novo, a few miles down the lagoon, was out of bounds, however, and the two Portuguese slavers found there were also sent up to Sierra Leone under a prize-crew. Lagoon-side gossip told Irby that several more ships were loading at Lagos, also now banned to Portugal, and in that port a final three were captured. Seven prizes, with several hundred Liberated Africans, had resulted from one short patrol.[4]

The new Felony Act brought a mini-boom to West African slaver-hunting, for it authorised colonial governors to commission armed ships, in effect their own little privateers, to enforce it. Armed colonial schooners were soon patrolling the waters off Sierra Leone, looking for enemies of all types and nationalities, bringing in bounty of war and slavers indiscriminately. The number of slave-ships they detained showed clearly the continued volume of illegal trade. It was simple to evade the British patrol, for one frigate and a few schooners operating out of Freetown could do little on a long and busy coast. 'In the Rio Pongus', Judge Thorpe reported to the Colonial Office in 1812, 'those renegade [British] factors, who a few months since renounced Slave trading, are still supplying those fast-sailing Ships and Schooners that come under Spanish Colours & American navigators & who proceed with such alertness that this Cargo will be landed and the Slaves put on board in Forty eight hours'.[5]

A new slaving business had just appeared on that river. Its mistress was Mary Faber, daughter of a former American slave who had fought for the British and sailed in 1791 from Nova Scotia. With her husband, the North American sea-captain Paul Faber, Mary was setting up shop under the patronage of Mongo John. 'The Mongo', the Fabers and the others had watched what colonial officials, a Vice-Admiralty court and the Royal Navy could do to enforce abolition. It had not been sufficient to frighten them out of the rivers and into Freetown, to attend church and trade in rice and cloth.

Governor Thompson ceded office to Governor Captain Edward Columbine in 1809, and went back to England to publicise his concerns about the corruption, as he saw it, of the abolition campaign in Sierra Leone. Governor Columbine sought to take abolition peacefully beyond the colony and into the territories on its borders. The man he chose to help him was the former American slave John Kizell, who, unlike Mary Faber, had chosen the legitimate route to prosperity.

John Kizell had been captured as a child in Sherbro country, a hundred miles south of Freetown, and sold into slavery in North America. He had fought for the British in the War of Independence and returned to Africa from Nova Scotia a thoughtful, educated, Christian adult. In 1810, Governor Columbine sent him as envoy of abolition to the Sherbro chiefs. Letters of introduction stated his mission.

You must be sensible that the Slave Trade cannot be carried on much longer and therefore I earnestly hope and entreat that you will turn your views to the cultivation of your land . . . I hope you will allow my friend, Mr Kizell, to have a sufficient portion of ground, or territory, for him to build a town; and to point out to you the proper mode of rearing those articles for trade which will supply you with European

commodities . . . I shall leave the transaction entirely to yourselves as
I do not intend to send a single European to live in Mr Kizell's intended
town, but I shall furnish him with tools, &c. for cultivation.[6]

The mission had started well. At the Banana Islands, just off the colony's
south-west coast, Kizell met Mr Cleveland, a former – he said – slave-dealer
who had renounced the trade and who promised to 'give me land for such
a noble work'. Across the narrow straits into which the Shebar River
debouched, he encountered reluctance. The Tucker clan ruled here, and they
had no time for abolition. 'They inquired, if you come up to stop the Slave
Trade, what shall we do for a living? I answered, You and your people, as
the governor says to you, must all work, as other people do.' It was not a
good pitch. At the upriver town of King Safer there was outright rejection.
Safer would not let Kizell read the letter himself, but sent for the British
slaver Mr Crundell who took one look and 'immediately cursed and swore,
and raved; he told the king and his people, the governor [of Sierra Leone]
was a nuisance. "He is like Buonaparte, he wants to take the country away
from you."' The palaver ended in threats of violence and Kizell's hasty
departure.

Despite this doubtful reception, Kizell bought land on Sherbro Island and
called it Campelar: a stretch of verdant green behind a tropical beach where
turtles' eggs hatched beneath the coconut palms. Within the year, he was
running a small fleet of boats between here and Freetown, doggedly working
at the replacement of old trade with new. It was to John Kizell and his strip
of land that another remarkable man turned in 1811.

Captain Paul Cuffe was already well known in his native New England.
The son of a Native American woman and an African-born slave who had
bought his own freedom, he had gone to sea at an early age. It was his
conviction that trade, along with the Christian faith, was the key to Africa's
betterment and he had filled the hold of his brig with American goods to
sell in Sierra Leone. He and his black crew spent three months on the African
coast, meeting officials, visiting schools and chapels, distributing Bibles to
settlers and native chiefs, making notes on the British colony and what lessons
might be learnt for an American model. Cuffe suggested another generation
of black Americans should bring fresh blood and trade to the colony and find
on British soil the opportunities they did not enjoy in the land of liberty.

John Kizell eagerly recommended Sherbro as a site to house such a group:

the land there, he wrote, 'is so fertile in some places, that it would surprise any man to see what a quantity of rice [the natives] will raise in a small spot . . . They do not work hard except when they prepare their plantations which is during about two months in the spring.'⁷ Telling Kizell he would see him again soon, with black Americans to settle these promising lands, Captain Cuffe left Africa in April 1812 with a hold full of Freetown goods. He was making for England to ask for a licence to trade between the USA, Britain and Sierra Leone. His plans were ruined by the war which broke out two months later.

'Free Trade and Rights of Sailors!' was American President Madison's disingenuous war-cry; Congress voted funds and the drums began beating. The chance to acquire British Ontario in the north and Spanish Florida in the south was important in rallying troops and raising a war-chest but the American temper had also been vexed by disputes at sea: the impressment of seamen from American ships; the British embargo on American trade with neutral or enemy states; and, finally, the condemnation of too many American ships in British courts, forfeiting their profits to the British Crown. On 18 June 1812, America declared war. For having returned via enemy territory – Sierra Leone – Captain Cuffe's ship was seized, and was restored only after the president's personal intervention. For the time being, his proposed annual visits to Sierra Leone, taking American emigrants and supplies to Africa, bringing African goods to Britain and America, were on hold.

Another man surprised by the news of war was American (he said) George Cooke, a former employee of the slaver Benjamin Curtis on the River Pongus. Cooke had just paid £20,000 for a factory there. He said it traded only in legitimate goods – ivory, gum, hides, timber – and maybe it did. Any business valued at £20,000 was worth investigating, however, and enough illegality flourished elsewhere on the Pongus that bounty-hunting was easily disguisable as law-enforcement. Governor Columbine had gone home and his successor, Governor Maxwell, was a more combative character.

Judge Thorpe pointed out the complete illegality of Maxwell's planned raid. The River Pongus was over 100 miles outside British jurisdiction and Maxwell had no authority to decide what business African rulers carried on, or permitted to be carried on by foreign tenants, in their own territories. Maxwell ignored him. He would later claim that he had exceeded his authority because he had misunderstood its limits – he was a simple military man – and because of his excessive zeal for abolition. It was done with brio: in

March 1813, three packed troop-transports ascended the river as far as Bangalang, blowing up the factories that studded the banks to either side. They established their camp in the village of a chief who had taken the British side – for payment, it would seem – seized George Cooke and 2¼ tons of his ivory (to add to the 4½ tons taken from other factories), loaded it into ships' boats and sent it away downriver. Casks of spirits followed, and cloth, guns, trinkets – all the other normal articles of exchange in African trade. Then they set fire to his compound and left. While Cooke and other accused factory-owners waited in Freetown's gaol, their goods were auctioned outside, the proceeds given as prize-money to the soldiers and seamen of the expedition. George Cooke claimed American nationality but no one believed him. He and two other factors thought to be British were convicted of slaving, sentenced to fourteen years' transportation, and sent to Britain to await shipment to Australia.

The British government was preoccupied by fighting in Europe, the West Indies, the North and South Atlantic and now on the Great Lakes and the eastern coast of America. Governor Maxwell's expedition was a minor raid from a minor colonial settlement and it raised no alarm in London. HMS *Thais* visited the coast in 1812 and blew up a few more factories at Cape Mesurado, 200 miles outside the limits of British authority. And when HMS *Ulysses* arrived in the autumn of 1814, Captain Browne's actions, too, seemed to confirm that the colonial enforcers had right as well as might on their side. With three ships under his command and the authority of the navy in his ensign, Browne oversaw the swift capture of thirty slavers, the release of 1,820 slaves and the accumulation of nearly £50,000 in prize-money. Some slavers were legitimate prey, under rules of war or the Portuguese agreement, but much of the bounty came from a repeat raid up the Pongas in which the last of the factories were ruthlessly destroyed, their goods carried off and their owners either chased into the bush or brought to Freetown gaol. The frenzy only came to an end in early 1815 when Browne's ships left the coast to get supplies from the naval depot at St Helena, and learnt there that Napoleon had escaped from Elba and landed in France. Captain Browne sailed immediately for Britain.

The looting was no more legal done by the Royal Navy than by Governor Maxwell's colonial schooners, yet this repeated, thorough, brutal destruction accomplished what Judge Thorpe's courthouse had not managed: it convinced the British traders that it was time to give in. The first to renounce the trade, in return for financial compensation from the British government, was Benjamin Curtis, who 'sent in a tender of his allegiance' to Freetown in early 1814, 'with a promise of obeying the laws of Abolition'.[8] In May that year, Governor Maxwell wrote that the notorious old slave-trader John Pearce, too, had given up the slave trade and was trading in rice with Freetown. As further pledge of his sincerity, his son Sebastian had been sent to the Church Missionary Society establishment on the River Nuñez to be educated in the new piety. By the end of the year, most other slavers had followed. Mary Faber, Mongo John and a few others still held out but by 1815, slave-traffic in the Pongus was almost extinct for the first time in two hundred years.

By the time Captain Browne reached Britain, Napoleon had been defeated at Waterloo and Europe was tentatively at peace. In July 1815, Buonaparte tried to board a ship for the United States but was stopped by the British blockade. In October, he left for St Helena, the remote, beautiful South Atlantic island where he would die in 1821. As representatives of nations who had just laid down their arms met to decide the terms of peace at the Congress of Vienna, one last, grand campaign remained to be fought.

Nations trading in the Mediterranean had long paid an annual tribute to the Barbary States of North Africa – Morocco, Algiers, Tunis and Tripoli – to allow their ships to pass unmolested. During the Napoleonic Wars, however, the Dey of Algiers had taken to seizing and enslaving whatever seamen his fleet could bring in. These much-publicised 'Christian slaves', about whom thrilling and terrible tales were told, were now to be rescued. The Americans went first. They had already fought the dey in 1804 and after making peace with Britain in December 1814, American ships went back to North Africa to rescue their kidnapped citizens. The following year, a combined Anglo-Dutch fleet bombarded Algerian ships and harbour defences, one thousand more slaves were handed over and the practice of centuries came to an end.

When British delegates at Vienna suggested that a similar international force be deployed off West Africa to stamp out the other 'vile traffic', however, they found that ransoming black slaves from white, Christian masters did not hold the same attraction as rescuing white slaves from the Muslim tyrants of Barbary. There was a nodding of heads and hidden yawns, rolling of eyes at the British crusade in which no one else was interested, and a pious but meaningless declaration: that those around the table considered the universal abolition of the trade in Negroes to be particularly worthy of their attention, being in conformity with the spirit of the times, and the general principles of our august Sovereigns, who are animated in their sincere desire to work towards the quickest and most effective of measures, by all means at their disposal, and to act, in the use of those means, with all zealousness and perseverance which is required of such a grand and beautiful cause.

It was gracefully phrased, but meant little. For the time being, only Britain was willing to send ships to the other, darker, slaving coast. No one else wanted the task, and few had the means to take it on. The fleets of Spain, the Netherlands, Denmark and Sweden were shattered. The United States was making noises about expanding its navy, alerted to its weakness by its recent war with Britain, but even its proposed new total of ships was far below British strength. France still had a considerable fleet, but many of her ships were unfit for service and her administrators were resistant to their deployment on foreign adventure. All these countries had seen their treasuries emptied by long wars and without the years of abolitionist pressure to back a costly, self-denying project, none would withhold work and profit from their citizens. The lonely task of leading the campaign to which the Congress of Vienna had given its tepid approval thus fell to a British naval officer.

Captain Sir James Lucas Yeo was thirty-three. He had joined the navy as an eager ten-year-old midshipman, and had fought off Spain and in the Caribbean and, most recently, had commanded the fleet which defeated the Americans on the Great Lakes. 'You are hereby required and directed to put to sea', ran his new, peacetime orders

and proceed without delay to the coast of Africa . . . in proceeding down the coast you are diligently to look into the several bays and creeks on the same between Cape de Verd [sic] and Benguela, particularly on the Gold Coast, Whydah, the Bight of Benin and Angola, in order to your seizing such ships or vessels as may be liable thereto, under the several Acts of Parliament prohibiting the slave trade . . . and you are to use every other means in your power to prevent a continuance of the traffic in slaves . . .[9]

The breezy tone of these instructions can only have been imparted by some desk-bound clerk who had never looked at a chart. Between Cape Verde* in the north and Benguela in the south, these being more or less the limits of West African slaving, there lay some 3,000 miles of little-known, less-charted coast. 'Several' was a laughable description of the profusion and confusion of tiny bays and secret creeks clustered at intervals along that enormous stretch, from all of which slaves might be loaded. No warship could enter these, for the surf at the mouths was high, the currents contrary and the channels narrow. Ships' boats on 'detached service' would be needed. The ship would anchor on the far side of the surf and a cutter, whaleboat, gig or jolly-boat, manned by an officer and a dozen men, would be sent off for days or weeks at a time with muskets, knives, water-casks, a box of hard tack and a tarpaulin against the heavy dews, their mission to explore the hostile inlets and flush out the slavers who hid in their malarial depths.

Outside the slaving rivers, there were almost no natural harbours. The view from deck of the West African coast was of hazy, surf-bound, palm-bound, endless beach. For generations, ship-to-shore relations here had been conducted from foreign vessels anchored well out, their messages, gifts and cargoes ferried by African canoemen through the tremendous surf. Men had gone mad with the monotony, and the rolling, nauseous swell on which they waited as business was done beyond their view, in unknown bribe, raid and palaver.

This was the coast for which Commodore Yeo sailed in late 1815 in his forty-two-gun frigate *Semiramis*, arriving at a colony which had grown greatly in size if not at all in charm since the *Derwent* came eight years before. Down by the waterside, 'Kroo Town' had emerged: a colony within a colony, inhabited by men of the Kru tribe who came up from villages on the Grain Coast. They were a wild-looking lot to a newly arrived British seaman, 'distinguished by a tattooed arrow on each temple, with its point to the eye; and almost all of them have the front teeth of the upper jaw filed to a point, or some portion of each tooth removed . . . Their only article of dress is a piece of printed cotton cloth round the middle [and] a fetish which is commonly the tooth of some wild animal, fastened round the ankle or wrist.'[10] They were, one seaman explained, 'carried by all the African cruisers to do the

* Cape Verde here means not the group of islands, but the cape on the African coast from which those islands take their name.

dirty work and work in the sun'.[11] These tough and agile men, immune to heat and fever, would be as invaluable to the Royal Navy as they had been, indifferently and for generations, to slavers and anyone else who required their services. When they had made enough money, they returned to their villages, bought wives and retired.

Commodore Yeo had thought a squadron of small slaver-catching cruisers would follow him to the African coast but at the last moment these were diverted to guard the lonely emperor at St Helena. The *Semiramis* and the sloop HMS *Bann*, sent 'on particular service', were deemed, along with the colonial schooners, sufficient to police the illegal trade with the vague authority of the Congress of Vienna's declaration behind them. They were not.

'I have twenty reasons for disapproving the Abolition of the Slave Trade', one speaker had told the House of Commons in 1807,

> the first of which is, that the thing is impossible; and therefore, I need not give the other nineteen. Parliament cannot abolish the Trade: we might relinquish it; but to whom? To France, Spain, and Holland, and other countries, who will take it up and share it among them.[12]

The transatlantic trade had dwindled when the seas were full of men-of-war, manned by former slaver crews. Now it was reviving, and the sailors of Lisbon, Cadiz, Genoa, New York, Nantes, Liverpool and Plymouth were seeking jobs. One of the officers who had found himself on half-pay after the wars was Irishman Robert Hagan, an active, energetic and thoughtful officer still only acting lieutenant when peace ended hopes of promotion. In November 1815, he accepted command of one of Sierra Leone's colonial schooners. A small vessel reporting to an obscure governor was no glamorous command but it brought a salary and the prospect of bounty. To a seaman without connections, this was the best to be hoped for in peace. He made an immediate start, energetically penetrating the rivers and bringing in a clutch of Spanish slavers. By the time Commodore Yeo arrived, Hagan had made a name for himself in Freetown, and could advise the commodore on the tricks of the coast.

Behind Yeo came Captain William Fisher on HMS *Bann*. Captain Fisher was a flogger. He flogged at Palma: 'Punished Edward Skeller for Drunkenness with 12 lashes; Killed a bullock weighing 490 pounds', and at Madeira: 'Punished Jas Moir 24 lashes neglect of duty; Killed bullock weighing 219 lb', where he also took on seven sullen English convicts from Funchal gaol, some relic of the war which had left its flotsam and jetsam about the shipping routes of the world. He flogged again off Cape Sierra Leone: 'James Moir 24 lashes for disobedience of an order; Owen McGluck 12 lashes' for some crime now indecipherable in a log written by a tired man atop a swell, blurred by old salt.[13]

The *Bann's* first cruise took her south. 'As there have been no men-of-war on this coast lately', wrote one officer in January 1816

> the Spaniards have been carrying on the slave trade to a great extent; we have information of several now on the coast, and sail this afternoon in quest of a large Spanish ship, mounting 20 guns, belonging to the Havannah. . . . I hope we succeed in capturing this ship; there is little doubt of it, after which there will not be a creek nor corner about the coast which we shall leave unsearched. Our boats are fitted up and well armed for sailing where we cannot get in with the ship. I trust we shall be able to put a final stop to this inhuman traffic; at any rate it would be a great satisfaction to us hereafter to know, that we have done our utmost to do so.[14]

They were heading for the Gallinas, an infamous estuary a hundred miles below the colony's border. The Gallinas was a slavers' haven, protected by a bar too high for warships to cross. River-conduits poured in on all sides, bringing the captives of tribes who raided far into the interior for slaves. This had been a preserve of the British before abolition and hopeful observers had thought legitimate trade might take over this rare sheltered harbour. There was fertile country here, where tobacco, rice, pepper, coffee and sugar cane could have been grown, ferried down the rivers and exchanged for European goods to replace the trade in humans.

It had not happened. Instead, the Gallinas was falling again to the old trade and a greater concentration of the dishonest, the unscrupulous and the vicious were settling here than in any other estuary north of the Line.* Spanish slavers had arrived in place of the British, and the Vai chief Siaka

---

*'The Line' was the term generally used for 'the equator'.

was emerging as the most successful of several African, or part-African, leaders eager to trade: 'King Caulker', a mulatto slave-trader educated in England, now claiming American nationality; the Cleveland dynasty; and the ghastly, ghostly figures who flitted across the backdrop to many slaving stories: the Tucker clan, who were rich, cunning and loyal only to their own survival and profit. Down the secret waterways came not coffee and rice but great slave-canoes and over the bar came the vessels sailing again from Havana and Matanzas.

On 13 January, HMS *Bann* anchored outside the bar and sent her boats to test the surf. They crossed, and a huge sheet of still water opened up before them. Its green surface was pierced by numerous low, small islands, fringed with mangroves in which the dead wood of the interior lay bumping. At its head, three rivers penetrated the mainland to north-east, north and north-west, the latter connecting with Sierra Leone when the rains brought high waters, although the British did not know that yet. All around were the grim island-compounds of the re-emerging trade: a warehouse, a wharf, a cluster of round-bottomed canoes, a counting house, a harem and a barracoon guarded by high bamboo palings and tatty men with muskets. The first boat the *Bann's* boats stopped in the shallows was an American 'trading for slaves'[15] but with none yet aboard. The second was a Spanish schooner which did not heave to at their signal – a blank shot across the bow – but chose rashly to open fire instead. She was overpowered and a prize-crew went on board to take her and her cargo of slaves back to Freetown. The *Bann* sailed on down the coast. Two more Spanish schooners were taken, with 550 slaves aboard. A third ship seen and chased also flew the Spanish flag but, when boarded, proved to be American. She had been a privateer during the war, preying on British merchantmen in the Channel, turning slaver with the peace. There were 276 blacks aboard. They too turned back for Freetown.

A second cruise south began badly. On 29 January: 'Mr Hill, 36 lashes for mutiny; John Hawes, 24 lashes for insolence, Nathaniel Howard 12 for ditto; Mr Quirk, 16 lashes for neglect of duty and insolence; Robertson ditto for repeated drunkenness.' A captain flogging his own junior officers for mutiny did not run a happy ship and a monotonous cruise to the Gold Coast did not help: squalls and heavy rain decreased visibility; ships were stopped but had no slaves aboard; the crew was restless. This was an unfriendly coast. There were none of the usual port stops where men and officers could amuse themselves and let off steam. Hundreds of men cooped up in hot, cramped quarters became fractious. 'Feb. 8 punished John Leighton 12 lashes neglect of duty, Edward Nelson and John Sawman ditto.'

On 5 March, sharp eyes saw a distant sail and 'a great number of natives' on a beach. Suspecting that slaves were being gathered for loading, Captain Fisher ordered full sail and chased. First an American, then a Portuguese, flag was hoisted on the unknown schooner, then she swung side-on to the British and started firing. The decks of the *Bann* were instantly cleared for action and the two gun-crews rammed in shot. They fought for an hour, stepping smartly back from the recoil which could take a foot off, retching in the smoke returned from the blast. Rapid gunnery decided the outcome in a battle of broadsides, and the *Bann*, with every gunner aboard a veteran of the winning side, was the better drilled. A fourth round of British fire blasted away the schooner's rigging, her sails collapsed and the battle was done. With a British lieutenant in charge and British carpenters patching up the damage just done by their own guns, the captured *Temerero* left for Freetown, the Portuguese crew confined below and forty Negroes bought at Ouidah breathing fresh air and drinking fresh water on deck. Two of the *Bann*'s men were found drunk on liquor stolen from the *Temerero*'s hold. They were flogged. The *Bann* sailed on, and ten days later chased, boarded and detained another Portuguese schooner, the *San Antonio*.

Portugal's 1811 agreement with Britain had restricted the numbers of slaves to be loaded per ton and the *San Antonio* should have been carrying only three hundred. There were six hundred aboard, and any men aboard the *Bann* who thought abolition a piece of bleeding-heart liberalism must have changed their minds when they saw this slave-deck. Crawling among the Negroes packed and fettered below – there was not the headroom to stand – the boarding party retched and gagged and brought up thirty so near death that the *Bann* surgeon thought them 'irrecoverably gone'. 'In the midst of the sick,' he reported, 'lay a putrid corpse, and such a horrid stench, that Captain Fisher was apprehensive of a plague, and was obliged to take not only the crew, but 150 slaves on board the *Bann*, and make the best of his way to Sierra Leone.'[16] Thirty others, the Portuguese captain told them indifferently, had already died and been thrown over the side.

Now, making for Freetown in company with her prize, the *Bann* found what countless merchantmen had found before her. Sailing down the coast was easy, with light winds behind, carried on an eastward-setting current.

Cape Coast could be made from Freetown in a week but Freetown from Cape Coast could take more than a month and the return voyage was often made under more difficult conditions. The *Bann* was not only weighed down with an extra cargo of sick slaves and captured crew, but depleted by men on prize-ships.

On 9 March, one Portuguese prisoner died, his body heaved into the sea with a brief and unfelt blessing. They continued into the endless 'light airs' which left the ships, in the terminology of their logs, 'baffled'. Cat's-paws stroked the sails and left them flapping; the ship beat feebly back and forth to cover a handful of miles each day under the heat of an equatorial sun. On 23 March, 'came on a tornado', which crackled round the masts and beat its rain on the decks for twenty-four hours, forcing itself through the timbers to those crowded miserably below. Food and water ran low: by the end of the month, the Portuguese prisoners were on half-allowance. A week later, space was made in the log each day for note of water remaining: 26½ tons that day, 26 the next.

The surgeon did what he could but more slaves fell sick. Some died. In these slow waters, bodies sent over the side bumped against the hull, rolling slowly about the ship while men with boat-hooks nudged them away, for there was a horror of seeing even a dead man taken by a shark. At Freetown, seventy sick slaves were ferried ashore to the hospital and oranges were issued to the ship's company, who were suffering the constipating, enervating effects of salt meat and no vegetables. A week later, the other prize-ships arrived with four hundred slaves and the hospital was overwhelmed by another batch of the ill and the dying. At the end of April, the *Bann* headed for Jamaica, prize-money well earned, her tour of duty on the Slave Coast over and Africa thankfully left behind. On the coast she left, the illegal trade was booming.

In the busy colonial ports of the Caribbean and the Americas, the vague anti-slaving commitments of mother countries were dismissed. Spain, more than ever dependent on the great wealth of Cuba, would continue the traffic as long as her colonists wished. France, fighting to regain her position on the world's stage and with her own West Indian colonies to be supplied, would do the same. Portugal, despite the Regent's agreement, bowed to the needs of Brazilian plantations. Abolitionists had had greater hopes of the United States and, indeed, American coastguards and warships had been sent to patrol the Gulf of Mexico and the lawless seas off Florida and Texas, trying to stem the import of Negroes. American slavers did not only sail in American waters, however. Ships from Baltimore, New York and Philadelphia were also seen on the West Indian and African coasts, generally under the protective colours of Spain, and here there were no American warships to stop them.

Ships were arriving in Cuba 'on average 4–6 per week from Guinea' and 'nearly 100 American vessels' were reported 'fitting out at Havana for the slave trade'.[17] A short cruise down the African coast by a couple of British warships was insufficient to stop such numbers. Not only must more ships be provided, but the officers commanding them must be given more effective powers. Henry, now Lord, Brougham stood in the House of Lords to insist that these must include a mutual right of search. 'This might extend the principle established by the law of nations', he said, 'but, if ever the right of search for the contraband of war were justified by the law of necessity, it might fairly be contended for in the instance of the Slave Trade.'

This 'mutual right of search' was the agreement between two nations each to allow the other's navy to board, search and detain each other's shipping under certain circumstances. It would become the holy grail of Britain's anti-slave-trade campaign, but would take decades to extend to every slaving nation. Allowing foreign warships to board one's own was as hateful as allowing a foreign army to occupy one's country. Who would grant such power, in particular to the victorious and arrogant British, if not forced to it by bribery or threat? Portugal had given in, within limits, and in return for 'compensation'; so had the Netherlands, which outlawed the trade in 1814 and, pragmatic about the limits of its own resources, granted Britain the right of search four years later. But when Britain suggested the same to France, the idea was declared to be so disagreeable to the French government and nation that there was no chance of its being adopted. French Foreign Minister Talleyrand wrote carefully that the French king 'had issued direction, in order that, on the part of France, the traffic in slaves may cease'.[18] But when the West African island of Goree, seized by the British during the wars, was handed back to France, French slave-ships were soon sailing beneath the garrison's guns. Correspondence passed between Freetown and London, London and Paris: painstaking, incontrovertible lists of names, dates and numbers to prove the volume of French slaving. An inquiry was set afoot, the first governor was dismissed and in 1816, France sent warships to the West African coast, ostensibly to put down the trade.

Their presence provoked 'not the least appearance even of secrecy, nor the least fear of interruption' wrote a British merchant visiting Goree. 'Two of the last vessels which left this place with slaves, passed outwards at a time when three French vessels of war were at anchor outside the bar.'[19] The new governor had arrived with stern new orders from Paris but also with a cordial letter of introduction to M. René Dupuis, the Senegalese mulatto through whose hands most of the slave trade passed. His intention to continue the trade was 'known to every individual marching on two legs at Goree'.[20] Guadeloupe and Martinique, no less than Cuba and Brazil, were hungry for labour and prepared to pay for it and the African chiefs of the French colonial hinterland were already conducting eager negotiations. King Damel, the British merchant wrote, 'one of the more powerful chiefs of this part of Africa came to speak to slave traders here and is now burning and pillaging villages for slaves'.[21] In January 1818, Dupuis 'shipped from his wharf 252 slaves to the schooner *La Louise*',[22] commanded by an ex-French naval officer, bound for Martinique. The British could not stop her, for there was no mutual right of search; the French, it appeared, would not.

It was known on the slaving rivers that America, as well as Britain, had outlawed the trade, and pledged at the peace negotiations in December 1814 to 'use their utmost endeavours to promote the entire abolition of the slave trade'. But who had seen an American warship anchored off the African rivers? No one. Were any expected? Not according to the American slave-ship skippers who laughed when they were asked, and told their dealers not to worry. The US law banning the slave trade was printed and reprinted in the *Sierra Leone Gazette* in 1817 in the hope it might 'clear up the understanding of those wretches who well knowing themselves unworthy of the name of Britons now clumsily attempt to cling to America, such as Messrs Cook, Benjamin Curtis, Ormond, Faber, Lightburn, Pock, Laurence and other equally celebrated characters of the Rio Pongas'.[23] But law without warships to enforce it was useless.

As customers came flocking back across the newly peaceful oceans in defiance of law, treaty and pledge, supply increased to meet demand. Europe had exhausted itself in war and Britain and America had made a grudging, precarious peace but West Africans were still fighting. The source of the slave-caravans streaming to the coast was only guessed at by the whites who took them away. Too few Europeans had travelled inland to know of the wars of Yorubaland or the slave-raiding kings of Dahomey and Kumasi. Sixty thousand slaves were estimated to have been shipped from Africa during Commodore Yeo's first year of command, and fortunes were again being made from black ivory. The profits were staggering and the risks were few: a slave bought in Lagos for a few rolls of tobacco – about 12 shillings sterling, according to Yeo – would sell in Brazil for $400. One Portuguese slave-captain told Yeo he had made twenty-two successful voyages before being arrested. The couple of British warships sent to stem a trickle had found themselves facing a torrent.

It was not to be expected that the slave-brokers of the rivers Pongus, Nuñez and Sierra Leone would keep their word in the face of such temptation. When a vessel making for Mongo John's quays was boarded, it was found to be the property of Dr Botifeur, 'formerly an Englishman', as the *Gazette* said derisively, 'and now a Spaniard at the Havanah'.[24] Then came the sad news that Benjamin Curtis had returned to the trade. Taking advantage of his new welcome in Freetown, he had bought a schooner there and sold her to Mongo John, who had loaded her with slaves and sent her to Cuba. For a while, Curtis protested his innocence: 'you may perhaps think me very bold in writing to you but it comes from a pure heart, not altogether what you have heard of me, many stories have reached your ears which were not done by me etc etc'.[25] His son was less coy. 'Curtis Junior', reported the *Gazette*, 'was lately met at the bar of one of the rivers of the neighbourhood of this colony with twenty slaves on board a Schooner of his father's; a respectable inhabitant of this place expressed his astonishment at his carrying on such a traffic, to which he deliberately answered "there is more money to be made in selling slaves than rice".' On the River Nuñez, too, the trade was reviving. Sebastian Pearce, son of the old slaver John, had completed his education with the missionaries and returned to his riverside home. 'I am extremely sorry to inform you', wrote Sebastian to the new British Governor in Sierra Leone, Charles M'Carthy,

of the white traders in this river, that deal in slaves, namely Mr John Bateman and Mr Anthony Spanard. . . . The fact is, if you don't be sending in soon, they will be disposing of all their domestics. Since the death of poor old father, John Pearce, they have been trying their utmost to destroy his place, and they are till this very day.

Sir, I would esteem it as a lasting favour, if you will be good enough, as to send in for these whites in this river – not on account of me only, but morely on account of their carrying on the Slave Trade so briskly.

They have been down to the colony [i.e. Sierra Leone] several times, and confessed with their mouths, and even took their oaths, that they would not traffic in slaves no more; as for my part, I compare them to hippocrite. [*sic*] I hope you will send me answer by the first opportunity.

PS I am sorry to inform you of our mutual friend Jno Pearce. He died on 6th Oct, Mon. evening, about 8 o'clock, of what disease I cannot rightly say, but some says that he died of the dropsy.[26]

One trader whose defection caused the Governor Charles M'Carthy particular sorrow was Captain O'Kearney. He was a slippery sort, who had found employment in the dimmer corners of empire: a subaltern first in New South Wales, then Goree, from where he had drifted down to Sierra Leone. Governor M'Carthy sent him to the new village of Bathurst as superintendent, acting as magistrate over several hundred Liberated Africans. He did his job unremarkably, turning up in court, disentangling tales of vendetta and petty crime, dispensing some version of justice and filing the necessary papers, but after three years in the post went missing. The first reports that he was at Gallinas, trading in slaves, were disbelieved but a letter found aboard a French slave-ship detained there confirmed the truth. John O'Kearney, the note stated, '[does] agree to pay to Captain Guiot . . . 605 slaves, none to be under four English feet, to be as equally proportioned men, women, boys, and girls, as can be'.[27] Governor M'Carthy advertised a reward of $400 for the renegade's capture, but he was safe in his estuary, protected by the slavers' guns.

Yet it was neither renegade resumption of slaving by British citizens, nor the ready supply of slaves, nor even the wilful indifference of other countries which brought to an end the first post-war naval patrol. That was done by the decisions of two British courts.

Governor Maxwell's punitive expeditions up the River Pongas in 1813 had not been forgotten. Messrs Cooke, Dunbar and Brodie, the three factors sentenced to transportation to Australia, had been fighting their legal corner and they had powerful arguments to make. As Judge Thorpe had pointed out at the time, the expeditions were completely illegal, although it was not this, but a technicality, which eventually released them from their sentence: the clause in the Felony Act by which colonial courts could try slave-traders for felony had been based on a repealed statute so their conviction in Freetown was invalid. Only one had been transported to Australia. The others were released from the Portsmouth hulks to start their claims for damages.

Their release coincided with rising unease in the Colonial Office and the Admiralty courts over the legality of other British actions on the West African coast. 'There exists at Sierra Leone', declared Dr Stephen Lushington, committed abolitionist and Admiralty judge, 'a lamentable ignorance of the principles that govern the rights of nations in amity with each other.'[28] How could a British warship, he asked, board, let alone detain, the vessels of another country, whatever the pretext, if that country had not specifically authorised such a procedure? Given that only Portugal – and, more recently, the Netherlands – had done so, and then only in certain circumstances, British warships should be confining their activities to Portuguese, Dutch and British slave-ships. Similarly, how could British courts claim jurisdiction over citizens of other nations, whether breaking their own laws or not? No country had granted Britain that right. In Lushington's view, the capture of almost every slave-ship since 1808 – over one hundred – had been illegitimate, and the instructions on which detaining officers had acted were 'from the beginning to the end illegal . . . in violation of every principle of the law of nations'. One of these detentions was about to be challenged in the High Court of Admiralty.

In March 1816, Lieutenant Hagan had spotted a French vessel off Cape Mesurado, 225 miles south of Freetown. He had signalled her to heave to and had opened fire when she did not. These were the reactions of war, and the French skipper had felt them too: there was a bloody fight in which fifteen men were killed before the French hauled down their colours and surrendered. The prize, Le Louis, was Nantes-owned. She had come from Martinique for slaves and had already taken on twelve, picked up here and there along the coast between Cape Mesurado and New Sester. She had been condemned at the British Vice-Admiralty court in Freetown, her slaves had been liberated and Lieutenant Hagan had given her no more thought. However, the captain of the Louis knew Hagan had no right to act as he had, and he appealed the court's decision to the High Court of Admiralty in London.

By the time the appeal was heard there was a backlog of similar claims pending by Spanish, Portuguese and Americans. The *Louis* was a test case, and a great deal rode upon it. As the French captain's lawyers said, slaving broke no international law, whatever vague pledges had been made at Vienna or elsewhere. France might have outlawed the slave trade, but no British officer could compel a Frenchman to observe French law and no British Admiralty court had jurisdiction over a French vessel. The court's judgment, in 1817, was unequivocal, and reversed the decision taken in 1809 in the case of the American *Amedie*. 'A nation is not justi-fied', said Judge William Scott,* 'in assuming rights that do not belong to her merely because she means to apply them to a laudable purpose; nor in setting out upon a moral crusade of converting other nations by acts of unlawful force.'[29] The French captain was awarded compensation.

It was a vindication of law over force, but the judgment completely under-mined Commodore Yeo's mission. A few stray Portuguese or Dutch might be captured, but otherwise British warships must sail uselessly up and down, looking on as other nations carried off slaves with impunity. If the little fleet off Sierra Leone were not to cost Britain a great deal in compensation and apology, it must be reconfigured, its aims and powers redefined and the free-doms of war left behind. It must abandon privateering and be placed, defen-sibly, within the law.

It fell to the Foreign Office to give the patrol back its purpose, restoring by diplomacy what the *Louis* judgment had banned them from achieving by force: making foreign flags answerable to British naval officers. British ministers† abroad must add abolition to their agendas. Foreign governments must be brought to outlaw the slave trade to their nationals and a network of treaties must be created to bind and entrap. The mutual right of search must be laid thumpingly on every diplomatic table, and as many nations as possible be persuaded, forced or bribed into signing up. First, foreign governments must set a date at which slaving would be banned, with severe penalties for transgressors; second, they must reduce and define the area

---

*Later Baron Stowell.
†Diplomatic representatives abroad were known at this time as 'ministers' rather than 'ambassadors'.

in which slaving might continue until that date; and third, they must ensure the new laws were enforced. That meant allowing the British to enforce them, or sending out warships to do so themselves or granting a mutual right of search.

In 1817, the first treaty of the new era was made with Portugal, still the easiest of the powers to bully. The Regent reduced his country's agreed slaving waters even further, cancelled the right to frequent certain north-of-the-Line ports which had remained open under the previous agreement, and explicitly empowered the Royal Navy to act as police. He was paid £300,000, ostensibly as compensation for slave-ships detained by 'unlawful force' during the past decade. The same year, the impecunious King of Spain, in return for an even larger 'compensation' of £400,000, banned Spaniards from slaving north of the equator, granted the mutual right of search, and promised to extend the ban south of the Line in May 1820. It was thought he might use the money to send a Spanish naval patrol to West Africa but the new royal fleet was destined instead for Latin America, where rebellion stirred the Spanish colonies as it had stirred the British two generations before.

With these first agreements signed and paid for, a drop in the volume of slaving was expected, particularly north of the equator. However, treaties without enforcement were only pieces of paper, and there was no desire for enforcement in Bahia, Rio, Cadiz or Havana. The new agreements were no more self-policing than the 1807 Abolition Act, and with too few British ships to enforce them, they were immediately and widely flouted. Under them, Commodore Yeo wrote, the slave trade 'assumed a most perverse complexion: for Portugal . . . was allowed to carry on the trade south of the line, and Spain, north; so that no part of Africa was exempt from its pernicious influence'. In December 1818, a British merchant in Cape Verde reported that Portuguese colonial governors on the Cape Verde islands and in Bissagos were not just accepting slavers' bribes to look the other way, but were actively dealing in slaves themselves. 'Such flagrant breaches of the treaties', he wrote

> when British blood has flown in torrents in Europe for the independence of these two nations, when British generosity and Philanthropy has so lately paid large sums of money for redeeming the north of the line from this degrading scourge . . . hundreds of vessels are now taking slaves – even canoes from our rivers convey our brethren for sale to

the Rio Pongas – the Caulkers, the Clevemans [i.e. Clevelands], the Tuckers and all those vile wretches living near the Sherbro are employed in the same criminal speculation, yet our friends in Europe are congratulating us upon their treaties. Alas Mr Editor, speeches and declarations unsupported by armed vessels are of no avail.[30]

If Britain were to uphold her stated aim of extinguishing the slave trade, the Foreign Office must extend its network of agreements and the Admiralty must back them with more than just a few ships on 'particular service'. The West African Station, and the 'Preventive Squadron' which patrolled it, were to come formally into being.[31]

3

False Papers and Mongrel Vessels

In 1819 Sir George Collier, an experienced fighter of both French and Americans was appointed commodore of the new Preventive Squadron, patrolling the west coast of Africa. His orders came from the Admiralty, but his terms of engagement were increasingly dictated by the Foreign Office. The easier of Collier's tasks was to suppress the illegal British slave trade, already fast-diminishing. The more difficult was to enforce Britain's anti-slave-trade treaties with other countries. He and his officers were about to discover how many loopholes those complex documents contained and how much hard, dangerous cruising their enforcement would require.

Besides his flagship, HMS *Tartar*, the Admiralty provided Collier with six warships: HMS's *Thistle, Pheasant, Morgiana, Myrmidon, Cherub* and *Snapper*. They were to be deployed differently to the ships on the 'particular service' of previous years. The flagship would still leave for the West Indies during the rains, but the others would remain on the West African coast for two- or three-year commissions. The expense of seven warships was considerable, and was questioned by the many who could not see why the British taxpayer should be footing this bill, yet even seven were not enough. London still did not know the magnitude of the challenge and, even if it had, the outlay in ships and men necessary to patrol the whole beat outlined in 1816 for Commodore Yeo was unthinkable. The captains of the new Squadron would spend most of their commissions at sea, returning only briefly to Freetown or Ascension to repair, reprovision and convalesce, but their cruises would rarely take them south of the equator. Along the whole vast stretch from there to Benguela, the slave trade would be scarcely affected for another generation.

Each captain kept a heavy pile of papers ready for checking on his desk. These were the instructions which, in these post-*Louis* times, told him what he could and could not do in his dealings with suspected slavers flying the flags of other nations. When they took up their new duties in 1819, their parameters of action seemed to be these: Portuguese allowed below the equator, but not above; Spanish allowed above but not below, until May 1820, then nowhere; Dutch not allowed anywhere and can be stopped everywhere; French not allowed anywhere but cannot be touched unless there are grounds to suspect the involvement of British citizens, and then only with great caution; Americans ditto, but with even greater caution; everyone else, unclear.

The procedure laid down for bringing in a prize was this. As soon as a ship was detained on suspicion of illegal slaving, her crew, with the exception of the captain and one or two other officers, was taken on board the detaining vessel and landed at the nearest port. Two junior officers of the British ship, with a crew of between five to twenty men, were sent on board the prize to take her up to Sierra Leone, where the slaves were landed and lodged in the 'Liberated African Yard'. Prize-crew and slaver's officers went into lodgings to await their appearance in court. Ascertaining the legality of the capture was no longer the work of British Admiralty courts, but of new 'Courts of Mixed Commission' on which two British commissioners would sit beside two of the other nationality. These were to be established in Sierra Leone, Rio (for the Portuguese), Surinam (for the Dutch) and Havana (for the Spanish).

This apparently simple situation was nothing of the sort, however, and both hunted and hunters knew it. Where there were profits, there was ingenuity, and slavers would always find ways to wriggle through the treaties. Furthermore, over the whole picture lay the great shadow of recent war. The British were loathed both by those they had defeated – France and America; and, almost as much, by those they had defended – Spain and Portugal. Slaving appealed in part because it went against the will of Britain. Some slavers merely took a mild pleasure in provoking the old enemy and enjoying his splutters but others sincerely held and regularly expressed the conviction that the naval campaign was nothing but a cynical shield behind which British commercial interests in West Africa could expand. Impeding that campaign was a patriotic act on their part.

Control of the illegal slave trade had been brought nearer to police work and further from bounty-hunting. However, British officers making their cases before the Courts of Mixed Commission were still bound by one part of the old, pre-*Louis* system. As detained ships were still defined as prize, cases against their captains, agents or owners were brought not in the name of the Crown, but in that of the officer who had made the detention. If the commissioners found for the detaining officer, he got the bounty to divide among his ship's company as prescribed by Admiralty regulations. If they found against him, he was personally liable for damages.

The Dutch were the first of the foreign commissioners to arrive in Freetown and it was Lieutenant Hagan who tested their mettle. Colonial vessels could not detain slavers under the new treaties: only commissioned officers of His Majesty's ships could do that. Lieutenant Hagan was too valuable to lose, for he had greater knowledge of the coast than any officer of the new squadron. In 1819, he was finally confirmed in his rank and took command of the tubby little ten-gun brig HMS *Thistle*. In her, he detained two Dutch schooners in the Gallinas in October 1819, brought them in for condemnation and discovered how ingeniously obstructive the new courts could be. Hagan, eager to be back at sea, announced he would leave the case in the hands of a representative. There was anguished discussion. The treaty did not mention this proceeding, said the Dutch, and it could not therefore be admitted. When it was agreed to consult national governments, the Dutch gentlemen were left with time on their hands as correspondence sailed slowly between Freetown, London and Amsterdam and Lieutenant Hagan was left with two detained schooners on his, and dozens more slaving while he was stuck in Freetown. He protested, answers to his protests were made with as much delay and insolence as the commissioners could manage, and the two sides almost came to blows. When governments had been consulted, and the fruit of these consultations had finally been received, it would, of course, be decided that representatives were allowed. It had been done purely to waste time.

A ship detained on Hagan's next, delayed cruise gave the Dutch commissioners another opportunity for stalling. The *Thistle* was off the Grain Coast when the masthead saw a sail inshore. Hagan tacked and approached. Down went the boat with the boarding party and, from the other ship, down went canoes packed with slaves to be relanded, for slavers knew the terms of the new treaties as well as the Squadron. Only a ship with slaves actually aboard could be detained. If all slaves had been hurried off before a British officer set foot on her deck, she was untouchable. It was a race: coxswain swearing, bluejackets sweating at the oars, canoe after canoe shoving off as they approached. By the time Lieutenant Hagan scrambled over the side to tell the master his ship was detained, all but one solitary Negro were on the beach.

When the case against the *Eliza* came before the British–Dutch Mixed Commission, the Dutch commissioner agreed that she had been carrying slaves, that her crew had unloaded them in view of the British and that one had remained aboard. But the treaty stated slaves (plural) must be found. A slave (singular) was not mentioned. The ship was wrongfully detained, he insisted, and Lieutenant Hagan, as detaining officer, must pay damages. So furious was Hagan at this second attempt to subvert the treaty that, even after the Dutch commissioner's absurd interpretation of it was overturned on appeal, he personally sued the ship's master for perjury.

No cases involving Portuguese (which included Brazilian) shipping could be heard before their commissioners arrived in Sierra Leone and so appointments were found difficult. Captain Kelly of HMS *Pheasant*, calling at the Cape Verde islands en route to Africa, had been 'told by the governor' (a well-known slave-dealer) 'that the terror entertained at the Brazils of the climate of Sierra Leone was so great that the Portuguese Government was unable to prevail upon fit persons to go there upon any terms'.[1] It was a useful excuse. Portuguese prizes lay rotting in the river. When the *Pheasant* returned from her first cruise with the Portuguese slaver *Nova Felicidade* and eighty-one slaves, more than two years after the Portuguese treaty had been signed, there was still no one in Sierra Leone authorised to hear the case against her.

The governor of Cape Verde was not the only Portuguese official working in happy defiance of his country's laws. Others were doing the same on the equatorial islands of Principe and São Tomé, in the Gulf of Guinea and the rivers in what is now Guinea-Bissau, all of them old conduits for slaves, interconnecting with each other and, by creeks and narrow necks of land, with the rivers Pongas and Nuñez in Freetown's backyard. These rivers were a nest of busy slavers: agents bringing in captives, brokers sending them off in light vessels to the offshore islands, larger craft conveying them thence to Brazil. On Principe, Governor Fereira, his wife and his daughter were all enthusiastic slavers. Madame, as his fat wife was known, and Doña Maria, his daughter, specialised in the 'midget slavers' running between mainland and islands. The governor was more interested in the transatlantic trade and the *Nova Felicidade* was one of his ventures.

Any seaman confronted with his first slave-deck was shocked by the number of bodies packed into its space. The *Nova Felicidade* was a grim introduction to the trade's realities. 'The state in which those unfortunate creatures were found', said Captain Kelly, was

> shocking to every principle of humanity: 17 men shackled together in pairs by the legs, and 20 boys, were in the main hold; a space measuring 18 feet in length, 7 feet 8 inches main breadth and 1 foot 8 inches in height, and under them the yams for their support. One of these poor creatures was in the last stages of dysentery.[2]

Thirty-four women had even less space. Released, 'scarcely one of them could stand upon their legs, from cramp and evident starvation'. But although the government in Lisbon was sent all necessary proofs of the Fereiras' involvement, no action was taken. Governor Fereira, too, remained untouchable.

When the Portuguese commissioners finally arrived in Freetown, three years late, lo!, it was found that no duplicates of the commission authorising them to execute their new duties had been brought with them. Until Rio was notified of this and took action to send these out, it would be most irregular to sit in court. And when the commissions were eventually received, what had been a vacuum became a negative force, for they, too, were skilful in their interpretations of the treaty.

Among the first cases brought before Commissioners Altavila and Figaniere was that of the schooner *San Salvador*, one of the 'mongrel vessels' becoming a feature of the illegal trade. She had been bought by a Spaniard from a Baltimore shipbuilder on behalf of a Portuguese merchant in the Cape Verde islands, armed and freighted in Rhode Island, crewed by Portuguese, Americans, Italians and French with one P. C. Greene, an

American, listed as 'supercargo' but in reality her commander. The *San Salvador* had arrived on the African coast under a Portuguese flag in December 1819 and Mr Greene had gone ashore to buy his slaves, leaving First Mate Fletcher, also an American, in charge of the ship. A letter sent back from 'Peter Careful's, Big-town' ordered Fletcher north to the barracoons of the Gomez family of the Gallinas to 'see what slaves are collected from the gentlemen at that place'.[3] The *San Salvador* took on Gomez's slaves on 23 January; two days later, HMS *Myrmidon* spotted her prey and the slaver's crew, seeing the unmistakable masts of a man-of-war beyond the bar, pushed the slaves back into the boats and rowed for the shore. It was the same trick by which the *Eliza* had thwarted Lieutenant Hagan, but one of the *San Salvador*'s boats was caught before she reached the beach. With an enslaved Krooman in it, this seemed enough to make the *San Salvador* a legitimate prize and as she had been sailing under the Portuguese flag, with Portuguese papers, her case was taken before the Portuguese Mixed Commission.

First, the commissioners claimed that the ship was not Portuguese, but American, and thus her case could not be heard by any court or commission in Freetown. That did not stick, as the paper chain was too incriminating. The hearing began and the rescued Krooman deposed. Señor Gomez of the Gallinas had sold him for a hundred 'bars',* he said, paid in rum, gunpowder and tobacco; there had been twenty-two other slaves aboard the schooner; Mr Fletcher had offered him $100 if he would tell the British he was not a slave. Mr Greene's incriminating orders to Fletcher were read out and British commissioner Edward Gregory was satisfied the *San Salvador* could be condemned. The Portuguese commissioners, however, were not.

They were acting, they claimed, in accordance with the sixth article of the 1817 treaty, which stated that 'no cruiser, Portuguese or British, shall detain any vessel not having slaves actually on board'. As none had been aboard the *San Salvador* herself, but rather in her boats, the detention was illegal. Commissioner Gregory protested:

the facts of the Negro being on board when the captors approached; of

---

* 'Bars' was a nominal coast currency, which could be made up in a variety of items – guns, tobacco, cloth, etc.

his being, in their sight, put into the boat in order to evade them; and of his being taken in that situation; when viewed in connection with the ample proofs of the vessel having been engaged in an illegal slave-trading voyage, seemed to furnish sufficient ground of condemnation. Not to allow their force would be to defeat the very object of the treaty.[4]

He knew as he spoke that that was exactly what his Portuguese colleagues wished. Captain Leeke of the *Myrmidon*, they said, must not only restore the vessel and cargo but pay damages to the owners of the *San Salvador* for losses suffered.

In February 1821, HMS *Morgiana* stopped another Portuguese vessel in the Bight of Biafra and a boarding party found 'the incredible number [for such a vessel] of 396 slaves'.[5] They were north of the equator and it seemed a clear-cut breach of treaty. The master, however, had his story ready. These slaves were not taken on here, he said; they had been loaded at the Angolan slave-port Cabinda, south of the Line, with perfect legality, and winds and currents had pushed his vessel north of the Line. The boarding officers knew he was lying. Only four water-casks were empty, and in the long passage from Cabinda more would have been drunk. The surgeon examined the brands on the slaves' breasts and declared they had only just begun to heal and the slaves themselves said they had spent little time on board. The slaver and her sorry load followed the *Morgiana* north for adjudication.

By now, however, one Portuguese commissioner had found himself so fatigued by the climate that he had left Freetown and the commission could hear no cases in his absence. When Captain Finlaison of the *Morgiana* asked what he was supposed to do with his prize, he was told he must take her to the nearest Mixed Commission in which two Portuguese commissioners were sitting, and that was in Rio de Janeiro. Wearily, the *Morgiana* set sail with the slave-ship, her crew and the wretched slaves and the rest of the squadron grimaced: the absence of the *Morgiana* meant the preventative membrane must be spread even thinner, and one entire prize-crew had recently disappeared, no one yet knew how or where.

There were many ways for the men of the Preventive Squadron to die: the usual exit routes of disease and accident; the rarer incidents of shark and crocodile attack; and the growing, unforeseen consequences of criminalising the slave trade. Profit had not just spawned ingenuity in the courts. It was also spawning violence on the seas. Slavers now went armed and ready to fight their way through any patrol sent to stop them. Six months ago, HMS *Pheasant* had captured the Portuguese slaver *Volcano*, put a prize-crew aboard under Midshipman Castles, and seen them depart for Sierra Leone. They never arrived, and had been assumed, sadly, to have gone down in one of the tornadoes which shook the coast. Captain Finlaison was the first to learn of the real manner of their deaths, when he put in at Bahia en route to Rio and a man came aboard with half a dozen chickens for sale and begged to see the officer in charge.

The chickens were a ruse. The man was Quashie Sam, a Krooman who had been one of Midshipman Castles' prize-crew. He had been hiding on the outskirts of Bahia for two weeks, having already sought refuge with a British merchant captain but been repulsed. He had heard a salute fired in the bay, seen a British warship anchored there and seized his moment. Six weeks into the *Volcano*'s passage to Freetown, he told Captain Finlaison, Mr Castles was fishing in the chains, the crew were about their tasks above and aloft and Quashie Sam was below feeding the slaves when shots were fired on deck. Racing up through the hatchway, he saw Mr Castles slide, bleeding, overboard, hacked about by the Portuguese slaver-captain's cutlass. The shots had been aimed at the British quartermaster, now sprawled dead at the helm, and two men aloft in the rigging, both of whom fell into the sea. Two other Kroomen jumped overboard as the black cook and another Portuguese sailor killed the remaining British sailors, then turned, saw Quashie Sam and came for him, but only to force him below with the slaves and close the hatches over his head. Another black sailor was thrown down with him. At midnight, the slaver-captain told them that all the British were dead and the ship was on her way to Brazil. The slaves were once more slaves; as for the two black sailors, 'he would save their lives and sell them at Bahia, unless he fell in with an English vessel, in which case he must kill them to prevent discovery'.[6] In Brazil, Quashie Sam had been sold to a tobacco plantation, run away and made his way to the coast. He was brought back aboard the *Morgiana* to Sierra Leone and freedom. His story was a warning to prize-officers to guard their prisoners closely, and never let go of their weapons.

If the new treaties did not stop illegal slaving by the ships of Portugal and the Netherlands, they did restrict it to some extent. France and America, however, had refused to sign any agreement at all. Suspicion of the old enemy's motives was just too strong.

The combination of Commodore Collier and his Irish sidekick, Lieutenant Hagan, could have fed the paranoia of any French captain. George Collier had been commodore of the fleet which helped force the French evacuation from Spain and Lieutenant Hagan had served under him for six years. Together they had captured three enemy ships: a warship off Rochefort and two privateers. When they sailed in company from Freetown on the commodore's first cruise, French skippers filling their holds with labour for Guadaloupe and Martinique regarded them bleakly and wondered which war they were fighting: the new one against the slavers, or the old one against the French.

The *Louis* judgment of 1817, however, had given the French carte blanche to slave where they wished, and whereas they had previously confined their activities to Senegal, now they were seen sailing hundreds of miles to the south. Their captains did not even bother to dissimulate their purpose. When Hagan boarded two French vessels in the Gallinas,

> the commanders gave a very polite reception to their boarders, candidly avowed their object, one saying that his number was to be 150 slaves, and they were perfectly at their ease in an unreserved conversation which followed. When the boats left them, they pronounced their adieu with all the good humour of conscious security. The cargoes of these vessels had been landed and their traffic on shore was going on.[7]

Nor were French ships the only ones taking advantage of French immunity. 'The flags of France and America', Commodore Collier informed the Admiralty, 'are now generally adopting as the best cover to illicit slaving. The unpleasant situation this places his Majesty's officers under who are charged with preventing this traffic, must be evident to their Lordships and will, I hope, induce them to give me some specific instructions upon this head.' None arrived. With the colonial authorities at Goree complicit, there was little the Preventive Squadron could do against the French, although some British officers had already decided that if one side broke the rules, then the other could do so too.

Commodore Collier stopped at Trade Town on the *Tartar*'s next cruise south. There, he took aboard a few marooned American seamen, whose captain had died of fever, and left. Slavers? Certainly not, they said. In the roads, the *Tartar* lookout spotted a schooner, which, seeing the British frigate tack to approach, piled on sail and fled. Men on her deck were seen lightening ship, throwing cask after cask over the side to bob in the wake. It was a long, uncomfortable race. Other French captains might brave it out, merely refusing the British officers' request to board. This one was more cautious, for after the first cask had gone over the side, he was guilty not just of slaving, but of murder, and some unreasonable French magistrate might find the death of a few blacks a serious matter. When he finally hove to, a British lieutenant was rowed across with his waterproofed packet of papers proving rank and nationality.

The *Jeune Estelle* was from Martinique, her French papers were in order, but, although the British had no right to search her, Commodore Collier ordered it done anyway. Yes, he had taken on slaves at the Pepper Coast, Captain Sanguines said candidly, but they had all been taken from him by a Spanish pirate. It was a credible story but the boarding party was not sure it was a true one. The French crew was uneasy and there was a lingering smell about the ship, that essence of fear, sweat and excrement known to every seaman on the slaving coasts. Ignoring Sanguine's protests about the sanctity of the French flag, several British seamen went below to search but found nothing. Still they were convinced something was hidden. Down they went again and this time, above the soft slap of waves against the hold, a faint groan was heard from inside a stopped-up cask. The lid was ripped off and two little girls were pulled out, almost dead of asphyxiation. Among those who gathered round them, back on the deck of the *Tartar*, were the American seamen just rescued from Trade Town. We know these little girls, they said, casually incriminating themselves; they were among the slaves our captain bought before he died; he gave them 'to his mate, on his promise to perform the rites of Christian burial on himself'.[8] Just after that burial, Captain Sanguines had landed, armed, and carried off these two and fourteen more, claiming them as payment of a debt. The children, once they could breathe and speak to the Kroomen, corroborated the story.

Back to the *Jeune Estelle* went the boarding party: where was the American mate, Collier demanded, where was the American vessel and where were the other fourteen Negroes? Captain Sanguines would not say. Collier ordered another search of the hold. Jammed between two barrels, they found one man, fighting to breathe, and realised with horror what had been in the casks Sanguines had thrown overboard.

'You are breaking the laws of your country,' Commodore Collier told the slaver in disgust.

'What of it?' Sanguines replied. 'I know of more than forty captains trading slaves under the French flag,' and produced a receipt for the $8's worth of brandy and iron he had paid for the man just found. Given this proof that the slave had been 'fairly bought', and not from a British citizen or in British waters, Collier was forced to leave him aboard. It would be a waste of time sending Sanguines up to Senegal for adjudication. As soon as he was able, Captain Sanguines began a prosecution against Commodore Collier for 'illegal detention'.

Given evidence of such cases and under mounting pressure from Britain, the French government passed a law in 1820 which increased the penalties for slaving and in December of that year the French frigate *L'Huron* arrived in Freetown harbour. Her commander, Captain Chevalier du Plessis, seemed willing to put past hostilities aside. His English was fluent and he was happy to attend dinner at Government House with British officers, picnic in the hills and tour the Liberated African villages before setting off for the Bight of Benin. Surely, it was thought, some dent in the enormous illegal French trade must now be made. Was this not France's *Amelia*, come to enforce her felony law? But Captain du Plessis, for all his charm, seemed no more able, or willing, then his predecessor.

In HMS *Snapper's* last, brief cruise of 1821, she boarded seven French slavers around Cape Mount. One, an officer wrote,

> was a mere boat, though she had on board one hundred and fifty-three slaves, literally packed together: these poor creatures were in a truly pitiable state, and by their most expressive cries and gestures towards us, evinced their anxiety to be released. The feelings of our officers on this occasion need not, and indeed could not, be described; our sailors, not very familiar with laws or treaties, expressed their indignation in no equivocal terms on our permitting the schooner to proceed; they, of course, feel rather at a loss to account for the partiality shown to the French flag.[9]

Early the next year, Lieutenant Hagan suffered a grim déjà vu, falling in with two French vessels at the Gallinas. One was commanded by Captain Lempreur of the French Royal Navy, who 'came on board the *Thistle* in the full-dress uniform of his rank in the French service; and stated, amongst other things, to Lieutenant Hagan, that he had, a few days before, had the gratification of meeting an old friend and brother officer in the person of M. du Plessis, Captain of the French brig of war *L'Huron* and Commodore on this station'.[10]

The Preventive Squadron might rage against the fact, but in the absence of a treaty, a French squadron or a colonial administration which did not favour the trade, French slavers remained as inviolable under Commodore Collier as they had been under Commodore Yeo.

Commissioners for the new British–Spanish Mixed Commission arrived in July 1819. After they, too, had spun out the formalities, they began reluctantly to condemn the stream of Spaniards caught slaving north of the equator. However, in March 1820, two months before the date at which Spanish slaving was outlawed everywhere, the Spanish Commissioner of Arbitration, like the Portuguese, found himself so brought down by the climate that he returned to Cadiz to convalesce, saying 'he would not remain at Sierra Leone if his government would give him £100,000 per annum'.[11] As the Spanish treaty, like the Portuguese, had no provision for cases to be heard in his absence, and he had left a strong protest against any ad hoc provision being made to do so, any British captain detaining a Spanish vessel was stymied. His absence mattered less than it might have, in fact, for the expected rich harvest of Spaniards was not gathered in after May 1820. Flags of convenience had sheltered illegal British and American slavers since 1807 and now the Spanish, too, turned to the nationality game, secure in the knowledge no Spanish man-of-war would come checking their documents. All they had to do was call in at the busy, venal Portuguese islands, buy some documents and call themselves Portuguese for the duration.

In July 1821, HMS's *Snapper, Pheasant* and *Myrmidon* sailed from Sierra Leone to Ouidah in the Bight of Benin. At this date, Spanish and French slaving was theoretically banned everywhere, and Portuguese slaving was banned north of the Line. The three ships' detentions showed how much those bans were worth: French, Portuguese and Spanish slave-ships were everywhere. Only one was surprised with slaves aboard, a Portuguese loading in the River Calabar, and she was sent up to the Mixed Commission. One of her compatriots, the *James & Philip*, was well known to the officers of the

Pheasant who boarded her off Ouidah. She had previously been the Dutch *Maria*, condemned for slaving by the British–Dutch Mixed Commission, sold at auction as prescribed by the treaties, and bought by an Englishman acting as agent for a Ouidah slaver, who had sent her straight back into the trade. Altogether, the vessels fruitlessly boarded were estimated to be fitted up for six thousand slaves, and as soon as the British warships turned back for Sierra Leone, they sailed with impunity. That year alone, 190 slave-cargoes left the Bonny and another 162 were loaded in the Calabar.

The *Thistle*, in from patrolling the coast north of Sierra Leone, brought the sad news that there, too, the trade had fully revived. 'The renewal in the traffic of human beings on [that] coast', Governor Charles M'Carthy of Sierra Leone wrote to London, 'must be viewed by every friend to humanity with deep regret; accompanied as that renewal has been with cruel wars amongst the hitherto peaceful natives: the arrival of a Slave ship in any of the adjacent rivers is the signal for attack, the hamlets of the natives are burned and the miserable survivors carried and sold to the Slave factors.'[12] The heaviest traffic was from Goree to Bissao; further south, the Nuñez and Pongas, 'not long ago considered too near this colony to be approached with impunity by Slave vessels', were again 'entirely under the control of renegade European and American slave-traders'.

At the end of Commodore Collier's commission in 1821, he found himself entangled in the snares of Portuguese hypocrisy. On his last cruise, his boats had found a Portuguese skipper buying slaves from the slave-dealing chief Duke Ephraim of Duke's Town in the River Bonny. Ephraim cheerfully admitted to having promised the Portuguese captain three slaves who had not yet been paid for and were still in his barracoons. Certainly the British could take them, he said, why not? As long as they paid, he did not mind who had them. With a *Tartar* prize-crew aboard, the Portuguese *Gaviao* was sent up to Freetown and her own officers taken aboard the *Tartar* to follow. In Freetown, Collier found his orders to sail immediately for England but the *Gaviao* was still toiling up the coast and had not yet arrived. At the British–Portuguese Mixed Commission, Collier cited his orders to leave, filed his plea against the master of the *Gaviao* and asked the court to hear evidence from himself, his officers and the *Gaviao* crew brought up aboard the *Tartar*. Alas, the Portuguese commissioners could not: procedures did not allow it; their hands were tied; no evidence could be heard until the *Gaviao* herself arrived. On the morning of 17 June, the *Tartar* headed for Britain. Later that day, the *Gaviao* came into Freetown harbour.

Collier had appointed a Mr Walsh to represent him in court. However, the Portuguese commissioners regretted that nowhere in their instructions was there a clause providing for a detaining officer's agent to cross-question witnesses and no, Mr Walsh could certainly not read the written depositions. The case against the *Gaviao* was declared unproven, she was restored to her owners and the court turned to the claim those gentlemen then made for compensation from Collier. As he was not able to appear (being in the Bay of Biscay) it went against him by default. He was ordered to pay £1,520 13s 9d in damages.

Too many officers had been penalised for carrying out what were their orders. Most unfortunate of all was Captain Willis of HMS *Cherub*. The master of a Havana slave-ship whose slaves Willis had sent up to Freetown appealed the ship's condemnation, and a London court agreed that Willis had acted wrongly. He must compensate the Spaniard not only for the detention but also for the loss of his slaves, who had scattered and could not be found by the time the court ordered them restored to their buyer. There followed the distasteful business of valuing the slaves as property: had they been sick or strong, damaged or complete, old or young? For exceeding his powers, Captain Willis was ordered to pay £21,180. That was the law of prize, and it would remain so until 1848, when lawyers for another Squadron officer sued for compensation forced the British government to accept liability in such cases. Captain Willis was ruined.

It was small surprise, therefore, that Commodore Collier's final report to the Admiralty was written in the same tone as Commodore Yeo's: pessimism mixed with anger. If other nations did not participate in the active prevention of the slave trade, he insisted, the British law was a dead letter. The French knew it, the Portuguese, Americans and Spanish knew it; even the slave-traders on the edge of British waters knew it. However much and proudly politicians and journalists in London might speak of the power of the British flag, many in the West Indies and on the West African coast held it in contempt. The interference of the Royal Navy had been added to other hazards run by the slavers: tornadoes, piracy, insurrection, disease; but it had not destroyed the trade any more than any of these had done. He might have added – and perhaps he did in private – that unless British naval officers were given protection from personal loss, they would soon be forced to look the other way as much as the officers of other countries.

4

Bad Blood

During Commodore Collier's command of the West African station, only one other government seemed willing to take real measures against the illegal trade. Forty years later, President Joseph Roberts of Liberia would speak about his country's birth. 'The programme of the founders of the American Colonization Society, as I have always understood it,' he said, 'was

1st. To establish on the shores of Africa an asylum where such of her scattered children, as might choose to avail themselves of it, would find a free and happy home. 2d. That through the instrumentality of a colony thus established, composed of men who had themselves been the victims of cruel servitude, additional facilities would be afforded for the extirpation of the slave trade, then rampant, with all its attendant horrors, at nearly every prominent point along that Western Coast. 3d. By means of Christian settlements, in the midst of that barbarous people, to introduce the blessings of civilization and Christianity among the heathen tribes of that degraded land.

It was a charitable reworking of history, made when the colony had flowered into an independent republic and the mother country had finally outlawed slavery on her own soil. It might have described the motives of Paul Cuffe and John Kizell, but it was far from the truth.

Liberia was born from the holds of the *Elizabeth*, an American merchant ship which left New York in February 1820. She carried a collapsible sawmill, wagons, wheelbarrows, ploughs, guns and ammunition, cannon, fishing nets, a small barge, two dogs who hated each other on sight (their fighting would almost cause a mid-ocean duel), the Reverend Samuel Bacon of the American Colonization Society, three of the Reverend's colleagues (all white) and eighty-six free black American 'workmen' (about one-third of them children). Among them was the Reverend Daniel Coker. 'Surely', he wrote, 'this expedition is in the care of God . . . my soul travails that we should be faithful and if we arrive that we should be useful in Africa.'[1] What was surer still was that they were no longer welcome in America.

Slavery had been abolished only in the northern states of America, where an 1820 census returned a total of 233,000 free Negroes. Free they were; but unequal and unwanted, living in a white society which no longer had a use for them and ascribed to them all the usual attributes of an underclass: fecklessness, dirtiness, a tendency to thieve and lie, indolence, viciousness, too many children. Assimilating freed Negroes into white society was unthinkable. Allowing them contact with their still-enslaved siblings was dangerous, for they would contaminate the enslaved with ideas of liberty; but so was leaving them to fester and breed alone in their ghetto, for who knew but that the 'San Domingo virus' would spread and the horrors of the Haitian revolution be repeated on American soil. What, then, was to be done with them?

'Every thing connected with their condition, including their colour, is against them', wrote Reverend Finley, minister of a New Jersey town in which 1,500 free Negroes lived, 'nor is there much prospect that their state can ever be greatly ameliorated, while they continue among us. Could not the rich and benevolent devise means to form a Colony on some part of the Coast of Africa . . . which might gradually induce many free blacks to go and settle, devising for them the means of getting there, and of protection and support till they were established?'[2] These ideas took root in the American Colonization Society, formed in a Washington coffee house in 1816. The ACS brought together some of the republic's most powerful men and power spoke with a united voice: the free blacks must go. Agents were sent to visit West Africa in 1818, where they met John Kizell and learnt of the wonders of Sherbro Island.

The publicity surrounding the Colonization Society's programme, along with inadequacies in the American abolition law of 1807, brought the subject of the slave trade before Congress again. New, severe legislation was passed whereby the transatlantic slave trade was equated with piracy. If enforced, it would bring impressive results. President Monroe was also empowered to send warships to West Africa and money was voted to resettle freed or rescued slaves in some West African spot. The pioneers aboard the *Elizabeth* had been given free passage out on the understanding that they were to prepare a settlement for the many predicted to follow.

On 9 March, they anchored in Freetown and naked Kroomen flocked out in their canoes, weaving between the captured slave-ships in the harbour. 'I stood on deck and looked at these children of nature', Daniel Coker wrote, 'till streams of tears ran down my cheeks . . . thank the Lord I have seen Africa.'[3] Their next visitors were 'the officers of the different British vessels', who 'acted very friendly'; and then an American Methodist, Mr Perry, who 'was so happy at seeing us, he could not contain himself, but shouted and praised God. He and Mr Bacon took a hug.' On 20 March, they landed on Sherbro Island and found the good Mr Kizell had prepared a few huts to shelter them until a mainland site was bought and sturdier homes erected.

The USS *Cyane*, first warship of the tentative new American anti-slave-trade squadron, arrived in Freetown just after the *Elizabeth* left. An ungracious peace had been made between Britain and America in February 1815, the causes of war left largely unresolved. Ill feeling festered. Six years ago, the USS *Cyane* had been HMS *Cyane*, sloop of the Royal Navy, seized by the Americans from under the nose of Sir George Collier's own squadron. She had been incorporated into the United States navy and it was, one American seaman would write, 'the exquisite pleasure of "rubbing it into the English" that led the government to send the *Cyane* to cruise on the scene of her capture from the English, especially as she would frequently be sailing in company with British war ships also engaged in suppressing the slave trade'.

The *Cyane*'s officers were well received in Freetown, where primitive versions of the entertainments offered by older ports were emerging. There were amateur theatricals and concerts, excursions and hunts. Marines gave dinners for naval men and naval men gave them for the colonial regiments; horses raced on the sand and picnics in the hills were determinedly written up as *fêtes champêtres* in the *Gazette*. 'During our stay,' wrote home

American Captain Edward Trenchard – who had opposed Commodore Yeo on the Great Lakes six years ago – 'the European gentlemen who were residents at the place treated us with utmost respect, striving who should be most forward in attention and hospitality.'[4] Trenchard had brought with him a band of musicians – the sort of jovial folly allowed to captains, kings of their little domains – who 'played every day for practice and on all festive occasions'. Dinners aboard the *Tartar* with Americans as guests – hosted by Commodore Collier, who had, with Lieutenant Hagan, captured a rich Charleston vessel during the war – were followed by dinners aboard the *Cyane* with the British as guests, and clearly music soothed, or at least drowned out, any surly asides about better late than never, mad monarchs and slave-owning in the land of liberty. The officers of the *Cyane* passed a convivial week before heading south.

Trenchard found the emigrants on Sherbro Island already suffering, and recommended they immediately move elsewhere. John Kizell had built his huts unasked, and expected no payment; he had sent the tired arrivals twelve chickens and a bushel of wheat and joined them in prayer and thanksgiving, but his land was disastrously chosen: not only unhealthy and ill-provided but surrounded by as much bitter water as first Granville Town, then Freetown, had been. 'Had I authority to do so,' wrote the Reverend Samuel Bacon, 'I could take a vessel lying within the floating of one tide, say 25 miles from us, in the Shebar, under American colours, taking on slaves.'[5] Captain Trenchard did have the authority, and, after a brief visit to Sherbro, he exercised it. Off the Gallinas, he found '7 sail, 1 brig and 6 topsail schooners, close in shore. On perceiving us, they made all sail and stood off; it being nearly calm, I instantly despatched the *Cyane*'s boats, properly officered and manned, in pursuit, who succeeded in taking possession, and bringing alongside 6 of them.' Two of the detained ships flew the Spanish flag, one the French and one the Danish but the other two were American and one of these was rashly commanded by Midshipman Andrews of the US Navy. This young man, seeing the *Cyane*'s cutter approach, 'attempted to make his escape to the shore in his boat, but was pursued, overtaken and brought on board'.

At first he assumed an air of indifference, and totally denied his vessel to be American, or his being concerned in the slave trade; but after finding we were in possession of his papers and going to make a prize of him, his confidence forsook him, and he acknowledged his vessel was American and engaged in the traffic of slaves.[6]

A brief patrol of Sherbro and the Gallinas showed the *Cyane*'s dismayed officers just how far their countrymen were still involved in the trade: at least six vessels detained there were from Baltimore, Charleston and New York. The same six also showed how difficult it would be to prove it. The United States had anti-slave-trade agreements with no one. Whatever American officers suspected to be the true nationality of the vessels waiting for slave-cargoes, built along American lines, crewed by men with American accents, they could board, search and detain only those flying the American flag – or the British one, on Commodore Collier's informal say-so – and few would fly the Red Ensign or the Stars and Stripes in sight of a warship. Most American ships, Captain Trenchard wrote, were 'so completely covered by Spanish papers, that it is impossible to condemn them'. They sailed from the USA to some port in Cuba

with a cargo of blue and white cottons, India checks, nankin, powder, tobacco, &c. where they make a sham sale of the vessel, for the purpose of procuring a set of Spanish papers. The officers make oath that the cargo . . . has been landed, and procure the requisite certificates, whilst every article has remained untouched on board. They then take on board a Spaniard, who passes for the captain, though perhaps this is his first voyage to sea, hoist the Spanish flag, and proceed to the coast of Africa, north of the line, keeping three log books, two in Spanish, one true and the other false, and one in English. Having obtained their human cargo, and escaped the vigilance of the cruizers on the coast, the next plan is to arrange the log book to be produced in Cuba, which must shew that the slaves were shipped south of the line, and the vessel with her cargo is then admitted to entry. When overhauled by the English or Patriot* privateers, they exhibit American papers, and when by the Americans, Spanish papers, by which means many escape capture and condemnation.[7]

* i.e. South American.

'I sincerely hope', Trenchard added, 'that government have revised the law giving us more authority. You have no idea how cruelly these poor creatures are treated by the monsters engaged in taking them from the coast.'

While the *Cyane* cruised the coast, Samuel Crozer of the ACS was setting off across the Shebar straits to the mainland. The ACS committees planning this voyage, working with no knowledge of palavers, ritual, tribal hierarchy or slaving networks, had reached the hopelessly optimistic conclusion that land could be bought, the settlers moved across and the business of clearing and building begun before the rains set in towards the end of April. As Governor M'Carthy of Sierra Leone had warned, however, Crozer found that the local chiefs wanted nothing to do with the project, for a community of free blacks was no more welcome here than it was in New Jersey. Whatever was said by agents who came with promises of neutrality, however much they swore that God, not politics, guided their hand, these settlements for free blacks reeked of abolition and that threatened custom, dynasty and wealth. By the time Mr Crozer returned to Sherbro Island, empty-handed and newly wise, the rains had come: dense, thunderous downpours to drench the colonists through their feeble roofs of thatch, sending up steamy mists from which clouds of mosquitoes emerged and attacked. Already they were weakened by lack of food, for the *Elizabeth*'s supplies had not been enough to cover this long, unforeseen stay, and suffering diarrhoea, for their water supply had gone bad.

Sick in mind, body and heart, they quarrelled and John Kizell sadly watched the experiment fail around him as the rain fell and the camp fell with it into bitterness and despair. 'Some would not be governed by white men', he wrote, 'and some would not be governed by black men, and some would not be governed by mulattoes; but the truth was they did not want to be governed by anybody.'[8] The malaria killed them off, one by one, black and white. When it killed Samuel Crozer, the Reverend Bacon decided he must go to Sierra Leone and ask for help. He died on the way. Daniel Coker, leader by default, gathered a group of colonists together and sailed for Freetown. Only a rump remained on the island, determined they had not left America for African freedom only to be thrown on British charity.

* * *

Cruising southward to find more American slavers, the officers of the *Cyane* had also looked out for a more suitable spot for the colonists. They thought they had found it at Cape Mesurado,[9] a long, narrow, densely forested tongue of land, 3 miles across at its widest point and extending 30 into the ocean. Either side of the isthmus, a river debouched: the Junk to one side, the Mesurado to the other, both of them old slave-conduits. This was the land the Americans wanted and Lieutenant Matthew Calbraith Perry held discussions with 'King Peter' of the Dey people about a possible cession. When the *Cyane* returned to America, Captain Trenchard reported Mesurado to the ACS as the 'most elligable situation for a settlement'. The result was that the ACS agents sent to Sherbro to replace those who had died brought orders that Sherbro Island be abandoned and Mesurado acquired. The last of the *Elizabeth* group left on Sherbro, now regretful and ready to leave their huts, were brought to Freetown and by April, Kizell's land was empty. The only Americans left there were dead ones, disintegrating under their crosses in the marsh.

Over one hundred American blacks were waiting in Freetown when the next American warship, USS *Alligator*, entered the harbour with the ACS agent, Dr Ayres, and more black emigrants aboard. The *Alligator*'s commander, Lieutenant Robert Field Stockton, a well-connected New Jersey man, was only twenty-six years old but already a veteran of ocean and conflict, especially with the British: grandson of one of the signatories of the American Declaration of Independence, noted for sterling service in the recent war, in which he had earned the name 'fighting Bob', and an ardent picker of fights with British officers.

For Lieutenant Stockton, fighting the British was pleasure as well as duty. After the peace of 1815, he had sailed aboard one of the ships which battered the Dey of Algiers, an expedition much to his taste. Cruising in the Mediterranean after this, he had racked up the astonishing total of *three duels in six months* – all with British officers, all turning on some offence to Stockton's acute sense of national honour; all, according to his own accounts, ending in the unmanly defeat of his opponent. Not, therefore, an obvious candidate for collaboration with the British Royal Navy, Stockton had nonetheless lobbied for the *Alligator*'s command. Returning to America from the Mediterranean duelling spree, his ship had run down the West African coast, and what he saw of the slave trade had persuaded him he wanted to be part of its suppression. He was perhaps disappointed to be offered a 'friendly and hospitable' welcome from Governor M'Carthy, who advised him the natives of Mesurado would be found 'gravely hostile to abolition' despite knowing that this American at least would heed no warnings from the British.

Lieutenant Stockton had been authorised to hold further talks with King Peter, this time accompanied by arms. Again, Peter refused to sell and said his decision was final. Lieutenant Stockton did not agree, and employed guides to take him to Peter's Town where a second meeting was held at which American pistols were held to African heads. King Peter and his council parted with Cape Mesurado in exchange for guns, furniture, a bundle of mirrors, rum and cigars worth about $300. A similar collection of goods was put together for Peter's overlord, 'King George', who 'resided on the Cape and claimed a sort of jurisdiction over the northern district of the peninsula of Montserado', or at least told the Americans he did.

The village thus brutally acquired was to be Monrovia, capital of Liberia, land of the free. The American colonists sheltering in Freetown packed their bags again and set off down the coast, passing and leaving behind their miserable former home on Sherbro Island, sailing onwards into the hot south-east, with flying fish on the decks and sharks in their wake. Some were hopeful, others apprehensive, but even the most fearful had not expected the occupation of Mesurado to be opposed so soon and with such determination. Lieutenant Stockton might have thought he had cowed King Peter but King Peter thought otherwise. As their ship came to anchor in the Mesurado River, the emigrants saw a native army encamped on the beach. Their first three months at Mesurado were spent, not on the dubiously acquired soil of the cape, but on one of the islands in the mouth of the river, out of the reach of spears and arrows. They named it Providence Island, and waited, dispirited and bitter, until another rescue mission should come. Again, one after another succumbed to fever; again, fresh water ran out; again, the rains came to plague them and no warship appeared off the cape to beat away King Peter's forces.

USS *Alligator*, gone to cruise elsewhere on the coast, was as stunned by the volume of illegal slaving as the British ships *Snapper*, *Myrmidon* and *Pheasant* had been on their own summer cruises. Stockton, given information of American slavers in the Gallinas, had found two schooners at anchor there. The *Jeune Eugenie* and the *Elize* both flew the French flag but he seized them nonetheless and sailed on to Trade Town. There he anchored quietly in the roads to observe two other schooners also flying French colours, also thought to be American. Shortly after Stockton's arrival, an officer of one, the *Daphnée*, was heard to hail cheerfully from his cutter and was invited on board for a chat. Realising his visitor, a M. Guoy, was under the impression that the *Alligator* was in fact the *Jeune Eugenie* come to join him, and that Lieutenant Stockton was a fellow slaver, the officer did not disabuse his guest until he had burbled out sufficient information to incriminate his ship. His mouth closed abruptly when Stockton produced his commission and ordered an *Alligator* boarding party to take possession. An American officer had no powers to board a French ship but Stockton was, he would explain, 'satisfied from the external appearance of this vessel', as he had been of the *Jeune Eugenie* and *Elize*,

> that she was an American bottom, and of that description of vessels called, by way of distinction, Baltimore built vessels: and being fully convinced she was concerned in the slave trade, I presumed of course the colours she had hoisted were assumed for the occasion, and not true; for it was well understood that the slave trade had been denounced by both nations whose protection she appeared to claim.[10]

Nor was there any doubt that she was slaving: her captain was ashore purchasing slaves, the crew testified she had picked up 'a cargo exactly suited to the slave market' for which there were no records on board and the logbook was falsified. 'These are among the reasons,' Stockton would continue, 'which led to the conviction that no faith or credit ought to be given to her papers.'

As British officers had already found, such workmanlike assumptions – even where accurate – would not stand up to French lawyers. Nor had Stockton bargained with the determination of French (or American) crews: the *Daphnée*, *Mathilde*, *Elize* and *Jeune Eugenie* all set off for America under prize-crews but only the *Elize* would arrive. A few days out to sea, the captured slavers overpowered the other *Alligator* crews and turned around. A favourable wind had them back off Trade Town in two days, their slaving voyage scarcely inconvenienced. There the American prisoners were politely lodged while the slave-ships resumed their business. By July, six hundred Negroes were on their way to Guadaloupe, packed on their hams in the steaming holds, the American sailors accommodated rather better above. From Point à Pitre, the Americans made a crestfallen voyage back to their own coast, sent on their way with many ironic good wishes.

In July, the *Alligator* was joined by the USS *Shark*, commanded by Trenchard's old lieutenant, Matthew Perry, whose cruise was as eye-opening, and frustrating, as the rest. First he stopped a slave-schooner belonging to the governor of Guadaloupe, but had no powers to detain her. Then he chased the *Caroline*, another French vessel, just out of the Gallinas and sent three officers to board her. 'The overpowering smell,' wrote a shocked midshipman, 'and the sight presented by her slave deck, can never be obliterated from the memory.'[11] There were 164 Negroes packed into a space 15 by 40 feet each tucked into the other with the children lying on top of the adults' bodies. They were naked, and shaven of head and body hair to prevent lice. 'Their bodies were so emaciated, and their black skins were so shrunk upon the facial bones, that in their torpor, they resembled so many Egyptian mummies half-awakened to life.' Brought face to face with the reality of the illegal trade, 'I never saw the sympathies of men more deeply moved than were those of our crew. We hoisted up a cask of water, and some bread and beef, and gave each poor slave a long drink and a hearty meal' but they could not detain the ship. Commander Perry harangued her captain on the cruelty of his business, even obliging the man to sign a pledge 'to abjure the slave trade forever', but the slaves could not be rescued and the pledge was doubtless tossed over the side as soon as the Americans had gone.

Back in the United States, Lieutenant Stockton found himself in tangles familiar to the officers of the British squadron. The French Minister to Washington was furious that an American warship should have boarded ships sailing under the protection of the French flag. Only the *Elize* had arrived, and that vessel the Frenchman 'demanded . . . should be given up, asserting, at the same time he deprecated the traffic [i.e. the slave trade], that it was the right of the French government, to judge of the conduct of its own subjects, and to punish their infractions of its laws'.[12] The presence of only three French citizens aboard amid a host of Americans, the verbal evidence of M. Guoy and her crew, the fact that although 'she was built in the U.S. they could not shew any legal proof of a transfer from her original owners', the fabricated logbook – none was of any weight. In the absence of a treaty authorising him to do so, no American officer might board any ship flying the French flag. Whether she was truly French; whether she was breaking the laws of France, America or humanity – these were not at issue. Parallels with restrictions on British actions towards ships flying the American flag were ignored and the *Elize* was restored to French jurisdiction.

Despite what he and other American officers were reporting, Lieutenant Stockton knew there was much resistance at home to believing the extent of American duplicity on the coast. 'It is possible', he wrote to the Secretary of the Navy Department in May 1821,

> there may be some difficulty in persuading men generally, to believe in the adroitness and fraud with which this trade is prosecuted. They have almost reduced it to a science, and heretofore in the disguise of Frenchmen, and with the facilities afforded them in the West Indies, have made certain calculations with regard to their success, laughing at the exertions of all christendom to put an end to it.[13]

Many believed allegations of American slaving on the West African coast to be British propaganda, and even the findings of the *Cyane*, *Shark* and *Alligator* could not persuade them to accept a mutual right of search. When the exasperated British Foreign Minister asked the president in 1822 if he could imagine anything more atrocious than the slave trade, he replied, fatuously, 'Yes. Admitting the right of search by foreign officers of our vessels upon the seas in time of peace; for that would be making slaves of ourselves.' Whatever the good intentions of the American seamen who had seen close-up the horrors of the coast, they were scuppered by orders from above.

The American squadron was withdrawn in 1822 and would not reappear for twenty years.

Alone on the coast again, the British Preventive Squadron entered 1822 with a new commodore, a new flagship and the same depressingly enormous task. Two thousand rescued slaves reached the crowded settlements of Sierra Leone that spring and summer alone; but everyone knew that thousands more had got away. 'The traffic in slaves has not decreased,' the commodore wrote to London:

nor do I see how it can whilst it is supported by European protection in the most open and avowed manner, and defended by force of arms. Were the British ships, employed on this coast for its suppression, allowed to act with freedom, it would in a short time be so cut up and harassed, as not to make it worth the risk, trouble and disappointment which would inevitably follow.[14]

The comments of the squadron's officers were not ignored but their partners in the campaign, the diplomats, were forced to work at a pace dictated by unwilling negotiators, the slow settling of post-war administrations into new positions and alliances, and the inbuilt delays of a time when communications were held up by snowfall, or the speed of horses over potholed roads. George Canning, who became Foreign Secretary in 1822, did his best. That year, Britain, France, Russia and Prussia met at the Congress of Verona and Britain tried again to force a precedent in international law. Each country, said Canning, could separately declare the trade piracy and 'upon the aggregate of separate declarations, a general law [could] be incorporated in the Law of Nations'. The proposal foundered on French antipathy and the others' indifference. Far more productive was a new 'Equipment Clause' in the agreement with the Netherlands which would virtually eradicate the Dutch flag from the slaving seas.

'Whereas', ran the agreement reached with the Dutch in December 1822, 'it has been found by experience, that vessels employed in the illegal traffic, have unshipped their Slaves immediately prior to their being visited by the ships of war', thus evading the treaties, henceforth 'if there shall be clear and undeniable proof, that a Slave or Slaves has or have been put on board a vessel for the purpose of illegal traffic . . . such vessel shall be detained.' This would end the mad dash of ships' boats to reach a slaver before the last slave had been thrown overboard or canoed ashore. But the 'Additional Article' was far more important. Far away in Amsterdam, Canning had shouted and banged his fist on the table to have it accepted, for this changed the nature of the naval campaign from capture to detection. It consisted of a detailed list of the 'outfit and equipment' of the ship which was henceforth to be 'considered as prima facie evidence of her actual employment in the Slave Trade'.

If a ship's deck had open gratings, rather than the closed hatches used on normal merchantmen, she was deemed a slaver, for their only purpose was to allow air to circulate among slaves below. If detaining officers found shackles, bolts, handcuffs or an 'unreasonable quantity of water' – more than a merchantman's crew could be expected to need – or even empty casks to hold water (unless it could be proved that these were for palm oil), she was a slaver. Too many 'mess-tubs or kids', the tin vessels used to give slaves their farina and rice, were incriminating. So was 'having on board two or more copper boilers or even one of an unreasonable size', or too much farina or maize, staples of the slaves' diet. 'Unless rebutted by satisfactory evidence upon the part of the master or owner that the vessel was otherwise legally employed at the time of detention or capture', she would be condemned and declared as lawful prize.

The 'Equipment Clause' was to become as central to the condemnation of slavers as the mutual right of search, and in recognition of this, both Portugal and Spain refused to accept it. Portugal did agree that proof of there *having been* one or more slaves aboard was sufficient for condemnation; Spain merely agreed to take it all under consideration, which might indicate acceptance in several years' time, a hint that another bribe might swing it, or burial under fear of Cuban disapproval.

Illegal British slaving also received another blow that year, when an important loophole was closed. The Felony Act of 1811 had not prevented indirect participation in slaving and evidence had been amassing of continued British involvement – not by seamen and shipowners, this time, but by merchants and financiers. A huge volume of 'trade goods' was of British manufacture, and these goods were transported in British ships, insured by British firms, to Bahia or Havana for sale to the Brazilian or Spanish merchants who exchanged them for slaves in West Africa. The Slave Trade Consolidation Act was designed to prevent all this. Britons might no longer, with 'prior knowledge' of the trade for which their goods or services were intended, 'fit out, man, navigate, equip, dispatch, use, employ any ship, vessel or boat' for the trade; 'loan or advance, or become guarantee or security for' such trade; be a partner or an agent; ship 'money, goods or effects' to be used in the trade; or 'insure . . . slaves or any property or other subject matter engaged' in the trade.

The Dutch Equipment Clause, the Portuguese agreement and the Slave

Trade Consolidation Act were all useful weapons in the Preventive
Squadron's armoury. They came, however, when time for slaver-catching
was limited. Other events had overtaken the ships on the West African
coast.

5

The Fever, the Deys and the Ashanti

There were elements of West African service which no British government could influence. One was the reaction of local people to foreigners arriving to settle, trade, farm or evangelise, threatening custom and profit. Another, more immediate, threat was the havoc wrought by the climate on the European constitution.

The most feared killer on the Slave Coast was not the slaver, the slave-ship, the shark or the 'cannibal kings' and ju-ju men of legend. It was 'the fever': malaria. Here was the source of the old tales: the White Man's Grave; *beware, beware, the Bight of Benin! There's one comes out for forty goes in!* – the silent garrisons and ghost-ships swinging to anchor; the graveyards full of pathetic memorials to babes, youths and the few white women who ignored the warnings and followed their menfolk out. In Guinea, 'death,' wrote Surgeon Alexander Bryson, 'in the form of fever or miasm [*sic*], lurks in every corner, hovers round every bush condensed and concentrated through the absence of light and heat, rises, emanating from the debris and decomposition around'.[1]

The new commodore, Sir Robert Mends, came to the African coast in early 1823 in his new flagship the *Owen Glendower*. In early March he was off the River Casamanca, north of Sierra Leone, sure two or three slavers were anchored at a village upriver under protection of the Portuguese governor. As the warship was too large to enter the river, volunteers were requested for detached service. Crews were formed of midshipman or bosun commanding a dozen or so men and eight of the *Glendower*'s boats put off early one morning to row for the estuary, leaving the frigate hidden over the horizon. By the time they reached the shore, the sun was up and, said Midshipman Binstead, in charge of one of the boats, 'dreadfully oppressive'. They continued at the oars all day. 'Really knocked up' after 'a fagging night's pull' of nearly 70 miles, they reached the village at three in the morning, 'pulled very quietly along under the huts' and came to rest. 'All hands were now glad to lay down which we did but could not long continue so as we were too annoyed by mosquitoes and sandflies.' Binstead's own face and arms were 'so swollen that I was in great pain and misery' and some of the men scratched themselves so badly 'they were perfectly unable to move or see'. Dawn came and a wretched huddle of huts emerged from the mist but 'to our great annoyance and disappointment',[2] no slavers. They had rowed 140 miles in terrible heat, suffered hundreds of insect bites and had nothing to show for it. This was detached service up the African rivers.

By May, the *Glendower* was off the River Congo and 'all the midshipmen were making out their wills in the event of slipping [dying]'.[3] On 13 May, the frigate headed out to sea, 'fearful of being seen from the shore or all the slavers would land their slaves', and her boats rowed for the river. There was a moment of triumph at dawn, for a Portuguese ship boarded by one officer had 320 Negroes aboard; and another of disgust when he was reminded that here, south of the equator, the Portuguese were still entitled to slave. 'I have never met with a more horrid description than my messmates gave me,' Binstead wrote, 'of the wretched state they were in, actually dying ten to twelve a day. All the men were in irons and the women under them by a small partition.' When the 'king of this place' appeared to ask whether they wished to 'make trade for slave', they were in no mood to be courteous. He did 'not appear at all pleased' by their short reply, although he was willing to answer Binstead's questions. How, the young man asked, does it all work? '"Suppose you give me musket or coat," the king said, "I give you good slave man or woman."' But where did that slave man or woman come from? 'I learnt from this monster that in the interior there are thousands of small farms to which they send men from here to purchase slaves for cloth, tobacco and powder and if, as they say, "no make trade for sell man, we go at night, lay in the bush and catch man, woman and child then sell them here to Portuguese."'

In June, the *Glendower* was cruising off the River Bonny in filthy weather. In such an enormous river, with its hundreds of creeks, boats could be away from their ships for weeks at a time. 'They would be provisioned for four-teen days but sometimes we didn't see them again for a month,' one seaman explained. 'When their provisions ran out and there was no sign of the ship they had to try and fall in with another cruiser.' On 16 June, the boats of the *Glendower* surprised a Spanish schooner with her slave-cargo part-loaded. When they saw the British, 'every soul jumped overboard to make for shore' and by the time the British came alongside, the ship was empty. They took her, nonetheless, and towed her to the town where those who had been made to jump overboard were being held, took on sixty – mainly children – and set off downriver to find the *Glendower*. Now the rain really set in, churning the waters, reducing visibility to a few yards ahead. 'I felt myself completely fagged out,' Midshipman Binstead wrote, 'and couldn't find the ship. We anchored for the night. I have never experienced such heavy rain in all my life.' At daybreak, they set off again, 'almost despairing of ever seeing [the *Glendower*] again', and spent another night anchored in the river, bitten by mosquitoes and sleeping in wet clothes. The following day, the mist lifted a little and 'to our great satisfaction we saw the ship at nine. We arrived on board with many bad cases of sickness and fever', and sixty chil-dren to be fed, clothed and tended.

By early July, they were in the New Calabar River, where the boats spotted a Spanish schooner which had fired on them a few days earlier. Under flag of truce, one British boat landed at the town where she was anchored to demand that the king hand over both ship and slaves. 'If not,' the British officer said, 'we shall land and burn this town.' He agreed. 'We made the king', Binstead wrote, unaware other officers had been sued for doing the same, 'put a few slaves on board prior to our boats going alongside which slaves being found would condemn the vessel.' When they demanded the rest the following day, the king refused. 'We anchored off the town, threat-ened to blow it down if the slaves were not immediately sent off', Binstead records, and, unsurprisingly, they arrived very soon: 141 women and chil-dren, some no more than three years old.

A Brazilian merchant later confirmed what the Bonny chief had described to Midshipman Binstead, and what this scene in the New Calabar suggested: that most slaves procured south of the equator were not the product of war but of simple sale, often by their families; or of having been pledged for a debt gone unredeemed. 'A negro', said that merchant, considers it a disgrace to have been born a slave, to be a debtor or criminal, or to have been sold by his father; he will therefore always tell you that he has been taken in war. I have asked the same question, over and over again, both on board slave vessels and in the barracoons on shore, and have received the same reply; and I have been amused by the derisive shouts that these replies called forth from the other slaves.

There were no derisive shouts here. 'I could not but feel for the poor creatures', Binstead wrote, 'to see them torn from their relations. To see father and mother fighting for their children was enough to draw pity from the coldest heart. To hear their cries and lamentations; all such I hope never again to see.' But they could not be left here, with those relations, for they would be sold to the next ship in; and better the exile of Sierra Leone than the exile of a plantation in Brazil.

With these women and infants also on board the *Glendower*, the ship was 'truly miserable'. The rain was still heavy, there were vicious thunderstorms and 'upwards of 200 naked slaves laying about, most of them sick . . . also several bad cases of fever amongst our own crew'. It always came on the same way. 'Headaches, pains and sick stomach, also pain in the back and loins', wrote one of the countless ship's surgeons who struggled against the disease. 'The skin is moist and there is a sore mouth, a foul tongue and diarrhea . . . delirium, which occurred about the fifth day, was usually fatal.'[4] The treatment was brutal, where there was any treatment at all: 'bleeding and opening the bowels with calomel and jalap'.[5] Sharks appeared about the *Glendower*, 'owing to the number of poor fellows that have lately been thrown overboard'.[6] On 19 July, the midshipmen's mess suffered its own tragedy. 'Departed this life Mr Richard MacCormac, midshipman. A most amiable young man, beloved by all his messmates.' Binstead wrote:

> I much feel the loss of so worthy a fellow. We were great friends and always on service stationed to the same boat. He died of the African fever, which had attacked him while him and myself were away in the boats up the Old Calabar. At 8.30 enclosed his body and sewed up in a cot, ready to commit to the deep.

They were badly short of food. With so many slaves to feed, the *Glendower*'s company was put on half-, then quarter-, allowance. 'Very anxious to arrive at some port,' Binstead wrote; 'little or no bread in the ship.' Three more weeks went by with no port found and Binstead himself 'was taken unwell with a headache, attended also by ophthalmia', the 'pink-eye' – inflammation and temporary blindness. It was one of the commonest of slave-deck diseases. 'The surgeon took 2lb of blood from me and supplied blisters to my hand', Binstead wrote. It was a treatment which can hardly have helped a man on one meal 'of bad oatmeal' per day, but he recovered despite it and, leaving the horrible Bights at last, was 'anxious to see some vessel from England'. They had had no news since leaving five months before and his mind 'was very uneasy at not hearing from home'. They saw none, however, just a continuation of the wretched coast now hated by all aboard, and more sharks in the wake for the 'poor fellows' still 'dying by the day'. 'Our mess now consists of six members,' he wrote on the last day of August, 'having when we left 27.'

Too short-handed to continue her work in the mangrove swamps and stagnant lagoons, the Glendower took her slaves to Sierra Leone, then made for Ascension, which had just been struck by another deadly African fever.

Malaria was not the only equatorial disease which could decimate a ship's company or a European town. Another, well known to the Royal Navy, razed the coast in 1823. HMS Bann's new commander, Captain Phillips, came into Freetown in March to reprovision his ship. They were taking on stores when the merchantman Caroline was reported at the bar, showing the white flag of distress. When three men of the Bann went down in the lighter, they found a terrible scene. The Caroline had left Freetown, healthy, a few days ago and gone trading down the coast. All but three of her crew had since died and those three were too weak to let go the anchor or bring in the sails. The Bann's men moored her, unbent her sails and disembarked her cargo, took the sick and dead to the hospital and returned aboard their own ship, southwardbound on her next cruise. Two days later, the first of them reported sick.

The man who stood shivering in the surgeon's berth complained of a high temperature, chills, aching bones and the symptom he least wanted to see: 'a yellow hue to the flesh'. The devastating yellow fever, known to seamen as the 'yellow jack', was aboard. In its swift, unsparing course through the system of man after man, blood rose from the mucous membranes of eyes, nostrils and anus. Frothy, black, blood-filled vomit was coughed onto the sickberth floor and inside, invisibly, liver, kidneys and heart gave way. The doctor could do little. His patients suffered days, sometimes a week, then died – or recovered. The strength of a man's immune system rather than the surgeon's ministrations dictated the outcome.

The pestilence spread like fire through Freetown, the wharves falling quiet, the streets empty; and down the coast, spread by ships and caravans, jumping from settlement to settlement, barracoon to barracoon. Convoys wound their way to Protestant cemeteries and all who could left for the hills, the islands or the sea. One Freetowner wrote home before he fled:

> That *dreadful scourge* the yellow fever has been brought into this colony by the ship *Caroline* . . . and out of a population of about 110 Europeans, nearly *eighty* have fallen victims to this dreadful disease; upwards of 250 blacks have also died of it; our streets are literally deserted . . . while writing this I have just learnt that our worthy Chief Justice was just taken with the black vomit last night and cannot live many hours. I am so alarmed that I shall leave this scene of wo [sic] tomorrow for the Isles of Los . . .[7]

Captain Phillips had decided to take his stricken ship to the healthy South Atlantic airs and hospital of Ascension. It was a hideous passage. Every day, some wretch in his hammock began the 'vomiting like coffee grounds' which presaged the end. The ship hove to, so undermanned that her movements were slovenly and slow, and the corpse was heaved over-board, a few words said by Captain Phillips until he was too sick to speak, and then by Lieutenant Saumaurez. On 17 April, those still fit enough to be on deck sighted Ascension, rearing from the sea, then the huts and cannon of the little garrison in Georgetown. A cluster of shipping was gathered in the bay when the *Bann* came in with the yellow quarantine flag flying, thirteen of her company dead and dozens of others sick. By evening, the medic of every ship which carried one had been brought to the little shoreside hospital with his chest of physic and lint, to help the few harassed nurses and the garrison doctor tend the men lying in corridors and courtyards, some delirious, some unconscious, some already dead. By the time the *Glendower* arrived with her own quota of sick, damaged men, those still healthy had left the sick in Georgetown and moved up the mountain, creating a cordon sanitaire of scrub and rock between their new camp and the mass graves and fever below. Eighty of the *Bann's* 120 men had died and the *Bann* had just left for Brazil in a last-ditch attempt to leave the yellow jack behind. Soon there were men from the *Glendower* in the overcrowded hospital and among the bodies disintegrating under lime. Commodore Mends joined them in September. A few weeks later, his teenage lieutenant son followed him, another victim of detached service up the malarial rivers.

In November, the *Sierra Leone Gazette* ran and reran the text of a new colonial Act 'for the preservation of White Seamen while in the River Sierra Leone'. Henceforth, no white man, whether employed by the Royal Navy or private merchantmen, was to be ordered, or allowed, to undertake 'such laborious work as must expose [his] life or health unnecessarily in this climate, and ought to be exclusively performed by Natives of Africa'. Masters and commanders were obliged to serve 'daily and regularly . . . a sufficient quantity of good and wholesome provisions' and 'not less than half a pint of wine, or a quarter of a pint of spirits' daily; and 'fresh meat or fresh fish [with] good yams, cassada, potatoes, eddoes, plantains or other vegetables'[8] at least twice a week. It was well meant; like so many other measures taken by concerned officers and officials in the days of scurvy, then typhoid, then malaria, it probably helped seamen's general health; but it would not save them.

The *Owen Glendower* had taken prizes west and east of Cape Coast, but had spent valuable time on Ascension. The *Bann* was recuperating in Brazil. The doughty *Thistle*, in which Hagan had been quietly, doggedly, catching slavers for four years, had been broken up, her timbers defective. Hagan himself would leave the coast in April 1823, having taken forty slave-ships and released four thousand Africans from slavery. It left only HMS *Cyrene* and the colonial schooners, which were not authorised to detain slavers under the treaties, to carry out the Squadron's principal work. They were not enough to crush a thriving trade.

In October 1822, before the epidemics struck, King Siaka of the Gallinas seemed to have bowed to British force. That month, HMS *Cyrene* had taken a Dutch vessel and a French one sailing in company to the Gallinas, where slave-cargoes awaited them. Anchoring outside the bar, Captain Grace had sent in three armed boats with a request that Siaka hand over all slaves awaiting his two prizes. The boats were fired upon as soon as they entered the river, but managed to land on one of the islands and turn the guns they found there on their attackers. By the time they re-emerged from the estuary, three British seamen were wounded, one was dead, the *Cyrene* was still anchored just outside and other armed British ships could be easily summoned from Freetown. King Siaka did his sums and sent out a message. He had been away at the time of the attack, he wrote; the European captains in the river were entirely to blame for the death and injury caused, for they had given his men rum and guns, and told them not to let a single Englishman leave the river alive. With these explanations came 64 adult slaves and 116 children for liberation.

By 1824, however, with the Squadron weakened, King Siaka and his clients were more confident, and men were arriving each month to claim their share in the rich illegal trade. Among them was Pedro Blanco of Malaga, who would retire a millionaire twenty years later, now a mere jobbing seaman in the slave trade, taking some ships to Cuba, piloting others into the slaving creeks between Sierra Leone and Monrovia and learning the ways of the Gallinas, sea and land, better than any other in his trade. He and the other incoming Spaniards were a new breed in the rivers, attuned to the logistics of organised international crime, for such the illegal slave trade was becoming.

'Merchants from Havana', explained a Liberian merchant,

> sent out agents to establish their deposits of goods and permanent barracoons. The double and treble call for slaves soon dispopulated the immediate Interior, when it became urgent for the natives of Gallinas to extend their wars further into the Interior. And in a few more years, this river was surrounded with wars, but as the slave factories supplied them with powder and guns, they made headway against a multitude of enemies.[9]

Here were the foundations of the vast fortune Pedro Blanco would amass, and of the multi-island compound he had begun building in the estuary. He established private quarters at Lomboko, a village straddling the river where it entered the lagoon, as guest of King Siaka, and headquarters on Dombocorro, an island near the mouth of the estuary. Further in, another island would soon house his sister Rosa in 'solitary and penitential' splendour. On another, a seraglio was being gathered 'within whose recesses each of his favorites' – daughters, wives and slaves of his clients – 'inhabited her own separate establishment, after the fashion of the natives'. The first of the great Blanco barracoons were going up, guarded by Spanish and Portuguese sentries, a 'wretched class of human beings upon whom fever and dropsy seem'd to have emptied their vials', standing at either end of the barracoons with their guns and bloodhounds, or perched in lookout seats 50 feet above ground to watch for the masts of warships. This fortified estuary would hold out against British assault for many years. Its success, and the famed riches of the men who worked inside it, inspired many young men with fortunes to make.

Slave-wars had broken out again to either side of Sierra Leone, and in the vast hinterland of the Bights. In Sherbro and the Gallinas, old and new brokers sold guns and bought captives from all sides, with Siaka's kinsmen and mercenaries as their eager partners. Along the river banks Siaka's hunters went, penetrating tributaries of the Shebar and Sherbro, and the jungle behind. Entire villages were fallen upon and the occupants bound, marched to collection points for embarkation in boats and canoes, marched again across necks of land to the estuary barracoons, and taken away to the Caribbean. Those few British officers still patrolling could not detain the French whom they boarded in Shebar and found awaiting the fruits of war. No warship was available to catch the Spaniard reported by a timber-merchant visiting the River Nuñez in November 1824. The slaver's arrival, he wrote, 'has completely unhinged the natives'.

> Government should either keep these people away, or else give up the abolition at once: it is useless doing things by halves. The natives will never have their minds settled to legitimate trade, while a slave ship can now and then come into the river – bring her whole cargo of bafts,* cloths, tobacco, and rum on shore, and say to the people, here take this, divide it amongst yourselves, but bring me 100 prime slaves, as has been the case in this instance. Another vessel is daily expected for the same purpose.[10]

Nor was there anyone to send against the Portuguese agents raiding here and marching their booty north for shipment. Sometimes there were

*Lengths of Indian cotton.

kidnapped Sierra Leoneans among their captives: stray children whose lives had held unimaginable turmoil, taken off slave-ships and parcelled out to 'countrymen' who took them to the Bullom shore opposite Freetown and sold them back into slavery. Women were snatched from fields and riverside laundries; men were ambushed as they sailed in boats carrying timber and grain. HMS *Cyrene* alone could do little, whatever weapons the diplomats gave her, however brave the men she sent ashore in small boats to face malaria, the fire of slavers and their rum-crazed African partners.

The American colonists had managed to land on the cape bought by Lieutenant Stockton with his bundle of fancy goods, and had since been under continual attack. They had hardly been able to build shelter for themselves when an American merchantman brought another thirty-seven colonists, a moderate supply of stores and the Reverend Jehudi Ashmun of Vermont, who prayed for guidance and took charge.

The rains were upon them again: great sheets of water falling to lie stagnant, breeding disease. Within five weeks, Mrs Ashmun was dead and the Reverend ill. Here, the healthy were those who would have been considered incapacitated anywhere else. Some days only two were fit for duty. Between them they had forty muskets and little ammunition. Under Ashmun's charismatic leadership, and with immense labour, the heavy guns were brought over from Providence Island and men, women and children went out in work parties, to fell by hand the dank and heavy forest around their village and create a clear space across which the Deys must advance without cover to attack, and a hedge of timber and brushwood which they must climb if they did so. Twenty men kept a sick, frightened watch each night and those still fit in the mornings helped raise a structure which the Deys watching from the forests, shimmying in by night to spy, had never seen. A Martello tower like the ones built to repel Napoleon from the Kent and Sussex coasts was slowly being erected on the extremity of the Cape.

On 10 November, King George and a Dey army crossed the Mesurado River. Ashmun rose from his sickbed to inspect and exhort; the work parties staggered out to bring back more and more wood for the protective hedge and the sick set their trembling hands to adding cartridges to the pile. At dusk, scouts came in with news that between seven hundred and eight hundred warriors were half a mile away, and advancing. Just before dawn on 11 November, they attacked, broke through the guard and advanced at the run with spears in their hands. Several colonists were killed then and there. The rest of the picket was forced away from their cannon and the whole colony would have fallen had not four houses on the outskirts been raided and found full of coveted goods. When the Deys turned to plunder, the colonists fired cannon into their midst. That was the turning point: half an hour later, the signal for the Deys to disperse and return home was heard from beyond the trees.

The next attack came, in greater numbers and with greater determination, on 30 November. Three attempts to batter the fortifications down were made in ninety minutes, with one man killed and two wounded within, and Jehudi Ashmun shot three times through his clothes, but unhurt. Outside the palisade, the Americans' guns killed in swathes. Inside, a penknife and a piece of priming wire were used to prise bullets from flesh, for there were no surgical instruments. The Deys retreated again, their dead left scattered outside the palisade, and the colonists waited.

On the night of 2 December, the British colonial schooner *Prince Regent* was sailing past Mesurado with a prize-crew returning from Freetown to the Gold Coast. They were startled to hear the roar of cannon from this lonely coast, followed by unmistakable musket-fire. The officer of the Monrovian watch, alarmed by a rustle or a shout, had opened fire. The alarm was false, but the response fortuitous, for it brought the company of the *Prince Regent* to see what was afoot. Their officer went to see the Dey chiefs, found them ready to negotiate and induced them to appoint Governor M'Carthy as arbitrator of their differences with the Americans. Twelve British seamen volunteered to stay in Monrovia when the *Prince Regent* left. Within two months, all twelve were dead of malaria. On 31 March 1823 the USS *Cyane* was seen approaching the peninsula with stores and another group of colonists. The *Cyane*, however, had called at Freetown on her way, and brought the yellow jack with her. As man after man went down, her captain decided he could remain at Monrovia no longer. The colonists were alone again to face fever and hostility.

Sir Robert Mends's death on Ascension had left the coast without a commodore. HMS *Bann*, back from Brazil, was at Cape Coast Castle and awaiting the arrival from Britain of her new commander, Captain Filmore. He came out in October 1823 as passenger on the gun-brig HMS *Swinger* and, learning that Mends was dead, assumed command of the flagship *Glendower*. It was the briefest of commands. The African coast did its grim work swiftly, and the surgeon told him to go back to England if he wished to save himself. He left the Castle in January 1824, giving command of the ship to young George Woollcombe, first lieutenant of the *Glendower*, until the arrival of a senior officer. Woollcombe's was an unusually hectic first week of command. The day after Captain Filmore left the Squadron in his hands, word came straggling into Cape Coast Castle that a hostile Ashanti army was on its way.

Along the Gold Coast was a string of dilapidated British forts – slaving factories in the old days, then property of a private trading company which, since 1822, had been brought under the authority of the Crown. Two African peoples, the Ashanti of the interior and the Fanti of the coast, claimed control of the hinterland. For generations, the Fanti had imposed restrictions and duties on Ashanti merchandise sent down to brokers on the coast. The Ashanti, invading kingdom after kingdom in their march from their inland capital of Kumasi towards the goal of direct access to the sea, had become an immediate threat. Groups of Fanti, fleeing the advance of their raiders, had sheltered in British territory, treaties and interventions had failed and a reluctant Ashanti king had come under pressure from his chiefs to make war on the foreigners. The small British Gold Coast fort of Anamabo had been attacked and a sergeant of the West India Regiment, accused of insulting the Ashanti king, was captured and executed by an Ashanti state executioner. His head, jawbone and arm had been exhibited in Kumasi. A British attempt to seize those responsible failed. As the Squadron struggled with disease and slavers, regiments were arriving at the Gold Coast garrisons at Governor M'Carthy's request, one from the Cape of Good Hope, others direct from Britain. On 20 January, M'Carthy left the Castle at the head of 170 men of the 'Royal Cape Coast Militia', an unsoldierly bunch of traders, workmen, about 250 unorganised Fanti and a few stray others. On the banks of the River Adumansu, they met 10,000 Ashanti soldiers. Only 61 of the colonial militia survived the encounter.

It was not at first clear whether M'Carthy was among them and the immediate question for Lieutenant Woollcombe and Major Chisholm, senior army officer at the Castle in M'Carthy's absence, was how to relieve him or cover his retreat. It was thought 'there was a probability of his coming down with the remainder of his forces',[11] Woollcombe wrote, to the British fort on the coast at Sekondi, and the *Owen Glendower* set off there. A few had indeed made it that far, but then been slaughtered. When Woollcombe and two officers went ashore to seek information, the locals would not let them get to the fort and the British sergeant besieged inside it; indeed they turned so hostile that Woollcombe had to make a run for the boats. He returned later with marines and 'small-arms men in hopes of drawing them out and burning the town but they came on in such numbers' that two marines were killed under the fire which opposed their landing. They tried to burn the town, but the thatch was too wet to catch fire.

Having returned to the Castle to await more definite news of M'Carthy, Woollcombe wrote two hasty letters to catch a vessel returning to England. One was to Admiral Bedford with a copy of Filmore's sailing order appointing him acting captain. The other was to his family. 'I hope,' he wrote home, 'the Admiral will confirm [the order] I have now command of a frigate under my orders and the *Swinger* under my orders to be a Lieutenant again would make me mad.'

Every man on the West African coast wanted to make prize-money, but Woollcombe's need was urgent. He was the eldest son of a large and impecunious Devonshire family, and his father and siblings had as much investment in his success as the man himself. His sisters had been left without a dowry and his brother William was an army officer on half-pay, one of so many unemployable country gentlemen attempting to live on a small – if unearned – income. What George could achieve in the Preventive Squadron would make a material difference to his sisters' marriage prospects and his brother's future employment.

Only after the ship carrying his letters had left for England did the news come that M'Carthy was dead and the enemy advancing. It was a terrifying moment; but one when young men might make brilliant moves, be mentioned in dispatches and secure their future. A power struggle erupted. When Captain Filmore had left the *Bann* for the *Glendower*, that ship's first lieutenant, too, had seized the chance of acting command. He was George Courtenay, and he believed himself senior in the service to George Woollcombe, whatever their respective acting positions in the squadron, and was not going to miss this opportunity any more than his rival. 'I had embarked 200 men', Woollcombe wrote his uncle in fury,

> on board the *Owen Glendower* under the command of Major
> Chisholm . . . to go up to destroy [Sekondi] when the *Bann* joined
> and Captain Courteney [*sic*] chose to call himself the Senior Officer
> on the Station, put himself onto the *Owen Glendower* and appointed
> myself to the *Bann* . . . and now I stand at risk of being superseded
> by either Captain Prickett when he comes out on the *Victor* or by
> Captain Bullen who is appointed to command on the station . . . it
> will be disgraceful to now do duty as a Lieutenant on a ship I have
> commanded.[12]

In March, one of the handful of survivors from the Adumansu rout appeared at the Castle. He was Mr Williams, merchant turned militiaman, and he had spent two months shut in a hut with four severed European heads, M'Carthy's among them. Two other men had been with him at first. They had been executed. He had been released to bring the news to the British.

George Woollcombe in the *Bann* brought confirmation of M'Carthy's death to a stunned and frightened Freetown. It was, wrote the *Gazette*, black-bordered for weeks, a 'heart-rending and afflicting intelligence'.[13] The flag on Fort Thornton was lowered to half-mast, minute guns were fired sixty-five times – one for each year of M'Carthy's age – and all officers were ordered to wear black armbands for two months. Woollcombe's own attention had turned to disturbing news from home, for a letter awaited him in Freetown. His grandfather was dead; family finances were in chaos and his brother William was considering going back on active service. Some good fortune had come, however, after the disappointment of thwarted command at Cape Coast. 'You will be glad to hear', he wrote home

> that on my passage [to Sierra Leone] I had the good fortune to capture
> a brig under Brazilian colors with 324 slaves on board. She has not yet
> arrived but she was a very dull sailor I have no fears about her. I am
> told there is no doubting her condemnation.
>
> My share of prize money will be 1200 pounds but as prize money

is always a long time before it is paid, it will be of no use at present when it is so much wanted. William says he has applied [for] full pay I almost wish he may not succeed as I am sure he never will enjoy anything like comfort by returning to the army and as he must go to the bottom of the list he can have no chance of promotion.[14]

As to his 'dear Sisters', who would be left 'very badly situated'

let what was intended for me go to them if by that means I can add to their comfort. I assure you it will add to my happiness. I have my pay from my position which even if I should not be confirmed to the rank I am now acting in will always keep me above want.

The *Bann* was in Freetown because the new commodore, Sir Charles Bullen, was due. He would expect all ships not urgently required for defence to muster there to meet him. Another veteran of French and American wars and friend of the dead Commodore Mends, Commodore Bullen would bring with him the desperately anticipated news of who had been promoted, or confirmed in an acting rank; and who had not. Should the news be bad, Woollcombe wrote, 'I hope I have sufficient philosophy in me to bear with it'.

Commodore Bullen arrived in the frigate *Maidstone* in May, bringing with him the fast-sailing HMS *Victor* and excellent news for Woollcombe personally: that 'I was to continue in command of the *Bann*, Lord Melville [of the Admiralty] having placed me first on his list for promotion'.[15]

Commodore Bullen had no time for the *fêtes champêtres* and dinners with which Freetown greeted its important guests. He sailed south immediately with HMS *Victor* and HMS *Bann*, and found little had changed since Yeo, then Collier, then Mends – all dead, Sir Charles may have reflected – made the same voyage. Rivers and coast were thick with slavers, playing all the old games of deception. 'Scarce a port was visited,' Bullen reported, 'but where the wretched beings were lying in chains ready for embarkation as soon as the opportunity offered.'[16]

The Bights of Benin and Biafra, now banned to Portugal and Brazil, were still full of their flags. Portuguese authorities on the offshore islands still supported the trade, the multiplicity of rivers which emptied into the delta still brought hundreds of slave-carrying canoes from the hinterland and on the other side of the ocean, thirteen slavers left Bahia in one month alone, all bound for these illegal waters. The *Maidstone* found four Brazilians here clearly preparing to receive a slave-cargo but, without slaves aboard, none could be detained. Chasing but losing another Brazilian off Lagos, the *Victor* fell in instead with a tiny schooner, aptly named the *Piccanniny Maria*. She had come from Gabon with twenty-three slaves lying on water-casks with only 18 inches between their faces and the deck above. Six were already dead. This was one of the 'midget slavers' owned by the daughter of Governor Fereira of Principe.

By far the worst offenders, however, were the French. The *Maidstone* 'never saw a vessel but she chased and came up with, when the first gun to heave to was the signal for the [French] Flag to be hoisted'. One Frenchman, boarded in the Old Calabar, 'conducted himself in the most insulting and insolent manner when visited by our boats'. Eight were boarded in two days in the River Bonny, 'fitted up for slaves, & would take away in all about 8000'. All were untouchable; they should not even have been boarded. Off Principe, too, 'the French engross all the trade in slaves', wrote another officer home. They had recently boarded, illegally, the slaver *Orphée* 'in a state that would have made your heart ache to have seen. The rascals had the men chained by the necks, or nearly all of them; the rest, by the legs, to the deck; and to add to the horror of the thing, the bolts were riveted':[17] they would be in that position and that filth until they made Martinique. 'The groans of the poor sufferers nearly unmanned me, when I desired them to be released, I thought I should have choked, never were my feelings so much hurt.' The men of the *Victor* saw worse when they stopped a Frenchman further north. Making for the slaver in ship's boats, they saw the French crew descend and pull for shore, leaving their slaves below. Before the bluejackets could get aboard and take control, the ship was wrecked in the surf. All on board drowned in their chains.

George Woollcombe's command of the *Bann* was as brief as others in that season of deaths and shuffles. In June, he was offered and eagerly took command of the *Victor*, a faster-sailing ship. His first, distressing capture in her was the *Diana* of Brazil. 'Of all vessels I was ever on board of', he reported, this was in the most deplorable condition: the stench, from the accumulation of dirt, joined to that of so many human beings packed together in a small space (the men all ironed in pairs) was intolerable; and to add to this scene of misery, the small-pox had broken out among them; nine had died before we took possession, and one almost immediately after our first boat got alongside.[18]

A *Victor* midshipman took her up to Freetown, where she was put in quarantine off Fourah Bay, for twenty-three more slaves died on the passage up, and the smallpox still raged.

The *Maidstone* and *Bann* separately boarded another Brazilian slaver, the *Dos Amigos*, as she hovered off the Guinea coast, but neither 'could touch her as the slaves, which were then assembled on the beach, had not been put on board'. But the *Victor* got her, running her down between Principe and São Tomé, where, at their own request, Woollcombe left the captain and crew. One seaman begged to come with him: he was a 'domestic slave' in Brazil, and this was his opportunity to make Sierra Leone and freedom. The *Dos Amigos* was in worse shape even than the *Diana*. 'The filthy and horrid state I found her in', Commodore Bullen reported on visiting Woollcombe's prize, 'beggars all description: many females were far advanced in pregnancy, and several had infants of from four to twelve months of age; all were crowded together in one mass of living corruption, and yet this vessel had not her prescribed complement by nearly 100.'[19]

Last of the many Brazilian prizes yielded by the summer's cruises was the *Bella Eliza*, caught by the *Bann*. It took her seven weeks to reach Freetown, during which 'our brave officers and men', wrote the *Gazette*, shocked at the size and condition of the ship when she arrived, 'together with 371 wretched beings, [were] confined within the narrow compass of a vessel said to be 148 tons burthen [suffering] from the want of water and provisions . . . all hands must, in two days more, have perished'.[20]

When reports of all the Squadron's cruises were in, with numbers of those rescued and estimates of those who got away, the results of the death, the disease, the hard sailing and the suffering were heart-breaking. 'Disheartened and justly incensed', wrote the *Gazette*, 'must our officers and men have been to see, that notwithstanding the fatigues they are undergoing to . . . abolish this traffic, the Trade was flourishing under their own view.'[21] Time and resources necessary for slaver-chasing, however, were as limited under Commodore Bullen as they had been under Commodore Mends.

The *Maidstone* had broken her slaver-catching cruise to visit Cape Coast Castle, and found the garrison still in distress, with the militia and surviving regiments camped in groups outside, awaiting the next attack. HMS *Driver* had brought out Colonel Sutherland to take command in May, and for five months the men of the *Driver* were engaged in restoring the castle's patchy defences. Sutherland had immediately gone to join Major Chisholm where his men were stealthily cutting roads through the bush to reach the Ashanti camp. Another battle had been fought on 21 May, in which the Ashanti were driven back, but two days later, a 'fetish boy' appeared at the Castle with a message: build your walls higher; land all the guns and men you may from your warships, but the king of the Ashanti will throw every stone of your building into the sea.

Five thousand refugees had fled to the Castle, bringing disease and famine with them. There was not enough room to dispose of the corpses and, with smoke from Ashanti fires visible over the trees, they could not be carried outside the walls for burial. Dead and dying lay together in the streets. Siege prevented stores being brought in overland; garrison, towns-people and refugees were all dependent on vessels coming down from Freetown with rice, flour and medicine. Most of all they needed ammu-nition. Commodore Bullen was told that even the lead gutters bringing rainwater to the town's cisterns had been cut up to make bullets, leaving the women to make dangerous voyages to a stagnant pond beyond the walls to fetch water. This, at least, the ship could remedy: the *Maidstone*'s crew were set to making hoses to siphon the water in safely.

At the beginning of July, a troopship came from Britain with rein-forcements, many accompanied, disastrously, by wives and children who joined the sick and starving in the Castle yards. The governor of Danish Accra, a few miles to the east, sent in his own hastily gathered army to assist. On the night of 11 July, an Ashanti attack was repelled. The men at the guns did not know it, but one lucky shot had grazed the Ashanti king in his palanquin and he was convinced the British knew where he was. He would not mount again. On the 12th, the attack was smaller; and on the 13th, the Castle waited and no attack came; nor on the next two days. Then came confirmation: the Ashanti army was withdrawing to Kumasi, ravaged by the same diseases which had attacked the castle.

They had survived, but at huge cost. Of the two companies of white soldiers who came from the Cape of Good Hope in April 1823, only one man was still alive by the end of 1824. Of those who had come out from England in November 1823, eight had survived; of the 101 men brought just before the Ashanti attacked, forty-five died during their first week.

Fever had struck the *Victor*, too, and Commander Woollcombe took his ship to São Tomé to recuperate. He wrote home from here, fearing 'accounts of the *Victor* being in a very sickly state may find their way into the papers'.

> I must also tell you I have had an attack myself but a very slight one it has debilitated me a good deal but I am now recovering very fast and I hope very soon to be quite recovered. I hope this will make you all easy . . . In one of my letters to [his sister] Jane I said if I get ill I will return but I trust they [his sisters] will not consider my not doing so now a breach of promise as was I to give up my ship now it would be an insuperable bar to my ever getting another.[22]

Returning to convalescence and safety in Britain when there was still bounty to chase and the golden chance of command was unthinkable and Woollcombe was still making feverish calculations of bounty due and how it would best aid the family.

> My share of prize money or bounty money for [recent prizes] was ten pounds a head so then to the captors will be 2763 15 my share being 3/8 of the whole. We also get half the proceeds of the sale of the vessel but that will scarcely pay expenses of condemnation so that it perhaps will not be quite the sum I have stated but I don't think it can be much below. I am this particular in stating this as it is an additional reason for me to insist on what I wrote to you about before I allude to my giving up all claim to any things that must be intended for me by my father. William made known to my mother my wishes and I have a letter from Jane saying they will not allow it but I must . . . insist that it may be so.

Promotion, promotion; prizes, prizes: such was the thumping rhythm of thought in a poor lieutenant's mind, even sweating, yellow-skinned and under fire.

News of the suffering on the coast had indeed reached Britain, in letters received from sick and frightened soldiers, seamen, marines and their families. The Ashanti war was a complicated business and Britain's own role in provoking it was not easily explained. For many at home, it was just another element in the West African campaign waged against slaving and barbarism, and support for this was wavering. For each triumphant anecdote of a slaver taken, there were long lists in the papers of men dead of the fever or killed in action. The press gathered the news of death and disaster and informed the country; the Colonial Office held urgent meetings with the Admiralty and more troopships left England with garrisons to reinforce the Gold Coast forts. When they returned with more despairing correspondence, half of those who had sailed on the outward voyage were already dead. Invalids, widows and orphans evacuated from Sierra Leone and the Gold Coast were disembarked into quarantine at Portsmouth and London. Despatches from the Gambia came home: one whole garrison was dead of the fever and the town it protected was in fear of attack from the local chief, who threatened to return to the slave trade unless the British renewed his 'dash.'* HMS *Swinger* had been found in the river with her commander and seven men dead, and seven slavers anchored around her, awaiting their cargoes.

And then, just when the African experiment was at its most unpopular, news reached the Colonial Office of an unauthorised expedition to quell the old troublemakers back at work just beyond the colonial borders.

Charles Turner, an old hand at colonial affray, had become Governor of Sierra Leone and the Gold Coast settlements in July 1825. His response to the outbreak of slave-wars was swift, and new. He knew that if he could not defeat the slave-brokers themselves by force or threat of sanctions, he must divide and conquer, persuading the Africans with whom they worked to forsake them and throw in their hand with the British. To do so, he must offer more – in cash, now, and promises, for the future – than their slaving patrons could. By the end of the year, he had concluded a treaty

---

* 'Dash' was the African 'Baksheesh': somewhere between a tip and a bribe.

with African slave-brokers, or the landlords of European ones, around Sherbro and the Gallinas, in which wars between them were brought to an end under British guarantee: if either attacked in the future, the other could call on British help.

'Whereas a cruel and destructive war has for several years raged', Turner's treaty ran, and many 'defenceless inhabitants' have been 'cruelly murdered or sold into slavery', further, since 'violent outrages' had been committed on 'property and persons of British subjects engaged in lawful trade and commerce, plundering the one, seizing and selling into slavery the others' and the war had 'already approached the frontiers of the colony', their overlords 'have, of their own free will and accord, stepped forward and thrown themselves and their countries upon the protection of his Excellency the governor-general of Sierra Leone and the British Government, as the surest means of saving themselves and subjects'. Banka, king of Sherbro, and Queen Ya Comba of Ya Comba, represented by Thomas Caulker, had 'ceded, transferred and given over . . . the full, entire, and unlimited right, title, possession, and sovereignty of all the territories and dominions to them respectively belonging'. These territories and dominions, covering 70 miles of land to the south of Sierra Leone, were renamed Turner's Peninsula. This was to be the 'forward base' for British actions against those now officially agreed to be the common enemy.

Boats went out to the French slavers anchored around the Plantain and Banana Islands and officers called up to the captains that their vessels were now in British waters where their trade was forbidden, and they must leave. Slaving crews caught ashore on new British territory escaped across the new border with the Gallinas, where the factors would shelter them and organise their passage home aboard returning slavers.

Turner's actions were disallowed, his treaty unratified. Since 1808, the Colonial Office had been discouraging all local attempts to expand British responsibility in West Africa. Britain had had to acquire some territory for rescued slaves to be resettled, but the borders of Sierra Leone should have been its strict limits. The anti-slave-trade patrol, as far as the government and its officials in London were concerned, was to float off Africa, fighting seaborne foreigners, not to engage with African peoples on African land: one need only look at Cape Coast Castle to see the folly in that. Other people – in the Gold Coast, Sierra Leone, Monrovia and the satellite settlements springing up beyond – knew that abolition could not be so neatly contained by naval patrols and colonial borders. Engagement on land must follow.

6

Two Captains

While Charles Turner was making his fruitless treaties on land, and Lieutenant Woollcombe was hoping for promotion at sea, other men were looking to Africa as a source of wealth and adventure. The exploration and exploitation of the continent – the great 'opening-up' of the nineteenth century – was to become inextricably linked with the suppression of the slave trade. Greed for the profits of illegal slaving continued to attract many men and some women, but missionary endeavour, legitimate merchant adventuring and a love of exploration brought others. Explorers, evangelists, legal traders and abolitionists soon found themselves treading the same path. Among those who felt the lure of Africa in the 1820s were Captain Hugh Clapperton, Scottish explorer, and Captain Théophile Conneau, French by blood and Italian by birth, who would become one of the coast's most notorious slavers.

'Some things', wrote the *Sierra Leone Gazette* in September 1823, 'appear involved in inextricable obscurity.'[1] The occasion was the publication of yet another pamphlet on the course of the Niger, an obsession of nineteenth-century explorers on a par with finding the North-West Passage. Its long, twisting course had baffled explorers and theorists determined to settle where, exactly, it reached the sea; whether the great river known to enter Timbuktu from the south-west was the same as that which rose 200 miles inland, north-east of Sierra Leone.

'There may be such a region in the interior of the Continent, as the

Caspian Sea, and it's [*sic*] environs', the *Gazette* continued. 'There may be such accumulations of water as the lakes of Canada, even in the torrid zone, where great part of those of the Niger may be wasted by evaporation . . . there may be an opening in the Kong Mountains, through which it passes . . .', it might be a continuation of the River Congo. Each of these theories had its own supporters, but one idea was gathering consensus. 'Whether the Niger and Congo be the same, or separate rivers, their waters seem to have been designed by Providence as a great means for promoting the intercourse amongst the Nations inhabiting the interior of Africa; and may be the means of producing greater effects than any that have yet happened amongst them – their civilization and conversion to Christianity.' These were the words of an anonymous correspondent to the *Gazette* but they expressed the growing interest of a loose but influential group: missionaries, merchants and the Royal Geographical Society.

In 1795, the Scottish doctor Mungo Park had gone up the River Gambia, struck off into the unknown interior, found the Niger's source in the highlands and traced its first 200-mile stretch towards Timbuktu. Ten years later, exploring further, he had passed that city, gone round the great bend where the river turns south-east and entered present-day Nigeria. His murder at the Bussa Rapids was one of Freetown's – and Regency Britain's – favourite whodunits. Since then a score of curious, courageous, Africa-obsessed young officers on half-pay had wrapped themselves in Muslim robes and left the Barbary States to cross the Sahara. Their missions were almost interchangeable: to enter Timbuktu, the distant, shrouded city which had taken tenacious hold of the European imagination; to discover the fabled (and, as would transpire, non-existent) Kong Mountains; to reach the shores of Lake Chad; and to fall in with the Niger and trace its flow to the ocean.

In 1822, the thirty-four-year-old Scot, adventurer and naval officer Hugh Clapperton travelled as companion to a surgeon optimistically appointed British consul to Borno, in what is now north-east Nigeria. The two joined forces at Tripoli with the explorer Dixon Denham, also making for Timbuktu, and travelled south together. The surgeon-consul died shortly afterwards, another victim of African fever, Denham went east to explore the shores of Lake Chad and Clapperton went alone into the slave-owning, slave-trading Muslim empires. He reached Sokoto in March 1824, the first European to do so, and was greeted by a vast crowd.

Usman dan Fodio had died in 1817, leaving his empire partitioned between his brother Aduallahi and his son, Mohammed Bello of Sokoto. Over twice-weekly audiences, Sultan Bello and Hugh Clapperton took to each other. The African was a noble-looking man in his mid-forties. A little plump, he had neat features, a curling beard and great dark eyes and lived an apparently simple life: dressed in cotton robes and a turban arranged in the Tuareg manner, with a fold across his lower face. He was attended not by palace guards and courtiers but by elderly slaves. His state and private rooms were plain. He was the superior of the two in intellect and many of his questions about theology and science left Clapperton floundering. He was fascinated by Clapperton's telescope, for he had a wide knowledge of the stars and constellations. He also appreciated the compass and demanded a detailed explanation of the sextant. Here, at least, the naval officer could satisfy him. Their most common conversation, however, was how to open communications between the landlocked Sokoto empire and all those peoples, goods and teachings beyond. They discussed the possibility of a British consul residing in Bello's capital, with a European physician in his suite; and the encouragement of European merchants, bringing European goods: more of these sextants, compasses and telescopes, tableware and cutlery, furniture and textiles, and guns, guns, guns. If such men could be brought, the sultan suggested, he would welcome them at his court, and, in exchange for this offer of British friendship and commerce, he would – or at least Clapperton understood him to say he would – ban the external slave trade on which his empire had grown rich.

Clapperton left Sokoto with ostriches, the sultan's gift for the zoo at Windsor Castle, and a letter in which his proposal to the British government, or Clapperton's understanding of this, was outlined. Sultan Bello, Clapperton believed, wished to open diplomatic and trading relations with Britain and to this end wanted a British consul to take up residence at a 'seaport' in his empire named as 'Raka'. He also wanted the delivery of certain 'presents' (mainly guns) which were to be brought to another named port, thought by Clapperton to be near Ouidah. In return, he would ban the trade in slaves from his territories 'to the African kingdoms of Atagher, Dahomy, or Ashantee'.[2]

This proposal seemed to chime with the British government's promotion of 'legal commerce' in the fight against slaving. It had worked – if partially – in Sierra Leone, years ago; could the practice now be extended to other areas of the vast slaving lands of Africa? The towns of the Lagos lagoon had been identified as likely ports to export palm oil, the raw material of soap, candles and lubricants. Several former Liverpool slaving-houses were turning to this new trade, employing the same ships, captains, men and intimate knowledge of the Guinea coast that had turned them a profit in the days of slaving. Their merchantmen took out salt, rum and all the goods which used to buy slaves and distributed them according to the old patterns of credit and collection.

The first resident British palm-oilers – 'palm oil ruffians' as they were called for their understandably defensive, sometimes offensive, behaviour in an area where they were unwelcome – had built their wharves on the lagoon at Badagry and a few ships already left with palm oil instead of flesh in their holds. If the supply of slaves from inland kingdoms such as Sokoto and Dahomey could be halted by extending this and other legal commerce, the barracoons of the Bights would decay, the slave-ships be turned away empty and the task of the Preventive Squadron and the government of Sierra Leone made easier, and cheaper.

In 1825, Clapperton returned to Africa to have another try at tracing the Niger's last, southward run to the sea. This time, he went as the British government's new envoy to the sultans of Sokoto and Borno. He left Portsmouth aboard HMS *Brazen*, bound for West Africa to start her commission with the Preventive Squadron. Also aboard were fifty soldiers, twelve convicted smugglers who had traded military service at Sierra Leone for transportation to Australia, the explorer Dr Dickson and Clapperton's remarkable young Cornish manservant, Richard Lander.

At Lagos on the Slave Coast, the River Ogun penetrates the coast and runs due north. An immense series of lagoons streams off into the mists of its delta, providing secret inland waterways running parallel to the coast. Here, hidden from the eyes of the Squadron, the great slave-canoes glided between the factories of Popo at the far, western end past Porto Novo to Ouidah and Lagos in the east. At Lagos lived a gang of slave-brokers as filthy as their brethren in the northern rivers. They claimed not French, Spanish or American blood, but Portuguese and Brazilian. These gaggles of decadent, Africanised men lived in courteous semi-autonomy, often more powerful than their landlords but preserving the decencies of obeisance. There was an exception to the Brazilian regime at the far western end of the lagoon. George Lawson, of mixed British and African blood, had been steward on a British slave-ship in the old days but, since abolition, had settled ashore and claimed sovereignty over a part of the lagoon. Thousands of slaves were brought to these ports by the slave-making kingdoms of Sokoto, Ashanti and Dahomey and Clapperton believed that Sultan Bello's 'seaport' must be located nearby.

HMS *Brazen* entered the Bight of Benin in November 1825, and a low schooner under Spanish colours was seen close inshore. Boarded and inspected, she was clearly about to pick up her cargo. When her captain confessed that slaves were waiting for him at Little Popo, a legal route to detention opened up. The factor, waiting with his lines of manacled slaves at that dismal lagoonside harbour, was dismayed to see his buyer appear under British escort. A Briton aboard a merchant schooner at Popo was watching.

'As soon as the officers [of the *Brazen*] landed from the ship', he wrote,

the slaves were demanded to be given up; but the king obstinately refused to deliver them. The officers then briefly told him that, unless they were immediately produced, his town would be cannonaded, he himself and his son taken prisoners, and the slaves seized by main force. This seemed to alarm him a little, and induced him to pay a little more respect to the imperious summons of Englishmen; and the unfortunate people were shortly after ordered to be liberated.[3]

The 231 emaciated, naked and manacled men, women and children thus illegally liberated 'evinced the liveliest joy on being made acquainted with the favourable turn in their affairs, and the gratitude they displayed to their deliverers was natural and sincere'. 'A *nation is not justified* . . .': the reproving words of the High Court of Admiralty had been ignored and Captain Willis had laid himself open to reproof, even prosecution. Thanks to his defiance, or arrogance, these 'poor creatures' had been rescued from death by hard labour in Brazil; his men had been given the fillip of prize-money falling due at the end of a dangerous cruise; and British authority had been asserted.

It was too dangerous for Britons to travel alone from Little Popo, for anyone connected with the country of abolition was a target. Clapperton, Lander and two companions went to Badagry, where the palm-oilers lived, hoping to find information about Raka. Dr Dickson, the other explorer, disembarked at Ouidah, where the Brazilian Francisco Felix de Souza extended his usual courteous welcome to visiting foreigners, on whichever side of the slaving debate their passport placed them.

The enigmatic Francisco de Souza was the best-known slave-dealer on the Guinea coast. Stories of his origin and arrival in Africa were told in all its slaving ports, especially Ouidah, the town which he had dominated for many years. De Souza was thought to have come to Africa 'in the year 1792, in his 24th year'[4] as governor of the Portuguese fort in Ouidah and had since become a private trader, the most successful of an Afro-Brazilian community which had settled and intermarried with local families. Many tales were told of the man:[5] that he had fled Brazil as the result of a crime; that he used black magic to subdue his rivals; that he 'wished it supposed that he was a Spaniard by birth, and was always treated so in courtesy and styled Don'. In 1818, he had helped place King Guezo on the throne of Dahomey, the great slave-raiding kingdom to the east. His reward was the title of Cha-cha, chief slave-broker for the thousands of captives which resulted from Guezo's annual slave-hunts across the borders of his kingdom.

De Souza was the most powerful man in Ouidah, and one of the most mysterious. His house was huge and luxuriously furnished and his hospitality famous. Yet he mixed little with the guests enjoying his largesse for he was 'a man of strange, sullen, and solitary habits, never appearing amongst the captains he entertains but at dinner, and then seldom speaking to any of them; he holds a most absolute and arbitrary control over them all . . . they are as much under his command, as is the ship of war under the admiral'.[6]

When this man offered his escort for the journey to Dahomey, Dickson accepted. He would be safer with de Souza's stick than with a regiment of redcoats. Captain Willis of the *Brazen* promised to send the heavy baggage after them and left. His guests might lay the foundations of a new type of commerce in the interior but as yet there were plenty more slaves on their way to the coast and plenty of slavers in the Bights for the *Brazen* to chase and detain.

In Cuba, another bright young man was dazzled by the lure of Africa, and the tales of men like de Souza, living in gilded palaces with slaves prostrate at his feet, hundreds of women in his harem and the power of life and death in a nod of his head.

Théophile Conneau was a war-baby born about 1807 to French parents in occupied Italy. He had grown up multilingual, cunning and utterly without scruple. His cocky memoir, *A Slaver's Log Book*, was published under the name of Theodore Canot. It is typical of a sailor: in turns sentimental, technical, lascivious and chilling, with much dashing action in which Captain Canot, as he styled himself, is always the best and bravest. Nonetheless, much of it is corroborated by more reliable Admiralty papers and it gives an entirely credible description of a ruthless young man's introduction to the illegal slave trade.

In 1826, Conneau found himself in Havana, not yet twenty but with a couple of transatlantic voyages and a great deal of coastal sailing already behind him. In this hot, decadent city the heart of the slave trade beat seductively. 'The riches of Havana are immense', wrote an awe-struck British naval officer:

Of the city of Havana it might be said, as of Lima in times long past, that it is paved with gold. Fancy what must be the wealth within its walls when one solitary individual, who keeps a small grocer's store and grog shop, has been able to guild [sic] the most splendid palace for a café, equal, if not superior, to our first clubs in London and outdoing anything in the shape of a café even in Paris.[7]

Everyone in Cuba was involved in the slave trade, from the Captain-General – the colonial governor – down. Here, the abolition promises of Madrid were laughed at, and, secretly, Madrid laughed with these richest of colonists, whose sugar, coffee and tobacco kept the mother country afloat in her sea of debts. In the bay of Havana was a squadron of Spanish warships, paid for with the £400,000 British bribe meant to wean the Cubans from slavery. In fact, the ships were sent not to enforce the treaties, but to take on the armies demanding independence in Vera Cruz and Cartagena de Indios. Lying among the Spanish frigates were sleek slave-schooners built in Baltimore and Philadelphia, glinting and gleaming in the sun, and British warships sent to report on them. 'During my idle hours,' Conneau recalled, 'I often sailed about the harbour, amusing myself at the sight of the men of war and the sharp-built slavers. . . . The slavers in particular attracted my curiosity . . . and admiration.'[8]

Whatever Spanish ministers might promise, they would do nothing which might cause disaffection among the men who ran their Cuban plantations like little tsars; the hostesses who threw parties of an extravagance scarcely known in Europe or America; the glamorous slave-ship officers and their well-paid, ruthless crews; and the host of officials, merchants and two-bit tradespeople who lived on this island like lords, for anyone with a spare peso here had a share in a slave-ship.

Like everyone else, the kind Italian grocer with whom Théophile Conneau lodged in Havana had a share in a slaver. The night before she sailed for Africa, he invited his young guest to the captain's farewell party. 'On our arrival on board, we met all the owners of the vessel, some nine in number,' Conneau wrote. 'The Captain, who had a share in her, gave us a superb déjeuner prepared from the shore. Champagne and Lafitte were the only succulent liquids used to moisten the luxurious repast.' Infatuated, Conneau importuned the friend who had taken him with 'a thousand questions in regard to the slave trade, the mode of obtaining a cargo, the outfitting, the compensation to the Captain and officers, the dangers of the cruisers . . . that night my dreams placed me on board a slaver hard chased by John Bull, so much had my ideas been quite captivated by what I had seen on board'.

What Conneau found out was already well known to the British squadron and the British Commissioners at the Havana Mixed Commission, whose miserable task it was to hold colonial officials to the Spanish anti-slave-trade agreements. The game of chase and denunciation had already become ritualised. Incoming slavers put in at one of a hundred bays, creeks and rivers, unloaded swiftly, and marched their stumbling slaves to whichever plantation had ordered them. The next morning, an agent waited on the private secretary of the Captain-General and 'in comfortable vis à vis relates the happy landing of the contraband, depositing in the meantime on the table the necessary rouleaux [rolls of bills] which contain the 51 dollars head money'. Next morning, 'a small slave is sent, or its equivalent in Spanish ounces, as it is well known that government officials prefer the gold to mortal flesh'. When the British commissioner found out that another party of slaves had been landed, he would wearily make his complaint, the Captain-General would exclaim in shock and a detachment of dragoons be ordered to gallop forthwith to the plantation and stop the terrible event. Alas, they were invariably too late or discovered that the British had been misinformed.

The generous Italian grocer also found Conneau his first slaving berth, aboard the *Areostatico*, sailing under a gay Catalan captain and chief mate. Her crew – Spaniards, Portuguese, a Frenchman and two Slavonians – were 'jailbirds and the refuse of the press gang', for the Spanish squadron had taken the best of the island's sailors. The vessel was armed against pirates and loaded with four kegs of coins and 'all the necessities for the comfort and maintenance of a slave cargo'. On the day of sailing, 'we gave a grand déjeuner and left la Havana under a shower of blessings'.

Forty-one days later, a black pilot guided the *Areostatico* up the River Pongus to a safe anchorage beyond the shifting channels. Here, the captain went ashore and reappeared with Mongo John, Paul Faber and some sixty followers to escort them to Bangalang, 'a pleasant spot at the head of the river', said Conneau, enjoying his adventure, where they would start the overtures of trade.

It took a month to load wood and water, collect the slaves, all children, and stow them aboard. During this time, Conneau and Mongo John discovered a liking for each other, and a mutual passion for liquor and tales of adventure at sea. One injudicious excursion to the Mongo's harem was forgiven, although John, having retrieved his guest from the ladies' embraces, pointedly 'advised me to steer a straight course for my quarters, as he said his cruisers kept a strict lookout in the premises'.

When the last little slaves had been brought from the hills, Conneau was told to begin stowing them aboard. The *Areostatico* was not large enough to have a slave-deck, so mats were strewn over the firewood in the hold. This was where 108 children would spend a month at sea. It was standard stowage: there was not enough room between mat and headboard for them to sit, so 'we made them lie down spoon fashion,' wrote Conneau, 'one in the other's lap; on the starboard with the left side down, and on the port vice versa'. It was his first lesson in slave-management. When the ship slipped away, black pilot again at the helm, there was a shout: the children had not been manacled and one or two, uncaring in their desperation, had pushed up the hatches and leapt overboard. The hatches were fastened shut and the vessel left.

Théophile Conneau was not aboard. Mongo John had invited him to stay behind as secretary and storekeeper, paid 'one slave per month or its value at the rate of forty dollars per head'. It was not a large wage, but made more palatable by a love affair with Esther, a 'blushing quadroon' in Mongo John's harem. She was the daughter, she told him, of a mulatto mother and white father, 'a missionary from England', who 'had abandoned his profession for the more lucrative slave traffic, and, after collecting a large quantity of slaves, left for America', abandoning wife and child as well. At first, Conneau's responsibility extended only to the Mongo's legitimate trades in rice, ivory and palm oil. His days were spent making inventories and his nights, more excitingly, in the arms of Esther. The dry season would bring the caravans from the interior and the start of the real work.

In Futa Jallon, the traders were on the move, preparing for the annual trek to the coast. This year Ama de Bella,* second son of a chieftain well known to Mongo John, was entrusted with leading his father's caravan. Forty slaves – prisoners of war taken in recent slave-hunts, household slaves no longer wanted or wives given in redemption of debt – were lashed together; two women accused of witchcraft were haltered and led by the neck, as was an apostate from Islam and another who had killed his son. Others, brought not as merchandise but beasts of burden, carried food, water, gold, cloth and ivory. With his two principal wives in a curtained litter, soldiers, a train of slaves and a bleating, shoving mass of livestock, Ama de Bella left his father's town to squat for a time on one of the roads to the coast, sending out ambush squads to detain the smaller slave-traders also making their way to the sea. Size added to the prestige of his caravan and 'absconding debtors' were netted: he was able to 'sequester a certain tribute' due his father from tribesmen 'which could never be collected otherwise'. Nearing the coast, they stopped to disguise the sick slaves. A 'mineral drug peculiar for its power to bloat the flesh' was ingested, and lemon juice, rum or red pepper forced down with it to produce sweat and 'give a luster to the skin'. These were old tricks of the trade, but with eager new buyers coming every year to the coast, there might be greenhorns ahead.

When the first reports came to the rivers that a Fula trader was on his way, the barkers – men 'employed by factories or chief traders to seek and meet strangers in the interior and induce them to bring their produce to their patron' – went out with presents and promises. Bangalang won. Gunshot from the hills announced the caravan's approach and when the smoke from Mongo John's answering cannon cleared, Conneau saw a great crowd of tired and filthy travellers. First came the young chief and his suite; 'next came the principal traders and their slaves, heavy laden with produce, followed by some forty captive slaves secured by rattan bands. Then came some fifty

---

* This, at least, was Conneau's rendition of his name.

bullocks, a large quantity of sheep and goats. The women followed next, and a large tame ostrich closed the procession.'

Conneau was not entrusted with the vital business of examining and bargaining for the slaves but 'as I wished to be instructed in the rudiments of my profession', he said, 'I watched my employer with avidity in all his operations'.

As each slave was brought in, the Mongo examined them from head to foot and as they were perfectly naked, no part was spared. Male and female, young and old, all underwent long manipulation. This was done to ascertain the soundness of their limbs. Every joint was made to crack; hips, armpits, and groins were also examined. The mouth was duly inspected and when a tooth fell short it was noted down as a deduction.

Then came the trading: on the first day, hides and rice; on the second day, livestock; on the third, gold, ivory and slaves. Male slaves, Conneau recorded, were bought for between $18 and $20. When selling women, 'we made a deduction of 20 percent when above 25 years old, but if young and well built with favourable appearances of fecundity, they commanded a price equal to a prime man. . . . A pregnant woman, or one with a baby at the breast, brings a trifling more.'

During the evenings, when trade was done, Conneau and Ama de Bella sat talking. The young African was a devout Muslim and knowing that believers could not, in an Islamic country, be condemned to slavery, Conneau wondered 'in what manner they could have collected so many slaves'. The Koran, Ama de Bella explained, 'permitted the sale of bondservants

and from that source many were yearly exchanged for European goods, which in return supplied them with the means of carrying on the wars commanded by the Secret Book – to conquer and subjugate all tribes to the true faith. In order to carry out more fully the commands of a true Mahometan to destroy all unbelievers, they had recourse to the cupidity of the white man, whose milder religion authorized its votaries to enslave the African.

With the gunpowder just acquired in exchange for his slaves, Ama de Bella 'hoped in the next rainy season he would be able to carry on a large war against different small tribes'. The two men parted good friends, the African leaving a 'volume of the Koran illuminated with the sandals of the Prophet', the Italian presenting him with a double-barrelled gun and promising the next dry season would bring him to Futa Jallon.

Conneau was ambitious. Before the first rains came, he had moved on from Mongo John's employment, gone into partnership with an English merchant and forged his own links with customers and suppliers. His new partner, Edward Joseph,* had come out to Africa with Governor Turner, fallen into debt and fled Freetown, briefly taken work with Mongo John but left to establish himself in legal trade. He was, Conneau said,

> a true admirer of African beauties. He not only loved the country but
> admired their customs and their language, which by the by he spoke
> well. Native dishes he preferred to roast beef and plum pudding; he
> delighted in the African melodies and would fall into ecstasies at the
> philharmonic sounds of the discordant tam-tam. Even African barbarity
> had its charms, but what captivated him most to an African life was
> the Asiatic custom of polygamy and the dolce far niente of the natives.

When Conneau sent his first small vessel off to Freetown, loaded with palm oil to buy 'English goods', Joseph's contacts came in useful.

As Conneau came to understand how deeply the institution of domestic slavery was embedded in West African life, so he understood how it had come to feed international trade. In Africa, he explained, 'where coin is not known, the slave is made a substitute for this commodity, and in each district a positive value is given him which is passed for currency and legal tender'. They were walking banknotes. 'If a man wishes to purchase a wife, he pays the amount in slaves; another wishes to purchase a quantity of cattle, he tenders in payment slaves. Fields of cassava, rice, or yams are paid in slaves.' Behind this African mint was a set of African bankers,

> native brokers . . . such as exist in all countries where slavery is permitted
> and whose business is to run the country in search of this or that kind
> or quality of slaves for different patrons; the strong man to replenish
> the phalanx of a War Chieftain, the neat boy for a servant, or the

---

* Spelt Jousiffe in some documents.

adopted child for some old unfruitful Queen, or the handsome maid for the harem of an African Lord.

Some Africans were slaves from birth; others became enslaved, for this was the penalty of many crimes. 'The creditor or bankrupt shares the same fate. The murderer, the manslaughterer, or the highway robber is condemned to the same punishment, with the addition that his family and near relations follow him in his captivity.' With them went witches, adulterers, barren women and gamblers; and the disabled and the mentally ill, 'as there are in Africa no madhouses, no hospitals or houses of refuge'. Some domestic slaves may have had sentimental value for their owners but many did not.

Many are exchanged for commodities which the whites have introduced, and a native will sometimes dispose of a slave for a barrel of rum to celebrate a marriage or a funeral. A female will sell her domestic to ornament herself with a new string of coral or any other gewgaw. The bad crop of rice is also the cause of many exchanges, where a favourite slave is made to pay for the needy provisions.

All these, brought by the 'native brokers', passed into Conneau's and Joseph's hands.

But the real richness of their barracoons still came from war, for here African and foreign greed had intermeshed perfectly. 'Three quarters of slaves shipped are the produce of native wars', Conneau thought,

which are partly brought about by the great inducement and temptation of the white man. . . . England today sends to Africa her cheap Birmingham muskets and Manchester goods, which are exchanged at Sierra Leone and Accra, on the Gold Coast, for Spanish or Brazilian bills on London. France sends her cheap brandies, her taffeta reds, her Rouen cottons and her quelque-chose, the United States their leaf tobacco, their one-F powder,* their domestic spun goods, their New England rum, and Yankee notions, with the same effect or the same purpose . . . these wants, desires and luxuries have

* gunpowder.

become an indispensable necessity to the natives and the traffic a natural barter.

For the other young men adventuring in Africa, things had gone disastrously wrong.

When the captain – now signing himself Abdullah Clapperton – with Richard Lander, the two doctors, and their servants left the *Brazen*, he had hoped to find Sultan Bello's men waiting somewhere nearby to escort them to Sokoto. None had come, nor any word of them. Bello's name was known, but no one knew of any seaport named Raka. It was the first indication that Bello had promised more than he could, or would, deliver. If Bello did not send for them, however, then they must travel to him, and so the party left Badagry in canoes, on 7 December, accompanied by an adventurous British palm-oiler and a Hausa interpreter. With large umbrellas held over their heads for protection and status, they moved like stately mushrooms around the bends of the Gazie creek and spent their first nights sleeping beneath the magnificent stars on red sandy clay, fatally unprotected by nets. It was the only time they would sleep comfortably, or in health.

Sokoto lies 500 miles from the sea. Between the river and the open savannah, they had to cross thick forests which made for hard and miserable walking. Clapperton was imprudently trying to break in a pair of new boots. 'We could not see the heavens over our heads,' he wrote, 'the path winding in every direction.'[9] Horses were scarce. They could buy only one, which Clapperton and Dr Pearce were to ride alternately, but no saddle came with him. 'My slippers being down at the heels,' he recorded, 'I soon lost them off my feet when I got my legs and feet miserably cut, and soon getting galled by riding without a saddle I had to walk barefoot – this was really if possible worse for when ever I crossed an ant path my feet were as if on fire and they drew blood from every quarter and I hobbled on with a stick.'

Five days after they left the coast, with fewer than 50 miles covered, Dr Morrison was babbling with fever. Two days later, Captain Pearce and Richard Lander were also sick. Soon, Dr Morrison turned back for the coast, where he died on 27 December, the day that Captain Pearce also expired in the forests. Captain Clapperton was so ill that he could take no part in the burial ceremony. Richard Lander, scarcely fitter than his employer, supervised the digging of the grave, the building of a structure over it to keep out scavenging animals and the erection of a wooden board at its head.

They felt better as forest gave way to savannah, the malaria in remission and new horses procured. At Jannah, they were able to participate in the dances and receptions of the court. Then it was the road to Engwa, a beautiful tract of small hills and valleys, stockaded towns and grassy plains; then a range of bare granite hills. Every now and again a caboceer* would emerge with some immense train behind him, and there would be singing and ceremony and palaver. Clapperton fell sick again, with diarrhoea and a severe pain in his side. The fever came back time and again and he shut himself up in grass huts to sweat it out. They rode overnight to escape the sun but this exhausted him too. 'Halted at 4', he wrote,

> and lay down on the ground till 6 as I was from fever sickness & pain in the head no longer able to bear the motion of the horse – I had no covering & though the morning was raw & the ground wet I arose much relieved of my sickness & familiar exhaustion – there are times when a man will take any remedy what ever may be its future effects – such was my case and even if I had had to die by my laying on the wet ground I could not sit on horse back nor could I stand.

Malegueta pepper was chewed, rubbed on a piece of cord and applied to the captain's skin to bring the fever out. When they entered the mountain passes, someone gave the captain peppery medicine which produced severe nausea for half an hour but then left him feeling well for the first time in weeks.

A crowd escorted them into the Oyo capital, where they were received by the king under a great umbrella, backed by a dense, laughing crowd of his women. Privately, he assured them he was 'glad that white men had come at this time, and now, he trusted, his country would be put right, his enemies brought to submission, and he would be enabled to build up his father's house, which the war had destroyed'.

Everywhere there were slaves. At Yarro, Captain Clapperton accepted the offer of one of the chief's daughters for his use during his stay, his anti-slavery principles put aside, or thought irrelevant, in this case. At Bussa, they spent some days trying to find out whether any of Mungo Park's papers had survived. The happy times ended at Kano. These were the lands where Ali Eisami had been snatched by Usman dan Fodio's raiders a few years

* a headman.

ago, and they found them again 'in a state of dreadful agitation'. The peaceful Arabic empire whose culture and arts had impressed Clapperton was threatened by war: sovereignty over the ancient states of Hausaland was under dispute by the two sultans who had been friends last time Clapperton visited. On the border which divided them, an army was massing. Whole provinces on either side were in insurrection against one or the other imperial master and there were rumours that the silent, dangerous Tuareg were on their way from the north, stirred by the promise of war. Leaving Lander at Kano with the baggage, Clapperton hurried on to Sokoto with only the 'gifts' which Sultan Bello had requested from Britain. Troops were gathered outside the city walls and there was no time for the quiet courtesies he remembered. Conversation was replaced by manoeuvre and drill. Communication with the outside world had lost importance given the urgent business of defending the empire, but it was not only war which had changed Bello's attitude towards his guest.

Since Clapperton's last visit in 1824, rumours had reached Sokoto that the British had set their sights on Hausaland and that these occasional expeditions by officers claiming adventure, exploration, hatred of the slave trade and love of the hunt were the devious prelude to invasion. This tactic, the whisperers said, had been used to bring unsuspecting India under the British heel. Bello might have disbelieved these drifting fancies but he could not ignore information brought to him from Kano. Among the baggage left there with Richard Lander was a bundle of muskets intended as the British government's present for the ruler of Bornu: friend last time Clapperton had visited, now enemy. The muskets could not, in time of war, be allowed to reach their recipient. Guns were so scarce here that an extra handful could decide the outcome of battle. Unseemly episodes followed: the sultan tricked Lander into bringing the baggage to Sokoto, then stole the muskets; Clapperton refused to accept his apology or explanation; old African friends fell away, seeing the British visitor had become a dangerous companion. Clapperton, his health deteriorating, fell into depression. 'I never saw him smile afterwards', Lander would report.[10]

In February, as the decisive battle was being fought in the dustbowl of the Borno border, Clapperton briefly rallied, and went hunting. The next day, he collapsed: malaria, dysentery, malnutrition and exhaustion claiming his last strength. He died on the morning of 13 April 1827, supported in Lander's arms, a rattle in his throat, 'sitting up and staring wildly around;

some indistinct words quivered on his lips, he strove but ineffectually to give them utterance, and expired without a struggle or a sigh'. Richard Lander, left quite alone, buried the captain 5 miles out of town under a wooden plaque inscribed with the words 'and he was left alone in his glory' and read the service over his grave. Around him, coffles of human war-booty were beginning the long march to the coast. At the end of April, Richard Lander set off the same way. Nothing had been heard of Dr Dickson since he left Abomey; and the course of the Niger, which Lander was sure they had been within miles of discovering, remained a mystery. He found one thousand slaves penned in five factories in Badagry, 'chained by the neck to each other, waiting for vessels to take them away'. Their Portuguese owners not only refused to take Lander's messages to the coast but 'denounced him', he claimed, 'to the king as a spy sent by the English government'. Custom required him to drink gri-gri water – a noxious drink – to prove he was telling the truth. 'If you come to do bad,' the king's priests told him, 'it will kill you; but if not, it cannot hurt you.' He got rid of the worst of it by making himself vomit repeatedly, and it was concluded he must be 'under the special protection of God'.

Still the Portuguese refused to carry his messages but gossip filtering to the coast alerted a merchant captain in Ouidah to the presence of a distressed Englishman among the slave-pens. Captain Laing of the *Maria* went to find him, paid the ransom demanded – six Danes guns, 1 barrel powder, 8 romals, 10 'Glasgow Danes' (a measure of gold); presents to two messengers consisting of '2 guns and 1 taffatee'* (a total, with expenses of canoe hire and the bill for Lander's subsistence while at Badagry, of £61) – and transferred Lander to HMS *Esk*, homeward-bound after two years on the African station.

On land, the new envoys of abolition – explorers, evangelists and legal traders – had been defeated by the forces of the slave trade. Until more resources were sent to penetrate up the rivers and to force paths overland, the abolition campaign would remain in the hands of the naval patrols.

---

* Danes guns are Danish muskets; romals are forked stock whips; a taffatee is a length of linen.

7

Two Lieutenants

The Preventive Squadron approached the end of its first decade larger, stronger and better equipped to deal with illegal slaving carried on under foreign flags. The British Foreign Office had continued to make and amend anti-slave-trade treaties. The British Admiralty had increased the number of ships and the colonial government of Sierra Leone was doing its best to support them. Yet more slaves were traded in the late 1820s than when the first squadron left for West Africa in 1819. The resources put in by the world's most powerful nation still seemed insufficient to suppress the trade, and in the last years of the decade, a violent new element appeared in the slaving seas which would hinder the squadron's campaign even further.

When Charles Bullen replaced Robert Mends as commodore of the Preventive Squadron in 1824, he had nine ships under his command. The largest was his flagship, the forty-six-gun frigate *Maidstone*. Then came the *Atholl*, twenty-eight guns, and the *Brazen*, twenty-six; two twenty-gun corvettes, the *Bann* and the *Esk*; then the brig-sloops *Victor* and *Redwing*, each carrying eighteen; and lastly the two twelve-gun brigs, *Conflict* and *Swinger*.

They had been put together as a squadron from bits and pieces not being used elsewhere, rather than as a unit composed to meet the conditions and requirements of West African service. This was a hard coast for ships on long commissions, sometimes running upwards of 80,000 miles in four years. Timbers shrank under the hot sun, and if not caulked in time for the rains, the decks below were inundated. Hulls were eaten by remora – suckerfish which attached themselves to the timbers. Ropes dried and frayed in the hot winds. Seamanship and discipline were still superb, for these ships' companies had learnt their skills at war but the Squadron's ships were outclassed by those of the slavers. The *Conflict* and *Swinger* were so slow they could rarely catch one in chase; the *Bann* and the *Esk*, more commodious vessels, were 'Seppings-built': practically a solid mass, coated with cement and tar, caulked outside and in and thus guaranteed to have as little 'give' in the water as possible. It meant they were solid and safe, but it made them slow. The *Maidstone* frigate was fast, but could not patrol effectively inshore or upriver, for her keel was too deep and her tall masts too visible. Many slavers, on the other hand, were purpose-built for the task: lean, low, fast, with sails bent low and broad to weather tornadoes; small-timbered; their beams held together by screws which could be loosened under chase to give them more play.

Occasionally one of the faster British ships took one of the slower slavers on the open seas, trusting to seamanship in the chase, gunnery when the prize came into range and ferocity in hand-to-hand fighting when she was boarded. Sometimes information or luck allowed slower warships to corner a slaver with cargo aboard before she got her anchor up, unfurled her sails and made swiftly away. Officers in charge of 'dull (i.e slow) cruisers' might attempt to disguise them as merchantmen by dressing a few men in the red jerseys of merchant sailors and sending them to stroll about the deck. On seeing a slaver, a commander might run in the other direction under full sail – leaving one ship's boat discreetly behind him. If the slaver captain fell for it, thinking the warship had spotted another slaver and gone in chase, he might enter his anchorage, load his slaves and be taken by the boat left lurking, for whatever the bluejackets lacked in resources, they made up for in courage.

Most slavers were still taken by boats on detached service, the accepted means for young men to find relief from the boredom of patrol and, if they were lucky, derring-do and bounty. Such expeditions could be dangerous and uncomfortable, as Midshipman Binstead of the *Glendower* had found. 'At night', wrote one young officer,

the boat was sometimes a very trying place to live in. Anchored up a creek, with a rain awning over the top, no fresh air could get in or foul air out, and the total of 70 occupants inside, including 30

black men, worked out at about 10 cubic feet per man – a condition which is, I understand, impossible for a human being to live
in. We managed to live but it was not pleasant, and I was always
glad when the morning came. We should have liked to bathe, but
as a crocodile rose to everything that was thrown overboard, bathing
was not permissible. The hippopotami during the night were a source
of annoyance; they breathe so noisily through their wide-open
mouths.[1]

Commodore Bullen was unimpressed by the quality of his ships and, finding
the Admiralty unwilling to provide better ones, decided to buy himself a
private slaver-catcher superior to any in the squadron. In late 1825, the
Maidstone's boats took a beautiful Spanish schooner with 292 slaves aboard
off Lagos. She was condemned by the Mixed Commission, put up for auction
in Freetown and bought back by Commodore Bullen, 'on my own account',
he wrote to the Admiralty: first, 'for the shelter and comfort of the officers
and crews of my boats when detached on distant service in this unhealthy
climate, to prevent, as much as possible, their contracting fever from being
exposed to the tremendous heat by day and the heavy dews by night';[2] second,
as poacher turned gamekeeper.

Bullen renamed his new pet the *Hope*, and gave her to his second lieutenant, William Tucker, with a midshipman, an assistant surgeon, eighteen
bluejackets, five marines, eight Kroomen and an ambitious itinerary: to patrol
the Bight of Benin, and keep particular watch over Badagry, Lagos and
Ouidah.

In September 1826, the *Hope* put into Ouidah and began the routine
business of boarding the ships lined up at anchor there. Twelve were
owned, chartered by or consigned to Francisco de Souza. None had slaves
aboard, although several were 'forward with their preparations' – yams
loaded, slave-decks laid, water-casks ready. One of these was the *Principe
de Guinea*, a beautiful, purpose-built slaver from the shipyards of
Philadelphia, bound for Rio de Janeiro. Brazilian ships taking on their
slaves illegally north of the equator tended to head straight for the Line
when they left, to reach the safety of legal waters as soon as possible.
Calculating the course which the *Principe* would take when she left Lagos,
Tucker retreated beyond the horizon and ordered all sail furled. There the
Hope drifted, her thin, naked masts scarcely visible against the sky. They

waited. It took the crew of the *Principe* only three hours to load their cargo by night, slip anchor at dawn and be away, appearing over the horizon at first light just where Lieutenant Tucker had said she would be. They chased her for twenty-eight hours, and fought a bitter battle for two and a half more, until three of the *Hope's* guns had been blasted from their mounts by enemy fire, Lieutenant Tucker himself, wounded, was firing the long gun, and three men were being operated on by the assistant surgeon below. Tucker was faint from loss of blood when he finally brought the *Hope* clashing and grinding alongside. Midshipman Pengelly led the boarders over the rail, the surgeon leaving his patients below to follow, cutlass in hand. A brief and ferocious brawl ended the chase. On the Brazilian deck, thirteen were dead and a dozen wounded; below, three of their seamen had died, and, during thirty hours in which no one had taken food, water or aid to the Negroes on the slave-deck, eleven slaves were near joining them.

When the *Principe* was condemned by the British–Brazilian Mixed Commission in Freetown, six hundred Africans were given a new life. For de Souza, it was a minor inconvenience: eleven more ships had been waiting at his wharves, and each represented enormous profit. Nor was her loss permanent. At the auction house, merchant captains, Squadron officers, civil officials and well-known slavers all lounged in company, discussing the vessels on the stocks, raising a languid hand to bid. The *Principe* was knocked down to an agent from Ouidah. There was no law to stop it; there were profits to be made; it was business.

Lieutenant Tucker took one other prize in the Bight of Benin, the Spanish schooner *Paulita* with 221 slaves aboard. Her capture was easier than that of the *Principe*, but her voyage to Sierra Leone was worse, for there were smallpox and dysentery on the slave-deck, and twenty-eight black corpses were jettisoned on the way. Reaching Freetown in December 1826, both Tucker and Midshipman Pengelly learnt that the *Principe de Guinea* had earned them promotion, and sailed for home. Commodore Bullen's commission, too, was ending and he had no further use for the beautiful little ship he had bought on his own account. She, too, went up for auction and, as Bullen, Tucker and Pengelly were returning to Britain, the *Hope* was returning to her old trade, for she, like the *Principe*, had been snapped up at auction by the slavers.

* * *

In 1827, Sir Francis Augustus Collier[3] replaced Bullen as commodore of the Preventive Squadron, commissioning the frigate *Sybille* as his flagship. Collier was a keen, hard man to work for. He had seen service aboard Nelson's flagship at the Battle of the Nile and he clung to old standards and old ways. His previous command had been against the pirates who infested the Gulf of Persia and this experience would be of use in his new anti-slave-trade brief. Piracy was on a dramatic increase on the Guinea coast, in the Gulf of Florida and along the sea-routes to Brazil and the Caribbean. In its legal days, the slave trade had been generally carried on by merchant captains who considered themselves gentlemen. These men observed a certain code of behaviour towards each other, if not towards their cargoes. Except in times of war, when merchant shipping was caught up in a free-for-all between belligerent nations, captains of legal slavers had not preyed on each other's shipping or poached each other's cargoes any more than had captains of ships carrying tea, sugar or coffee. This changed when slaving was criminalised, growing more dangerous but concurrently more profitable. Legislation, treaty and the British-led patrol had dissuaded the law-abiding from slaving. Those left were tough and ruthless, willing to arm and fight the British or each other. By the mid-1820s, the Preventive Squadron's campaign was only one of many wars in the rich and crowded slaving seas, and sometimes they became entangled.

America and Britain were at peace but other quarrels still raged between the Old and New Worlds. A mania for independence had spread across Latin America and the King of Spain, as obsessed with his lost American colonies in the south as George III had been with his in the north, would not let them go. The fleet which Théophile Conneau had seen in Cuba was one of many sent to subdue the colonies, and alongside them went the privateers, licensed by royal marque to seize and kill. The 'letter of marque' was a means for governments to augment their national navies temporarily without going to the expense of building their own ships and recruiting their own men. In time of war, the captain or owner of a private vessel obtained a letter of marque from the government which authorised him to attack enemy shipping on behalf of his country. These documents were internationally recognised and all maritime nations used them. Captured ships were brought before an Admiralty Court, which determined whether or not the detention was legal, and the prize was divided between ship's company and state. King Ferdinand VII issued many letters of marque to enable Spanish ships to attack his former Latin American colonists and the new republics were fighting back: not only against Spain, but also, interminably and with indescribable complexity, among themselves. Privateers swarmed from Cartagena to the River Plate and the Spanish Main was as full of buccaneers as it had been in the grand days of Philip and Elizabeth.

New games of empire and dominance were being played, new borders fixed, territories grabbed and dynasties founded. A privateer captain might sail confidently with a Latin American letter of marque issued by one government and only learn at sea, from someone with more up-to-date information, that that government, and possibly even the country it ruled, had ceased to exist. His papers were worthless and he was a pirate if he continued to sail under their protection. The coasts of Africa had been drawn into these battles and strange ships under unknown flags, or no flag at all, cruised each other's path. Those which could not pick up a slave-cargo because British cruisers were watching the ports had begun to wait across the horizon to waylay some departing ship, take its cargo and throw its crew overboard. From everywhere came reports of rakish brigs which ran up a succession of flags and bore down on ships sailing between Rio, the West Indies, West Africa and Europe, stealing whatever cargo was aboard – bullion, tea, sugar, silk, Negroes, it little mattered. They brought with them a violence new even to the Slave Coast.

The Brazilian *Defensor de Pedro* left Rio for Africa on a legitimate slaving voyage but her crew turned pirate, abandoning their captain when he went ashore to arrange the purchase of slaves. In February 1828, they attacked the British merchantman *Morning Star*, homeward-bound from Sri Lanka with invalids and a rich cargo aboard. Raising the British flag, the pirates approached then opened fire, boarded her and murdered her captain, most of her crew and several passengers. This was a particularly bloody instance of disrespect towards the flag of what was supposed to be the world's most powerful navy but other distressed British ships were appearing in West African harbours with their anchors thrown overboard and their rigging cut away in attempts to escape a pirate's chase. The entries were multiplying on *Lloyd's List* of merchants falling prey to privateers, mainly under Colombian and Buenos Airean colours, but sometimes those of France, Portugal and America, whose flags were no more immune from hijack than the British ensign. When slavers preyed on each other, no heart bled in the Admiralty or the City of London but when they preyed on British merchant shipping, the Royal Navy had to act.

*   *   *

Commodore Bullen's report on the squadron's last cruise gave his successor an idea of the volume of illegal shipping on his station. Just over four and a half thousand slaves had been liberated under Bullen's command. Seventy-two of the *Maidstone's* company had died of fever, she had run through twenty-nine lieutenants, four pursers and two surgeons and Bullen knew that however many slaves had been rescued, far more remained captive. One captain estimated 30,000 Negroes were in barracoons, awaiting embarkation.

Shortly after arriving on the coast and mustering the squadron, Commodore Collier left for his own first cruise of the Bights, and spotted one of the most notorious of the Brazilian slavers. The *Henriquetta* had 548 slaves aboard and was making her sixth voyage in two years between Bahia and the African coast. She had already transported over three thousand Africans and made her owner a profit of £80,000. Outmanoeuvred at last, she surrendered to the deadly fire of the *Sybille* gunners and was taken to Freetown, where a British traveller went aboard her crowded decks with his notebook. 'The spectacle', he wrote,

> was humiliating in every sense, and the immediate effect upon the olfactory nerves was excessively disagreeable and oppressive. We found the officer who had charge of the vessel confined to a small space in the after-part of the deck near the tiller. The pressure of this dense mass of human beings was suffocating, and the crowd was so great that one poor slave who had fallen overboard in the night, on the voyage, was never missed until the following morning.[4]

When the *Henriquetta* was sent up for auction, Commodore Collier followed his predecessor's example and bought back his prize, renamed her *Black Joke* and made her tender to the *Sybille*. There was great competition for her command: Lieutenant William Tucker had 'made commander' for his spectacular detention of the *Principe de Guinea* and there were plenty of eager young officers bursting to emulate him. In early 1828, the *Black Joke* was given to Collier's brightest young officer, William Turner (a bewildering number of junior officers were called William) formed in the same adventurous mould as Tucker.

Pirates were on Lieutenant Turner's mind on 1 May, when the *Black Joke* fell in with a heavily armed brig flying Spanish colours off São Tomé.

Her captain claimed that she was the *Providencia*, and two Black Jokes (a ship's crew was customarily called after its vessel in this way) rowed their master's mate across to check his papers. He found a letter of marque from the King of Spain authorising him to hunt down South American rebels. It also bore the scribble of Commodore Collier, who had boarded two days earlier and signed an 'order to cruise', indicating he accepted the papers as authentic. The boat returned to the *Black Joke* with a Spanish lieutenant and five Spanish seamen aboard. 'Why is your captain holding my men?' Lieutenant Turner asked, and the Spanish lieutenant in reply asked to see Turner's own identifying papers. A British ensign, British uniforms and British accents were no longer proof of identity when lawless crews assumed whatever nationality suited them best. William Turner did not know that the *Providencia* herself had been hunting down a particular Colombian privateer for some time and her captain suspected the *Black Joke* of being that Colombian, expertly disguised. Arrogantly, Turner refused to produce his commission, although the Spaniard had fourteen guns to the *Black Joke*'s one, and twice as many men. The Spanish request was reasonable, as was his second suggestion that fifteen Black Jokes be exchanged with fifteen Providencias, and they sail in company to Principe to sort the question out. When Turner refused this suggestion too, the Spanish ship opened fire and when the firing stopped two hours later, Turner got his men back but the *Black Joke* was in tatters.

It was not a good beginning, but Lieutenant Turner retrieved his pride two weeks later, taking his first prize off Ouidah despite being again outgunned. She was a Brazilian brig with eight guns, a crew of forty-five men and 645 slaves crammed suffocatingly below. The name on her documents was *Vengador*, but she had previously been the *Principe de Guinea*, captured just as courageously by William Tucker two years ago and sold back to de Souza at auction. It was the first in a string of brilliant captures which made the *Black Joke* the pet of the squadron, and the *bête noire* of the slaving marine.

All slavers in the Bight of Benin were on the look-out for two ships that summer: the fast-sailing, boldly commanded *Black Joke*; and the pirate schooner *Presidente*, notorious for pouncing viciously on the unwary and the slow. She was commanded by a Portsmouth outlaw, crewed by ninety-five men of different nationalities and criminal pasts, and she sailed now under South American colours, now under Spanish, Portuguese or Yankee.

Juan Rodriguez was a captain in the army of Buenos Aires, then an independent city-state rather than part of Argentina. He had been fighting the Brazilians in one of the endless wars of the Plata. Taken prisoner on the Brazilian–Uruguayan border, he paid his own ransom and took ship back to Buenos Aires, only discovering at sea that that ship was a pirate and bound for the Caribbean. He was landed, destitute, at St Bartholomew's, along with various prizes the pirates had taken en route, and left to make his own way back to South America. He had fallen in with Captain Prouting of Portsmouth, who said he was bound for Buenos Aires and offered the young man a lift. Only when Prouting seized a Portuguese merchantman and murdered her crew did Captain Rodriguez realise he was aboard a second pirate and approaching Ouidah.

Francisco de Souza, like most large-scale slavers, ran a fleet of merchant ships up and down the coast, bringing supplies to his barracoons and ferrying trade goods to his agents. As one of his ships, the *Nosse*, left Ouidah in late August, her Portuguese captain, Juan Maria Evangelista, saw a stranger bearing down on him. American then Portuguese colours were hoisted, a shot was fired across his bow and a hostile boarding party approached. The *Presidente* had got him. In custody in the pirates' gunroom that night, his own captured vessel and another prize both following in the *Presidente*'s wake, Evangelista felt the buck and snap of a ship responding to canvas. A third ship, his captors told him, which Captain Prouting believed to be carrying bullion to Gibraltar, had been spotted, and a new chase was on.

The *Black Joke* had also approached Ouidah that day, under disguise of a Brazilian flag, to see which of the usual suspects were there. A couple of miles off the bar, men in her sails saw three vessels sailing out to meet them. One they made out to be heavily gunned and signalling orders to her two consorts. Lieutenant Turner, guessing the *Black Joke* had been recognised despite her Brazilian flag, raised the British ensign instead and hailed the advancing schooner with a shout. There were no games of courtesy and subterfuge in this fight, no display or demand of documents, only a deadly and immediate broadside tearing across the water, and the *Black Joke*'s smaller reply. Three ships to one was an unequal contest, and Lieutenant Turner did not stay and fight, but stood off out of range. As yet, neither he nor Prouting had realised what they had taken on. On board the *Presidente*, Rodriguez was summoned. "'You are a soldier", said Prouting to Captain Rodriguez. "Yes, Señor", replied he, "Then by —, you shall command our marines, if we bring that speck into a fight."'[5]

Away they went into the ocean and the falling night, the *Presidente* tracking the *Black Joke* and her prizes trailing behind her. Juan Maria Evangelista, brought up from his prison to watch the chase, would later recall in the Old Bailey that they sailed for hours under every inch of canvas they could keep up, the British ship at times less than a pistol-shot ahead, gaining a yard, losing two, gaining, losing. When moonlight illuminated the sea, the *Presidente* was still on the *Black Joke*'s tail, but the two other vessels had fallen behind. The contest was one on one: the *Black Joke*'s drum beat for action, the watch below raced on deck, Turner tacked and positioned his agile vessel athwart the schooner. From this position, his gun might sweep devastating fire down her deck from stern to bow – had the man at the pirate's tiller not also acted ably and fast, twisting the ship out of the *Black Joke*'s range. For an hour they turned about and about in the graceful, deadly dance of fighting ships under sail, their bulk and volume belied by ease in the water and the sharpness of the work which altered sails and positions to the second – until the *Black Joke* turned, the wind filled her sails and again she shot away, the pirate following. Moonlit grapeshot and musketry over the stern wounded the British ship, but did not bring her down.

Seeing her so close at hand in the bright light of the moon, Evangelista realised what the pirates had taken on: that, he shouted in panicky warning at Captain Prouting, was no merchant brig; that was His Majesty's brig *Black Joke*. 'I don't care a curse,' said Captain Prouting, 'as soon as they come near me, I'll fight them like hell.' ('Oh d—n,' Evangelista would be reported as saying fearfully, 'dey be all mad to fire on de British flag – sure to be taken and hung up at de yard-arm.') Prouting had nothing to lose: he was British, and he had fired on a king's ship. His decks were cleared for action, men stationed at the bow and along the rails with muskets. As boarding seemed inevitable, a beautiful shot from the *Black Joke* shattered the pirate's boom, cut through her rigging fore and aft so the sails came tumbling down, and killed the man at the wheel. Shrieking bluejackets came over the side. Amid the flapping, suffocating canvas on deck, Captain Prouting fired his long guns into the scrambling mass of invaders before he was killed. The deck was a shambles. His crew did not fight on, but hauled down their flag – now that of Buenos Aires – and surrendered. When a head count of the dead was made, the British found they had killed thirty pirates, and lost one man of their own.

While the pirates were put in irons and taken below, and work began on repairing the damage, Lieutenant Turner was in Captain Prouting's cabin. If more evidence had been needed of the ship's trade, he found it here, in a book in which the pirate's signals were laid out. When the *Nosse* came into sight at daybreak, her pirate prize-crew unaware their captain had been waylaid and killed, Turner signalled her in private code to close. Close she did, and was captured, Evangelista and his own shaken crew reunited.

It was William Turner's last action in command of the *Black Joke*, for news of his promotion reached the coast and he was ordered home. In less than a year, he had overseen the liberation of more than 2,000 Africans. He sailed home in the same ship as the men of the *Presidente*, accused of piracy and on their way to trial in Admiralty courts.

It took two months to complete their interrogations. At first, Juan Maria Evangelista had declined to testify unless he was 'assured of remuneration' but he changed his mind when the court fined him £100 and sent him back to Newgate Gaol. In their defence, the prisoners claimed to belong to the state of Buenos Aires and to be acting with the authority of its government. Buenos Aires, being at war with Brazil, had authorised the *Presidente* to seek out and take Brazilian vessels. As Britain had recognised Buenos Aires' independence from Spain six years before – partly in exchange for a commitment to abolition of the slave trade – any letters of marque issued by its government must be regarded as valid. As for the prisoners' assertion that they had believed the *Nosse* to be a Brazilian ship and thus a legitimate target, who could disprove it? All thirty-eight were released.

8

A Costly Grave

Governor Charles Turner's 1825 treaty with the Sherbro chiefs was broken within months, possibly weeks. The inevitable news was brought to Freetown in January 1826: the slave-wars had begun again, the brokers of the Gallinas were also involved and principal responsibility for this renewal and extension of hostilities lay with the Tuckers. James and Harry Tucker were experts at this sort of dirty work, but they were now operating on what Governor Turner, not yet informed by London that his treaty would not be ratified, considered British territory. As he planned a second expedition south, determined to bring the Tuckers back for trial and leave no devious middle force between Britain and the chiefs who signed abolition treaties, HMS *Leven* sailed into Freetown with Captain Fitzwilliam Owen aboard, convinced that he and God between them could save the African continent. Captain Owen saw the links between exploration, colonisation, Christianity and abolition more clearly than Captain Clapperton. He expressed them far more explicitly than the Colonial Office and the Admiralty found comfortable.

When HMS *Leven* arrived in Freetown in February 1826, she had already been almost four years on the African coast. Captain Owen had been ordered to undertake an enormous cartographical survey for the Admiralty. This was badly needed. The officers of the Preventive Squadron, working without Admiralty charts, had to peer at the land and send their boats in to determine where they were. *Swallows and Amazons* methods were used to distinguish the apparently identical inlets and river mouths. Sester was recognised 'by a hill in the interior, and the land appearing double', the entrance to Lagos River was 'marked by a Big Tree'; that of Ambriz by 'A Remarkable Pillar of Granite'.

Owen's orders of 1822 had been as grand in their scope as those issued to Commodore Yeo in 1816. He was to make a survey of 'the entire Eastern coast of Africa, the Western coast of Madagascar – the islets and shoals inter-jacent – together with the Western coast of the Continent from the Zaire to Benin, and from the Rio Grande to the Gambia'. The voyage of his two survey ships was marked by the usual avalanche of death and disease, for the fever was as dangerous on the east coast as the west and chose its victims in the same way: 'the mortality', wrote the ship's surgeon, 'was confined to those who had slept ashore and those on the river surveys'.[1] They succumbed in their dozens: where there is a Morley Bank, a Point Durnford, a Watkins Creek or a Fisher's River on the nineteenth-century British map of East Africa, there a man of Owen's little squadron died.

Owen had left England as an abolitionist, but only of the type any decent man of his generation might be: it was his belief, but not his passion. Commitment was no more axiomatic in the navy now than in 1808. At Rio, provisioning en route to East Africa, more than twenty of his seamen had deserted, seduced by the offer of better-paid work aboard slavers fitting out in the bay. They were rounded up and flogged. Owen later set the date at which he became a zealot against the 'hellish traffic' as that on which he entered the East African harbour of Quilimane.[2] This was the entry point to the great River Zambezi, which a party of Levens was to survey. But cartographers, botanists, officers, passengers and seamen – even those who had tried to jump ship in Rio: all forgot the plans of exploration in the horrors on show here.

Once this had been the grain basket of Mozambique. Now it was utterly blighted by the detritus of slaving: the ghastly warehouses where slaves awaited departure, the moaning processions in the streets, the bodies of those too old or weak to work, discarded on the streets and wharves to die untended. This was hell. 'Those places where peace and agriculture had reigned', Owen wrote, were now the 'seat of war and bloodshed' where 'contending tribes are now constantly striving to obtain mutual conflict prisoners as slaves for sale to the Portuguese, who excite these wars and fatten on the blood and wretchedness they produce'.[3] After seeing the careless destruction wrought by Portuguese, Brazilian, Arab, African and conscienceless others of many and mixed nationality, Owen decided he must do something about it: unilaterally, but in the name, and beneath the flag, of Britain. 'It is to me', he wrote,

> as clear as the sun, that God has prepared the dominion of East Africa for the only nation on earth which has public virtue enough to govern it for its own benefit . . . The presence of a single Englishman in authority would prevent the continuation of any traffic in slaves which on this coast we pay a hundred times more in our endeavours to dam the torrent than would be necessary to possess ourselves of the source and turn the stream, and this without force or injustice . . .[4]

Thus began Owen's one-man British protectorate of Mombasa. It lasted three years before London, aghast at this extension to its African responsibilities, forced him to close it down, but Captain Owen remained an enthusiastic interventionist. Governor Turner's acquisition of 'Turner's Peninsula' mirrored his own vetoed plans and Owen was happy to help the governor with his second punitive expedition. In February 1826, the *Leven* accompanied a fleet of colonial schooners carrying troops and supplies to the River Sherbro. Captain Owen was aboard Governor Turner's gig as it sailed upriver to see the Tuckers' bush-town blown apart by British marines. To Governor Turner's rage, the Tuckers slipped away and could not be found, but this second foray up the Sherbro did succeed in showing local chiefs, hovering between obedience to the British and obedience to the slavers, that the balance of power was shifting. It also killed Charles Turner himself, who died of the fever in March. Government passed to Sir Neil Campbell, and bets were made in Freetown on how long he would survive it.

The wars between Kussoos and Sherbros, the treaties signed by monarchs with strange African names and the dirty machinations of Tuckers and Clevelands, were barely comprehensible to the British observers who followed events through newspapers, parliamentary debates and letters from sons, husbands and fathers. To them, it appeared that little news but death came from the West African coast: a continual, lugubrious roll-call of the dead from settlements whose inhabitants did not expect to live a year. Fever had killed most of the recent victims, but bullets and knives had taken others – shot and wielded not only by foreign slavers but also by those whom the Squadron's supporters had believed it to be liberating: the African brethren, whose disparateness, internecine aggression and enthusiasm for the slave trade were never fully realised at home.

There had always been vociferous opponents to the campaign in Britain. They were a fluctuating and multi-party group. One steadfast lobby came from the 'West Indian interest' who thought they were protecting British Caribbean colonists; other protesters, at various times and for various reasons, simply thought British governments had no business spending taxpayers' money on solving other people's costly problems. The Squadron should be withdrawn, they said, the West African settlements closed down, and the African continent and those who traded with it, in whatever currency, left to their own devices. Every year, there were squawks of outrage and disbelief when colonial expenses were voted in Parliament and this year's Freetown budget was announced as greater than last. 'Given the enormous havoc of the climate on European health,' said one MP in May 1827, 'it is ridiculous that the government continues year after year to vote money to its maintenance.'[5] *The Times*, while careful to condemn the barbarities of slaving and laud the personal courage of British seamen, was influentially critical of the project. 'What benefit', it asked later that year, '[has England] ever yet extracted from the pestilential posts she occupies on the western coasts of Africa? And what real advantage has she yet conferred through them upon the Negro people?'[6] The suppression of the slave trade was an 'infatuate policy', a 'mixture of quackery and hypocrisy which has instigated a certain class of people to press upon government the retention of a costly grave for British subjects, by nicknaming it a school for the civilisation of negroes'.

Even those who believed the Squadron must continue its work, regardless of the cost, were wondering if Freetown had not been badly chosen as its home port. Much attention had been given to a report which Governor Turner sent home on taking office. So many Negroes had been liberated by the Squadron, he warned, that the old arrangements for their reception and settlement in Sierra Leone were becoming inadequate. 'Very shortly', he said, Freetown would 'become a very large and unwieldy mass of people'.[7] Hitherto, Liberated Africans had been dispersed into the villages spreading up to the mountains, 'where they have been for years supported in idleness by the Government', but as the land there had not yielded enough to feed them, many were heading for 'barbarism' in the woods or returning to Freetown to beg in the streets. He had tried parcelling them out as agricultural labourers to private 'landlords' or employing them on public works

but 'those used to not working, do not want to do so'. The superintendents employed in the villages might mean well but were not suited to
circumstances: 'for example, there is no one to teach agriculture'; and the
officials of village and town alike were generally incompetent. Worst of
all, the grotesque expenditure of life and money had hardly dented the
number of Africans selling each other into slavery, or that of foreigners
taking them off. In Freetown itself, a visiting officer found twenty-eight
people in the gaol accused of kidnapping and selling their fellow
Freetowners. 'Most of these inhuman villains', he said, 'are manumitted
slaves themselves, and in several instances relations or countrymen of their
unfortunate victims.'[8] One man had been 'kidnapped from the colony three
times before and liberated as often, owing to the different vessels in which
he was embarked having been, fortunately for him, captured by HM ships
Brazen, Maidstone and *Esk*'.

Captain Owen's survey-ships *Leven* and *Barracouta* had divided the
mapping of the West African coast between them, with the young
Lieutenant Vidal taking the *Barracouta* along the southern stretch. The
Preventive Squadron had extended its patrolling to the Bights and
the equatorial rivers, but had hardly reached the Angolan coast: some of
the African brokers there still did not even know their trade was under
attack. In January 1826, Vidal was at Benguela, entering the southern
extremity of the beat defined for Commodore Yeo. Here, the Portuguese
governor told him indifferently that ten thousand slaves left the town each
year. At São Paolo de Loando, further north, the number was '18 to
20,000 . . . chiefly to the Brazils'. It was only at Cabinda that Thomas
Boteler found 'the natives . . . have heard of men-of-war, fighting at sea
and seizing slaves', but even here were confused as to their purpose: 'they
hold them in great dread, and imagine that their crews are rogues who
seize indiscriminately all vessels that they meet with . . . war-ship no make
trade – no dash notting – sail ebery where – look ebery ting – ab plainty
gun – plainty white man – eatee too much – What e do?'[9]

As they approached the Gulf of Guinea, coasting the monotonous
littoral of Gabon, Lieutenant Vidal found his hosts becoming coyer on
the subject of the slave trade: 'well knowing the antipathy of the English
to [it] and their activity in suppressing it', they were 'fearful of making it
too much the subject of conversation'. One Jack Romando, pilot to HMS
Pheasant several years ago, came aboard when they touched at the tiny

island of Corisco, got drunk and obligingly wrote a list of the various goods recently paid for slaves, enraging the local chief, who feared such indiscretion might bring a punitive visit from the British and the blame of his fellow dealers for inviting it. From the low, densely inhabited coast of Cameroon, fleets of small canoes darted out of the reddish haze, offering fish for cloth. Once a canoe-party of chiefs came, 'distinguished by the elevated chair on which they sway, and the umbrella borne over their heads', but they turned quickly back. 'They had supposed us to be a merchant vessel, and were much chagrined when they found out their mistake; for, as a man of war brings no trade but, on the contrary, tends to curb it . . . so she excites no other feeling than fear, and a hearty desire to get rid of her as quickly as possible.'

In the Bights the picture was different. Here they knew exactly what the British ships were doing, and how successful they could be when circumstances allowed. When the *Barracouta* anchored in the River Bonny, she found French and Spanish slavers alongside the palm-oilers from Liverpool. Provisions were swiftly provided by King Peppel 'in order to get rid of us, for such is the dread there of a man of war that the presence of one, even off the river, occasioned an instant stagnation of the trade within'.

Before the Preventive Squadron was created in 1819, most slave-ships were brought in from north of Sierra Leone, or the coast between there and Cape Mount. Now the Bights were the real theatre of war. This change had created difficulties, for a slave-ship and her human cargo had to be brought 1,000 miles before the legality of the detention could be determined and the slaves released. Detained slavers spent more time beating up to Sierra Leone from the equator than they would have done crossing the Atlantic to Brazil.

'There is perhaps', wrote Naval Surgeon Bryson, 'not any condition in which human nature may be viewed in a more revolting aspect than in that of a crowded slave-vessel, with dysentery on board. . . . The effluvium which issues from her decks, or rather prisons, is peculiar and sickening beyond conception, and is generally perceptible at a great distance to leeward.'[10] The horror of a vessel awash with shit was no longer confined to the Middle Passage; this was the condition of many being taken up to Sierra Leone, with British prize-crews aboard these stinking, floating cesspits, crouching on slave-decks to take off shackles clogged with excrement, hosing decks and bodies covered in sores, separating sick from well, dead from sick; all this before cooking vast meals from limited supplies, rationing water, finding blankets and old clothes to cover nakedness; and then navigating a boat overweighed, undermanned and often ill-found through difficult waters. If headquarters were moved from Freetown to some position nearer the Bights, the lives of those who undertook these horrible duties would be saved, and less money wasted. This idea, long suggested by naval officers, was finally being taken up in earnest.

A degraded string of islands hugged the sea-route to Brazil from the Bonny and the Calabars. The Spanish islands Anobón, Corisco and Elobey were specks in the ocean across the equator; the middle two, Principe and São Tomé, were Portuguese-governed; northernmost and closest was Fernando Po,[11] abandoned by its eighteenth-century Spanish occupiers after a short and fever-ridden experiment in plantation. It emerged as the mountainous, black-soiled top of a submerged volcano, abruptly misshapen where the platform miles below had slipped. Despite its proximity to the slaving rivers and the corrupt islands, Fernando Po had remained aloof from the slave trade. Its indigenes were the Bubi people and in its hills lived a maroon community perhaps two thousand-strong of escaped slaves from Principe and São Tomé. A British plan was cohering around this Spanish-claimed African isle which was, its supporters said, the perfect headquarters. Mixed Commissions, government, courts and all other colonial apparatus should be moved here, Freetown should be left to languish in its petty corruption and disease, and seamen be spared the long prize-voyages which had killed or incapacitated so many.

In 1826, the *Quarterly Review* summed up the prevailing view with the optimism Britain often showed for an utterly inappropriate place to found a colony, as well as a cavalier attitude to the freedom conferred on rescued slaves.

A day or two at most, from any situation in the two bights, would be sufficient to carry [liberated slaves] to Fernando Po, where they might be employed in cutting down timber, preparing billets of wood for the steam-vessels, and clearing the ground for cultivation. In the present state of this island, the savage natives produce the finest yams in the world, and appear to possess abundance of fowls. A refreshing breeze constantly blows over the island from the Atlantic; it has plenty of good anchorage in more places than one, and abundance of clear, running water; and it is so situated, as to overlook and command the whole Bight of Biafra and the numerous rivers that fall into it.[12]

Naval voices were joined by medical ones. The improvement to health, it was thought, would come from the 20 miles of sea which separated Fernando Po from the mainland. The 'miasmata' of the swamps and mangroves along the coast and rivers did not span the straits, so the island, they said, should not suffer the repeated epidemics of Freetown. Commerce agreed. The palm-oilers of Badagry were being joined by others in the Bonny and the Calabars. While their ships remained anchored at Duke's Town, Creek Town or Bonny, their captains dining with Duke Ephraim, King Eyo or King Peppel, their tenders cruised the coast, picking up palm oil as they had used to pick up slaves. A strong naval presence to protect them would be welcomed, as would a safe, healthy offshore harbour.

There were nay-sayers in Freetown, which would lose its status and much of its income along with its courts, government and shipping. But all other voices seemed to converge and agree, and in January 1827 the Admiralty looked for a seasoned officer to supervise the foundation of an experimental settlement on Fernando Po. Captain Owen, just returned, seemed tailor-made for the task, at least to those who did not know he was accountable to God rather than the British government. He was 'not on any account', the Colonial Office told him sternly, 'to deviate from the execution of the Special Service at Fernando Po . . . for the purpose of looking after vessels employed in the Slave Trade',[13] although what that Special Service was had not been entirely decided when he left for Africa. The Admiralty was under the impression that all other West African bases would be closed once Fernando Po was up and running; the Colonial Office said the island was not to be a colony but only a naval base and town for Liberated Africans living under British jurisdiction, but did not make this clear to Owen; and no one remembered to tell the Spanish, who still claimed sovereignty over the island, that they were moving in (let alone the estimated 50,000 Bubi indigenes).[14]

Owen's frigate, HMS *Eden*, left Plymouth in company with the troop transport *Diadem*, sent to replenish the constantly dying regiments, and a clutch of passengers. Shuddering and praying in their berths during unseasonal Channel gales were the Reverend Davy and his wife, a missionary couple on their way to Sierra Leone. He was to undertake conversion, she the education of the female young 'not only in the mere education of letters', but in the domestic arts – which Mrs Davy would impart by permitting her pupils to do her housework – and 'all the moral duties of civilized society'. Also aboard was James Holman, famous in his day as 'the Blind Traveller': a former naval lieutenant who had lost his sight during service, and taken to restless travel and the writing of exhaustive, exhausting, narratives of his journeys. He was an extraordinary and admirable man but one suspects from the relentless Gradgrindery of his writings that he would have been wearing as a companion.

Beyond the Cape Verde islands, temperatures soared and the English sheep in their thick wool became so miserably hot that Owen ordered them slaughtered and the mutton salted down. Then the maize seed taken on at Madeira became so damp in the hold that it had to be tenderly carried on deck each day to air to prevent its germinating before arrival. They reached Freetown in September 1827, and Captain Owen heard that Governor Neil Campbell, too, had died of the fever. The *Eden* did not stay long in the stricken town. As the ship was being cleaned, and water taken on, Owen learnt of a semi-derelict steamer in the harbour, the *African*, 'formerly . . . employed in the Colonial service on this coast, but lately been laid up for want of repair' and now 'half full of mud and water'. He had her rescued, repaired and painted in double-quick time and filled her with 60 black soldiers of the Royal African Corps, 160 'skilled artisans' and 100 'black labourers' who would do the grunt work of settlement. It was a neat example of wasteful Sierra Leonean sloth against the energy and can-do-ism of Fernando Po.

They reached their new home in heavy rain on 27 October and were greeted by a flock of long canoes, their oarsmen tattooed, wearing conical straw hats and smeared in yellow clay, holding up yams and asking for iron bars. By the end of the month, with the *Eden* still in the bay fending off islanders whose curiosity was becoming tiresome, Owen had worked out the topography of the island and decided the shape of his settlement. A clutch of thoroughly naval names was pasted on: Maidstone Bay, enclosed by Cape Bullen and Point William, fed by the Barracouta River, was to be the principal anchorage; on its south-eastern side, on the Point William peninsula (opposite Point Adelaide), the village of Clarence[15] was to be built, named after the Lord High Admiral, later King William IV.

On 25 December, Captain Owen took formal possession. There was great ceremony: the colonists divided into their constituent parts and marched, to bugle, drum and fife, to the flagstaff on Point William to see the colours hoisted and hear the captain speak.

In obedience to the orders of his Royal Highness the Lord High Admiral, I directed the first operations of clearing the land on this point [Point William] to be commenced on the first day of November last, and on the tenth and twelfth following, purchased from the native chiefs, and from the tenants of one small part of that ground which I desired to occupy, the full right of property and possession, for which iron was paid to the amount of three bars, and land-marks fixed by the native chiefs, to shew the extent of ground so bought.

Therefore, in the name of God, by whose grace we have been thus successful, and for the sole use and benefit of his most gracious Majesty, George the Fourth, King of Great Britain and Ireland, I do, by this public act, take possession of all the land bought by me as aforesaid, under the future name of Clarence.

God Save the King![16]

By mid-January 1828, two house-frames had been erected near Point William to serve as a hospital, and 17 Edens, suffering from supperating ulcers, were transferred to its bare wards.

A month later, three Royal Naval ships sailed into Clarence Bay with the *Sybille*, Commodore Collier's flagship, in the lead. The visit was not a success.

At British Accra, Collier had put ashore a young Scottish midshipman on a three-year leave of absence. He was Thomas Park, son of the Mungo Park who had gone missing while exploring the Niger in 1805,[*] determined 'to travel into the interior, and search for his father',[17] whom he thought might not be dead, but held prisoner by the tribesmen of Bussa. The *Sybille* had sailed on to Cape Coast Castle and joined company with HMS *Primrose* and HMS *Esk*, which had just picked up Richard Lander and learnt of the death of Captain Clapperton and the wars of Sokoto. Almost as distressing to Commodore Collier was the sight of Commander Harrison of the *Diadem*,

---

[*] Or possibly January 1806.

transferring his troops from Fernando Po to the depleted Castle garrison, and doing so bearded. Collier was not an officer to appreciate his men going native. The commodore 'would not receive him in his Fernando Po costume; and being unequal to contend with the higher powers, [Harrison] yielded to the alternative of removing his beard, in preference to subjecting himself to the consequences of his superior officer's displeasure'.[18]

Harrison was uncomfortably caught between superior officers. Leaving England, Captain Owen had encouraged all his officers to cultivate their beards 'for the sake of the advantages, which, from experience, [he] considered were to be derived from it. In the first place,' he said, 'all the Arabs wear long beards, and they are held in much respect wherever they sojourn among the various African nations. They also command respect, because they are generally worn by the old men of their own country.' This seemed to be confirmed when 'on our first arrival', James Holman wrote, 'the chiefs of Fernando Po advanced with delight to rub beards, with all those among us who wore them.' Commodore Collier did not share that delight. When he crossed the straits to inspect the new settlement, he was severely displeased to find Owen and the rest of his officers not only bearded but in 'a state of tropical undress'. This, he said, was 'unbecoming conduct' – a serious allegation against an officer – and hot-tempered letters passed between Owen's half-built verandah and Sir Francis's quarterdeck.

Even the stiff-necked commodore could not find fault with the slaver-catching of the first, fast-moving and successful six months of the settlement's life, for Captain Owen had entirely ignored the Colonial Office's instructions to leave that business alone. The resurrected *African* steamer had caught two Brazilian prizes on her voyage from Freetown to Fernando Po and eager junior officers had since been unleashed on the Bights and returned with seven hundred slaves and several ships. Two of them – renamed *Cornelia* and *Portia* for Captain Owen's little daughters – had been incorporated into the fleet and sent back into the rivers. There were no Mixed Commissions in Clarence to determine whether this spate of detentions was legal. A few ships were sent up to Freetown, Owen informally approved others, failed to declare certain of the smaller ones and sent a few, illegally, to the Admiralty court at St Helena. By March 1829, the population of Fernando Po stood at 1,277 and food supplies were low. Having 'made bankrupts of the natives in the yam market', the British were having to procure them elsewhere. The sheep which might have started a flock had been made mutton on the voyage out and there were no cows. The *African* was sent up the Old Calabar to buy cattle to found a Clarence herd. She anchored off Duke's Town in company with two Liverpool palm-oilers and a Havana schooner awaiting her slaves.

Duke Ephraim of Duke's Town was always ready to embrace new commercial opportunities. Although he still 'most strenuously supported' the slave trade, he had invested heavily in palm oil and received Captain Smith of the *African*, accompanied inevitably by James Holman, at one of the evening levees he held every day 'for supercargoes, and Captains of vessels, to talk over "news". Upon these occasions', Holman wrote, 'he discovers an acute knowledge of his own interest', part of which, that hot March night, was that the British on Fernando Po were short of food. Smith and Holman slept 'in the Duke's English house, where his visitors always sleep, but none of his family' and learnt the next morning that a schooner which had 'secreted herself further up the river' had dropped down after dark, loaded a cargo of slaves during the night and got away. A couple of days later, Captain Owen himself arrived, rather tactlessly, aboard an ex-slaver taken leaving the duke's river. He went to pay his respects to the duke who, wrote Holman,

> received him very civilly, but suspiciously, for, notwithstanding their great professions of friendship for the English in general, and their real regard for some particular individuals, who are regular traders to the country, the consideration of the profits they derive from the slave-trade, prompts them to feel no little annoyance at our interference in their lucrative commerce. They already perceive that our new settlement at Fernando Po, is calculated to interfere with their proceedings, and they have clearly expressed their sentiments upon the subject; not, however, without clothing their observations so cunningly as to avoid giving offence. 'What for,' said one, 'white man come to live in black man's country? What for can't white man stop in own country? Much better for white man, than black man's country.'

Canoes took Owen, Smith and Holman upriver to Creek Town the following day as guests of King Eyo, to dine on Calabar chop – 'a dish consisting of any sort of meat stewed in palm-oil, and highly seasoned with pepper' – eaten from English china, with wine drunk from English glasses; and spend the night in a 'wooden framed English house', furnished with English sofas, mirrors and a chandelier, all sent out to the present king's father by a Liverpool slave-merchant in the old days. Owen then returned to Fernando Po but Captain Smith, remaining to barter for bullocks, was there to see the slaves brought, as soon as Owen had gone, 'to wash themselves in the river . . . chained in pairs, the right leg of one to the left leg of another'.

Despite Captain Owen's zeal for abolition, his treatment of the Africans liberated on Fernando Po was as autocratic as Governor Ludlam's twenty years before, and marginally less legal. The slaves were now free, of course, in one sense; but only as indentured labourers, pressed men, married women and the peasants of 1820s England were – not very.[19] In April 1828, a Spanish schooner (masquerading as French) had been brought in with one hundred slaves on board and the Brazilian *Voador* with 230 children. 'The black mechanics and labourers, and their wives', brought from Freetown, 'shewed the greatest anxiety to take one, two, or more of these children under their protection, although they had been previously told that they would not receive any additional allowance for their support. One woman remarked that, as she had left her child at Sierra Leone, she wanted another in its place, to carry at her back.'[20] Other boys were put 'under the protection' of civil and military officers. But there was not the population on Fernando Po to absorb a large number of adult 'apprentices' and so the rest Captain Owen co-opted into labour parties and set them to building roads, docks and gardens on 'an allowance of sixpence per day, and their provisions'. The Frenchman who had commanded the 'Spanish' schooner was so enthused that he offered his services as overseer, and thus the slaves who had last week seen him at the helm of the ship taking them into slavery now heard him ordering them into the jungle paths to render them passable. Surely they must have been as bemused about their change in status as the *Derwent* Recaptives of 1807.

Most bent to this labour as they had bent to labour ordered by others all their lives, but not all. Small groups were reported missing in the mornings. Four *Voador* slaves ran the day they were landed and made for the hills, hoping the maroons might shelter them. One returned to Clarence a month later. He and his comrades

had lived in the bush by day, emerging at night to steal yams, and proceed on their journey, until . . . being at some distance up the mountain, they were fiercely attacked by the natives with spears, and stones thrown from slings. In this rencontre, one of them was killed, and another taken prisoner; while he, and his remaining companion, effected their escape, by taking different directions: they never, it appeared, met afterwards.

It was not an unhappy outcome for the administrators: 'that the islanders are [evidently] unwilling to give shelter to runaways', wrote Holman, was 'an occurrence by no means unsatisfactory, as the newly liberated Africans desert very frequently, and sometimes in small troops, so many as nine having been known to go away together'.

If Owen's experimental settlement had lasted long enough, it would have run into hideous diplomatic tangles, for his treatment of captured slavers and slaver-ships was illegal and aggressive. It was not legality which closed this experimental chapter, however, but the eternal, inevitable fever. Low-lying Clarence was no more immune to malaria than Freetown and soon the other, ghastlier plague washed up at its shores.

In May 1829, the *Eden* had sailed from Fernando Po to Freetown, taking Liberated Africans and slaver-crews for trial. Learning the yellow jack had hit town again, she left hastily, but too late. Forty-seven of the *Eden*'s 130 men succumbed on the return passage to Fernando Po, 'dying daily', her surgeon reported,

amidst almost incessant rain and frequent tornadoes, accompanied with much thunder and lightning; the main-deck was crowded with sick, and constantly wet. The moral effects of these scenes became palpable in every countenance; while from the want of medical atten-dance, the surgeon and two assistant surgeons having died, it was impossible to pay the attention to the ventilation of the ship, or even to the personal comforts of the sick, which their situation required.

Only three officers were still standing when the *Eden* reappeared in Clarence Bay, bringing the Freetown sickness with her.

For a month, Owen attempted to contain the disease, removing the *Eden*'s sick to quarantine, clearing out and fumigating his ship. Fifty more died as he did so. By mid-July, sick himself, he had realised the fever would not be contained and left with the survivors for St Helena. Forty men were left behind at Clarence 'but we expect', wrote one officer, 'to find most of them dead on our return'.[21] The voyage was as terrible as that of the *Bann* five years before.

> Imagine a set of poor wretches lying upon gratings on the deck, some dying, some dead, some delirious, some screaming for water to quench their parching tongues, and no one to attend to their call; others calling on their wives and children to bestow on them their last blessing. Of 173 officers and men who left England in the ship we have only 6 officers and 11 men left.

As Owen left, his grand plans for settlement defeated by disease, Colonel Nicolls of the marines, governor of Ascension, arrived to take command. The Colonial Office had realised that Owen was a loose cannon, his aggressive anti-slaving bringing more difficulties than rewards, and had ordered Nicolls to take his place, unaware of the epidemic which would greet him. The soldiers, marines and wives who came with him from Ascension sickened. Three of the newly arrived medics had to be landed in their cots and within the week, two of them were dead. The work of settlement petered out; there were not enough able bodies to heft spades and dig roads. Those still fit for work spent their time burying the dead. A macabre joke was spawned, and written into the island's duty book, the sole order to appear there during the months of sickness: 'Gang No. 1 to be employed in digging graves as usual. Gang No. 2 making coffins until further orders.' The population of Clarence shrank to a tiny rump and the Bubi suffered worse.

In a squadron of 792 men, 202 died of the yellow fever as it spread from Freetown down the coast and from ship to ship. Ships fled the smokes which hung about them, softly piling on deck and clinging to their shrouds, and made for the clearer airs of Fernando Po, Ascension and St Helena bringing fresh waves of sickness with them. Out in Clarence Bay lay vessels abandoned, or so undermanned that they could not be worked. On the *Sybille*, Commodore Collier and his surgeon took what precautions they could. At sunset, when the drifting red mists approached, every man was handed a specially devised costume to keep the wet air from his skin. 'All hands', said one irreverent midshipman, 'looked like so many polar bears',[22] wrapped head to foot in blanket and an all-covering frock and trousers. Their costumes were useless against the remorseless disease. Man after man died: taken ill with violent vomiting one day; dead the next. Twenty died in July; forty-seven more in August. Fever struck Tom Collins, the *Sybille*'s old sailing master, as they approached Principe, and killed him twelve hours later, as they anchored in West Bay.

Tom Collins was an old-timer; he had no family of his own, or none that anyone knew of; the ship's company stood for kith and kin, the *Sybille* was his home, his only possessions those in his sea-chest. On a silent deck, his coffin was weighted with shot and there were many volunteers for the ship's boats which rowed him out to sea on his final voyage. The strongest were chosen, an officer served as chaplain for the chaplain was sick and those who could left their hammocks and went on deck to speed Mr Collins on his way. Vast, dark cloud-banks blotted the sky as the boats pulled away. When they halted on open water, the men raised the oars and the officer stood shakily to read, but it was too dark to see his Bible. He blessed the coffin with brief, remembered words: 'we therefore commit his body to the deep', and it was hoisted and steadied. They let it go as the first thunderclap shook the water and the first green lightning lit the scene, but it leapt half out of the water again and turned end-on as the storm let loose its strength, the thunder broke, and broke again, the coffin sank and reappeared with a thunderous rattle, bouncing horribly on the surface of the water as something appeared to pull from beneath and the body appeared to resist, desperately returning to the light. Defying their officer's orders, the oarsmen turned and pulled for their ship. They thought the Devil had come for Tom Collins's soul.

The ghastly spectacle off West Bay deepened the fear aboard the *Sybille*. Hysteria worked its way through the ship, and men tripped and dropped things and came to a morose, unlistening stop despite the officers' bawling. The master was dead, the purser was dead, 105 officers and men were dead or too sick to rise and those left had lost hope. Commodore Collier went among them, heartening and exhorting where threatening had ceased to have effect but it was Dr M'Kinall whose actions remained in the minds of survivors. He had told the men too many times to remember that the fever was not contagious, but they would not believe him: how could they? They had seen man after man go down, and there were no miasmic mists or rotting river-weeds to blame for it here on ship, at open sea. They respected the doctor but they did not believe him. And so, unable to find words to persuade them, Dr M'Kinall stood by the berth of one delirious man with a wineglass, caught his nauseous, frothing vomit and drank it in full sight of men who had massed silently to watch. Then he stood, walked about the ship, chatted and showed himself to everyone who was still alive enough to know he was a man and not a hallucination. But even Dr M'Kinall's continued good health did not convince them.

When Captain Owen returned to Fernando Po late in the year, he found its white community reduced to four officers and two women. All the others were dead. He was convinced this was the fault of Colonel Nicolls, heading a conspiracy against the establishment of Fernando Po. The colonel, confronted by a thwarted messiah, defended himself against this mad idea, but the discussion ended by his running into his house and barring the door. When Owen attempted to break it down, Nicolls threatened to shoot him. Captain Owen abandoned the island once again, taking with him all the stores and labourers he could collect, determined to make his reports to London and save his reputation. Colonel Nicolls struggled hopelessly to keep the settlement going but it was impossible. Fernando Po would be abandoned four years later, having proved a costlier grave even than Freetown.

Nor did young Thomas Park survive his adventure. 'Without any knowledge of the world', the Europeans later said sadly at Accra, he had taken no one's advice, heard no one's warning.

> He lived for three months in the town, and though he had frequent invitations to take up his quarters with the Europeans, he preferred remaining in a hut with designing natives, who plundered him. There he indulged in drinking spirits; married an Accra wife by way of learning the language; and took long walks in the heat of the day, with a view of hardening himself. The consequence was . . . that when he set out . . . his constitution was already completely broken; he was thin and weak; he caught a fever after a few marches; and fell another victim to African discovery.[23]

9

Cuban Customs, Brazilian Buccaneers

The two biggest markets for slaves at the end of the 1820s were Cuba and Brazil. Cuba was still a colony of Spain but Brazil had become independent of Portugal in 1825. In November 1826, the Brazilian emperor had made an agreement with Britain to abolish the slave trade, partly in acknowledgement of British recognition of his country's independence. However, that agreement had not diminished the number of slaves crossing the Atlantic to Brazil any more than the earlier ones made in the name of Portugal. Spain, too, had put no further resources or commitment into forcing Cuba to observe the abolition treaties signed in Madrid a decade ago. Still the only danger posed to the slave-ships sailing weekly for Havana, Matanzas, Rio and Bahia was the British naval patrol, and many were prepared to defy it.

Théophile Conneau, for one, saw nothing wrong in breaking the laws of his own country or anyone else's where there was money to be made in black gold. In 1828, however, his business suffered a setback. Early one spring morning, 'the voice of my servant calling on me at my door to rise and save myself' woke him 'from a very pleasant dream'.[1] His factory was alight. Within hours, its wooden huts and palisades were burnt to the ground, his precious stores destroyed in the fire. He had to barter the Negroes in his barracoons for emergency provisions. It was a warning. Two years before, Conneau had been drawn by the profits of a booming illegal trade to the River Pongus. His early employment with Mongo John had ended and older traders on the river felt threatened by the factory he had set up there in partnership with the English outlaw Edward Joseph. The Ormond clan had struck back and Conneau was being warned to take himself elsewhere.

Mongo John himself was old and his grip on the trade had loosened even before the newcomers set up in competition. Slights, absences from his table and his hearth, a furtive murmur among his women and empty wharves at Bangalang all proved he was no longer chief-among-traders. He brooded, and drank too much, visited the seraglio but left frustrated and sure his women mocked him. He began playing silly games: promising one thing but delivering another; giving slaves bought on Conneau's credit to other captains; speaking openly of treachery and revenge. Distrust grew. Slaves were stolen by one captain from another; raids were carried out and bodies found in the river; servants were bribed to inform; factors went armed not only against the British but against each other. One morning the body of Mongo John was found outside his seraglio, 'in one of the vegetable patches, stretched out among the cassava plants, a pistol in the left hand still loaded'. It was supposed the old man had committed suicide, and after the funeral ceremonies, the Mongo's family came looking for the man they believed had driven him to it. Théophile Conneau decided to let matters cool. The obvious place for him to go was Cuba.

Having arranged his affairs with Edward Joseph, Conneau therefore left for Havana. He sailed for Freetown and, under the noses of the British, who could do nothing to stop him, 'purchased a schooner condemned by the Mixed-Commission Court' and crewed her with 'prisoners from prizes and men of all nations', the patrons of Freetown lodging houses whose proprietors did not care if their customers arrived aboard a warship, a merchantman or a slaver. Next he needed a cargo of slaves – to sail to Cuba without one would be nonsensical, a waste of a voyage – and one of his new crew provided the excuse to acquire one quickly and cheaply. A French slaver, said this man, lay in the River Nuñez, her cargo almost complete. She was commanded by a man who had until recently been her mate: a thief, liar and assassin who had poisoned the captain and seized the ship. It was an opportunity for the self-serving reflection and inverted honour in which Conneau excelled. 'I believe', he would write, 'that the slave trade was never carried on with the punctuality that all smuggling traffics should be, and gentlemen commanding slavers have in general forgotten that title when accidents or misfortunes deprived them of their cargo.' There was no honour among these thieves. 'As I was not different from others of the same cloth,' he admitted, pleased with his own roguery, 'and I then loved a little excitement ∴ . . I considered in my Don Quixotish opinion that my mission was to redress this Captain's death and chasten the villainous mate.' A river-pilot was kidnapped and forced with a knife to his throat to take them upriver to where the 'villainous mate' was carousing with the king. His 197 slaves were stolen, several men were killed and Conneau headed out to sea.

It was July: the current and strong south-westerlies were against him. After ten days he was still off Cape Verde when a strange sail was seen to starboard. A musket-shot through his mainsail confirmed she was a British warship. In an unregistered vessel, without documents or the protection of any nation's flag, Conneau risked the pirate's penalty of a noose from the yardarm if he fired back. 'Every sail was trimmed to the best advantage and the position of our slaves changed, sometimes a little more forward or more astern . . . every encumbrance from the deck was also thrown over the board.' After a few hours, the British ship fell away, another man-of-war outsailed by another slaver.

Now they caught the wind and the first islands of the Antilles were soon in sight. This, in Conneau's perverted view of his trade, was normally a moment of 'merriment', when slaves were

liberated from their shackles and allowed [in daytime] free intercourse with the females. The tank of water is also left open at [their] disposal and from this moment forward these men who were subjected to close confinement as dangerous enemies are now permitted to mingle with the crew their former masters . . . our sailor, with the generosity proverbial to his caste, distributes with the independence of a millionaire to his Black friends his last shirt, reserving to himself only a clean suit to land with. The women . . . are rigged out from the Captain's, Mate's and Petty Officers' wardrobe, and sheets, table cloths, and spare sails are soon torn in strips to adorn their loins . . . black emigrants, who dress in this masquerade and with new expectations before them, forget in part their long privations.

But this time the expected scene of laughing blacks and generous whites was spoiled by a sullen crew. This was a ship short on trust: crewed and commanded by pirates and thieves who respected each other no more than their cargo, and treated each other worse. Those taken by force in the River Nuñez were planning to serve Conneau as he had served their mate-turned-captain, and that man had served his own: Conneau was to be marooned and his crew would sell the 197 slaves for their own profit. He learnt of the plan from an informer, and the repercussions were bloody. 'Several flagellations took place' during 'investigations' and following the 'court martial', where Conneau was the only judge, four were 'given their discharge' and two were put in irons. The punishment of the ringleader

> I left to the crew, who cast votes as the punishment to be inflicted to him. . . . Several were for [killing him], while others were for making a raft and setting him adrift. As I considered both these punishments too cruel, I proposed to chastise him in the same manner as he wished to serve me; and next morning I landed him with two shackles on his feet on Turtle Island on the north side of St Domingo, with provisions for three days,

and sailed on.

Even in Havana, it would cause some embarrassment for the governor and his officials if an unregistered vessel carrying illegal cargo should sail brazenly in under command of a criminal, so Conneau landed on a beach on the island's southern coast and set off for the city of Santiago to find 'an honest merchant' to whom he could entrust his slaves. Local information led him to a Catalan dealer, who took charge of the case.

> That day the Governor was informed of my arrival and the total number of the Africans was also duly reported. The Commander of the Port was also applied to, and in a blank page of his port register was inscribed the name of my schooner, as having sailed from that port six months previous. A registrar [sic] and a blank muster roll were then furnished to secure an unquestionable safe entry in port.

Thus was the small matter of piracy resolved. Two days later, Conneau's ship, 'now a Spanish property under the name of Santiago', a little homage to his hosts, 'was sent into the harbor under charge of a pilot who was to act as her Captain – a formality necessary for the satisfaction of the boarding officer', and soon after disposed of at a 'sham public sale'.

The ship taken care of, it was the turn of the slaves, given '48 hours to recruit and acquire a stately walk'. Then the seamen shaved the heads of the younger men, used soot to dye the hair of the older ones, thereby 'transmutated from grandfathers into decent prime fellows', and marched them into Santiago, where they were 'comfortably housed in a store to be sold at retail'. Conneau, 'consider[ing] the business management in perfect hands . . . took a stroll in the country for a month'.

'The island of Cuba', wrote the British clergyman Robert Walsh, 'seems now the *refugium peccatorum* for every ruffian, and the spirit and practice of the buccaneers revived there at the present day.'[2] Walsh knew nothing of Théophile Conneau, still small fry on the international scene. He was referring particularly to the Cuban ship *Veloz Pasagera*, sometimes slaver, sometimes pirate, notorious from West Africa to the Gulf of Florida. An old Spanish warship, she was one of a new breed of giant slaver and every ship of the Preventive Squadron was looking out for her.

The Reverend Walsh was returning from three years in Rio as chaplain to the British minister there. He had been shaken by his own reactions to a first sight of slaves in the flesh, strewn about the wharves like so much rubbish, 'entirely naked, with the exception of a covering of dirty rags tied about their waists'. Some he saw 'yoked to drays, on which they dragged heavy burdens . . . chained by the necks and legs'; others were 'lying on the bare ground among filth and offal, coiled up like dogs'. The effect, he was appalled to note,

> was to shake the conviction I had always felt, of the wrong and hardship inflicted on our black fellow-creatures, and [to wonder if] they were only in that state which God and nature had assigned them . . . it was not surprising that people who contemplated them every day, so former, so employed, and so degraded, should forget their claims to that rank in the scale of beings in which modern philanthropists are so anxious to place them.

It was only when he had seen slaves playing with great discipline in a military band, and selling their wares in the streets 'all very neat and clean in their persons, [with] a decorum and sense of respectability about them, superior to whites of the same class and calling', that he recovered faith in his convictions. 'The white man', he reminded himself, 'made a slave on the coast of Africa, suffers not only a similar mental but physical deterioration from hardships and emaciation, and becomes in time the dull and deformed beast I now saw yoked to a burden.'

Walsh knew of the *Veloz Pasagera* from Captain Arabin of HMS *North Star*, ordered from West Africa to Rio to pick up the British minister, Viscount Strangford, and take him home to England. After three years on the African coast, the *North Star*, Walsh wrote, was 'a perfect menagerie, with different kinds of monkeys, parrots and paroquets, which every one was bringing home to his friends; and I was awoke in the morning by such a concert of chattering and screaming'. Monkeys and parrots were endearing creatures. The vast swarms of ants were not, nor the cockroaches, so large that Walsh thought when he encountered his first they must be some species of small African bird; nor the centipedes which unfurled 5 slithering inches from between the boards. In order to 'encounter these plagues', Captain Arabin 'had taken six of a certain species of spider on board, which feeds on cockroaches'. The spiders had colonised the ship: 'in every angle of the timbers, in my cabin a huge one had taken up his abode, his body nearly as large as a walnut, and his legs radiating from it in a circumference of seven or eight inches'. Walsh handed his man a bottle of rum, ordering him to 'immerse in it every crawling thing he can catch' and went to chat with the officers on deck while the servant pounced and swatted.

Wildlife also ruled the mess, even at the captain's table. Biscuit taken on at Freetown with larvae in the flour had 'generated living insects' during the passage to Rio, 'which burrowed in the bread, and filled it with curculios and different animalculae'. All seamen automatically tapped their biscuit on the table before raising it to their mouths, but tack which walked by itself still took guests by surprise: Walsh was fascinated to find that 'when a piece of it was laid on the table, it began to move by its own internal living machinery'.

Viscount Strangford had negotiated the 1826 agreement whereby, in exchange for British recognition of Brazilian independence from Portugal, the Brazilian emperor would abolish the slave trade by 1830, regarding it from that date as piracy. Strangford kept himself to himself aboard. It was Captain Arabin who explained to the interested clergyman the particular difficulties of dealing with Brazilian slave-ships until the happy day of abolition should come. 'The instructions sent to king's ships as to the manner of executing the treaty of Brazil', noted Walsh, 'are very ambiguous. They state in one place that "no slave ship is to be stopped to the south of the line, on any pretext whatever". Yet in another, a certain latitude is allowed, if there is reason to suspect that the slaves on board "were taken in, to the north."' Practice seemed to have established that detention was legitimate if the slaver were detected to the north, and chased across the Line, but not if sighted when already to the south. The cost of establishing this working rule was the heavy penalty paid by Captain Murray of HMS *Atholl*, who had fallen foul of Brazilian lawyers. He had proved that slaves on one Brazilian slaver were loaded north of the Line but the detention of the ship when spotted four degrees south of the Line was nonetheless held illegal. While the case was being heard by the British–Brazilian Mixed Commission, the rescued slaves escaped their ship in the river and scattered. Captain Murray was found personally liable for their value, set at £61 5s.

Captain Arabin had been one of many British captains to board and search the *Veloz* during her trips to the African coast, and interrogate her disdainful Spanish captain, Don José Antonio de la Vega. The full-rigged *Veloz*, well armed and plentifully crewed, was larger than any ship in the Squadron except the flagship *Sybille*. She could hold over one thousand slaves, but her capacity was also her weak spot. Embarking such numbers took time and all slaves must be embarked at once, for if she were stopped with a partial cargo, up she would go to Freetown. Thus for months she hovered off the coast, dipping in and out of the Ouidah roads for wood, water and rum, boarded and boarded again by sweaty British officers; tacking back and forth while her agents on shore gathered slaves in some stinking clutch of barracoons for loading and swift departure. By April, when the *North Star* left Africa for Rio, there were rumours that the cargo of the *Veloz* was nearly assembled somewhere on the lagoon: a few more coffles from the interior, a few more negotiations, a fleet of canoes assembled, and on, or about, 1 May, according to information from a spy ashore, she would load and leave. Arabin, therefore, was laying his return course from Rio with that of the *Veloz* to Havana in mind: if all went well, the two ships would meet mid-ocean, and although 'in every way inferior in force and firmness to the armed slaver', the *North Star* would take the Cuban on, her crew impelled not only by a 'sense of duty', but also by the knowledge that 'in case of success in this instance, [they] would share

16,000*l* prize-money'. It would be a glorious end to the *North Star*'s African commission.

Men and officers drilled every day: there was none of the gradual relaxation which characterised some homeward voyages. Boats rowed out targets for the gunners to aim at; marines practised musket-fire to cover boarding parties, and young gentlemen and bluejackets forced each other back and forth along the deck in cutlass drill. As the point approached where the ships' courses might intersect, chase and bounty dominated conversation. On 22 May, the captain and his guests were 'talking of this pirate at breakfast and the probability of meeting her in this place, when, in the midst of our conversation, a midshipman entered the cabin, and said in a hurried manner that a sail was visible to the north west on the larboard quarter'. There was a rush for the deck where those with spy-glasses made out a three-master approaching. The stranger, still many miles off, was seen to change course, coming into the wind to bear down directly on the *North Star*. For an hour, the two sailed on a collision course, then the stranger suddenly veered away, filled her sails and ran before the wind. The chase was on.

For hours they went, the stranger 'doubling in all directions, and every moment seeming to change her course to avoid us', Captain Arabin with a glass screwed into his eye, every man on deck staring after the sail which represented £16,000. When only four miles separated them, and the stranger's decks were visible to the naked eye, Arabin ordered a gun fired as signal to heave to, then another when no notice was taken of the first; and when that, too, was ignored, one of the powerful long guns in the bow was loaded and everyone who could raced to the forecastle to watch the ball ricochet over the waves. It fell short and a Brazilian flag was seen going up the other ship's mast, for slaving captains knew the advantages of the Brazilian treaty as well as British captains knew its failings. They had covered 100 miles in chase when the light faded, and the stranger faded with it.

But Captain Arabin knew his game and all night the *North Star* clung to her course. Occasional glimpses of the ship ahead were sworn to by men aloft, staring into the hot night after their bounty. Dawn came, they had gone 250 miles in chase and there was a speck on the horizon. The wind was rising again and all morning, spirits rose with it as the speck became again a definable shape: hull, masts, sails and, by midday, a pivot gun amidships, a crowded deck and a cluster of cauldrons on the bow. When two British shots struck water alongside the *Veloz*, she finally hove to.

Bluejackets gathered at the rail, clamouring to board; officers slithered into the boats, shoving arms into the sleeves of the uniforms necessary to satisfy the treaties, adjusting hats. On the deck of the slaver, a 'ferocious-looking fellow, with a scourge of many twisted thongs in his hand', stood over the grating through which the first British boarders peered at the dark mass below. 'As soon as the poor creatures saw us looking down at them', Walsh wrote, 'their dark and melancholy visages brightened up . . . they immediately began to shout and clap their hands . . . they all held up their arms and when we bent down and shook hands with them, they could not contain their delight.'

The captain this voyage was not de la Vega, Arabin's old adversary, but José Barbosa, equally well known on the coast, his face scarred from a previous shoot-out with a British warship. As he was brought aboard the *North Star*, there was an altercation on the *Veloz*: the British officers were insisting the blacks be brought on deck, the Spaniards were protesting. The hatches were opened and the Reverend Walsh was first excited, then sickened, to see the black mass 'swarming up, like bees from a hive, till the whole deck was crowded to suffocation, from stem to stern, so that it was impossible to imagine where they could all have come from, or how they could have been stowed away'. Fifty-five, the Spanish said, had died and been thrown over-board since they left the African coast; another 500-odd were now on deck but the last did not come up until the boarders brought them in their arms. 'On looking into the places where they had been crammed, there were found some children next the sides of the ship, in the places most remote from light and air; they were lying nearly in a torpid state, after the rest had turned out. The little creatures seemed indifferent as to life or death, and when they were carried on deck, many of them could not stand.' Walsh was appalled; but the men of the *North Star*, accustomed to the horrors, told him this was one of the better-run slavers they had seen. They brought a tub of water for the adult slaves, who rushed for it 'as if they grew rabid at the sight of it'; and took some in cupped hands to the little children, who looked at it milky-eyed and apathetic and had to be persuaded to open their mouths.

Aboard the *North Star*, the Spanish captain was 'pacing the deck in great agitation; sometimes clasping his hands, and occasionally requesting a drink of water; and when asked whether he would have any other refreshment, he replied, turning his head and twisting his mouth, with an expression of intense annoyance – nada, nada – nothing, nothing'. The interrogation began.

How many slaves were aboard? The correct number per tonnage: the British were welcome to check. Where had he loaded them? South of the Line, naturally. Why did he not heave to when ordered? He thought the *North Star* was a pirate. None of this would have prevented his detention had Barbosa been sailing under the flag of his own country. But he was equipped with Brazilian papers and however much Arabin and his lieutenants pored over them, and although everyone knew neither Barbosa, his ship nor her owners were born in, lived in or had any other than the most tenuous and venal connection with Brazil, the documents allowing him to carry slaves could not be faulted.

As they rocked on the mid-ocean swell, the slaves lifted their faces to the air, chattered, and drank. The little children started to sit up and look about; and Captain Arabin consulted his officers. They knew the British–Spanish Mixed Commission would reject the case. The slaves were counted. Barbosa, as he said, had not broken the tonnage rule. Black seamen talked to the slaves on deck and came hopefully to report that some said they were taken on at Badagry, north of the Line. Would their testimony be accepted by the Brazilian Commissioners? Everyone knew it would not. Finally, the water-casks were counted on both ships. It would take three weeks to beat up to Freetown and they did not have enough water to keep the slaves alive that long.

Nine hours had passed since Barbosa came aboard the *North Star* and night had fallen again before Captain Arabin acknowledged he could not keep his prize. He let the Spaniard return to his own ship, his impeccable papers restored. The swarm of slaves who thought they had been saved were sent back, pleading and crying, into the hold, the little children crammed again against the suffocating timbers. The hatches shut above them. The *North Star* turned to sail for Portsmouth, her crew grim and silent; the *Veloz Pasagera*, hers exultant, for Havana. 'It was dark when we separated,' wrote Walsh, 'and the last parting sounds we heard from the unhallowed ship, were the cries and shrieks of the slaves.'

'A slave pays to government,' Robert Walsh had found in Brazil, 'ten per cent on the first price, and the same sum every time he is purchased again.'

> On proceeding into the interior, he pays five and a half milreis when leaving Rio, and five and a half on passing the Rio Peto, and thirty

ventems on crossing the bridge of the Parahiba, so that every one sold at the Vallongo for 250 milreis, and brought up to the Minas Geraes, and there sold again, pays to government 61,600 reis, or about 8*l* at present currency. If, therefore, out of the number imported into Rio, 30,000 be annually sent up the country, the whole will produce to government a revenue of 240,000*l* per annum from Rio alone.

According to Viscount Strangford's agreement, this immensely lucrative business was to end on 1 January 1830. On that date, all slave-trading by Brazilian ships was illegal, both north and south of the Line. Between signature and the stipulated deadline, the Brazilian trade reached panicky levels. About 200,000 slaves were brought into Brazil, in ships adopting whichever combination of flags best covered their voyage. As the deadline approached, efforts were made to gain extra days, minutes, seconds of legal slaving time. The last official clearances for slave-ships were issued in Rio on 31 October 1829, but in London, the Brazilian envoy begged, then demanded, that the Preventive Squadron not be unleashed immediately. Familiar reasons were brought out: some ships might have cleared before 31 October for a slave-voyage, he said, but have been detained for many reasons – his examples filled page after tedious page of correspondence – and thus the Squadron must be ordered to hold off to allow completion of voyages by slaver captains anxious to obey the new law but caught by weather, wind, tide, a shortage of food, of water, sickness among the crew, contingency, circumstance, the hand of God . . .

The Foreign Office caved in. Orders reached the African coast that Brazilian ships with slaves aboard might not be stopped until 13 March 1830 and even if 'they should be found at sea subsequently to the said 13 March 1830, they will not be liable on this account to be treated as pirates'. This was the greater blow, for equating their trade with piracy would truly have kicked the Brazilian slavers, and all who borrowed their flag, into submission. This last-minute amendment struck at the heart of the treaty, for now Brazilian slavers could get away with the derisory fines, the non-existent imprisonments and the valueless reproofs by which France and America continued their illegal trade.

Nonetheless, and despite the last-minute wriggles and hedges, the lucrative Brazilian papers issued to captains of all nationalities would cease to guarantee immunity if they were actually caught at sea, with slaves, by a

British warship. Had the *Veloz* crossed the path of the *North Star* a year later, Barbosa would have been sent for trial, 555 Africans been saved, a British ship's company made richer by £16,000.

After that nine-hour encounter with the *North Star*, the *Veloz Pasagera* had sailed safely on and landed her surviving slaves, not in Rio, as her papers stated, but in Havana. She did not need to make clandestinely for a small bay on the southern coast, like the pirate Théophile Conneau, but merely exchanged her Brazilian for a Spanish flag and sailed in. On her next voyage to Africa, however, she could no longer sail under the shelter of a Brazilian flag and Brazilian papers, but must take her chances to outsail or outwit the Squadron. In August 1830, reports were passed to the British by their spies on the African coast that the great ship was back, crewed by 150 men who would fight their way through any encounter.

HMS *Primrose* had just arrived at Ouidah, come from south of the Line with encouraging news. It seemed that the ban on Brazilian slaving was having some effect. In the Bay of Loando, *Primrose* officers had 'heard that Spaniards, Portuguese and Brazilians [had] all destroyed their forts on the southern coast and given up slaving there'.[3] As unhappy corroboration of this, they also learnt that a local king had recently brought sixty slaves to the coast and finding no buyers, 'ordered them killed, as he could not afford to feed them'. HMS *Primrose* was one of the few British ships which could match the *Veloz* in speed. In three years on the station, she had taken many prizes but suffered much from last year's yellow fever epidemic, her old captain and many others left dead in the Ascension graveyards. A still-debilitated crew was now commanded by William Broughton, twenty-six years old, bright and well-connected. His first lieutenant was the immensely experienced Edward Butterfield, a young man who had taken his turn commanding the *Black Joke*, been promoted to the flaship *Sybille* for gallant action aboard her and stayed on the African coast when that ship sailed for home.

On 2 September, the new Commander Broughton was ordered to hunt down the *Veloz*, known to be planning to load her cargo soon and then softly, silently, slide over the horizon. He had been only four days in command when the lieutenant of the watch brought word of a strange sail spotted. Through a five-hour chase in haze and squall, she was identified, with exultation, as the *Veloz Pasagera*. This time she would have to fight or run. By midnight, the ships were in hailing distance as they slid past each other on opposite tacks, but there was no answer to Commander Broughton's shout, nor any when a British gun fired in warning. Only a sharp musket-volley brought the *Veloz* to and then her ports were seen to be open, with a light showing in each. Her gunners were ready at their posts.

'What ship are you? Whither bound?'[4]

'Going to St Thomas for wood and water.'

Lieutenant Butterfield was sent aboard and received politely enough by the first mate, who explained the captain was ill. As Butterfield said he would take a quick look below, however, Captain de la Vega appeared in the companion-way and said flatly:

'No possible.'

On the gundeck, visible over de la Vega's shoulder, the huge, well-paid crew was in position, their guns shifting to keep the *Primrose* covered as she drew ahead, fell back; drew ahead, fell back. Butterfield knew two of the men staring back at him: they had been aboard one of the slavers he had taken in the *Black Joke*.

'My ship is His Britannic Majesty's ship *Primrose*, and I am come on board to search you. Do you understand me?'

'No possible.' Three requests were refused.

'If you will not allow me,' said Butterfield, 'I shall have to go back and report it to my captain, and you know what the consequences of that will be.' No reply; only the scrape of the shifting guns.

Butterfield returned to the *Primrose*, and a Spanish speaker went to the rails with the hailer, to say a boat was coming with an officer to inspect the ship. Answers came from the *Veloz*: they did not understand; he might be a pirate. 'Wishing', Broughton would report, 'to avoid the effusion of blood by a night action with a vessel crowded with slaves, I remained by her until morning', rocking side by side, drawing away, drawing near.

'This is His Britannic Majesty's ship *Primrose*,' he bellowed at the dawn, 'and I want to send a boat immediately to examine you.' Again, into the defiant silence and the slap of the waves: '*Este es un navío de Su Majestad Británica y voy a mandar inmediatamente una lancha a inspeccionar*', and then: 'If this is not complied with in five minutes, I will fire at you.'

'I can't help it,' de la Vega finally called across the water, in faint and petulant English, 'you can do as you please. If you fire, I will fire too.' An Italian voice came from behind him: 'And we will all go to hell together!'

Two British broadsides were fired while a boarding party gathered in the rigging to leap over the prize's bow, but the slavers were also gathering in defence. A long swell heaved under the vessels, smashing them together then tearing them apart before the men could take hold of the other ship's stays and swing across. William Broughton was at the head of the first group to board and took a slaver's pike in his gut and an axe blow to the top of his arm. Lieutenant Butterfield leapt across the body slumped unconscious on the deck, urging the rest to battle, and in ten minutes' vicious, bloody fighting 'carried her', Broughton wrote shakily, 'with a loss on our side of 3 killed, and 12 wounded; the Velos [sic] had 46 killed, and 20 wounded, out of a crew of, as near as I could ascertain, 150 men, of different nations'.[5] The foredeck ran with blood. On the slave-deck, there was terror and jubilation mixed. There were 550 living slaves aboard, and five dead, killed by the British broadsides which had liberated the rest.

Dr Lane, still convalescing from the yellow jack, came light-headed and shaking to sew up the hole in Commander Broughton's intestine. Grapeshot had torn through the flesh of two British seamen; musket-balls had lodged in some and must be tweezered out, with the splinters of bone around them; others had been holed by pike or bayonet. From the *Veloz Pasagera* they carried Captain de la Vega untenderly for the doctor to amputate his arm; then the twenty men of his crew who had been shot or slashed in the British onslaught. Six died of their wounds.

It was a brutal action, and the *Primrose*'s last on the West African station. She turned for home as soon as she had left her prize at Sierra Leone, taking with her twenty-two of the *Veloz*'s crew to be tried for piracy in Britain. Like the men of the *Presidente* against whom Lieutenant William Turner had testified two years earlier, they were found not guilty and returned to Havana at British expense, to be tried there by the Spanish courts for breaking the slave-trade laws. No one thought for a moment they would be convicted.

10

Black Jokes and High Jinks

As the Squadron entered its second decade of service, it was clear to the Colonial Office, the Foreign Office and the Admiralty that the illegal slave trade was flourishing. Treaties had been made with all the major slave-carrying nations except the United States but only the Swedish and Dutch had ensured they were properly observed. The Courts of Mixed Commission were working effectively in Sierra Leone and Dutch Surinam, but not in the more important slave-ports of Rio and Havana, where the attempts of British commissioners to prosecute slavers ran up against too many local interests.

Overt British participation in slaving had been almost completely squashed: the odd British-born seaman turned up on captured slave-ships but the days of George Woodbine were over. Not all Britons, however, had given up slaving completely, and legislation designed to prevent indirect participation in the trade had not been effective. The more unscrupulous corners of the City and the industrial towns still surreptitiously insured and financed slaving voyages, or exported their beads, guns and cotton to men whom they knew would sell them on to the slavers. Periodically, too, press and Parliament were goaded – usually by lobbyists for the endlessly aggrieved West Indian interest – to question the expense of the Squadron and the death of British seamen in a cause that Britain had no direct need to champion. So far, the small but persistent band of critics had not succeeded in having the Squadron recalled and the anti-slave-trade campaign wound up, but they were tenacious and well placed.

Captain Fitzwilliam Owen's idea of Britain's 'civilising mission' would later take a strong grip on the British imagination, but as yet the influence of missionaries and legal traders was confined to a few tiny colonies along the West African coast, and had made no impact on the slave-raiding peoples of the interior. The anti-slave-trade campaign was still almost exclusively in the hands of the British Squadron, where commissions were hard and dangerous. Some officers, however, still eagerly sought a West African commission. In an unusually long period of peace, the Preventive Squadron was the only naval service that offered bounty, excitement and promotion. One of those who launched his naval career with the Squadron in 1829 was thirteen-year-old Naval Cadet Edwin Hinde.

'Dear mother', Edwin wrote home that August from an ill-lit and crowded midshipmen's mess in Portsmouth Harbour:

> I know that a letter from me will cause you a great deal of pleasure, particularly when I tell you that I am quite comfortable and that all the officers are exceedingly kind to me, and I would have slept very well all night had not one of my messmates (as is always the custom) let me down, and when I woke, behold I lay prostrate on the deck, along with my bed, however two boys picked me up and made me comfortable for the rest of the night.[1]

Edwin Hinde had just joined HMS *Atholl*, commissioned by Captain Alexander Gordon and due to depart for West Africa. Family connections had secured the berth, for Mrs Gordon was a friend of Edwin's 'Aunt Steer' of Pall Mall. Thus did a favoured naval career begin. Captain Gordon would take an interest in the child and both ladies would keep a distant but benevolent eye on the level of 'dear Edwin's' pocket-money and the state of his wardrobe. Mrs Gordon had sent him £5 to pay his mess bill and 'hereafter', he told his mother, 'I must give one sovereign per month, and five shillings to the marine that waits upon me'. As his pay was only £1 2s per month, only an extremely lucky run of prizes would keep Edwin from relying on family support for a considerable time to come.

In September, HMS *Athol* was at Tenerife taking on supplies. She left with her 'hen coops well filled', Edwin informed his family, 'besides a good fat sheep in the pen'. Many landlubbers going aboard ships wrote of their surprise at finding the deck both nursery and zoo: hen-cages piled by the wheel, livestock munching and defecating on the foredeck, boys everywhere – running, swinging on ropes, fighting when the lieutenants were not looking, shimmying up the masts, attending open-air lessons in French, mathematics and navigation. It was a wonderful place for an active and intelligent boy, if the men entrusted with his training were kind and his mess was not run by bullies. It was a terrible one for any poor child forced into the navy against his wishes, seasick and cold, averse to horseplay and longing for his mother. Edwin, signed up for three years, was ebullient. 'The more I see of the sea life', he wrote to his father, 'the more I like it . . . '

The *Athol* seemed fortunate when she took her first prize, a French schooner with 472 slaves aboard, before she even reached Freetown, but her officers had not yet learnt the subtleties of the nationality game. By the time the ship made harbour, Captain Gordon had learnt that 120 of the slaves had been 'rescued' from a Spanish slave-ship 'wrecked' some-where on the coast. He intended to liberate these 120 at Freetown and send the ship and other slaves to Goree, for trial in a French court. However, once ashore, the master and mate swore she was Spanish, and as certain of the ship's documents were written in Spanish, and there were Spanish names on her muster, Captain Gordon agreed to send her before the British–Spanish Mixed Commission. He had been hoodwinked. The *Athol* had left again before the hearing came on and, predictably, the slaver's officers reverted to their original nationality, declaring them-selves ready 'to swear that they had previously been induced through fear to state that she was Spanish but that they were now ready to swear and prove that she was French'.[2] The Spanish commissioners refused to hear the case and as the French (or Spanish) vessel left Freetown under her French flag, 'she was instantly seized by the Collector of Customs for being in British waters, and condemned in the Admiralty court': but as prize not to the *Athol*, but the British Crown. The nationality game had cost them bounty on 352 slaves. Admiralty meanness over the payment of prize-money was notorious. Another, inventive example of this had just become known to the Preventive Squadron.

It was standard practice in older squadrons for captains to buy their own tenders. Since Commodore Bullen bought the *Hope* – ex-*Principe de*

Guinea – at auction in 1826, this practice had also been adopted by the Preventive Squadron. Officers assumed such vessels were subject to the same rules and privileges as Admiralty-commissioned tenders and that any prizes they took on detached service would swell the bounty of the mother ship. The Admiralty, however, had raised objections.

Commodore Collier had bought three ex-slavers to serve as tenders. One of these, the *Paul Pry*, was 1,500 miles from the *Sybille* when she seized the *Donna Barbara*. There was no doubt of the Brazilian captain's guilt: he had 357 slaves aboard, loaded north of the Line; but there was plenty over the authorisation by which the *Paul Pry* seized his ship. The *Paul Pry*'s normal commander, Lieutenant Harvey, was briefly absent on business at Sierra Leone when the *Donna Barbara* was taken and the commander at the moment of the detention was only an acting – not commissioned – lieutenant. Lieutenant Harvey, returning in the nick of time to see the *Paul Pry* and *Donna Barbara* rocking in company, knew his subordinate did not have the authority to detain slavers. He, however, did. A farce ensued: the Brazilian was formally released by the man whose rank did not allow him to detain and formally recaptured by the one whose rank did. When Harvey took the slaver into Freetown, she was condemned and he applied for his share of the bounty from her sale. Now, however, the Admiralty demurred. Could a private tender, asked the judge, operating so far from the mother ship, be regarded as part of His Majesty's squadron? At the first hearing, it was ruled it could not; that the squadron's tenders were 'used by Sir A. Collier as a protection to the crew of the *Sybille* detached to Sierra Leone against the climate',[3] but could not make detentions under the anti-slave-trade treaties. Any bounty due on slavers they detained would go to the Crown. Commodore Collier led the protests. In two years' time, the ruling would be overturned, but they were demoralising years for the men running the gamut of malarial coast and slavers' guns on detached service. There were mutters. Who did the fighting, after all? Who had a musket-ball in his shoulder and a cutlass wound in his thigh? Not the stiff-collared, deskbound pen-pushers in Whitehall, still less King Billy, whatever his boasted naval connections.

Naval Cadet Hinde, whose income consisted mainly of pocket-money supplied by others, was enjoying himself. In February 1830, he went aboard his first prize, taken between Fernando Po and Principe, flying French colours but thought to be Dutch. Second Lieutenant William Ramsay, Edwin and twelve seamen took the vessel and her 227 slaves to Sierra Leone. 'Here you may think I was unhappy,' Edwin wrote to his mother:

> but on the contrary I never lived better in my life. We lost 12 slaves who died in the passage however the slaves are not so miserable as you would suspect, in general they are merry and often come on deck. They used to sing and dance, but to let you have an idea of our living, coming up, I will give you an account of how we passed the day: I used to get up at four o'clock, at six a good cup of coffee was brought to us. At eight a magnificent breakfast, of three or four dishes of fresh meat, dressed by an excellent French cook, then I worked my days [sic] work, longitude &c., at twelve a glass of ale, at three an excellent dinner and dessert of guava jelly and brandy fruits and a glass of liqueur, then tea. At ten I turned in for the night, unless some bad weather or squalls came on, then I had to turn out to shorten sail.[4]

Three weeks' beating up to Freetown were in vain. The Dutch Mixed Commission refused to accept the claim to Dutch nationality. Lieutenant Ramsay immediately and 'prudently took her to sea', a brother officer wrote, 'and gave her up to the master; but I am afraid there will be some words about her, as the French Commodore arrived the day after she sailed'.[5]

In Freetown Edwin found a single letter from his mother, the first he had had since leaving Portsmouth. 'I am almost in despair,' he wrote immediately back, 'about not receiving any letters, of all those which you have written, only one has reached me, which is very provoking for letters here so far from home are a very great comfort.' His mother had complained of his silence, but Edwin assured her it was not his fault. 'I always think of your pleasure in receiving a letter from me, for I judge of you by myself, and there is not pleasure for me, so great as that of hearing from home, it has frequently happened that all of my messmates have received two or three letters and I was the only one deprived of that comfort.' He gave her excited news about slaves and navigation lessons and how wonderful Lieutenant Ramsay was, taking 'great pains in teaching me navigation which I find very easy and very amusing'.[6]

The *Athol*, patrolling the Bights, resorted frequently to Principe to rest and provision, and the island became a holiday camp for Edwin and the other boys: dinner every so often in best bib and tucker with Captain Gordon, who sometimes required French conversation to keep them in practice; playing with Governor Fereira's poodle; learning to swim on the beach ('this is the only place on the coast where you can bathe on account of the enormous quantity of sharks', as he tactlessly told his mother).

> We have plenty to do on board here: in the forenoon we have school where we learn our navigation . . . in the afternoon we all go off on the quarter deck, are exercised in knotting and splicing under the chief boatswain's mate which is very amusing, and at night we keep our watches and the captain has given orders that we are not to be allowed to sleep during the four hours, however sometimes my eyes get rather too drowsy and I fall asleep in some corner or other out of sight.

The only annoyance was the mosquitoes by which they were 'almost ate up'; they were 'worse than the gnats in summer in France'.

> I have been recommended by the surgeon not to wear flannels not being accustomed to it . . . since I left home I have not had occasion to trouble the doctor a single time . . . I have completely got rid of those nasty headaches which used to trouble me so often at home . . . There are now three vacancies for midshipmen, and as there are three youngsters on board, the Captain has promised to rate us all as soon as our year is up, which will happen in two months . . . give my love to Granny and all at home.[7]

When Commodore Collier's commission ended in 1829, he did not auction his property back to the slavers but bequeathed the *Black Joke* to Captain Gordon, Senior Officer on the coast until the next commodore arrived. William Ramsay, recently promoted first lieutenant, was given her much-coveted command. 'I believe', Edwin wrote, 'I am going in her of which I am very glad as Lieutenant Ramsay is a great friend of mine . . . I expect we shall take plenty of prizes', but that bubble was burst: 'I am not going in her, as I expected', he wrote dolefully a month later, 'for the Captain thinks I

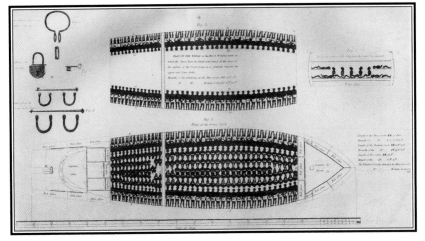

Plan of the slave ship *Vigilante*

'Slave Deck of the *Albanez*', by Lieutenant Frank Meynell

Captain (later Commodore) George Ralph Collier

Midshipman
Cheesman Henry Binstead,
HMS *Owen Glendower*

Richard Lemon Lander

HMS *Black Joke* chasing the slave-ship *Almirante*

House of King Bell of the Duala in Cameroon, 1841

Madame Fereira's House at Prince's Island, 1841

Prince Badahun (King Glele) and King Guezo, Dahomey 1856

SLAVE BARRACOON.

A barracoon in the Gallinas such as those found and destroyed in
Commodore Charles Hotham's raid in 1849

A canoe used to embark slaves in the Gallinas, capable of carrying 200 slaves
below, and rowed by twenty to thirty rowers, 1849

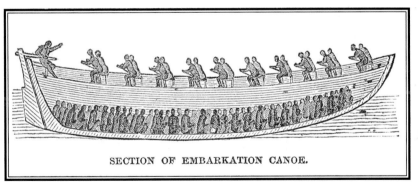

SECTION OF EMBARKATION CANOE.

Liberated slaves on board HMS *Daphne*, c. 1870

am not old enough yet.'[8] His disappointment was brief, for the *Black Joke* was so successful that nearly all her officers left with prize-crews and Edwin was sent aboard. He loved it. 'We live more comfortably here than on board the ship', he wrote home.

> Besides keeping a better mess, we have the comfort of a larger airy cabin. I am not idle . . . besides keeping 8 hours watch, I have to work the Days work and chronometer every day, to see the spirits served out morning and evening and to go to the masthead every four hours to look around . . . Instead of wearing our uniforms on board of the tender we all wear duck frocks with coloured collars and cuffs the same as the men, because we are very seldom in harbour and then only for a few hours we cannot get our shirts washed and these frocks are made to stand scrubbing with a hard brush and salt water, besides in case of going into action, the officers cannot be distinguished from the men, and the Spaniards receive a very great reward for every officer they kill, and as they are very good small arm men, it would be difficult to escape.[9]

His first month aboard in August 1830 was nonetheless a frustrating one.

> We have twice been on the point of having an engagement with the slavers: we were cruising off the mouth of the Bonny river, expecting a large Spanish brig with 18 guns and 600 slaves. One afternoon a sail was reported, we all made sure it was the Spaniard when we made him out to be a large brig standing under all sail. We instantly made sail in case: we found that we were coming up with him fast, so we beat to quarters and got everything ready for action, however when we came close to him we were very much disappointed to see him fire a blank cartridge and hoist French colours. Mr Ramsay and I went on board and found that he had 420 slaves and when we told him that we would take him he got into a rage and made us prisoners, however upon seeing the *Black Joke*'s guns, and all the men at their quarters he got quite civil and let us go on board again very quietly, however as he was a Frenchman we could not take him.

Four other French slavers in the Bonny River were boarded that month and 1,622 slaves went unrescued because their buyers could not be touched. Another 'had no slaves on board'

> but he took us for a pirate in the night, but the next morning when he saw that it was an English man of war he was very civil and made us a present of a dozen of claret and a demijohn of wine but the Spaniard that we were cruising after got away in the night while we were chasing the French brig.

Whatever the past enmities between their countries, slavers were all on the same side against the British.

The new commodore was John 'Magnificent' Hayes, just arrived in the frigate *Dryad*. This was a ship bursting with talent. The commodore's respectful nickname had been earned years ago, when, by superb seamanship, he had saved the *Magnificent* battleship from wreck in the Basque Roads. Unusually for a senior officer, Hayes had trained as a shipwright before joining the navy. 'He combined', a *Dryad* lieutenant said, 'with a high reputation as an officer, a scientific mind and the kindest of tempers, a perfect knowledge of seamanship in its superior as well as subordinate branches. . . . He could build, rig, govern and sail the ship with equal ease and credit.'[10] The tender which accompanied the *Dryad* from England, the *Seaflower*, was his own innovative design. His second-in-command was scarcely less celebrated, at least on this station, for Commander Turner of the *Dryad* had been Lieutenant Turner of the *Black Joke*, whose capture of the *Principe de Guinea* was still spoken of on the coast with admiration.

The *Seaflower* was commanded by Lieutenant Henry Vere Huntley, a man of initiative and skill, but weighed down by bitterness about his professional prospects. 'Though [the abolitionists] raved over the existence of the slave trade,' Huntley wrote, 'there were not more than half a dozen ships of war [in the squadron] and those of the worst description.'[11] He was out of love with the whole project. 'The whole attempt is a melancholy failure – it has been fully proved that as yet the endeavour of England to extend Christianity and civilization in Africa, has only resulted in an enormous loss of life, talent, and treasure.'

This was not the worst of his grievances, however, for he, rather proudly, was of an old Tory family and power in Britain had just swung to the Whigs. They would pass the Great Reform Act of 1832, which enraged so much of the squirearchy from which Huntley came, and, in 1833, would abolish slavery throughout the British Empire. The shift of government patronage had left young Henry, in his own eyes, out in the cold when promotions were discussed: he stood 'no chance of being favoured by men who governed upon the express determination of serving only those who supported their political views'. Thus it was with 'much gratification' that he had heard from Commodore Hayes that he was to command the *Seaflower* 'because it gave an hourly prospect of forcing for [my]self, that which a Whig government would not willingly give [me], namely promotion'. With ten Kroomen taken on, Huntley left the *Dryad* at Freetown and sailed for the Bights, and his first visit to Ouidah.

Like most British officers, Huntley was fascinated by Francisco de Souza. At Ouidah, he carried out the usual frustrating round of visits to ships he could not detain, although this did serve 'in the language of the kennel', said Huntley, ever the squire, '"to flesh the young hounds"'. He took the opportunity to wander up to the famous compound – house, guest house, barracoons – and ask the usual curious questions about the riches its plain walls were rumoured to enclose; the habits of its little-known, much-feared owner and how his fawning pack of tame captains spent their idle days between their trips to sea. 'At dawn', he was told, 'slave captains stroll on the colonnade to smoke cigars until breakfast is on the table; de Souza is not seen until late in the day; they have tea, coffee, claret, Guinness and Bass, bread, fruit and preserves, set out on exquisite china and glass.' The day passed in indolence until four, the hour of dinner, when everyone dressed in clean white clothes and 'a sallow, corpulent, heavy featured man of sixty five or seventy years of age approaches'.

His large dark eyes have hardly lost any of their early lustre, at a glance he recognises every one at the table, and notices all that is passing, hardly without a sign, he takes his seat, and motions for the assembled captains to do the same – this is De Souza – his apparel, unlike that of the others present, is a loose dressing robe, with a small velvet cap on his head, from beneath which his long hair is flowing, hardly even yet turned grey, his linen underneath not carefully changed and his large loose trowsers trail over his slippers which he wears without stockings; not a syllable escapes him during the dinner at which he is sedulously attended by some Africans . . . De Souza is very moderate at the table in every way, and stays there but a short time.'

It was a far better mess than that offered by the *Seaflower*. Huntley had discovered that the gift of command came at a price on this station. He hated the patrol and the monotony of the coast – 'a mere sandy beach hardly higher than the surf which rolls upon it . . . at long intervals a few scattered huts denote a Negro town' – and the lack of company. 'For the first time in [my] life', he wrote, he found himself 'without a companion . . . to speak with in [my] unemployed hour.' Closest to his own rank aboard the crowded tender was the assistant surgeon, then the midshipmen, and Huntley could not unbend sufficiently to forge with them the relationship Ramsay had with Edwin Hinde. Many commanders shared his frustration: 'cruising, cruising, cruising and very unprofitably too', another wrote, bored even with the sight of 'an elephant pacing the shore a stone's throw of the ship', with sending a boat on shore and 'being obliged to throw stones at the leopards gathered',[12] with everything to do with the African coast.

There were more ships in the Squadron than there had been a decade before, but they still fell in with each other only seldom – when the commodore had fresh instructions to impart or when a new senior officer took command – and only then experienced company outside their own claustrophobic, exhausted society. On visits to Freetown or the Gold Coast, ship-to-shore communication was often banned because of fever. On the few occasions men did go ashore, they found the ports of West Africa were a disappointing contrast to those of the West Indies, the Mediterranean – indeed any other station. A few donkey rides, the odd hunt, the always diverting spectacle of naked women but nothing like what was offered at Port Royal or Gibraltar. 'If I go on shore there is nobody to speak to but a parcel of black fellows,' Edwin Hinde wrote mournfully home, 'who hardly understand what you say.'[13] In such a place, where hospitality and shelter were scarce, it was difficult to remain aloof from the sophisticated enemy, especially its more sporting members.

Even three decades into the campaign, not every Squadron officer found his principal motivation in hatred of slaving. Captain Harry Keppel of HMS

Childers came to West Africa in 1837 with a romantic view of the trade. Many slaver captains, he still believed,

> are superior men; some belong to good Spanish and Portuguese fami-
> lies; generally young. I believe that many of them take command of
> these vessels for the excitement of the service [and] come to the
> coast of Africa as much on pleasure as business. The little Spanish
> I picked up . . . enabled me to converse freely with these agreeable
> young roués who, if they did not carry slaves, easily kept our cruisers
> employed by drawing their attention from the coast to chase these
> yachtlike slavers.[14]

Keppel, though as shocked by the misery of a slave-deck as the next man, had more in common with the bounty-hunters of the early years than the zealots of recent ones. The *Childers* was in Freetown only long enough to water and take on Kroomen, and then left in chase. Keppel may have been new to the coast, but the man at the masthead was not. A sail to the north being seen on the horizon, he had climbed up to have a better look: a square-rigged vessel, he yelled, sailing before the wind; and, a little later – a man-of-war; later still – an eighteen-gun sloop (he could tell from counting the number of cloths which made up one of her sails); and finally – it was just out from home.

'How can you tell?' roared back Keppel from the waist.

'The three midship cloths of her foretopsail are discoloured.'

'What the deuce has that to do with it?'

The lookouts at the stranger's masthead were new hands. Their stomachs had not yet adjusted to the coastal swell and the result was all over the sails. The seaman's laconic diagnosis turned out to be correct.

Off Cape St Paul's, having boarded one Portuguese slaver awaiting her cargo, the *Childers* spotted a second ahead, towing two large canoes. She too, however, was ambivalent in nationality and ownership and as the death-rate among prize-crews beating up to Sierra Leone was so high, a captain must be sure of his prize. The *Dos Amigos* was released and Captain Keppel, recognising her commander, Captain Canieras, as one of the 'superior men' of the trade, was delighted to accept his invitation to dine aboard his slave-ship.

A couple of months later, the *Childers* revisited the *Dos Amigos* at Little

Popo, where Captain Keppel had been told another Spanish schooner under Portuguese colours was leaving with three hundred slaves aboard. They spent fruitless hours waiting but the Spaniard did not appear: the British had one spy-network along the coast, but the slavers had another. Keppel made the best of his visit to the lagoon by provisioning and watering and courteous Captain Canieras lent his great slave-canoes to take off the bullocks, water, fresh fruit and vegetables. Would the officers and stewards sent to buy them care to spend the night in the comfort of the *Dos Amigos*, whose cabins and menus were so much better than those of the cramped and overheated *Childers*? They would. 'The only return we could make for his courtesy', wrote Keppel, enjoying the joke, 'would be to capture him when he had embarked his slaves.' They never managed it.

The *Childers* touched at Ouidah later that month, and found there, among the anchored slavers, a vessel commanded by a scarred and one-armed Spaniard, Captain Barbosa. He sent across an invitation to breakfast and relived, over cigars, the battle he had had with HMS *Primrose* when in command of the *Veloz Pasagera* – since bought back by her original owners, he assured the British officers who were his guests, and slaving again – and the more recent fun just had here at Ouidah, helping a slave-schooner escape HMS *Saracen*.

Other games played with slaving captains were less amiable. 'If a man-of-war lay in a port full of slavers,' one naval officer wrote,

> as I have seen at Whydah, with ten or a dozen slavers at one time, so long as the man-of-war was in sight they would not ship their slaves; directly the man-of-war was out of sight they shipped their slaves and every vessel in the harbour would weigh their anchor and set sail. The cruiser would probably chase the wrong ship, and after having chased 100 miles would be laughed at by the master of her and told that he only did it as a *pasatiempo*.

Meanwhile the unhappy Africans must 'be suffered to be collected together in the factory like cattle, until the numerous cargo is completed ... shipped and subjugated to every horror, and to all the degradation of the slavehold'.

This happened to Henry Huntley when one slaver led him out of the lagoon into a night-long chase, before heaving-to well out to sea and inviting him aboard, laughing, to show him an empty slave-deck.

'So you have no slaves on board?'

'No captain, none this time, they are all waiting for me in the barracoon,' was the cool reply of the Spaniard, with a flippant manner and tone.

'Then why have you given me so much trouble?'

'I wanted to try rate of sailing with the cruiser,' said the captain laughing.

'Well you have gained that knowledge and you will now pay the price of it', said Huntley:

and I immediately gave orders to the senior midshipman, to go on board the slaver with ten good hands, unbend his sails, unreave his running rigging, throw overboard his guns, and every other offensive weapon, and gunpowder – make his crew get the chain cables on deck, see that the inner end was secured, then let go both his bower anchors, and run the whole of the cables out to the clinch, the vessels being far beyond reach of the bottom of the sea.[15]

And he abandoned the slaver, thus completely disabled, to her fate.

Ladies played a coyer hand in these games. Governor Fereira of Principe was dead but his portly widow still happily combined slaving with flirtatious hospitality. When the *Seaflower* dropped anchor in the bay, Henry Huntley was summoned by a slave with the words 'Madame want to look captain, he come', given coffee and pastries and questioned as to the health of 'the old Commodore [Collier] of whom she was very fond'. When the *Childers* sailed in, Captain Keppel also found this 'kind and hospitable lady of rather dark complexion'[16] delighted to receive his officers. They were given the usual tour of the bay, Madame waddling ahead under a large umbrella with a cluster of slave girls about her. 'I never saw a set of people more happy and contented', the British captain wrote approvingly. They stayed for dinner, of course, brought to table by 'lighter skinned boys', all born round the coast at West Bay, 'where British cruisers go for wood and water'.

Both men knew perfectly well that Madame received British officers not only for their company but because she had what Huntley called an 'amiable little investment' in many slavers out of Ouidah and preferred the British to be anchored at Principe when these little investments were leaving for Brazil. They accepted her invitations nonetheless, for strange acquaintanceships were born in the desperate loneliness of the African station. When Huntley arrived at Principe with the news he had detained the Brazilian slaver *Atrevida*, Madame giggled and said 'in a laughing, good-humoured tone "suppose you know four live slave aboard for me, I think you no take him"'.[17] Huntley did not yield to her gap-toothed charm but others did.

One visitor to Cape Coast Castle noted the dangers of long exposure to the mores of the coast. 'It is imagined, rather generally in tropical climates', wrote Dr Madden, 'that hospitable hosts and hostesses are equally kind masters and mistresses to their slaves.'[18] He was referring in particular to Madame Fereira and strongly disapproved of the respect in which she was held by British officials, corrupted by the tropics 'where men's notions of right and wrong get frequently utterly confounded'. Several of Madame's slaves had taken refuge in Fernando Po and Sierra Leone since the British founded their settlements there. Her appeals for their return were ignored by Captain Owen but when Admiral Patrick Campbell, commanding at the Cape of Good Hope, took brief charge of the Preventive Squadron in the 1830s, he ordered Captain Craigie to round up her fugitive slaves in Freetown and take them back. To Craigie, who reluctantly did so, 'it was evident . . . that they would attempt to destroy themselves the first opportunity that presented itself to them'.[19] One of the women tried to throw herself overboard and although Craigie restrained the others to prevent them doing the same, one male slave managed to hang himself.

Madame Fereira's light-skinned houseboys were not the only uneasy evidence of British visits to the slave-quarters of forts and factories where bored and lonely naval officers were entertained by equally bored and lonely merchants and soldiers. Nor were their visits only to the forts and factories of the virtuous. Several of the African chiefs who had continued slaving nonetheless wished to maintain their friendship with the British who had so strangely gone over to the other side. Duke Ephraim could never quite make up his mind to the British being his enemy. Hearing the British were hard-pressed at Cape Coast Castle in 1824, he had sent up guns to help them fight off the Ashanti. In part, it was the enemy of his enemy being his friend in the long battle between inland and coastal leaders. But the duke had a genuine lingering fondness for his old comrades: his 'English house' was kept always ready for British guests visiting Duke Town in the Bonny.

European ladies were scarce on the African coast, where it was thought their constitutions rendered them more susceptible than men to the horrors of the climate. This was partly why officers and men looked forward so fervently to their time at Ascension, St Helena or the Cape Verde islands:

not just for the healthier air and a break from routine, but for the presence and company of ladies. The men preferred the more vulgar islands of Cape Verde, for there 'Jack', as he was affectionately or patronisingly known by his officers, 'can get a donkey to ride, something cooked up for his dinner, lashings of wine on which to get drunk, and aquadiente to make him insensible, provided the wine does not fulfil its duty; and last of all, there are plenty of black sultanas who will let him pillow his head on their laps'.[20] But the officers preferred to play on the islands of the South Atlantic, for the young ladies there were as bored as they, and both sides threw themselves into frenzies of hospitality and flirtation whenever they met.

'We had heard', wrote one officer, just come from a tour of the African coast where there was 'no killing the monotony', that 'the way to plunge into society' on St Helena was

> to give an entertainment of some sort, and ask all the elite . . . we boldly borrowed the Governor's list, and sent off cards, four days after our arrival, to 176 people for a quadrille party at the hotel! . . . Our ball went off splendidly; the ladies not only came and enjoyed themselves, but also sent us wreaths and naval devices in flowers, with which to decorate the room, and the garrison officers painted for us splendid illuminations . . . we decorated all our stewards with a blue ribbon upon which was inscribed [the name of our ship] in gilt letters . . . these were given next day to the lady each steward had most admired. A few days after our ball, the prize officers gave a grand picnic and all the young ladies wore the ribbons.[21]

The young ladies of St Helena were protected by fair skin and European blood; their company was delightful but did not satisfy the baser needs. African women, particularly those in servitude to expansive hosts on the African coast, were differently viewed, and used. When HMS *Childers* called at Cape Coast Castle, the officers went to inspect the 'native school'. 'Ma name George sar,' said one excited child, accosting the captain (whose rendition of his speech this is), 'son of Captain George C—, Royal Navy, sar.'[22]

11

The First Great Blows

A tiny British garrison had remained on Fernando Po when Captain Fitzwilliam Owen went home. Colonel Nicolls and a wretched, malarial marine corps still lived with wives and children in Clarence Cove, where warships and merchantmen gathered when they could, to escape the dangers of the mainland coast. It was a small post, but a vital one for the Squadron, for Nicolls received constant intelligence from arriving vessels of Spanish slavers awaiting slaves in this river, at this wharf; of French awaiting theirs in that river, from that factory; details of names, tonnage, numbers, destinations. It was all passed on to the Squadron. Where they could, officers took action. Frequently, however, the terms of the treaties forbade it. 'Were the dictates of humanity', wrote Surgeon Leonard of the flagship *Dryad*, 'not obstructed by the cold-blooded arm of the law',[1] then the ships patrolling the Bights would enter the rivers and drag them out, but with no slaves yet aboard, they were untouchable. The old game of cat and mouse was endlessly played.

The *Black Joke* was at Fernando Po in April 1831 when news came from a British palm-oiler that a large, well-armed Spanish slave-ship was taking on her cargo in the Old Calabar, with Englishmen among her crew. The ship sailed immediately, watched the mouth of the river all night and retreated over the horizon with topsails lowered when morning came. The slaver emerged and the long chase began. When Lieutenant Ramsay scrambled aboard the prize twenty-four hours later, Edwin Hinde was behind him. He wrote a lively account of the action to his brother.

I went on board with the full determination of shooting one of the Spaniards having no arms but a bad pistol. It was not the only way of killing one and I was determined to be able to say that I killed a pirate in action. However when I got on board, miserable dieta! (you will see that I have quite forgot my Latin) I found that the fun was over, owing to the vessels separating not more than 8 men got on board at a time until one got the vessels together again and lashed them, then we all jumped on board, I with pistol in hand, going to let fly at the first Spaniard I saw but unfortunately they had all run below. I ran forward to rouse the fellows up on deck and received a bite in the finer [*sic*] from a parrot, which I instantly hove overboard, so that all my bravery ended in the death of a parrot. However he gave me a good nip, so I can say that I was wounded in the action on the 25th . . . I suppose you have been having rare fun in England . . .[2]

Edwin Hinde was not the only young gentleman to distinguish himself. Mr Pearce, a midshipman scarcely older than he, his hat already holed by a pistol-shot, was knocked overboard by the cutlass of the huge Spaniard he had taken on, hauled himself back up a rope with his sword between his teeth and rejoined the mêlée. The fight was quickly over, the slavers surrendering to the customary violence of the bluejackets. Bringing up the slaves took longer. 496 adults had been bought from the imperturbable salesmen of flesh in the Bonny and the Old Calabar. The hatches had been battened down over them during the chase and those still living 'were found sitting on the heads and bodies of the dead and dying below'.[3] They shrieked for water and Ramsay ordered a large tub filled and placed in the middle of the deck. They rushed at it, trampling each other in their desperation. So many thrust and fought that 'their heads became wedged in the tub and were with some difficulty got out'. The sailors filled jugs to pass around but they had gone mad with thirst, and 'madly bit the vessels with their teeth and champed them into atoms'. There were 107 who were so ill that they had to be taken to Clarence Cove: there was no possibility of their surviving the passage to Freetown. As the boats ferried them to the shore, they tried to lap at the saltwater over the side.

Sixty died in Clarence Cove; another twenty-five on the passage to Freetown. Even to men who had spent years on the West African station, the condition of these slaves was shocking. The savages who had crewed the

Spanish *Marinerito* were taken to the island Anobón, 150 miles from the coast, and abandoned on the beaches there, without provisions, sheltered only by what they wore on their backs. The *Black Joke* was cruising off the Bonny a few weeks later when her men saw a drifting canoe and sent out a boat to investigate. In it were three of the *Marinerito*'s crew, starving, black-burnt and delirious. Nine of them, they told the unfriendly officers who plucked them from the sea and stood over them on the deck as they drank and drank, had built canoes, in order to row to São Tomé and board a slave-ship there. A heavy tornado came on; they were separated; the canoes with the food, water and their comrades were lost. For ten days they had eaten nothing, and drunk only what rainwater they could catch in their mouths. They were given passage to the mainland, but scant sympathy. 'One would discover', said Surgeon Leonard, 'a fearful retribution in this.'

Lieutenants Huntley and Ramsay saw an even worse case of brutality. Huntley, now in charge of the newer, faster tender *Fair Rosamund*, was at Fernando Po when another palm-oiler brought information that two Spaniards, heavily armed, were about to load slaves. At the mouth of the Bonny, Huntley found the *Black Joke* also waiting, for Ramsay had also heard the rumour.

'Ramsay,' said Huntley, 'is the news I hear true, about the *Regulo* and *Rapido*?' It was.

'Well, though this is not my station, you won't think me acting unfairly towards you, by staying to meet them, I'm sure, we have nothing like the *Regulo* and *Rapido* in the Bight of Benin.'

'I believe,' answered Ramsay, 'that the *Marguerita** will do my business in the way of promotion – and, my dear fellow, if there is to be any fighting, I hope you have the whole of it,' and he laughed as he so frankly put aside the question of poaching, as cruising on another officer's station is called.[4]

The two young men were eating salmon and Scotch marmalade aboard the *Rosamund* when the shout of 'Sail ho!' came. Ramsay rushed off to get his anchor up, the *Rosamund* got up sail and the slavers emerging from the

---

* i.e. *Marinerito* – British officers were famous for their cloth ear when it came to foreign languages.

mouth of the Bonny turned and shot back the way they had come. The *Black Joke* had twelve down from fever; the *Rosamund* had only twenty-two of a crew of forty-five. There were sandbanks everywhere. Crowds of merchant shipping obscured the chase, the British cheering the tenders on as they followed the slavers upriver, others booing. After seven hours' hard sailing, the slavers disappeared behind a sandy spit. Shouts from the masthead: canoes coming out for slaves; then slaves being thrown overboard. When the *Rosamund* rounded the spit, she saw the *Rapido* still offloading and when the last canoes were full, Huntley wrote, the remaining slaves 'were pushed overboard, shackled together by the legs, and drowned', the smooth river-water 'ruffled by [their] death struggles. Men, women and children were seen in great numbers, struggling in the water; by everyone on board the tenders; 150 of these wretched creatures perished.' Taken, the two Spaniards accused each other of breaking their 'previous pact to fight if approached by the small cruisers . . . the capture of the *Regulo* was utter ruin to [her captain], he had just before he sailed married, and his wife's fortune was wholly embarked in the vessel; he wore her miniature, which he seemed to idolise, but lookt at it, as upon one whom he had irrevocably ruined'.

This callousness was not unfrequent. Most men who had spent time on this violent coast could tell of such casual murder. It was but another 'instance', said those in the Squadron who felt their work went unsupported at home, 'of the additional inhumanity indirectly entailed on the slave trade by the benevolent exertions of England. Had our government been able to obtain from Spain, by the firmness and determination of her remonstrances, permission to seize all vessels under the flag *fitted for the reception of slaves*, this vessel could by no means have escaped, and no object could have been gained by the atrocious murder.'[5]

Gross flouting of the spirit of the Spanish anti-slave-trade treaties could only be stopped by the inclusion of an Equipment Clause, such as the Dutch had adopted, into the Spanish treaty and in 1835, two decades of Spanish prevarication came to an end. HMS *Trinculo* was patrolling off the Bonny when a sail was spotted and chased. The ship turned out to be armed and flying the Spanish flag. When Lieutenant Tryon clambered up from the boarding cutter, he found an officer of the French Royal Navy in command, who offered him a glass of champagne and gave him a message. 'Tell your captain I would have fought him had I been liable to capture', the Frenchman said, 'but I have no slaves on board. Tell him that he will find at Prince's

Island [Principe] the new treaty with Spain by which empty vessels may be taken.'[6] Away went the Frenchman east, to ship 600 slaves from King Bonny and take them to Cuba; and away went the *Trinculo* west, to find the new treaty.

The Spanish Equipment Clause marked a turning point in the Squadron's campaign. Spanish, or Spanish-covered, ships might now be stopped if they were only equipped for slave-cargoes, rather than already carrying Negroes aboard. At a stroke, it put 'the abolition of the Slave Trade', said *The Times*,

> which now almost solely flourishes under the Spanish flag, entirely in British hands, and the result may be readily anticipated. It may be hoped that in a very brief time the enormous expense attendant upon keeping numerous cruisers for this object in the most sickly part of the globe will cease to be necessary . . . at present, we employ a large force which is restrained by the regulations of the old treaty from acting with any efficiency; under the new treaty, a very small force will soon render the seas absolutely untenable even for vessels designed to deal in slaves.[7]

The latest increase in the Squadron's power was furiously contested along the coast. It infuriated King Bonny, used to seeing a long and profitable line of Spaniards at anchor in his river, awaiting their cargoes. He had already felt the ill-effects of British interference when they settled across the straits at Fernando Po. Now it seemed the Squadron would not leave him alone. In November 1835, HMS *Buzzard* fought and took a Spaniard with 280 slaves in his river and in December, the *Trinculo*, hanging about in the offing, captured another with 347 manacled Negroes aboard. In January 1836, he was enraged to be told that three of the *Trinculo*'s boats were approaching his wharves. When Spanish flags were hauled down on four of the ships outside his town, victims of the Equipment Clause, and four hated British ensigns replaced them aboard his waiting customers, King Bonny acted.

From the shore, his war-canoes were launched and Lieutenant Tryon of the *Trinculo*, leaving the last of the Spaniards, found himself surrounded and overpowered. By evening, he and eighteen bluejackets were locked in the Bonny slave-pens, a few Liverpudlian seamen from a palm-oiler thrown in after them. It was fortunate that one of the canoe men did not only take King Bonny's shilling. Fortified by a large dash, he got a message to the captain of the *Trinculo*, who set about lightening his ship to cross the bar:

18 feet of draught had to be reduced to 15 to get over and spars, spare sails, casks of food and water, cable, trunks, planks and ammunition all steadily came off. Quarter-inch by quarter-inch, the *Trinculo* rose until 2½ feet of weedy green keel appeared above the waterline. Nothing more could be unloaded: Captain Puget looked at the bar, across which a heavy surf was building, and decided to bump his ship across. She struck, and was lifted; struck again, shatteringly, and was lifted, and lifted again; the fourth huge wave took her into deep river-water on the far side with her masts rattling in their shoes.

Lieutenant Tryon and his party had spent four nights in the Bonny slave-pens when their ship appeared, anchored with Bonny Town in range of her guns, and loosed off four blank rounds. The king saw sense: all Britons were released without a fight and the *Trinculo* left with her four Spanish prizes trailing behind her.

The extension of the Equipment Clause to the Spanish trade would bring dozens of slaving fish into the Squadron's net, but not until it, too, had been tested and challenged and found wanting, been tightened and modified and explained. By May 1836, nineteen Spanish ships were already in Freetown, awaiting adjudication under the new rules. By September, there were twenty-six, clogging the bay, as

> from some informality or neglect at home [i.e. in Spain], the Mixed Commission could not proceed to condemnation [and] the slavers (availing themselves of an article in the old law, which says that final sentence shall be given in two months after the arrival of the slaver for trial, or the slaver shall then be liberated, unless the seizing party enter into bond to carry on the cause at his own expense . . . which responsibility of course our officers will not take upon themselves) are again at sea.[8]

Eight had already been released after a two-month detention, gone south to Ouidah, been given Portuguese cover and were back at the slaving game.

Théophile Conneau had just returned to Africa. Since leaving the River Pongas with his factory in ashes, he had captained slavers under various flags until he was caught in Senegal in 1832.[9] France, under a new government since the revolution of July 1830, was newly harsh towards slaving – partly to gain British recognition of the administration's legitimacy. The new government had not only agreed to the mutual right of search but had drawn up their own Equipment Clause and sent out a small squadron in 1833 to enforce it. Conneau was sentenced to ten years' imprisonment but had escaped his prison in Brest, returned to West Africa in 1836 and arrived in Freetown in time to 'witness', he wrote indignantly, 'the arbitrary proceedings of the English Government towards Spanish vessels trading on the Coast'[10] under the 'degrading treaty' for which he believed the Spanish minister had been bribed with £30,000. His stay in Freetown was brief, for the captain of an American brig needed a pilot and interpreter on a trip to supply the Spanish factors of the Gallinas, and offered Conneau the job.

If Conneau had been worried by Spanish slavers seen anchored in Freetown, his trip to the Gallinas reassured him that the latest agreement had done little immediate damage to the trade. On their first day, they sold 1,000 quarter-kegs of gunpowder to one Spanish factor; on the second, $5,000-worth of rum and tobacco to another who '[gave] drafts on London for the same'. The coast between there and Cape St Paul's was still dense with factories, fifteen thousand slaves each year left the Gallinas alone and yet Pedro Blanco, responsible for perhaps a third of that number, knew there was space for more wharves, more chains of Africans, more ships and more profit. All he had to do was dovetail demand and supply and in Théophile Conneau, he found the perfect man to help. When Conneau presented himself and recited his accomplishments, Blanco gave him the task of establishing 'auxiliary factories' on the River Sester to the south.

Conneau's new African home lay within the territory of the Prince of Bassa, who had worked aboard English slave-ships as a youth and had no objection to renewing his participation in the trade, his rent the usual dash plus a percentage on each slave shipped. In a few months' energetic work, 'a large and commodious two-story house near the sea beach was built' with 'two strong barracoons flanking the sides' and 'the whole country had changed its appearance'. A second little Gallinas had been born, Captain Conneau its attentive midwife.

On this beach, once isolated but for half a dozen Kroo huts, now counted two moderate-sized towns, and its inhabitants were amply supplied with employment from my factory. The Interior natives, confident of a ready purchase of their captives, soon found their way to the beach and in brief time the good Prince . . . sent expeditions against his neighbours, claiming redress for imagined grievances or payments from his great-grandfather's creditors.

Soon, ships from Havana, Matanzas and Puerto Rico were waiting beyond the surf. 'The demand of slaves became so great', Conneau wrote, 'that the country could not furnish us with sufficient quantity for the slavers in port.' More factories were set up in villages almost on the Liberian border. More beaches were transformed from fishing village to slave-camp, more children kidnapped by neighbours, uncles, strangers and mercenaries on the paths where they played.

With such success came attention from the Preventive Squadron and British warships were soon cruising back and forth beyond the bar. Three of Conneau's slave-ships were seized and taken to Sierra Leone in his first year of trading. More, however, got exultantly away to Pedro Blanco in the Gallinas, or directly to Cuba, for Conneau kept a Kroo spy aboard one of the British warships. When word came from him that the British were low on provisions and must return to Freetown, the preparations were made: the slaves, the canoes, the oarsmen all ready and the new little slaving village gathered to watch and wait on the beach, hoping for light winds and starlight. On one, early occasion, 'the moon was on its full and the sea, as usual on such periods, was terrific'. The canoemen were uneasy but 'the [British] cruiser had been gone six days and I hourly expected his return. The shipment, although dangerous, was indispensable.' They were induced by promises of double, even treble pay, to try. Only the smallest canoes could be used in such a surf, and the lightest oarsmen appointed to paddle them. Parties of young men were stationed along the beach to watch, and dive to the rescue of any that capsized. Seventy drenched female slaves reached the ship waiting on the far side of the bar, but by the time the male slaves were brought from barracoons to beach, the wind had risen and 'every other canoe was capsized. Negro after Negro was rescued by the swimming party.' Canoe-men and swimmers were exhausted; the wind was increasing, dusk approached and the slaver was 'making signal after signal for dispatch'. Rum could no longer persuade the oarsmen to pick themselves up off the sand and steer another craft through the rollers, but only two-thirds of the slaves had been shipped. 'I sent to the store', said Conneau for a small cask containing several pounds of Venetian beads called corniola or mock coral. Now this bead was the fury of fashion amongst the native women, and no greater temptation could be offered to bend them to one's will . . . the offer of one bunch for every head embarked brought the entire female force to my aid. Mothers, sisters, sweethearts took charge of the embarkation and forced the exhausted men to fresh efforts.

One hundred more slaves were packed in. Three drowned. Two days later, the British cruiser reappeared. 'I sent my compliments on board,' wrote Conneau, enjoying the joke, 'and begged to know if I could be of any service.'

The new factories of Sester were hidden behind a narrow, rocky entrance which kept the warships out. Open roadsteads, however, had become vulnerable to the powers conferred on the Squadron by the Spanish Equipment Clause. At Ouidah, slave-ships could no longer arrive fully equipped and ride to anchor with pots, decks, cauldrons and other incriminating items on board, awaiting only the canoes of human cargo to be away. Now the factories must provide, along with the slaves, everything necessary to sustain them on their voyage, and the ship must be equipped in a matter of hours – planks laid, supplies stowed, humans packed below – if she were to escape the patrol.

The Spanish commissioners and the slavers brought before them did their best to subvert the new agreement as they had subverted the old. If the Squadron could detain them on finding planks for a slave-deck, slaves would henceforth sleep on mats, hides or dried grass spread over casks in the hold. If large quantities of farina and rice were grounds for arrest, then slaves would be fed on dried beef, biscuit, maize and yams such as any ship's crew might eat. If there were great quantities of these foodstuffs, well, the provisioning for the crew had been generous: they did not know how long the voyage would be, where they would next be putting in, what would be available. Despite its defects and omissions, however, the Equipment Clause was too powerful a weapon for the commissioners and the Cuban slaving marine to defeat entirely. By the end of 1836, the Spanish flag was rarely seen on the slaving seas.

The *Black Joke*, pet of the Squadron, 'terror of slave dealers and scourge of the oppressors of Africa',[11] did not live to see the new era. She took her last prize off the Bonny only a few days after Commodore Hayes had her surveyed and condemned as unfit. She had been repaired many times, drawn up on the rough slip of Clarence and scraped, caulked and patched up, but this time her timbers were rotten beyond saving. When news of her condemnation arrived at Fernando Po, there were strange scenes on the island. Liberated Africans, 'sensible of the boon she has conferred upon so many of their countrymen', crowded round the commodore when he landed, 'hugged and embraced him, and entreated him not to injure poor *Black Joke* and urged their suit with all the warmth of a grateful recollection of what their favourite had done for them and theirs'. But Hayes had decided. In Freetown, she was broken up and burnt. For the men who had sailed in her, or cheered her into the anchorages to which she brought her many prizes, it was a sad day. In the Gallinas, they toasted the *Black Joke*'s end in Cuban rum.

If the Spanish flag had disappeared, Spanish slavers had not; nor had the total volume of slave-shipping diminished. Rather, the international slaving marine sought new protective colours. Those of France were unavailable, for the government which seized control in July 1830 had brought in severe new legislation which virtually extinguished the French flag on the slaving coasts. Those of the United States and Portugal, however, were still available on the busy, venal islands, where teams of forgers, seamstresses and procurers of amenable captains were industriously turning to this new variation on their trade.

The *Childers* saw dozens of Portuguese flags. Near New Sester, a Spanish slaver was overhauled 'who could not long,' Keppel wrote, 'judging by her smell, have landed her cargo. She had a Spanish captain and crew, but sheltered herself under the Portuguese flag; she was a sort of jackal, picking up cargoes for the larger vessels.'[12] But the Portuguese had signed no Equipment Clause and without slaves aboard the jackal could not be detained. Ten miles to the south, the *Childers'* pinnace boarded and searched the Cuban ship *Vigilante*, anchored in the roads 'with everything ready for a start: her fore topsail yard was hoisted to the masthead, her cat-fall was overhauled, and a luff tackle for weighing the anchor stretched along her deck'. 'The planks were arranged over the water casks, ready for the reception of her slaves' and what the bosun called their 'poo poo pots' were placed alongside but there were no slaves aboard. 'Had our boats waited two or three hours',

Captain Keppel continued, 'she would in all probability have been captured, with 400 or 500 slaves on board' but her captain, too, was able to produce the Portuguese papers which gave him safe passage. Between 11 January and 3 February 1836, Captain Keppel boarded thirteen suspected slavers flying the Portuguese flag on the lagoon, one of them commanded by de Souza's son. All were equipped for the trade. None had slaves aboard. None could be detained. Commander Hill of the *Saracen*, also boarding too many Spanish brigs under Portuguese colours, threatened one with detention despite his papers. 'I am the most unfortunate fellow in the world', wailed the Spaniard. 'This is the third vessel I have lost in two years. That blackguard at Porto Praya [on the Cape Verde islands] told me they were all correct, and I paid him a thousand dollars.'[13] The blackguard was right, for despite Commander Hill's threats, there was nothing he could do.

It was the same along the whole stretch of coast: the Portuguese flag, extinct on the slaving coasts since Brazil became independent, had reappeared everywhere. In the view of Surgeon Leonard of the *Dryad*, its reappearance was proof

in the most incontestible [*sic*] manner of the absolute folly of attempting to suppress the traffic under the existing treaties and laws . . . since the convention with Brazil came into operation . . . there is not a single flag of that nation to be found on the coast: but, what is the result? The Brazil trade is now carried on with the most perfect impunity under the flag of Portugal; and all that this convention has effected, concerning which there was so much exultation among unthinking philanthropists, is a change in the colour of a piece of bunting, or a shift from a worthless flag to one, if possible, still more degraded.[14]

'My neighbour,' wrote Governor Maclean of Cape Coast Castle in 1838, 'De Souza, at Whydah . . . declares, and with truth, that all the slave treaties signed during the last 25 years, have never caused him to export one slave fewer than he would have done otherwise.' Against massive connivance, and the smooth and easy replacement of one flag of convenience with another, what could the few, overstretched ships of the Squadron do? If the Spanish Equipment Clause were to retain its force, the Squadron must next be given the power to strangle the revived Portuguese trade.

* * *

Eight years of civil war in Portugal had left that country without a stable government with which to negotiate until Britain and France intervened in 1834 and restored constitutional government. In December 1836, the new government was obliged by Britain to outlaw the slave trade south of the equator as it had already done – legally if not actually – to the north, and to deploy its own anti-slave-trade squadron. The law it reluctantly passed was, however, largely a dead letter. Courts would not punish slavers and Lisbon did not have the power to overrule its colonial governors in Mozambique and Angola who simply suspended the new law on the breath-taking grounds 'that it would ruin their territories and was impossible to enforce'.[15]

The fake Portuguese were supplying not only Cuba, but a renewed demand in Brazil. As agreed with the British in 1826, Brazil had abol-ished the slave trade in 1830, and numbers imported into Brazil had, for a couple of years, been drastically reduced. By 1834, however, watchers had realised this was due not to enforcement of the new legislation, but to the glutting of the market in the panicky years before it came into force. Brazil had never been a country to 'breed' slaves: fresh importa-tions, rather than births, traditionally replaced those who died their brutal deaths in fields and mines. The Brazilian system, wrote a French resident, 'devours the blacks. If continued importation were not supplying them, the race would shortly disappear from our midst' and as such an outcome was considered utterly impossible for the maintenance of the Brazilian economy, importation began again. No one had an interest in enforcing the anti-slave-trade law; at every level there was corruption and connivance. In 1832, 19,453 slaves had been imported; in 1833, the figure jumped to 50,324 and in 1834 to 60,000. The only difference between the old, legal trade and the new, illegal one was that the illegal ships did not sail under the Brazilian flag.

In 1830, slavers serving the Brazilian market had fled to the still-avail-able Spanish flag. Since that had become subject to the Equipment Clause, they had unravelled a loose end in the network of treaties and begun flying Portuguese colours instead. No anti-slave-trade treaty had been made with Portugal since 1817, for the Portuguese flag had been replaced by the Brazilian and Spanish in the 1820s, particularly after Brazil became an independent nation in 1826. The matter of the Squadron's authority over Portuguese slave shipping had therefore been allowed to lapse, for there was too little of it, and it was still regulated by the outdated 1817 agreement which allowed the mutual right of search only north of the Line, and detention only when slaves were actually aboard. Portugal might have passed an abolition law in 1836, but that did not confer any extra powers on British warships: only another treaty would do that, and Portugal was resolutely opposed to signing one. The administration could not say so, outright, to the powerful British who supported them against domestic opponents. Instead, they agreed to negotiations, then constructed delays and obstacles for five years during which the Brazilian treaty of 1826 and the Spanish Equipment Clause were undermined by the availability of the Portuguese flag. This was the situation the British Prime Minister, Lord Palmerston, was determined to change, by force if necessary.

An old and much-liked officer returned to the African coast in February 1839. In late 1838, after a decade with the excise service, William Tucker, formerly of the *Hope* tender, was appointed captain of the gun-sloop *Wolverine* and made Senior Officer of the Squadron's Southern Division, covering the coast from Cape Lopez to Benguela. The first part of his command was notable for its tact. While, in Lisbon, the British envoy struggled to bring his counterpart to the negotiating table, in Angola, Captain Tucker signed a cordial agreement with the colonial governor under which, pro tem, they arranged matters between themselves. Portuguese and British ships, they agreed, would henceforth 'co-operate in taking slavers'. On the governor's say-so, Captain Tucker's officers – strictly enjoined to courtesy and discretion – might board suspicious Portuguese shipping in Angolan waters (as the Portuguese squadron just sent out might board suspicious British shipping); and Portuguese citizens who were found slaving would be brought for trial by Portuguese colonial courts. 'If the British government had treated the affair', said the Portuguese press, 'in the same manner as its agent on the West Coast of Africa', then the treaty fruitlessly sought in Lisbon 'would have been concluded and the desired extinction of that execrable traffic taken place'.

In the first place, Captain Tucker perceived that the Portuguese Government had made great efforts to carry into effect the decree of 10-12-36 (in which it promised to abolish trading south of the equator) which upon some occasions, with evident bad faith, had

been denied. In the second place, by offering his assistance [he] does
not mean to imply that the vessels of war which Her Majesty [the
Queen of Portugal] has sent to the coast of Africa are not sufficient
to effect that purpose.[16]

It was useful in cementing working relationships on the coast but this limited
right of search could not stem the enormous volume of illegal trading. In
June, the *Wolverine* chased one of many suspicious Portuguese ships upriver.
Her crew scuttled her before the British could arrive, 'intending', they said,
'to raise her as soon as the *Wolverine* left the river'. There was a time for
tact, and a time for action. 'Considering her in every respect a pirate',[17]
Captain Tucker axed her masts and cut through her sides and decks, leaving
her completely disabled.

Local agreements and limited measures were not enough for Lord
Palmerston. As Captain Tucker was taking forceful action up African rivers,
Palmerston was doing the same in London, requesting a bill be prepared to
'protect naval officers from actions resulting from the detention of Portuguese
ships'. This was the genesis of the Act for the Suppression of the Slave Trade
of August 1839, one of so many passed to stop up gaps, close loopholes,
mend the tatters of treaties unpicked by lawyers and venal officials – an
unremarkably titled piece of legislation but one which had more effect than
any so far passed on the Squadron's power to crush the illegal trade. It bore
all Palmerston's trademark contempt for foreigners and in particular for the
Portuguese.

'Her Majesty', the new Act stated, 'has been pleased to issue Orders to
her Cruizers to capture Portuguese vessels engaged in the Slave Trade.'
Detaining officers were henceforth 'to bring the same to Adjudication in the
High Court of Admiralty of England, or in any Vice Admiralty Court within
Her Majesty's Dominions, in the same Way as if such Vessels and the Cargoes
thereof were the Property of British Subjects'. At a stroke, the Portuguese
Squadron, the British–Portuguese Mixed Commissions, Captain Tucker's
careful agreement and Portugal's sovereign right to enforce her own laws
were swept aside. It passed the Commons without debate, but there was
protest from the Lords. The Duke of Wellington stood to speak against it:
had the bill's supporters forgotten the *Louis*? If Britain provoked other powers
too far – and America, the other great, illegal carrier, was again protesting
– there was a danger of 'universal war'. But it was too important to be aban-

doned and Lord Brougham found a courtly way through the thickets. He moved for an address to the queen proposing that 'British officers should first be ordered to capture Portuguese slavers and then both Houses would concur in whatever measures of indemnification were necessary'. On 15 August, it became law.

It was, said one naval officer, 'the first great blow'[18] against the illegal slave trade; 'the first time', another thought, 'when suppression became possible'.[19] It provoked howls of protest from Brazil and Lisbon; assault on British nationals in the streets of Rio and Bahia; enraged protestations of innocent merchantmen accused of slaving; but it ushered in the Squadron's three most successful years. The southern waters opened up to British patrol were given to three of the fastest-sailing vessels on the station, under three of the smartest officers. Commander Edward Butterfield, mate on HMS *Primrose* when she took the *Veloz Pasagera*, had been given the beautiful new *Fantome*. Henry Matson had distinguished himself chasing pirates on the coast in 1833, been promoted from mate to lieutenant for his gallantry and been given the fast little *Waterwitch*. Lieutenant George Sprigg joined them with the *Brisk* and, between them, they terrorised the southern coast.

Some Portuguese colonial officials were beginning to accept that the old days were gone but not all. 'After the new regulations', Butterfield said,

> implicit confidence was placed in the Portuguese authorities, and Loando and Ambriz were left in their charge: but there can be no doubt in my opinion that they all engage in the trade. When a slaver is going to sail, the Governor generally goes to his country house, and when he comes back he finds the slaver gone and makes a great fuss and offers a reward to catch them. We always closed in whenever we had information he had gone to the country and I do not think we missed once taking a vessel coming out.[20]

A tenacious inshore patrol by ships' boats, covered by a longer-range offshore patrol from the three warships, put some of the old southern slave-ports completely out of business. Between May 1840 and March 1842, forty prizes were taken and 5,360 slaves liberated. The Congo, at the northern end of the beat, was battered by repeated forays; Benguela, a collection of mud huts at the other, was shut down. It was a remarkable, and remarkably swift, success and the Portuguese flag was again swiftly swept from the seas – gone the way of the Dutch, Brazilian, French and Spanish. But it was predictable: as one nation was prevented from facilitating the illegal trade, the next stepped in. This time, it was not a nation which would agree to be bound by treaties with the British, still less would it submit to Palmerstonian force. The next to move into the vacuum was the old enemy of British arrogance and black freedom: the United States.

12

Willing Promoters and Partial Remedies

The Spanish Equipment Clause of 1835 and Palmerston's Portuguese Act of 1839 allowed the Preventive Squadron, approaching the end of its second decade, to take a far more effective grip on the illegal slave trade. Some slavers, reacting to the repeated attacks on their business, sought new protective colours and the Spanish and Portuguese flags were soon replaced by American. Others, however, sensing these two agreements had irrevocably changed the trade, began seeking alternative ways to make a living.

In late 1839, just after the Portuguese Act was passed, Captain Conneau left New Sester for London with his favourite slave-boy, Lunes. They took a steamboat to Greenwich, gazed with admiration at the cupola of St Paul's and attended the circus, where the boy was frightened by an elephant in the ring. Lunes took solitary walks along the Strand and came back to ask his owner why people shouted 'Jim Crow' at him. They passed two months pleasantly in touring and visiting, Lunes in his midnight-blue velvet livery attracting interest and invitations. He did not wear velvet with gilt buttons at home in Africa, he would tell the staring ladies, but a cloth like, look! this handkerchief, placed so. They blushed and giggled. 'November', however; was 'not a favorable month for strangers to visit London. Its damp and foggy days soon sicken a foreigner from the dullness of the gloomy city.'[1] Captain Conneau turned to business.

Before coming to Britain, he had undergone a change of heart, or so he would later claim, and turned against the slave trade. Knowing that Pedro

Blanco intended shortly to retire to Havana, Conneau had wished to say a personal farewell. On his way to the Gallinas, he had called at the factory established three years ago at Digbay, and found it working its predictable black magic. The chiefs of Digbay and the twin town of Petit Bassa were cousins, 'who for many years had lived in harmony and friendship' until Conneau brought a slave-factory and its riches to one but not the other. 'The two towns had fenced, fortified and barricaded themselves' and raids and retaliations had begun. The Petit Bassa chief had finally brought in Bushmen mercenaries from the interior who attacked during Conneau's visit, storming the town in the small hours, firing the houses of those who fled, seizing those who did not and obliging Conneau to watch the victory ceremonies.

On a beaten earth plaza, the dead and wounded were piled together. The principal wife of the Bushman chief led the massacre. She had come screaming into the village with twenty-five other women, dead drunk on a mixture of rum, gunpowder and blood, a foetus impaled on her knife. This she 'put aside for a *bonne bouche*, and now adorned with a string of men's genital parts, she was collecting into a gourd the brains of the decapitated bodies [while] the men carved the solid flesh from the limbs of the dead, throwing the entrails aside'. The uneaten flesh was wrapped in plantain leaves and kept. Even Conneau was shaken by these horrors.

'I freely accuse myself', he would write, 'of being the cause of these wars. I would not pardon myself if I had caused them with the knowledge of their consequences; I would not be thought a willing promoter of these barbarities.' This was written when he was living in America years later, presenting himself as one who had sinned but repented. He forgave himself too easily. His years on the coast, his friendships with suppliers, his long contact with captives: through all these he must have known of the atrocities carried out in the first stages of the trade, before the slaves reached his barracoons. He had paid a ransom of two slaves for himself and one for each of his Kroomen, and left for the Gallinas to find that Pedro Blanco had already departed for Cuba, taking a reputed fortune of $4,000,000 with him.

All this had caused Conneau to reflect.

I had now been in the slave trade several years. The furor for changes and emotions had cooled off, and the desire for a roving life had subsided to a degree of negligence for new sceneries. The losses, troubles and imprisonment never had deterred me before, but to witness the late barbarities inflicted on the wounded in a war of which I was the involuntary cause had sickened my heart with the slave trade, and humanity spoke louder every day in favour of a lawful traffic.

So did the changing status of the illegal trade: the widening system of treaties and the increasing strength of the Preventive Squadron; the Spanish Equipment Clause and Palmerston's Portuguese Act; the demands for similar strong actions against the Americans. All these were reasons for his presence in London that autumn: he was looking for a respectable partner in a new respectable enterprise. The person he approached was a Mr George Redman Clevering of Lime Street, who already owned three vessels trading between Africa and Europe. One of these, the *Gil Blas*, had brought Conneau to England, and judging by its presence in the Gallinas, delivering goods to Pedro Blanco's agent there eighteen months later, Mr Clevering may not have been entirely innocent of the workings of the old trade. Conneau's proposal was to start a legitimate factory at Cape Mount, just north of the American settlements, which he considered 'one of the most pleasant places from Sierra Leone to Cape Palmas' and whose king was in his debt for past favours. Once an agreement had been made with Mr Clevering, and Don Pedro was informed, he would leave New Sester and live a happy and honest life here beneath the Union Jack. 'Mr Redman, being an enterprising person, heard my proposal with interest, and after few days' consideration, proposed to enter himself in negotiation with me as soon as I would give proofs of having abandoned forever the slave traffic.' Mr Clevering was careful but despite this stipulation, they both knew the old trade could not be so easily disentangled from the new. When Conneau returned to New Sester in March 1840, having visited Havana to inform Pedro Blanco of his plans, he found the American warship *Dolphin* anchored at his door. During his long absence, Washington had been forced to confront, again, the embarrassment of American slaving on the African coast. The factories on the Liberian periphery were its first target.

There had been no US anti-slave-trade squadron on the African coast since 1823. For the past twenty years, American patrols had been confined to home waters, with desultory visits to Liberia once a year or so. With any right of search still officially denied the British, American shipping on the African coast had had an easy time. Since 1833, American immunity had been extended to other nations by a consul in Havana who did more, perhaps, than any other individual to salvage the Cuban slave-trade from the twin blows of the Spanish Equipment Clause and the Portuguese Act.

Consul Nicholas Trist was a well-connected southerner. From wealthy Louisiana stock, he had married a granddaughter of Thomas Jefferson and included congressmen, diplomats and judges among his Washington friends. He had arrived at the Havana consulate in 1833 as personal nominee of President Jackson. Trist was as hawkishly jealous of American independence as Lieutenant Stockton had been, including independence for Americans to break their own laws and help foreigners do the same if they wished. Both American legislation and Spanish treaties should have made it impossible, but during his time in office, American registration papers were on sale at Havana as openly as Portuguese ones at Principe and Cape Verde. By the end of the decade most of the Cuban slave trade was protected by the Stars and Stripes. Without enforcement, and in the absence of any international law enforceable by others, the partial remedies of domestic legislation and bilateral treaties left great, fertile gaps in which such as Consul Trist could sow and reap their horrible harvest.

Everyone knew what he was up to. They knew it in Havana, where the British commissioners tried endlessly and fruitlessly to intervene. In January 1839, they wrote to him wearily:

as it may possibly not have come to your knowledge we think it right to make you acquainted with the report, prevalent in this place, respecting the ship *Venus*, which arrived here the 4th August last from Baltimore, and sailed shortly afterward for the coast of Africa.

This vessel, you will no doubt remember, arrived and sailed hence under American colors, under which, it is said, she took in a cargo of negro slaves, and landed them within the last few days on this coast, about 860 in number. The report farther states, there are several American citizens implicated in this flagrant violation of the laws of the United States, and as the *Venus* may be hourly expected in the harbor, we would respectfully suggest to you, that such immediate steps may be taken on her arrival, as may lead to the punishment of such offenders.[2]

Similar letters had been passing between them since 1835, the British formally informing Consul Trist of what he had been instrumental in arranging; Consul Trist writing back of his surprise – no, his shock – at the utter 'oblivion or *innate ignorance* of the simplest applications (until then deemed by me self-evident,) of first truths, in regard to *international independence*', revealed by their letters. Such interference by one power in the affairs of another as their letter suggested – however cunningly presented as a mere offer of information – could only be answered by 'a rebuke, such as my command of language would have been severely tried in making commensurate with my sense of the insult'. How would they like it, he asked, if he informed them of the 'number of casks of shackles . . . of British manufacture annually exported to this island, some of which I have seen passing through the Custom House here, without attracting more notice from either officers or bystanders, than so many boxes of Dutch cheeses'?

They knew it in London. 'You will state to Mr. Trist', wrote Lord Palmerston when the latest dispatch came in from Havana, 'that if he can at any time furnish Her Majesty's Government, through you, with any information which may directly or indirectly enable Her Majesty's Government to enforce the penalties of the law against British subjects who may be concerned in the slave trade, Her Majesty's Government will feel most sincerely obliged to him.'[3] In the meantime, would the commissioners remind him of the British–American engagement of 1814 to 'use their utmost endeavours to promote the entire abolition of the slave trade'. There was nothing else they could do.

They knew it in the Cape Verde Islands, where Mr Barker, British consul, reported Trist had granted 'false bills of sale of vessels and passes to these islands', where Americans 'change their flag, and by a fraudulent sale, are for the time converted into Portuguese or Spanish vessels, and thus get a double set of papers. If overtaken by a British cruiser, they are American vessels, and cannot be searched; if, by any wonder, they should be spoken by an American cruiser, they are Spanish or Portuguese.'

They knew it at the Gallinas. 'The *Comet*' (an American ship), wrote Pedro Blanco from his Havana palace to the agent he had left behind,

> is on her way to you with the merchandise which you asked for and as you also wished that we should send to you, a month later, an American private boat, able to carry 250 to 300 slaves, to embark the

return cargo, we have taken care to purchase one, on purpose to send it to you with some rum and tobacco, prepared with the greatest economy. We shall also most scrupulously take care that the said vessel takes her papers in form, so that she may run no risk when she has to touch at Cape de Verd to change her rag [i.e. flag].[4]

They knew it in Monrovia, where Governor Buchanan wrote home baldly that 'the chief obstacle to the success of the very active measures pursued by the British government for the suppression of the slave-trade on the coast, is the American flag. Never was the proud banner of freedom so extensively used by those pirates upon liberty and humanity, as at this season.'[5]

And they knew it in North America, from correspondence sent in from all sides; and from the outraged reports in newspapers made by North Americans disgusted by this semi-official connivance in a trade they found repugnant. When the American flag was offered in 1835 to protect the enormous volume of the illegal Spanish trade, and again in 1839 to cover the Portuguese as well, the Squadron found itself facing an impossible task, and the US government a growing embarrassment. Something had to budge.

In March 1839, a prize-crew from HMS *Buzzard* sailed into Freetown with two Spanish vessels detained off Lagos with slaves aboard and flying what the *Buzzard*'s commander, Lieutenant Fitzgerald, believed to be false American flags. Fitzgerald had exceeded his instructions in visiting them at all, whatever his suspicions, and even if those turned out correct. Their crews were Spanish, with a sprinkling of Portuguese, and both had American papers and captains, who cheerfully admitted they had been hired solely to protect the vessels from capture or detention by British warships. The British–Spanish Mixed Commission refused to accept the two ships were Spanish, and would not try them. Neither would the British Vice-Admiralty court, where the chief judge had seen too many hands burnt in American fires. True, he said, if they were not Spanish they must indeed be American, but in that case no one in Sierra Leone was authorised to try them. What, then, should he do, asked the prize-master? There were no US cruisers on the coast to whom he could hand them over for American officers to sort it out. Either the *Eagle* and the *Clara* must be turned loose to carry their slaves whither they would and return for more, or they must be taken to America and tried by an American court. The prize-master took them back to Lieutenant Fitzgerald in the Bights, who decided he had no option but to take them to New York. In April 1839, the *Eagle*, *Clara* and *Buzzard* left for America.

HMS *Dolphin* arrived in Freetown the same month with two more 'American' slavers for a repeat of this farce. One had been found with slaves aboard; the other with slave equipment: 600 wooden spoons, 350 pairs of handcuffs and materials for a slave-deck. The man who claimed to be her skipper had once been Danish but had recently obtained American citizenship. Two of his crew were Englishmen, or ex-Englishmen, now also claiming American nationality; his papers were issued by Consul Trist, and he was in possession of precise, incriminating written instructions from a shipping agent in Havana.

> The main thing for you to do on this voyage is to be ready in case you are boarded by a man of war, to show your log book, which must be regularly kept from the time you leave here – your ship's papers, your charter paper, for the voyage, your ship's roll, and instructions; and you are, in that event, to take all command, with your American sailors, according to your roll – all the others are to be passengers. You are to be very careful that in any cross questions you do not commit yourself, and always stick to the same story. When the vessel is discharged, you must at once cut your register in two pieces – one piece you must enclose, direct and send to Messrs. Thomas, Wilson & Co., Baltimore – the other piece you will bring with you, and give to me when you return here. You must be very particular about that, and do not let any thing pass after the cargo is out, before you cut the register in two pieces, and be careful to keep them separate – throw one piece overboard if you are obliged to, by being boarded by a man of war.[6]

They, too, were disowned by the Spanish Mixed Commission and set off for New York, where the *Buzzard's* arrival had caused a small sensation, for she was the first British ship to sail into an American harbour with prizes since the American War of Independence. Lieutenant Fitzgerald was still awaiting an interview with the New York district attorney when a respectable, portly man walked the wharves inquiring whether anyone there spoke the African language Mende. The slave-schooner *Amistad* had been recovered in distress off Long Island and thirty-nine African males, four African children, a Creole cook and two imprisoned Spaniards found aboard. The Africans had been arrested on suspicion of mutiny and the ship towed to New Haven, Connecticut, where a quick-thinking abolitionist grocer had contacted a lawyer and the lawyer had contacted this man, Professor Gibbs of Yale, to identify their dialect. British seamen pointed him towards James Covey. Kidnapped from his Sierra Leone village as a child and sold to a Cuban slave-ship in the Gallinas, Covey now worked with the Squadron which had saved him. On Professor Gibbs's request, Lieutenant Fitzgerald released him to interpret for the group whose own three-year struggle for liberty was just beginning.

The *Buzzard* and her two prizes had left New York by the time the *Dolphin* arrived. The district attorney had decided their two captains could, as Americans, be tried. The vessels they commanded, however, he persisted in considering Spanish, despite the opposite conclusion of the Spanish Mixed Commission in Freetown, and thus outside his jurisdiction. Lieutenant Fitzgerald and his two cargoes were on their way back across the Atlantic. The prosecution of the *Dolphin*'s prizes was easier. Despite protest from Maryland's powerful slaving interest, the Baltimore shipowners were brought to trial, their ships confiscated and condemned. The judge on whose order this was carried out was a southern aristocrat, a slave-owner and supporter of the institution of slavery, but one who hated to see the American flag disgraced. Others thought the greater disgrace was giving in to the British.

HMS *Buzzard* re-entered Freetown on Christmas Day, alone, her men exhausted. Knowing his two prizes were ill-found, Lieutenant Fitzgerald had not wanted to make the long return voyage to Freetown and had tried his luck first at the British Vice-Admiralty court at Bermuda. This, too, had decided it could not hear the case against the Spanish (or American) *Eagle* and sent him away. On the last stage of this long, enraging voyage, the three ships had been caught in a tornado. The *Eagle* foundered and the *Clara*, blown off course, had been lost to sight. Her prize-crew managed to get her to Jamaica, where the naval surveyors condemned her as unseaworthy. In the eight months that Fitzgerald and his charges had been roaming the seas, the Spanish Mixed Commission had changed its mind. The *Clara*'s Spanish nationality was now accepted, and the commissioners said she would definitely be confiscated, if she ever turned up; likewise the *Eagle*, were she not strewn in pieces across the Atlantic. Much time, life and property would have been saved had they made the judgment eight months earlier.

British warships catching American slavers red-handed and escorting them across the ocean: this was the clearest possible indication that American law-enforcement was not working, but there was still no question of formalising the arrangement. President Van Buren had explicitly welcomed the arrest of the *Eagle* and *Clara* but when a stream of other detentions followed, he made it clear the point had been taken; would the British now back off, please. In early 1840, he ordered a 'competent' naval force to return to the African station. The USS *Dolphin* had left, shortly followed by the USS *Grampus*, and a pointed message was sent to London that July: that the president, given this new deployment of his forces, 'has a right to expect that positive instructions will be given to all Her Majesty's officers to forbear from boarding or visiting vessels under the American flag'.[7] First stop on the *Dolphin*'s six-month cruise was Monrovia, where Commander Bell heard the names of Théophile Conneau and New Sester at the table of Governor Buchanan.

Since the USS *Cyane* sailed away in 1823, leaving the Reverend Ashmun in charge, the Liberian settlements had grown out of their shaky, violent beginnings. More American states had sent groups of former slaves to found their own little coastal towns near Monrovia, bought with the usual collections of muskets, gunpowder and bead and settled with the usual epidemics of fever and attack. The southernmost of these townships was the peninsula of Cape Palmas, colonised by the unwanted black labour of Maryland. Two others lay between here and the capital, Monrovia: Greenville on the Sinoe River, populated by emancipated Negroes from Mississippi; and Grand Bassa, bought for blacks from New York and Pennsylvania, a huddle of huts on the edge of the jungle. Under Governor Buchanan's energetic leadership, these scattered, vulnerable settlements were uniting into a commonwealth of two and a half thousand souls, with sovereignty claimed from the Gallinas to New Sester. Bitter water still flowed with the sweet: pincered between these two notorious slave-marts, the American colonies, like the British, had found themselves in uneasy but constant contact with slavers. Budding commerce in ivory, oil and wood was still less profitable than that in humans, and all the more subtle subversions of purpose tainted Liberian society as they did that of Freetown. The successful African-American running his warehouse, dealing in legal goods, had more in common with a well-spoken and friendly slaver than either had with the ochre-painted blacks who attacked the settlers' farms and worshipped heathen gods. Credit, goods, services and company were all on offer.

Théophile Conneau admired the American experiment, and was both customer and employer. He had first visited Monrovia when Pedro Blanco sent him to buy tobacco for the new factory in 1836, and had been impressed by the 'village of astonishing asparagus growth', with stores built of brick, wharves which were neat and well run, two churches with 'competent bells', wide, clean streets and shops full of goods. There were 'all sorts of mechanics', he found, for 'the inhabitants have imported with them that Yankee mechanical genius which characterizes Americans in general – their former masters'.[8] There were also ladies. Conneau does not mention his long-term companion, Rosalie, in his memoirs, probably because he was married to someone else by the time they were published. Madame Conneau, as she was known on the coast, was one of two Georgia-born mulatto sisters. The other, Mrs McGill, was married to Dr McGill, official of the Maryland Colonization Society. The connection was a useful passport.

New Sester had become to Monrovia as the rivers Pongus and Nuñez to Freetown: an insolent canker, a sore on the margin, a persistent temptation to those colonists who did not want to be pioneers, to plant their seed and build their huts, teach and pray. Grand Bassa was just 14 miles from one of Conneau's factories, Monrovia itself a couple of days' sailing. As Harry Demane had slipped away and gone slaving and as Freetowners still snatched children and sold them on the Bullom Shore, now emancipated American blacks watched sorrowfully as huts were deserted in the night and rumours came back of this man seen whip in hand on Conneau's slave-wharf; that guarding his barracoons; another marshalling the work parties on his plantations.

Governor Buchanan was determined to disentangle legal from illegal trade. Commander Bell's appearance off New Sester was at his request, for Buchanan thought a naval officer, with guns behind him, might persuade the Prince of Bassa to expel the foreigners from his land and outlaw the trade. A first letter was not well received. 'I wish you would mind your own business,' the prince replied, 'and let me alone.'[9] A second, addressed to the factors themselves, was as naïve in its assumptions as the British communications of twenty years ago.

I have received information that you now have in your establishments on shore several hundred Negroes confined in barracoons, waiting for an opportunity to ship them off. Whether you are Americans, English,

French, Spaniards or Portuguese, you are acting in violation of the established laws of your respective countries and therefore not entitled to any protection from your Government. You have placed yourself beyond the protection of any civilized nation, as you are engaged in a traffic which has been made piracy by most of the Christian nations of the world. As I have been sent by my Government to root out if possible this traffic on and near our settlements on the Coast, I now give you notice that you must break up your establishments at this point, in two weeks from this date.

This was the moment that Théophile Conneau returned from Havana and took efficient charge. Conneau had more experience of the coast than Bell. He had seen the British attack in every way they knew how: guns, diplomacy, appeals to humanity, dash; and he had seen them repelled. The arguments set out in his reply to Bell's letter were irrefutable. 'First, Sir,' he wrote, grandly, 'under the doubtful pretext of the authority of your nation, you threaten to land and destroy our property on these neutral shores.' Then the blow which made any American abolitionist wince. 'You are pleased to inform us that all Christian nations have declared the slave trade piracy . . . why then do the Southern states of your great republic allow slavery, public auctions, transportations from one state to another . . . of civilized American-born Black subjects?' Thirdly, since when had Liberia been an American colony? The world, he wrote, had been 'always led to believe that these settlements of Liberia were nothing more than Christian beneficial societies, humanely formed by private and philanthropic individuals to find a refuge for the poor Black American-born that the free and independent laws and institutions of the United States cannot protect in their native country'. They had no right to claim the guns of the US Navy in defence of their philosophy, or even their borders. Lastly, he pointed out bluntly that if the *Dolphin* were to attempt any enforcement, 'many factories here would suffer by your unjust attack, which would give them an indisputed right to claim high damages from your Government'.[10]

The *Dolphin* retreated.

The real value of this second American experiment with an African patrol was in the information the two commanders gave to the Secretary of the US Navy, Mr Upshur. He had been asked to report to the president on the volume of illegal African slaving under the US flag, and how this might be suppressed, a report delivered when the ships had left for a second cruise. 'Their presence on the coast,' he wrote with facile optimism, 'will, in all probability, in a great degree arrest its progress, so far as it has been prosecuted by the assumption of the American flag, and do much to relieve the nation from the unmerited stigma of participating in a trade equally in violation of the laws of the United States and the policy of their Government.' (Sustained snorts and raspberries, one imagines, when copies of that report reached the British Admiralty.) 'It appears that the traffic in slaves is now carried on principally under Portuguese colors,' he continued, 'through the medium of slave stations, (as they are denominated,) established at different points of the coast, under the protection of the neighboring native chiefs, who furnish the slaves, and receive in return goods manufactured in England expressly for this purpose.'[11]

The compulsory dig shoehorned in, Secretary Upshur turned to the commanders' recommendations. They had been instructed to work in 'friendly cooperation' with the British and Lieutenant Paine of USS *Grampus* and Captain Tucker of HMS *Wolverine*, well-intentioned and pragmatic men, had quickly reached an agreement: each would detain suspicious vessels flying the other's flag until the other returned. It was eminently sensible, and banned as soon as the *Dolphin* and *Grampus* returned to America from their first cruise and Washington heard about it. No such course of action could be recommended to the president. Upshur preferred to address a less contentious point. 'Both officers are of opinion that, so long as these stations are permitted to exist, and this barter carried on, all attempts effectually to arrest the traffic in slaves will end in administering only partial remedies, which will but aggravate the disease.' The ships' second cruise was brought to a premature and dismal end by an eruption of fever. They caught one slaver, the first taken by an American warship in African waters in nearly twenty years.

Partial remedies: from all sides of the debate, it was agreed that legislation and treaty left too many gaps. If international effort were to have any meaning, it must be spread further and more thickly. America had been goaded into sending out two warships but their commanders only confirmed the inadequacy of American law-enforcement: meaningful co-operation from Washington was vital. Then there was Africa herself. Even if all flags and all customers were made subject to an anti-slave-trade convention, this would only be truly international if Africa were brought into it. Remedies would always be partial until Africa herself was cured of the slaving disease.

13

Blockade

In March 1840, HMS *Wanderer* dropped anchor in Freetown Bay. Her commander, the Honourable Joseph Denman, had already served on the African coast as lieutenant and been converted to active abolitionism by the horrors he had seen there. Promoted commander, determined in his views, made confident in his convictions by possession of a Lord Chief Justice as father, he was returning as Senior Officer of the Squadron's Sierra Leone Division, with charge of the coast from Cape Verde to Cape Palmas.

Commander Butterfield's little division, south of the Line, was achieving its successes over the Portuguese trade by following the old system of patrol. The different geography of Denman's beat suggested another system. 'My opinion', he said, 'is that the system of *blockade* is that which alone can be successful under any circumstances': a system of 'cruisers at anchor, generally within signal distance of each other', supported by a supply ship and 'an outside vessel'[1] to replace any ship which needed to leave its station. It was the system by which his generation's grandfathers had starved Napoleonic France and their fathers had kept US ships cooped up in New England harbours. If properly enforced, it would bring the factors to their knees far sooner than the chase and pounce of previous years. It would also, he knew, be horribly, sickeningly hard on his men and ships.

No vessel off Africa, thought Naval Surgeon Alexander Bryson, 'could remain more than a week or two at anchor with safety to the health of her crew'.[2] Everyone knew that the sick list was hit during blockade. Ships lifted ceaselessly, sickeningly on the rollers, anything not secured tumbled about and broke and those who never suffered nausea at sea felt it now. Blockade was 'killing to officers and men', wrote one captain. 'You can form no conception of what they have to undergo – for months at anchor, rolling terribly, the thermometer eighty-six degrees: no supplies of fresh stock except at long intervals and not sufficient vessels to ensure certain reliefs.'[3] More subtle wounds, too, were inflicted by the boredom and the sense of purposelessness – the ineffectiveness of a handful of ships against a vast, derisive conspiracy at land and sea. The madness of the coast hit slaver-catchers as it had hit generations of slavers in that grinding monotony and heat; the constant roar of surf, the sameness of the land as far as both horizons; the feeling of something sinister at work just over there, beyond the surf, the endless mangrove and the palms. All these, a blockading commander wrote, 'have an effect even upon the best organised mind that is sometimes distressing, and we have, I grieve to say, examples of the effect of these trials in the invaliding of officers and others from mental disorganisation'.[4] This was nonetheless the duty Denman wanted the ships of his division to perform.

HMS *Wanderer* covered the most notorious stretch of coast: from the southern boundary of Sierra Leone to the deathly Gallinas. The next stretch, covering Cape Mount, New Sester and Trade Town, was assigned to HMS *Bonetta* and HMS *Termagant*, patrolling sometimes within sight of Captain Conneau's verandah.

When Conneau had returned to New Sester from Havana to find the USS *Dolphin* at his door, he was sailing aboard an American ship and bringing back a cargo of Pedro Blanco's trade goods. As agreed with Mr Clevering, Conneau had visited Blanco in order to arrange his release from whatever contract bound them but found his employer 'in no humor to accede to my philanthropic views'.[5] Only a madman would abandon the Cuban slave trade in early 1840: it was sanctioned by church, society, tradition and national honour and made more money than any substitute conceivably could. Conneau had agreed to supply at least one more slave-ship from New Sester but was not deterred from his other plans. He began the construction of another small factory a couple of miles from his barracoons. Here he would trade only in legal goods. It was managed by one of the Liberians who preferred life across the border and one small spot of decency returned to the polluted waters of New Sester. Decency, however, still ended at its perimeter. Blanco's trade goods – 'the last cargo I intended ever to invest in slaves' – had been sent out on credit and the barkers were bringing their prisoners in.

The new blockade caught Conneau's factory with its barracoons ruinously full. 'Provisions became every day more scarce', he wrote, as the barkers brought in their captives and his barracoons swelled to bursting. 'The horrors of a famine were the daily topic of our conversation.' He offered more and more money for food, but there was nothing to buy. His scouts scoured villages ever further inland for rice and cassava; there was none left. The oldest and sickest slaves were set loose to feed themselves, if they could, but still there were too many. Calling the local chiefs together, Conneau told them he must release the rest when the food ran out and 'was implored not to take such a step', which would 'surely cause a revolution among their own people'. In Havana, slave-ships rode empty at anchor, savings tied uselessly up in them; or returned with half-cargoes or none at all, telling tales of the inexorable British line and the factories unreachable on its far side.

As the Cuban trade suffered under Denman, so did the Brazilian under Butterfield's different methods, and with fewer slaves getting through, their price rocketed on the Brazilian markets. The consequence was predictable. A horde of petty adventurers was soon putting out in 'the merest nutshells'[6] of boats for the golden voyage which, if successful, would pay all their debts, build them a mansion and buy a harem of quadroons to put in it. 'The Brazilian slave merchant', said Lieutenant Matson of the *Waterwitch*, one of the coast's astutest officers, 'buys an old vessel for a mere trifle; a small crew can navigate her, as she is always in fine weather; on her return she is crammed full of slaves, but little water is required, the wind is fair, and the voyage occupies only three or four weeks.'[7] Restrictions on numbers had been routinely disregarded when the Brazilian trade was legal; now that it was illegal, there were no restrictions at all. However many you could pack in, with the absolute minimum of water and food, was the number you took. When a slave cost 20 shillings in Africa and fetched £120 at Brazil, there would always be people willing to trade.

These appalling craft, once taken by the British, had to be patched up and navigated, with surviving slaves and prize-crew aboard, to the nearest court. One officer recalled seeing a Brazilian prize stagger into Freetown with its sails patched over with bedlinen. When the *Waterwitch* arrived at St Helena for one brief period of recuperation, Lieutenant Matson was the only officer left aboard. All others had been sent off with prize-crews. His most recent prize, taken slaving under the forts of Benguela whose governors were supposed to be stopping her, he had been obliged to put in charge of the gunner. No one else was left.

The Sierra Leone Division saw more suffering and fewer prizes as the regime imposed by Captain Denman took effect. At times the blockading ships upped anchor and sailed to reprovision, or rest and recover their health on Ascension, and rumours went round the factories that slave-ships were coming. Then, the single light of *coast clear* shone from island to island and bay to bay and sinuous, stumbling lines marched to where the canoes were ready and manned to run the surf. Sometimes the British turned and got there first, and then bonfires were lit on shore with gunpowder thrown in great flashes upon them to warn the slave-ships beyond to turn back, and try another day. The tired lines of slaves would turn and march back through the night to hunger in the barracoons.

Pedro Blanco had left for Havana but other, younger men still lived on the marshy islands of the Gallinas, making their fortunes. Two thousand slaves were cooped up there, ruinously eating. The rice to feed them was on the far side of the blockade and few slave-ships could crash or slip the British wall to take the Negroes away and ease the pressure on the store. When British ships' boats overtaken by bad weather in the rivers were attacked, their crews were viciously set upon. After seven months of this, King Siaka wrote to Governor Doherty in Freetown, his pen guided by the Spaniards with whom his fortune had become indissolubly linked. His was a free port, he said, open to all, and it was not fair that the British should blockade it because certain Spanish vessels chose to visit. Supplies of rice from Sherbro and the Plantain Islands could not get through the blockade, and his people were suffering. Governor Doherty ignored his protests. The blockade continued and the factories opened their doors. The weakest, the oldest and sickest were turned out to fend for themselves or die on the beach.

At New Sester, they were desperate. When only two days' worth of provisions remained, a merchant ship owned by Dr Hall, Liberian merchant, appeared in the bay. Conneau sought him out, 'informed him of the destitute state of provisions the whole country was in and begged him to relieve my very difficult position'.[8] 'Seven hundred measures of rice' arrived a few days later, got through the blockade by some combination of deceit and defiance. It was enough to keep Conneau's factory going until the Cuban slave-ship *Volador* slipped past HMS *Termagant* and took her slaves away to hell. Two other New Sester factors supplied most of them, then closed their establishments and left for Cuba, 'abandoning in disgust' the invalids and those of the slaves that could not be embarked. Conneau sent the rest and 'this', he would claim, 'was the last cargo I shipped'. His thoughts lay with Cape Mount, respectability and the factory he would establish with Mr Clevering of Lime Street.

On 5 November 1840, there was a commotion on the beach below his now almost-empty factory. A stranger was running his boat up on the sand, where 'the natives, believing her to be my boat, ran to the beach to protect her'. Her skipper was one of Pedro Blanco's men, sent with a letter acknowledging the safe arrival of the *Volador*, Conneau's commission of $13,100 and notice that a fresh cargo of trade goods would soon be arriving to buy more slaves, blockade or no blockade. Behind Blanco's man came a running, shouting party of British marines. When the locals attacked them, HMS *Termagant* fired her cannon in reply and Commander Seagram wrote a terse letter.

Sir:

The natives or Kroomen of your settlement having this day fired on the boats of Her Britannic Majesty's ship under my command while in chase of a Spanish boat with seven men going to New Cestros, I therefore demand the persons who fired on the boats to answer for the same; and should this demand not be complied with, I shall take such steps as I deem proper to procure satisfaction.

I have addressed you on this occasion, judging by the interference of those Blacks in your behalf, that they are instigated by you.

I have the honor to be, Sir, your obedient servant,
Lieutenant Commander H. F. Seagram

Conneau took his answer himself, appearing on board at sunset in surf-soaked shirt and drawers to assure Seagram that the firing had not been at his instigation, that he deplored it, that he had given up the slave trade and would be obliged if he could borrow dry clothes. It was dark when his explanations finished and the surf was running high. He accepted an invitation to sleep aboard and the following morning, Commander Seagram accepted one to visit New Sester. Prince Freeman, waiting at Conneau's house, 'observed I must possess some powerful ju-jus to attract the confidence of my enemies'. He was taken by surprise when Seagram sat and earnestly began dissuading him from the slave trade and astonished when Conneau backed up the suggestion for, as Conneau had told Seagram privately, 'it would be easier to travel safely to Timbuktu and back than to convince these chiefs of the impropriety of the slave-trade'. Sure Conneau was 'deceiving the Englishman for some cunning purpose', the prince signed his abolition treaty and Conneau gave up the few slaves left in his barracoons to Seagram. For this gesture of commitment to a new, legal life, he was promised safe passage to Cape Mount aboard the *Termagant*. When he raised the British flag, she would anchor in the bay and take him off; if the need were urgent, he must hang the flag 'Jack down', the recognised sign of distress, and fire a blank gun. Before Conneau could pack up his old life and begin on his new, however, shocking news came from the north.

In Freetown, a Mrs Grey had gone to Governor Doherty with a troubling letter just received.

'Respected Mother, Rosamia Grey', it began:

> I hope when you receive this letter it may find you and family well. I have to inform you that Mr Manna has catched me on your account, and is determined to detain me till you come yourself . . . I am now equal to a slave, because I do not know what will happen to me. Between now and night all depends on the good or evil heart of Mr Manna. Therefore you will lose no time in coming to my assistance on your account.[9]

The letter was from Fry Norman, rescued slave, Freetown washerwoman and British subject. She had heard that one of her customers was leaving for the West Indies without paying her what he owed. This man had gone to the Gallinas to find passage aboard some ship and there Mrs Norman followed him, her baby on her back, to get her money. She did so but was recognised and kidnapped. 'Mr Manna' was a son of King Siaka, and a tough customer, 'ready to fight all comers', one officer said. 'Wounded in the hip, he had a shortened right leg, had received a bullet through the groin and two through the right shoulder, besides the loss of two fingers of the right hand. He had not an idea beyond fighting and drinking, for both of which he was justly famed. He never moved out without two bards, both of whom sang his praises in the most lusty manner.' Mrs Rosamia Grey was somehow in this man's debt, Fry Norman had been her apprentice and she would serve as surety for payment. If not redeemed, she and her child would be on the next ship to Cuba. The Siaka dynasty did not realise what possibilities their latest casual violence offered.

Commander Denman was summoned to Government House. If he would support Governor Doherty's plan to rescue this British subject in distress and Siaka reacted as predicted, the *Wanderer* could repeat – legally – the long-ago successes of HMS *Ulysses* in the Pongus. He agreed, and ordered his ships from their stations to gather outside the Gallinas.

On 19 November 1840 a flotilla of boats floated over the bar and into the estuary. Instead of the expected cannon-fire from the factories and ambush from the mangroves, they found the waters alive with darting craft and shouting men. The Spaniards, forewarned, had decided to ferry their slaves off the islands and as far upriver as they could get them before the British came. Fleets of great canoes were disappearing into the creeks at the head of the estuary, making for the tangle of inland waterways which only the locals knew. Only a few at the tail-end were caught, and only ninety slaves of the several hundred known to be held here were rescued.

Just inside the bar was the little island of Dombocorro, the last African soil that thousands of desperate beings had trodden. Here the rescued ninety were landed, fed and interrogated. From here a letter went to Siaka, summoning him to palaver and demanding the immediate surrender of Mrs Norman and her child. The following day, mother and infant were brought across the green water. British sentries watched the shore for any activity and boats landed here and there to investigate the deserted barracoons. Then canoes were seen collecting on the bank and Prince Manna appeared, with a horde of chiefs and sub-chiefs and attendants. Siaka, they said, was too old and unwell to appear. Manna was entitled to speak and act for his father. Let the palaver begin.

Commander Denman spoke of the attacks on British shipping and citizens during the eight months of blockade. The chiefs protested strongly. None of these acts, they said, had been committed by them or their people. All had been the responsibility of the foreign slave-traders and to punish them for the faults of others would be grossly unfair. Since you say you have no responsibility for, or authority over, these men, said Denman, and they have committed these outrages to both our detriment, you will doubtless help me bring them to justice.

His demand was this: the British would destroy the Spanish factories all about them; Manna and his people must round up the slaves just taken away and hand them over. In return, the cloth, muskets, rum, beads and other precious articles piled in the warehouses would be theirs, as well as all those distributed as credit among the inland suppliers: enough, it was thought, to buy thirteen thousand slaves beyond the hills. Manna and his men went away, and discussed the proposal all night. Did their interest lie with Spanish trade or British guns? In the morning, they agreed to the British demand. And then, continued Denman at the new day's palaver, the slave trade will be forever banned in this river. To this, they said, in a great din of refusal and anger, they could not possibly agree. Such a course of action would affect many other interests and peoples, and how could they speak for those? There must be intertribal palaver, time, recompense . . .

Several hundred slaves were brought back down the creeks, rowed to Dombocorro by Manna's canoe-men, received into the British camp and fed. Some had been twelve months in barracoons, loaded and unloaded from canoes when the slave-ships came but could not get through. At night, fires were lit on the islands and darting shapes emerged from the warehouses carrying their bundles. Shadowy canoes made for shore, low in the water beneath the loot. Spaniards, waiting out the British invasion inland, saw distant clouds of smoke and wept. Decades of hard, dangerous, lonely work on this wretched coast were being lost. Golden retirement was gone. Destitution approached.

On 21 November, King Siaka made his reluctant mark on the treaty, the slave trade in the Gallinas was formally abolished and Dombocorro emptied itself of its occupiers, their rescued slaves and a party of wretched whites. As Denman told Doherty, 'all confidence between the Spanish and the natives in the river must now be destroyed' and the factors, sure their former friends would kill them as soon as the British left, had begged safe passage out. Behind the departing British, Manna's people partied many miles into the interior with stolen rum, firing stolen muskets into the air and draping themselves in stolen cloth and bracelets.

Destruction on this scale had never been seen on the slaving coast. 'We earnestly hope', wrote the jubilant Sierra Leone commissioners to London, ramming home the point,

> that the good thus effected will be followed up in that manner which will secure for the cause of Africa all the advantages which prompt and judicious measures would obtain; and that we may not now be doomed to witness the revival of the odious traffic at the Gallinas, as was the case in the river Sherbro, after the total destruction of the trade there in the years 1825 and 1826, by the late lamented Governor Turner; when the re-establishment there of that trade might, by a comparatively small and well-applied expenditure, have been prevented.[10]

Within a few panicky days, wrote Théophile Conneau, 'the arbitrary proceedings of Captain Denman were known to all down the coast'.[11] News of the new severity travelled from factory to factory, and ship to ship: at Cape Mount, the Bights, Ouidah, past the Congo and down the long surfbound beaches of Angola, factors retreated into the jungle as local people made off with their property. On the island of Corisco, where a Spanish factory had fired on the boats of HMS *Wolverine*, bluejackets went ashore with Captain Tucker at their head. 'I come this day to destroy the Spaniard's houses,' he told the local leaders, but 'if you permit any people to fire at English men o'war's boats again, I will come and destroy your place too.'[12] Commander Hill of the *Saracen* sailed into the Shebar River and demanded Harry Tucker sign a treaty. When Harry Tucker refused, a party of *Saracen* seamen and marines landed and found a deserted slave-factory. Fifty armed blacks appeared from behind it. They had been slaves until a day or so ago, they said, held here; then they were given guns and told to fire on the British if they approached. Willingly they gave up their muskets and went down to the *Saracen* in the bay. The factory was burnt and the British left.

There were smoke and ashes on the coast that month. Looting parties came from the hinterland for their share of the goods turned over to them by the British. Bodies littered the beaches, unintended victims of the blockade turned out to die. The last few slavers gathered in armed compounds, waiting for ships from Havana to take them off.

For Captain Conneau, the unexpected willingness of Africans to attack their old partners was Denman's fault: he had turned over the loot of the Gallinas barracoons to Manna's people and made the plunder legitimate. Only one Krooman broke the silence to warn Conneau that the Sester chiefs, too, already baffled by his dealings with the British, planned to loot him before he abandoned them. All his servants deserted him, wrote Conneau, saddened by the infidelity; 'my own servant Lunes, the one I had taken to England, left me with the rest, carrying my double-barreled gun'.[13] Cannon were placed at the corners of his barracoons, the Union Jack was hoisted upside-down, a letter was sent to the *Termagant* and Commander Seagram scribbled quick orders for his first mate.

> You are hereby required and directed to take charge of the factory of Mr Théophile Conneau and protect it during the embarkation of his goods and property ... The natives are in no wise to be molested or interfered with unless they should openly attack you, when of course your endeavors must be used to repel them. At sunset a watch is to be set for the night, and the men mustered in their blankets or warm clothing. The Kroomen of the ship under your orders you will employ to assist in sending off the goods, and I have confidence in you to leave all unwritten orders to your judgement.

The British got to Conneau just in time. Prince Freeman's men were gathering to attack when the first boat landed and twenty-five marines marched up the beach. They took Conneau and all his goods off early the next morning and left as the first of the looters entered his abandoned factory.

Captain Conneau had cut his losses. 'Lieutenant Seagram', he would remember, had become 'now more friendly than ever'. Seagram was far from the first naval officer to fall for the charm of a well-spoken slaver who swore he had seen the light. He had offered not only a lift to Cape Mount but to 'preside at the intended purchase' of land, 'thus making the title more valuable to me', Conneau said, 'as the treaty would be signed and witnessed by a British Commander, while on the part of the natives, the epaulettes and sword of a Naval officer would give the affair more importance'.

Making north as the sun went down, there was a happy shout from the masthead and Conneau, who had been on the other end of the chase several times, was given the opportunity to watch one from the chaser's deck. 'Sail ho!' he said, 'is a magic word on a cruiser. Every man dropped his tin-can pot of tea to stretch his neck toward the desired object. Briefly a Petty Officer who had gone in the fore top with a telescope reported her to be a brig with raking masts and white sails, therefore she was pronounced a slaver.' But the breeze had died with the sun and neither ship moved during the long, hot night. 'From one end to the other', Conneau wrote, 'nothing was heard but their whispers, some praying for wind, others wishing for breeze, while the Commander, Doctor and Purser were mentally cursing the calm and their hard fate which deprived them of promotion and a large share of prize-money.'

At dawn, the prize came into view, becalmed some miles away. Three boats went down and shot away towards the slaver, all senior officers aboard them. Seagram had left the doctor and the purser in charge, recommending them 'to follow the boats in case the breeze should spring up, but recollecting that neither were sailors, he begged me', wrote Conneau, 'to point out the necessary manoeuvres in case of need'. From this unaccustomed position, Conneau saw his brother-slaver fire a blank gun to warn he would resist, and heard 'a faint hurrah from the boats, who now pulled with long steady stroke to the enemy'.

Smoke obscured the fight to those left aboard the *Termagant* and Conneau pondered the

> vicissitudes a man often encounters in a short time. Here I was, placed on the deck of a British armed brig with the trust of her maneuvers while in chase of a vessel who for what I knew then might have been consigned to me. Had she arrived twenty days sooner, I would probably have given her a full cargo of slaves. This day, circumstances had placed me in a position to assist in sinking [her] if necessary . . . [but] my heart rebuked me at the idea of taking arms against men who had perhaps broken bread at my table.

He did not have to. The British boats had been beaten off and were returning. Four men had been injured and three killed as the first two boats drew up either side of the slaver and attempted to board. The corpses falling back into the water overset the third, which drifted away and left her oarsmen struggling in the water. The slaver got away, picking up a lucky breeze, Conneau silently sending him good wishes.

They made Cape Mount the next day, Commander Seagram's head bound about in bandages. Here a river penetrated the coast, spreading 10 miles inland into a large and pretty lake. On its southern shore was Toso Town, home to King Fana-Toro, then aged 'seventy-seven rains'. The fertile headland between Toso and the sea was the land which Conneau wanted for his own. Fana-Toro and his son, known to Conneau as Prince Graye, were waiting for them. Witnessed by Commander Seagram, Assistant Surgeon Crawford and George D. Nobbs, 'Clerk in Charge', Conneau signed a 'title'.

'Know all these men by these presents', it ran – (six casks of rum, twenty muskets, twenty quarter-kegs of powder, twenty gallons of tobacco, twenty pieces of white cloth and twenty of blue, twenty iron bars, twenty cutlasses, twenty wash basins and 'twenty of many other trifling articles') – that 'all the lands under the name of Cape Mount' were assigned in perpetuity to Conneau and George Clevering Redman subject to the authority and dominion of her Majesty the Queen of Great Britain', along with 'the sole and exclusive right of traffic with my nation and people and with all those tributary to me'. Conneau called his estate New Florence, a homage to his birthplace. Commander Seagram would be reprimanded for his naïvety in putting his name to such a paper.

When Captain Conneau had sailed away and the rum from his storehouse ran out, Prince Freeman of New Sester was left wondering where he should next turn to secure his income, and the allegiance, status and power which went with it. The old persecutors seemed his obvious next patrons, swinging heavily in with new guns and new commerce to replace the old ones they had kicked out. Two months after Conneau left, Freeman signed his mark to an 'engagement' with Queen Victoria, represented by a naval officer temporarily turned diplomat, 'that the slave trade shall be at once and for ever abolished in the territory of New Cestros; that Englishmen may settle there for innocent trade; and that no white person resorting thither shall be harmed'.[14]

A few months later, 'Namar Commba, King of Cartabar in Gambia' also agreed that British ships might 'seize vessels or boats of Cartabar found carrying on the slave trade' and 'placed his country under [Queen Victoria's] protection'. King Bell of Bell Town and King Acqua of Acqua Town, both heavyweight slavers in Camaroon, negotiated a cannier treaty. 'In consideration of certain presents therein agreed to be made on the part of Her Majesty's Government annually for five years, there shall be an end of the Traffic in Slaves.' If they had got more out of abolition than Freeman and Namar Commba, they had also given more away. 'If it should at any time hereafter appear,' their treaties continued, 'that the Slave Trade contrary to Engagement exists in their territory, Great Britain will put it down by force.' The shape of the campaign's future was emerging in blunt words such as these, drafted by officers who presented their rough treaties beneath palm trees, appending signatures beneath some scratched cross by which the local chief promised – or so the officers hoped – to renounce the practice of generations.

On Christmas Day 1842, Governor Buchanan of Liberia wrote home. 'The most profound peace reigns still throughout the whole country adjacent to us; and as the slave trade is now shut out from Gallinas and New Cesters, we have a thousand miles of coast cleared of that most prolific cause of war, and may reasonably calculate on extending our peaceful influences during the next year more widely and successfully than ever.'

14

Commerce, Christianity and Civilisation

British public interest in the Preventive Squadron had been reawakened. Lord Palmerston's Portuguese Act had caused a furore and on its heels had come the scandal of American slavers detained by British ships. Finally, Captain Denman's triumphant actions in the Gallinas had reminded many that the Squadron was doing a noble job in Britain's name. Others, however, were reminded only that it was costing a great deal and provoking trouble with nations who might otherwise be friends and steady trading partners. Despite the successes of the late 1830s, a passionate public debate was under way by 1840 as to whether or not the Squadron should be withdrawn, and all its attendant expense of money and life be saved. Some said it had had no impact whatsoever on the volume of slaving, for this depended entirely on other factors, such as the price of sugar, cotton and coffee, measures taken by foreign governments to enforce their anti-slave-trade laws, and the fear in slave-owning societies of 'Africanisation'. Others disagreed, believing that slaving would reappear where it had been extinguished if British warships abandoned the African coast. No one, however, could argue that current preventative measures had fully worked. Despite all the efforts of the Squadron, the treaties, the 'extensions' of international law and the occasional collaboration of American, Portuguese and French warships, more Negroes were crossing the Atlantic now than before the trade had been banned. The question was: if the squadron, the bilateral treaties and the Mixed Commissions had not worked, where next should the campaign go?

White knowledge of the African interior, or at least of the coastal hinterlands, had increased since the Squadron was formed. The body of facts and impressions collected by explorers, missionaries, envoys and Liberated Africans had revealed a different character in the slave trade than the purely seaborne one ascribed it in 1819. A hundred tales had been told of the slave-raiding African chiefs who supplied the overseas markets and the endemic domestic slavery which facilitated their wars; of the Sokoto caliph whose system of plantation slavery rivalled that of Virginia and who stole the people of the Niger's upper reaches; of the man-eating, slave-slaughtering King of Dahomey, who terrorised the peoples of the river's lower waters; of the Fulani of Futa Jallon who supplied the Pongos and of the Mende who sent their captives to Siaka at the Gallinas.

Consensus was emerging that prevention must take precedence over cure and a new system must be found 'to arrest the Foreign Slave Trade in its source'.[1] These were the beliefs of both the leader of the ruling Whig party, Lord John Russell, and Thomas Fowell Buxton, the abolition movement's latest popular leader. Fowell Buxton had brought coherence, impetus and celebrity to the reviving public interest in the Squadron's campaign. He had lobbied vociferously for the abolition of slavery in the British colonies, made law in 1833, and acquired a large following. Tens of thousands had since read his book, *The African Slave Trade and its Remedy*, and meetings had been held around the country to discuss and petition for his plan. His thinking was this: that warships might harass and wound the buyers of slaves, but the trade would only be eradicated by forcing African suppliers to adopt the redemptive mores of Civilisation, Commerce and Christianity. The Squadron must be strengthened but the troops of the Lord must also be sent out to do their work. 'Let missionaries and schoolmasters,' Buxton said, 'the plough and the spade, go together, and agriculture will flourish; the avenues to legitimate commerce will be opened . . . civilisation will advance as the natural effect, and Christianity operate as the proximate cause of this happy change.' He had wanted a chain of British annexations from Mombasa round to the west coast, for only this, he thought, would force Africans to abandon the trade. This was vetoed, for it broke the first rule of British colonial policy: no expansion of territorial commitment. Instead, the government decided in 1840 to sponsor an expedition up the Niger, taking abolition to where the slave trade began: the raid and collection points far inside the continent.

The course of the Lower Niger had finally been confirmed in 1830 by

Richard Lander, returning to Africa with his younger brother John after the traumatic, first expedition from which he had returned alone. He and John had landed at Badagry, whose king they found more interested in the sacrifice of three hundred prisoners than the return of the man who had survived the gri-gri water, and set off on the 500-mile walk to Yauri, from where they would return downriver by boat to determine, once and for all, where the Niger met the sea. They canoed first to Rabba, where 'people stand gazing at us,' Richard noted with amusement, 'with visible emotions of amazement and terror; we are regarded, in fact, in just the same light as the fiercest tigers in England'[2] and onwards into storms, encounters with crocodiles and hippos and a sinister dwarf. But having survived one ambush, they fell to river-pirates who sold them to the King of the Eboes, who sold them on to the slave-dealer King Boy of Brass Town. Here they were treated barbarously: three days spent at the bottom of the royal canoe, footstools for Boy and his queen, before they sniffed salt in the air, felt the suck of the tide and realised they were reaching the sea. Richard Lander induced a British merchant captain to ransom them by promising he and John would work their passage away, replacing the many sailors sick or dead of malaria in the merchantman's crew. Despite this ignominious end, they had, finally, proved that the Niger flowed, through many mouths, into the Bight of Benin. Both Landers were now dead: John, of a disease contracted during his African adventure and Richard, of wounds received in an ambush on his last trip up the Niger in 1834.

This new geographical knowledge coincided with new technology. Steam had entered the Royal Navy and a slow programme of conversion was under way, with sailing ships being modified to carry engine rooms, coal bunkers and paddle-wheels. Steam was particularly suitable for small ships engaged on riverwork and coastal patrol, where deep keels were a hindrance, currents were difficult and winds capricious. It was ideal for West Africa, as long as enough coal depots could be established on the coast. Three new paddle-steamers were commissioned for the Niger Expedition, their construction and accommodation adapted for an equatorial river. They were flat-bottomed for shallow waters, but equipped with deep sliding keels which could be dropped into the hull at sea to stop their being blown across the surface of the water. Inside, iron partitions separated the accommodation into water-tight compartments in case the vessel grounded on rocks. Air was kept circulating through these by a cumbersome system of fans, worked by the engine when running and by hand when not, forced through an iron box on deck which

217

contained chemicals supposed to filter out 'miasmic gases' before it re-entered the ship.

Command of the new steamers went to Captain Henry Dundas Trotter, who had chased slavers on the West African coast seven years before; and the brothers William and Bird Allen. Their responsibility extended beyond naval duties, for they were also commissioners of Her Majesty, representatives of the young Queen Victoria as she extended the offer of friendship, trade and abolition, that holy trinity of African diplomacy.

'You will tell the Chief(s)', ran their instructions,

> that you are sent by the Queen of Great Britain and Ireland to express Her Majesty's wish to establish friendly relations with him; and to settle and agree with him for the extinction of the Foreign Traffic in Slaves in his dominions; and for the substitution instead thereof of a full and free intercourse and barter of all articles of innocent trade between the subjects of Her Majesty and those of such Chief, for his profit and advantage, and for the mutual use, comfort, and benefit of the subjects of both countries.[3]

They were to 'show to him'

> the advantages of putting down the Foreign Slave Trade, and of building upon the abolition a lawful and innocent trade. You will say to him, that his subjects will thereby be induced to cultivate the soil, to value their habitations, to increase their produce, and to behave well, in order to keep the advantage which that produce will give to them; that they will thus become better subjects, and better men, and that his possessions will thus become more full of what is valuable. You will impress upon him, that he himself will no longer need to make, or to keep up, quarrels with his neighbours, or to undertake distant and dangerous wars, or to seek out causes of punishment to his own subjects, for the sake of producing from the odious Trade in Slaves an income for himself. You will explain to him, that the people of his country will, out of the produce of labour in cultivating, gathering, and preparing articles for trade, bring to him more revenues, and be consequently more valuable to him.

They left England in April 1841 and entered the River Niger that August, hoping to offer their various inducements – education, trade, subsidy – to the chiefs of the delta in return for treaties, and reach Rabba before the water level started falling. 'We need not tell our readers', one German newspaper wrote,

> that the pretended object of this new and colossal enterprise of England is the abolition, or rather prevention, of the Slave Trade. But Europe is not to be cheated any longer by such pretexts . . . when events are ripe the mask will be thrown off, and the manufactures of those betrayed people [the Africans] will be immolated at the shrine of the Moloch of English commerce . . . it must be evident to every reflecting mind that Sierra Leone has been held solely as a stepping-stone to the conquest of Africa . . . young Englishmen are, under the pretext of love of adventure or antiquities, exploring every corner of the earth. [They] do not impose on us . . . why should young men who are not learned by profession consume their youth, their health and their fortunes, in hazardous expeditions from which they can derive nor expect personal benefit?[4]

They need not have worried.

In August, news reached the Squadron that Lord Palmerston had completely approved Commander Denman's attack on the Gallinas. He had announced it jubilantly in Parliament as vindication of the squadron whose cost and methods had been doubted by others, but never by him. Palmerston was sure Denman's methods were correct: 'taking a wasps' nest', he said, 'is more effective than catching wasps one by one'. He vigorously recommended to the Admiralty that similar operations 'should be executed against all the piratical slave establishments which may be met with on parts of the Coast not belonging to any civilised power'. What precisely the Squadron should do was left unclear in the usual confusion between Colonial, Foreign and Admiralty departments but Lieutenant Matson later explained how the new instructions were understood. 'Wherever we found slave barracoons erected', he said,

> we should endeavour to obtain the sanction of the native chiefs to destroy them; failing to obtain that consent we were in certain cases to do it without. However, it was never difficult to obtain that consent,

for it was always readily obtained for a very trifling subsidy . . . in every one of those treaties there was a stipulation that we were authorised to employ force, failing the execution of the treaty by the chief.[5]

Captain Tucker palavered with old King Peppel in the Bonny. In 1807, that king had threatened to seize all British ships in his waters. In 1823, he had told Commodore Mends he would outlaw the trade 'if the King of England would send him annually a seventy-four gun ship laden with goods'.[6] In 1841, he signed his mark 'that the Slave Trade shall be totally and for ever abolished' in his dominions. The price was a 'subsidy' from Great Britain of $10,000 per annum for five years. In New London, the Lawsons' compound at Little Popo, George Lawson's sons had forsworn the old trade and dealt only in the new, dragging their father reluctantly behind them. When Captain Tucker taxed George Senior, with shipping a cargo of slaves, he 'returned a submissive, and I must add a very proper answer, not denying the transaction alluded to, but promising faithfully for the future to abstain from exporting slaves'.[7] In December 1841, two of the major players on the Calabar, King Eyo and King Eyamba, also accepted a five-year pension from London, outlawed the external trade and empowered the Squadron to seize slave-ships in their waters.

Where the Squadron's approach to palaver differed from that of the Niger commissioners, now working their way upriver, was in its officers' readiness to blow up those who refused to accede to a treaty or later broke its terms. The Congolese and Angolan chiefs who received Lieutenant Matson were courteous, but under their protection eight thousand slaves each year left Cabinda alone and no treaty was forthcoming there. Marching through the jungle at the head of seamen and marines, Matson fell first on Cabinda, taking 1,075 slaves; and then on Ambriz, where he found another 240. £80,000 worth of goods were taken, and the barracoons were burnt to ash.

Only three vessels left Havana for Africa in 1842, and they, Matson wrote, were sent 'for the purpose of breaking up their establishments, and of bringing back whatever could be saved, either in goods or in slaves'.[8]

The Squadron's aggression had done enormous damage to life and property but the navy and its supporters thought this acceptable violence in the cause of abolition. 'I conceive', said Captain Denman, promoted for his work at the Gallinas, that the destruction of barracoons and slave places not in settlements belonging to European Powers would be justifiable all over the coast . . . upon the footing that the law of nations can afford no sort of recognition of the dealing in slaves by Spaniards in a foreign country. And secondly, that those persons were criminals by their own laws, and could not look for protection to their own government.[9]

This was dangerous reasoning and others saw things differently. The violence at Gallinas, Corisco and Cabinda was only one instance of a change of attitude noted in British officers patrolling in the early 1840s. The new hardline strategies inflamed old suspicions that Britain's 'humanitarian' operations were nothing of the sort: that blockade and treaty were not there to suppress the traffic in slaves, but to keep away other nations' merchant fleets. Previously, slavers had been deposited at British hospitals if injured, or returned to hosts who would give them a passage home: Governor Fereira at Principe or de Souza at Ouidah. Now, they were more commonly marooned on the nearest land, whatever their chance of survival. Captain Tucker, the most humane of officers to his own men, had no time for the sufferings of those whose cruelties, he thought, had put themselves outside that 'law of nations' to which Denman referred. 'They must bake their own bread,' he said. 'They know the risk and I have no compassion for them at all.'

In early 1841, when the coast was still traumatised by the Squadron's raids, a French merchant vessel put in at the Gallinas. No trade was possible, her captain said, 'inasmuch as the negroes of the country, being terrified by the threats used by the English, kept away'.[10] Sailing along the Gold Coast, he was surprised to see no 'native boats' putting out but learnt this was because 'for some time past, the British cruisers fired upon every boat they observed at sea, and that the negroes being terrified dared not appear. He claimed that the steamer HMS *Pluto* had entered the Gallinas just after he left, 'burnt and pillaged all the factories without distinction established on that point, and that afterwards to utilize the produce of their rapine, they had purchased 172 negroes'. This was a very twisted version of the real story: that Captain Blount had seen suspicious ships entering the Gallinas a few months after Denman's treaty was signed and found several factories operating upriver, armed and full of slaves. 159 captives had had the iron chains cut away from their necks by *Pluto* boilermen and the factories were burnt. But the French newspapers publishing the French captain's account did not know this, or did not publish it if they did, and French public opinion saw not suppression but bullying; not abolition but armed protectionism.

Certain British officers did not help their cause. Some, too long exposed to cynicism and brutality, regarded anyone on the slaving coast as unworthy of respect, let alone courtesy. Others simply had the Palmerstonian contempt for foreigners. When HMS *Cygnet* detained a French palm-oiler off Ouidah, her captain sent 'two men, without uniform', the French captain complained, 'in the costume of mechanics [who] instead of proceeding to search my ship, installed themselves in my cabin, and commenced a conversation with the passengers and crew'. Their manner of bringing him to had been unnecessarily aggressive, one of them was drunk and they refused to sign his journal, as required by treaty, confirming their search had turned up nothing. Another French captain complained that his ship was boarded by five boats of HMS *Madagascar*, bearing no flag. The British officer who came on deck was not in uniform, and his men 'carried off 20 tureens of preserved meat, and in fact everything they could lay their hands on'. The merchantman *Marabout* was treated worse: that ship was searched for four days, the captain claimed; his mate, stationed in the hold to prevent British sailors looting his cargo, 'was subject to every species of ill-treatment' and 'his crew remained during 23 days at the bottom of the hold of the English steamboat *Ardent*, on half allowance, and guarded by brutal soldiers, so that when [they] arrived at Cayenne it was difficult to recognise them'.

These tales were not just propaganda. 'Civility costs nothing', wrote an embarrassed British merchant resident on the coast, 'and would deprive foreigners of these eternal opportunities of insulting the service.' He had been asked by the Portuguese governor of Bissao to interpret for an officer of HMS *Brisk*.

The Governor of Bissao, Senhor Barretto, seeing an officer land from a boat with the British ensign and pendant, immediately put on his uniform to receive the visit; but seeing him enter the fort dressed in a pair of dirty blue trousers, a blanket coat, straw hat, with dirty shoes and stockings, he ordered the sentry to keep him at the door till he went and divested himself of his uniform, and put on his morning gown and slippers to receive him. [This] may serve as a hint to their superiors at home to enjoin a little more civility on the part of our officers in the discharge of their delicate duty on the Coast of Africa.[11]

There were too many other stories of disrespect and arrogance, and they were emerging as Anglo-French relations entered a delicate phase. The government which came in after France's 1830 revolution had conceded a mutual right of search in a treaty of 1832. It was to last ten years and when its expiry and replacement came before the French Chamber in 1841, there was a concerted attack on both previous and projected treaties. French seaports sent in their petitions, with lists of British insults and abuses; the newspapers were full of it; the Foreign Minister who argued for renewal was shouted down. Anglo-French disputes in Spain, Turkey and the Pacific heated the African debate and suppression of the slave trade became a pawn on a larger chessboard.

America, equally aggrieved by recent British aggression, had no treaty to renew. After the USS *Dolphin* and USS *Grampus* returned to the States, the British Squadron had continued to exercise a 'right of visit' on suspicious ships flying the American flag, insisting that there was a difference between this – boarding merely to ascertain nationality – and the 'right of search', which consisted of boarding to examine a ship's cargo and determine her destination. Americans did not agree, and continued to resent the intrusion. The accumulated grievances of the last decade burst out in the new: pushed forward, written up for pamphlets and fighting speeches, used by lobbyists and twisted by journalists, quoted in courts and chambers. Lieutenant Paine of the *Grampus* had urged official sanction for the co-operation he and Captain Tucker had found to be effective on the coast. Incorporated into a draft treaty, the idea was shouted down in the Senate. John Quincy Adams, who had secured the liberty of the *Amistad* Mendians and led the abolitionist campaign in Congress, stood to declare he would sooner go to war than recognise the principle of right of search by foreigners on American vessels, in whatever cause it might be carried out. No *Buzzards* would be tolerated in American harbours now. Heavy cannon were drawn up to the docks of New York lest they should be needed for any sudden (by implication, British) attack from the sea.

A scandal was developing in London that would fuel French and American hostility. If the Squadron represented official British condemnation of the slave trade, the trial of Pedro Juan Zulueta proved – to the gross embarrassment of the government – that British complicity still thrived; proof, said

223

the campaign's opponents with savage glee, that the British should set their own house in order before they interfered in anyone else's.

HMS *Saracen* had re-entered the Gallinas in early 1841, a few months after Captain Denman thought he had closed the estuary to slaving, and found Mr Clevering's *Gil Blas* and a second, more familiar vessel at anchor. She was now called the *Augusta*, but Commander Hill had previously known her as the *Golupchick*, sailing under Russian papers, and had sent her to Britain for investigation. There, the ship had been put up for sale by the Russian consul and bought by a British captain, Thomas Jennings, previously in the employ of the well-known slaver Pedro Martinez of Cadiz. Martinez was an associate of both Pedro Blanco and the equally notorious slaver Julian Zulueta of Havana. These three formed a tight-knit and mutually supportive group, represented in Britain by Julian's uncle and cousin, who ran a shipping agency in the City of London. Captain Jennings had acted on the Zuluetas' behalf in the purchase of the *Augusta*, then sailed in her to collect goods – cottons, muskets, tobacco and gunpowder – from one of Pedro Martinez's suppliers in Liverpool and gone to the Gallinas to deliver them.

In October 1843, Pedro Juan Zulueta, Junior, representative of the London firm, stood trial at the Central Criminal Court in London, accused of 'sending out a vessel for the purpose of trading in slaves'. Commander Hill of the *Saracen* and other Squadron officers had been summoned as witnesses for the prosecution and in the very hostile, sometimes insulting, questioning to which Hill was subjected, he remained unequivocal in his belief that the *Augusta* had been involved in slaving. To his personal knowledge, he said, Pedro Blanco had for years been African agent for Zulueta & Co. of London, drawing drafts on them which were 'current all along the coast'.[12] The *Augusta* had not been equipped for slaves when detained, but, Hill said, it would take 'a very short time' to fit her at the Gallinas: 'they may send out the water casks filled with water in two or three canoes; and if they do not choose to lay down a slave deck, they put mats upon the casks . . . they may embark 500 slaves in a couple of hours or upwards and be off.' Even if Jennings had not been planning to ship slaves, his cargo must have been intended for their purchase because although 'at most places on the coast there is both a lawful trade carried on and the slave trade, the Gallinas is an exception, the only exception I know, indeed; I know that from my own personal presence on the spot'. Other officers agreed. There was, they said, categorically, no trade but the slave trade in the Gallinas. 'The general course', said Colonel Nicholls, flatly, 'is to barter British manufactured goods for slaves.'

Yet Zulueta was found not guilty, for the evidence against him was circumstantial. Nothing could prove absolutely that the *Augusta*'s was a 'slaving adventure'. Officers' statements about there being no other trade at the Gallinas could not be taken as conclusive evidence of that fact; nor, if they could, that Zulueta was aware of it. The raking-up of material continued for two years, and incriminated – though not sufficiently for conviction – a shadowy army of Zuluetas and Cleverings: wealthy, respectable British merchants, bankers, lawyers and insurers involved in slaving. As Zulueta's own lawyer pointed out, it was not up to his client, as shipping agent, to enquire 'whether the persons to whom the articles were consigned ever traded in slaves'. Were such questions asked, 'it would annihilate one-third of the commerce of Great Britain'.[13]

For any who wanted to discredit the Squadron's campaign, here was ammunition. Which represented Britain's real wishes and interests, they asked, Squadron or City? Was the Squadron a feint, the government cynically offsetting the deaths of British seamen against the gains of British commerce? These were the bitterest of waters, and information flowed in that they were lapping happily at British feet elsewhere. The American minister in Rio, operating at the other pole of decency from Nicholas Trist, was sending reports to his own government not only of American involvement in slaving there, but of British capital and goods. The same depressing information came from Her Majesty's commissioners in Cuba. When the African Institution, an abolitionist charity, mounted its own investigation, it found that slave-collars and shackles were manufactured in Birmingham; that British guns were fired in the slave wars; and that Manchester and Glasgow exported £500,000-worth of trade goods each year. And when a Spanish slaver was reportedly supplied at Cape Coast Castle 'by a British Merchant, a Magistrate, with some of the Goods, not equipments, requisite for carrying on her unlawful Traffic', the Colonial Office demanded an explanation from the governor there. His reply was blunt and alarming. 'It is perfectly true', wrote Governor Maclean,

> and I have stated the fact at least fifty times in my official correspondence, that slave vessels (that is, vessels destined to convey cargoes of slaves from the leeward coast) do frequently anchor both here and at

Accra. But has Her Majesty's Government ever invested the authorities here with power to interfere with such vessels? We are neither at war with Spain, Portugal nor Brazil: by what authority, upon what pretext, then, could I prevent vessels belonging to those countries from anchoring at any of our ports?[14]

Commissioners of Inquiry had already visited the Gold Coast in February 1841 but their report had been deemed too damaging to be made public. Commissioner Madden named two large British firms as 'constantly employed' in the traffic: Zulueta & Co; and Forster & Smith, one of whose scions was Matthew Forster, MP, assiduous sitter on Parliamentary Select Committees, including that set up to examine the commissioners' own evidence.

Amid the growing governmental and public unease over covert British involvement, and a flood of complaints from French and American envoys that the Squadron regularly exceeded its orders, Lord Palmerston's Whig government was replaced by the Tories. The Foreign Office went to Lord Aberdeen, a more cautious man than Palmerston, and one with qualms about the legality of Admiralty instructions authorising the Squadron to destroy slave factories. Could it be proved that the 'trade goods' warehoused there were intended for the purchase of slaves, and no other, legitimate, commerce? The Attorney-General, like the judge in the trial of Pedro Juan Zulueta, believed the Squadron's evidence was not absolute proof of this, and his deliberations returned him to a larger question left uneasily pending by court decisions taken and reversed, actions justified and rebutted, damages given and withheld for decades: that of the justification – under British, 'international' or any other law – of carrying out independent operations on the territory of other powers, in this case that of the African chiefs. In February 1842, the triumphantly successful strategy of Denman, Matson and Palmerston was, in effect, pronounced illegal when the Attorney-General reported that he could not 'take upon himself to advise' that all the Squadron's operations were 'entirely justifiable'.

Blockading rivers, landing and destroying buildings, and carrying off persons held in slavery in countries with which Great Britain is not at war, cannot be considered as sanctioned by the law of nations; or by the provisions of any existing treaties . . . however desirable it may be to put an end to the slave trade, a good, however eminent, should not be attained otherwise than by lawful means.

Admiralty instructions, he said, must be changed.

Her Majesty's naval officers employed in suppressing the slave trade should be instructed to abstain from destroying slave factories and carrying off persons held in slavery, unless [the local powers] should by treaty with Great Britain or by formal written agreement with British officers, have empowered Her Majesty's naval forces to take those steps.

A failure of nerve or a scrupulous adhesion to the law of nations? That question resounds down the decades but there was no doubt about the reception on the African coast of the publication of the Attorney-General's conclusions, closely followed by Zulueta's acquittal: the Squadron had been disowned by its own government.

Wild rumours swept the African coast, Lieutenant Matson recalled, 'that the people had risen and obliged the Queen to turn out Lord Palmerston, because he wished to suppress the slave trade; that there was now a revolution going on in England to oblige the Queen to carry on the slave trade'.[15] Where they had been destroyed, the factories were resurrected; new palings laced with wattle springing up to house captives being brought again to the coast and trade cargoes being sent again from Bahia, Havana and Manchester. As the traffic regained the status it had enjoyed before Denman's attack on the Gallinas, vulnerable only at sea, African landlords thought again. 'Before I left the coast,' Matson said, 'in the beginning of 1843, the vessels were beginning to come over full of [trade] goods, and the very same men that had left the coast of Africa the year before I met returning from Brazil – men I was very well acquainted with, and who had relinquished hope of carrying on the slave trade.' By the end of the year, 'every factory in the Gallinas had been restored and was in active operation'.

In London, lawyers acting for the Spaniard Tomás Burón served a writ for trespass on Captain Denman. Burón was the owner of a factory in the Gallinas at which he claimed to have been 'lawfully possessed of certain slaves, goods, chattels, effects . . . to wit, 4000 slaves, of great value, to wit, of the value of £100,000, and of divers goods, chattels, effects' (their value put at £370,000) which Captain Denman had 'with force of arms, seized, took, and carried away'. He wanted compensation.

The Niger Expedition had also failed to withstand its various trials. Despite the precautions taken with the three paddle-steamers' design and equipment, they could not beat the climate. They had spent only two months in the river and the only solid achievement was to found a Model Farm 100 miles upriver. This was placed under Sierra Leonean superintendents who were to cultivate it while spreading the word and the faith and the British had continued into mounting ill-health. First to turn back, on 19 September, was the *Wilberforce*, for so many of her men were sick she was 'more like a hospital', wrote one missionary aboard, 'than a man-of-war'.[16] Captains Henry Trotter and Bird Allen went on, despite rising sick-lists, and reached Egga, where they found 'fifteen human beings exposed to sale': not to the white man, but to Africans of other tribes, for this was 'country where the influence of Islam was strong, and where slavery was an intertribal system, almost entirely without connexion with the white merchants on the far-distant coast'. They, too, turned back here, for not enough men were fit for service to take the ships any further. More sickened as they made their slow way back past the mudbanks, until neither captain could leave his bed and when the *Albert*'s engines stopped, there were no mechanics well enough to start them again. The expedition's botanist read the manuals and got them working after a fashion, and they bumped and drifted downriver with one officer fit enough to command. Even he had gone down with malaria when they reached the bar, and the surgeon commanded the Kroomen as they manoeuvred her roughly over it. Two months after they had entered the ghastly river, they returned to the relative safety of the sea.

15

Palaver and Presents

The early 1840s were the lowest point of the Squadron's six-decade campaign. Ill-will and cynicism surrounded it. There had never been effective support for its work from abroad but now there was outright hostility, and even support in Britain was wavering. Legal judgments and the fear of personal liability had banned the Squadron from aggressive operations on land, unenforceable treaties restricted its actions at sea, and its men were attacked by those whom they thought they had come to save. A few slave-ships were still taken, a few foreign officers defied their national stereotype and seemed genuinely interested in the cause, but the only strategies, if they could be called that, which had had even limited success were bribery and blockade. There seemed nothing else. The ships again rolled interminably at anchor, their men sick and frustrated, and again, suffering slaves were amassed in barracoons on shore. Now, added to the taunts of other nations that their work was a cynical shield for profit, the Squadron had the dismal knowledge that it was hurting the people it was supposed to protect.

'We increase the hardships of those run in the slavers', one officer wrote angrily home,

> and we besides land and attack and kill the black inhabitants themselves on the coast. For what? Because they will sell each other; those taken in their petty and eternal wars, or kidnapped, &c. Is not this horrible? But so it is and we are doomed to do these things by the

canting and ranting of the [abolitionists]! Every one of those Mawworms [hypocrites] should be sent out here to man the squadron. We should then see what would become of their egregious philanthropy.[1]

A famous, much-reproduced diagram of slave-stowage for the Middle Passage had shocked many people into joining the anti-slave-trade campaign, that such horrors might no longer pollute Christian nations. Now, forty years after the British and American abolition Acts, conditions were worse. 'In a space which a moderate sized French bedstead would occupy', a visitor to Freetown wrote,

I have seen 45 unhappy wretches packed, without regard to age or constitution, like herrings in a barrel. I saw them fed after they had been captured. On a shell about the size of a half crown piece was deposited a pinch of salt, for which a father and four children contended, each endeavouring to scramble a portion to eat with his rice. I have seen four children packed in a cask that I thought it impossible to contain one.

Slaver crews could no longer be marooned wherever the British wished. Some had to be kept for the passage to Sierra Leone in order to stow the slaves at night.

Our men are not sufficiently skilful to do this; I am told long practice is required. At the spot we are now blockading about 3,000 slaves have been collected by the agents for exportation, but the difficulties to get them away have been so great, that few have been known to be shipped for 12 months. Provisions have been exhausted, and dreadful expedients, if report be true, have been resorted to for subsistence. Among others, and the least revolting, is driving them into the woods every morning, like herds of swine, to pick berries. Again the slavers are obliged to make the most of the slightest opportunity that offers. Frequently the heavy surf on the open coast beach prohibits the passage of ship's boats, and sometimes also the native canoes; when this occurs, and the slaver is anxious to run his cargo, the unfortunate devils are dragged through the surf to the boats, anchored outside by lines attached to their persons. Men, women and children are served in this way; you may imagine what numbers must be drowned in such an operation. Prior to our interference, they could not afford to trifle with their lives in this way, as the supply equalled the demand; prices were low, and it was an object with the slaver to preserve all his cargo; the loss of a few slaves carried off the cream of his profits. Now a few survivors will give a handsome return.

There was one way out of the impasse in which the Attorney-General's judgment had placed the Squadron. As when 'unlawful force' had been outlawed in 1817, diplomacy moved laboriously but legally to take its place: if the British could not blow up foreign nationals' property, then African landlords must be induced, or bound, to ask the British to do it for them. It was the equivalent essential component in African treaties to the right-of-search in those with Europeans, and it was similarly slow and expensive to achieve.

Knowledge of how coastal African societies worked, and regulated their dealings with trading partners in the interior, had increased since the early days and it was those officers who appreciated the complex position of the coastal chiefs who were most successful in negotiations. In 1845, a shrewd and enquiring commander joined the Sierra Leone Division. Frederick Forbes had the reputation of being an intellectual among officers. He was interested in African languages, writing a monograph for the Royal Society on that of the Vai people of the Gallinas, and equally so in African manners and mores. He kept a journal during his years on the coast, distilled into a book on his return to Britain: *Six Months' Service in the African Blockade*; and he studied the customs which bound the chiefs, brokers and suppliers whom he met at palaver. Like Lieutenant Matson, Forbes appreciated the pressures on local rulers of peoples for whom slaving was not just any species of commerce, replaceable by any other. It was an old, semi-sacred custom and as such 'must be kept up, however much . . . disliked by the chief. The king is married into every family of note in his kingdom and cannot perform any national act without collecting the whole of the heads of these to "palaver"; and should he neglect to do so, or alter any established rule of the country, he is almost certain to perish for his temerity.'[2]

Despite all the setbacks and misunderstandings, treaties were still being negotiated, signed and sometimes even observed. In the River Cameroon, the kings Bell and Acqua had promised in 1842 to outlaw the slave trade. When HMS *Kite* arrived in June 1843, Captain Pasco was satisfied they had kept their word. That year's presents were therefore distributed as specified:

Calico, East Indian blue: 3,000 yards in 3 bales
Flints, musket: 2,000 in 2 casks
Muskets with bayonets and rammets: 720 in 6 cases
Coats, scarlet: 2
Swords with velvet scabbards: 2
Epaulettes, gold: 4
Belts, sword, crimson leather: 2
Case tin: 1
Rum, barrels of: 8
Powder, barrels of: 4

and the kings put in their request for next year's:

1 frame house, 2 bedsteads and beds, 2 easy chairs, 2 glass chandeliers, 2 mirrors, 2 hand organs, 2 blue frock coats, VR on buttons, 2 hats, gold band and binding, 4 pairs of trousers, 6 shirts, 2 pairs red boots, 2 large umbrellas, 2 British ensigns marked 'King Acqua', 6 small kegs of different coloured paints.[3]

'We visited all the ports in the Bight of Benin', another seaman recalled:

the Gold and Ivory Coasts, Accra and Cape Coast Castle. Sometimes we would have three or four black kings on board a day, signing Treaties; we would dress ship with flags and give them all a gun salute. The Captain used to send a message to the officers' messes and mess-decks that a black king was coming onboard and they should lock up all their valuables. They would come off in their state canoes, some with more than forty paddles, and tom-toms beating. Each was given a Purser's No. 2 jacket with a crown and anchor badge sewn on the left breast. They were served with a bottle of rum and biscuits.[4]

Some in the Squadron thought it all a waste of time. Henry Huntley, now governor of Prince Edward's Island, was scornful of the whole enterprise. He thought the treaties were expensively made and routinely broken. Others disagreed. 'An African chief is not, as is generally supposed in this country', wrote Lieutenant Matson,

> a kind of 'King of the Cannibal Islands', delighting in human sacrifices, and all that sort of thing; he is, generally speaking, a humane, shrewd and intelligent man. I have visited King Boy in the Nun, King Peppel in the Bonny, Duke Ephraim in the Old Calabar and the Chief of Benin, whose name I forget; and I could but admire, in most cases, the propriety of their conduct. I lived for a week in the house of King Bell in the Cameroons, and saw nothing that would shock the most fastidious taste, except perhaps the first day, when the soup was served in a utensil the proper use of which His Majesty did not know, but which was by far the most splendid thing of the kind I ever saw.[5]

Extending the treaty network to cover the whole coast would take years of tooth-gritting and persuasion. When first word spread of the new British tactic, many African rulers saw it more as a way to earn a quick dollar than as the basis for long-term collaboration. When a chief in the New Calabar was told a Spanish slaver had been taken leaving his river with 152 slaves aboard and the British would now like him to sign an abolition agreement, he 'very candidly stated that he would like it better to allow the slaver to enter, and for him to arrange with the man of war to take her on leaving and pay him a commission'. This was not allowed; when the British official insisted he give up slaving, the chief said he would 'sign book for that palaver' if he could get 'presents same as several of the other kings in the other rivers'.[6]

In these early years, few of the treaties lasted long. Some chiefs accepted their 'present' but never intended to keep their word. Others were dissuaded from renewal by their sub-chiefs or foreign tenants and slaving would re-emerge where it had been thought suppressed. The Chief of Ambriz refused his second year's subsidy from Captain Foote.

> I have to inform you that you can send for your goods, and that I feel myself very much obliged but will not accept your presents, for such is the will of my people, and also because I have been made poor by the

King of England and consequently I can use very well my slaves. You can accordingly send for your presents, as I will not receive presents from you who are not a friend of the Negroes and will not consequently give you ivory as I do to the Portuguese.

PS I send you two pigs for your dinner.[7]

At New Florence, Théophile Conneau was also experiencing the wrenching, braking, infuriating unwillingness of African partners to follow him into the new era. He had wanted to establish a farm to provide fresh meat and vegetables to passing shipping but it was not easy. Chiefs were not eager to befriend a factor who did not offer a cut in the profit of slaving, but the slower, smaller rewards of cattle, rice, fruit and oil. Conneau hired forty slaves for 20 cents per day and their food 'from the king and the neighbouring Chiefs' but they did not like the work of felling trees and clearing ground and disappeared into the bush. 'On remonstrating with the King on the indolence of his bondsmen, his answer was that white men were fools to pretend [i.e. demand] that a man should work from sunrise to sunset, and that every day. He said that was not Black men's fashion.'[8] Two other sources of labour presented themselves, and Conneau decided to tap them both. According to him, Commanders Seagram and Tucker had put in his head the idea for the first strategy. It was legal, but impudent.

'My Lord', he wrote, for this important letter with New Florence at its head was addressed to Lord Stanley, Secretary of State for the Colonies in London. Its gist was this: that M. Conneau would be very grateful if Lord Stanley could see his way to sending over one hundred Liberated African apprentices to clear his land, gratis. As a convert to abolition, with the friendship of British naval officers and the Union Jack flying hopefully from a palm tree on his premises, he was surely a worthy recipient. Waiting for a reply, he turned to the second. 'I left a man in charge of my hut to continue the labours, and I returned to Monrovia.'

Once Conneau had been banned from Liberian territory – although his dollars had always entered where he did not – but since his conversion to legal trade, he had become an honoured guest. He now lived only 70 miles from Monrovia and had been allowed to warehouse there the goods brought by the *Termagant* from New Sester. Two Negroes had also been 'secured by the Court as my apprentices'. What he needed was a vessel to trade along the coast, and in Monrovia he found, again, the carpenters, sawyers and blacksmiths to help him. A 25-ton cutter was quickly built, launched and courteously named the

Termagant. He returned to New Florence aboard her with stores, several 'mechanics' willingly embarked and a posse of labourers came aboard less freely: 'by force of double pay,' he explained, 'several natives sent on their domestics and inferior relations to give the finishing stroke to New Florence'. Soon his new, legitimate business was up and running. Within a fortified compound, several acres of crops had been planted. Over one hundred Africans sowed, carried and laboured. The large cool pens (which some visiting officers thought looked suspiciously like barracoons) were warehouses, he said, and they stood full. 'Native brokers' had been sent inland to advertise European goods in return for cattle, palm oil, camwood, ivory and hides. A pilot was employed to sail in the offing and alert passing vessels to the existence of a new establishment providing vegetables, fresh meat and hospitality.

Seaborne trade kept Conneau going during the first months of his new business. 'On the arrival of every war vessel, my boat boarded her offering my services and inviting the officers on shore. My offers were generally kindly received, and while I enjoyed the luxuries of their company, I reaped a liberal profit in furnishing the Pursers with fresh provisions and the ward room with small stores.' Officers would land for a day's shooting (boar was plentiful there), admire the lettuce in Conneau's garden, for this was a novelty on the coast and he was immensely proud of it; stay for dinner and perhaps the night, drinking, playing cards and talking over old adventures. Landside trade was not so good, for war had broken out between two of the larger towns of the hinterland and this had brought 'a perfect stagnation in the country trade'. Who would deal in rice and yams, or send their 'bondsmen' to work in Conneau's fields, when there was war to fight and prisoners to sell? The blow which most damaged this first experiment in legal trade, however, came from Conneau's new friends the British. 'I have to acquaint you,' wrote Governor Macdonald from Freetown, rather coldly, that Lord Stanley 'cannot sanction a compliance with your request to have a number of liberated Africans as apprentices in tilling your grounds, and further that he could not recognise the purchase of Cape Mount as placing that district under the protection and sovereignty of the British Crown'.

Conneau was furious. He had 'been flattered into the belief', he said, that Britain was now on his side, and he was to be rewarded for his actions by certain privileges. 'For the first time, I repented the confidence I had placed in the expectations and assistances promised by the officers of the squadron'. The 'English Jack' was petulantly hauled down, never to be saluted by me again, and in my fit of vexation, even the palm tree was chastised to the roots. The next day, a new pole commanding the full view of the harbour was erected, and there I hoisted a large tricol-ored banner with a white star in the center, which I caused to be saluted in presence of the King with a salvo of 20 guns from my eight cannons.

Walking the fertile shores of his lake, he decided he would not give up farming just yet. Agricultural tools were ordered from Britain, and 'forty youths' purchased. He would continue to grow coffee, and if it was slave labour which produced it, then on Lord Stanley's English head be it.

With attacks on slave-trading factories vetoed, it had become vital not only to urge treaty on African leaders but to return to the old, tired work of restraining their customers. Despite years of work, the international network of obligations and concessions was incomplete: as soon as one hole was stitched over, some international set-to or change of government seemed to rip another piece apart. In 1842, a new treaty with Portugal ratified what Lord Palmerston had unilaterally ordered in 1839. Progress had been made the same year with France when Lord Aberdeen had, to the Squadron's disgust, admitted that British ships had exceeded their powers on the west coast of Africa and, for this concession, France agreed to deploy her own Preventive Squadron: twenty-six vessels stationed between Cape Verde and southern Angola to search French shipping.

However, negotiations with the Americans proved, again, most disappointing. Like France, America had not only a history of grievance with Britain but several current points of disagreement, each of them bleeding into the others. Mutual efforts to suppress illegal slaving were bottom of the American list. Nonetheless, British envoy Lord Ashburton and American Secretary of State Daniel Webster managed to sign a treaty in August 1842. Ashburton's breakthrough was due to two new elements entering the negotiations: the first was courtesy, which had not been Palmerston's strongest point; the second was an offer from London to pay compensation in the case of ships which were detained and then proved not to have been involved in slaving. Britain and America therefore agreed

that each shall prepare, equip, and maintain in service, on the coast of Africa, a sufficient and adequate squadron, or naval force of vessels, of suitable numbers and descriptions, to carry in all not less than eighty guns, to enforce, separately and respectively, the laws, rights and obligations of each of the two countries, for the suppression of the Slave Trade.

Secretary Webster had asked the commanders of the USS *Dolphin* and USS *Grampus* to make recommendations for the squadron's deployment and they knew that two squadrons working separately would accomplish only a fraction of what two working together might achieve. They recommended that about fifteen small, fast ships be deployed and that they cruise in company with the British. Commander Paine also urged that his agreement with Captain Tucker be adopted: the mutual 'right of visit', to allow officers to board each others' vessels merely and exclusively to ascertain their nationality. The grievances of the past were too strong: the suggested clause was struck from the agreement. The squadrons were 'to be independent of each other' although orders should be given to the commanding officers to 'enable them most effectually to act in concert and cooperation, upon mutual consultation, as exigencies may arise, for the attainment of the true object of this article'. For the officers who had to interpret this temporising guff, what exactly they were supposed, or allowed, to do was as unclear as it had always been: what were exigencies, what was the 'true object', what happened if they disagreed during 'mutual consultation'? Commodore Foote of the British squadron must simply hope his opposite number was as reasonable as Commander Paine.

He was, in fact, the same Matthew Calbraith Perry who had cruised off Africa twenty years ago, then a lieutenant, now a commodore, and he had not changed his views. 'I cannot hear', he said, 'of any American vessel being engaged in the transportation of slaves, nor do I believe there has been one so engaged for several years.'[9] As far as he was concerned, he had been sent to suppress a non-existent trade, and his instructions, bluntly disregarding the 'true object' as understood by Lord Aberdeen and Lieutenant Paine, echoed this belief:

1. You are charged with the protection of legitimate commerce.
2. While the United States wishes to suppress the slave-trade, she will not admit Right of Search by foreign vessels.
3. You are to arrest slavers.
4. You are to allow in no case an exercise of the Right of Search or any great interruption of legitimate commerce.

The flagship given Perry for his first cruise was the frigate *Macedonian*, which, like the *Cyane*, had been captured in the war of 1812. A new treaty was all very fine, but let no one get carried away with ideas of collaboration. Instead of the recommended fifteen schooners, he was given two sloops of war and one brigantine. None was particularly unsuited to African conditions – no more so than the British vessels, at least – and they made up the stipulated minimum of eighty guns, but there were four of them to the British Squadron's twelve. Given this disparity in numbers, joint patrol was already difficult and Commodore Perry did all in his power to render it impossible, ordering his ships to cruise in convoy and choosing as his headquarters the Cape Verde Islands, some thousand miles from where an American presence was most needed. From this far northern base, his ships would occasionally put out together, visit Liberia, and return. Little wonder they did not take a single slave-ship, although they did blow up two 'native towns' implicated in violence to American merchants.

The Portuguese squadron kept south of the Line but the French and American squadrons, when they left the shelter of the Cape Verde islands, cruised the waters off Cape Mount and Liberia and, given the new spirit of collaboration and the old paucity of social opportunities, some fraternisation did take place. Strained dinners were held on board each other's ships or at the few areas of hospitality on the coast: Government House in Freetown or Liberia; the odd French or British merchant in the delta; the houses of lonely consuls and the verandahs of such as de Souza or Théophile and Rosalie Conneau. An American officer in Perry's squadron described one of these occasions.

> Dined on shore. Our captain and five officers, the master and surgeon of an English merchantman, and the captain of the French schooner, were of the party. It was a pleasant dinner. The conversation turned principally upon the trade and customs of the coast. The slave-trade was freely discussed; and the subject had a peculiar interest, under the circumstances, because this identical Frenchman, at table with us, is suspected to have some connection with it.[10]

That officer was cynical about the international campaign to suppress the trade and, in particular, its principal promoter. 'It is difficult to give unlimited faith to the ardent and disinterested desire professed by England', he wrote, 'to put a period to the slave-trade. If sincere, why does she not, as she readily might, induce Spain, Portugal, and Brazil, to declare the traffic piratical?' He was clearly unaware that Brazil had declared the trade piracy in 1826, so little effect had the declaration had; and had forgotten that though it had been piracy in America itself for two decades, not one American slaver had been hanged. Nor did the French and American officers confine their criticisms to British strategy off West Africa. Why should other nations believe the Royal Navy was deployed in the service of philanthropy here when it was blatantly deployed in the service of profit off, for example, Canton and India? The fragmented, inconsistent nature of pressure exerted elsewhere by Britain did not support her claims of disinterested action here.

Matters were not helped by a new scheme in operation at Sierra Leone. Slavery had been abolished thoughout the British Empire in 1834. It had not died a sudden death, however, but passed into a state of lingering degeneration. The British, alarmed by the prospect of an enormous, 'uncivilised' and newly free population, had converted their slaves to 'apprentices' and, as the scheme was largely in the hands of the new apprentices' former owners, it was open to obvious abuse. Still there were not enough hands to work the colonial plantations and in 1844, agencies were established at Sierra Leone to supply 'free labour' to British Guiana, Trinidad and Jamaica. Liberated Africans arriving off the ships which brought them in were offered the alternatives: they could stay in Sierra Leone, with the government stipend of 6d per day until they were established; or they could go to the West Indies to earn larger wages, with the option of returning when their contract expired. It was euphemistically called 'free emigration'. Among the first 250 'volunteers' were 76 just taken off a slave-ship, who were not even given the option of remaining in Freetown.

Any British round the dinner table could reply in similar wounding vein to such criticisms, however, for in the time it took Perry's squadron to capture not a single slaver, the British detained nearly one hundred. 'It is well,' wrote the same American officer defensively,

> that the public should be prepared for an inefficiency which can hardly fail to continue. . . . The French, like ourselves having no reciprocal treaties . . . are equally unsuccessful in making prizes. Eleven of their

vessels of war were stationed on the coast, during the period of our cruise, but effected not a single capture. England, by virtue of her treaties with the three nations above mentioned, empowers her cruisers to take slave-vessels under either of their flags. Hence the success of the English commanders; a success which is sometimes tauntingly held up, in contrast with what is most unjustly termed the sluggishness of our own squadron.

Collaboration was not much easier with the French, who were equally suspicious of British motives. Hostility was mutual: some British officers believed the French were there only to protect French trade, even, perhaps, the French slave trade. 'French co-operation,' one said drily, 'crippled us in all directions.' There was also a difficulty unpredicted in London but tricky to negotiate on the coast. The commodore

is almost the only officer among us who can speak French intelligibly or speak it at all; which makes our intercourse with the French ships of war here very awkward . . . a set of nods, winks, shrugs and friendly signs and grimaces – often a mere pantomime. This is laughable enough, but a real drawback to our thorough liking or understanding of each other. So, too, are we very shy of at all meddling with vessels hoisting French colours and let them pass . . . So that this fine laissez-aller complaisance increases the thousand chances of impunity and the running of slaves occurs as much as ever . . . with all our waste of life and waste of resources in the keeping up of this detestable force![11]

Frustration in the Squadron was worsened by the suspicion that its own government was not giving the support it should. Lord Palmerston was still out of office and his successors had a less muscular approach to foreign sensibilities. Palmerston's 1839 Act would be out of the question now; indeed, so far had the pendulum swung that the government seemed more protective of other countries' feelings than of its own seamen's welfare. *The Times*, although no fan of the African blockade, wrote disapprovingly of 'the policy, rather prevalent at the present day, of conciliating our foes by the sacrifice of our friends – a kind of ultra-fairness, which looks not to what is really just to all parties, but to what will appear just to those who are disposed to quarrel with us'.[12]

In 1844 Lieutenant Gray of HMS *Bonetta* stopped and boarded a vessel flying a French flag but which he believed to be a Brazilian he had been seeking for some days. She was not that Brazilian, but she was equipped for slaving; he did not detain her, as he explained to Commodore Foote, as he was not authorised to do so by the agreement with France. He, Foote and the rest of the Squadron were astonished when, on complaint from Paris, Gray was summoned before a court martial and found guilty of 'disobedience of orders' for stopping the ship at all. Professional collaboration, let alone harmony at the dinner table, was difficult in these conditions. The morale of the Squadron had never been lower.

New Florence was not flourishing as Conneau had hoped. The 'American colored man' whom he had appointed to oversee the slaves growing coffee had treated them so ill that several had run away and the land was neglected, but this was not why his fortunes were failing. 'On my first arrival,' he wrote, 'I had formed an idea that I could in one or two years open trade with the Interior.'[13] It had not been possible. 'The slave traffic only was thought of by the natives, and the little produce that is food in the vicinity was only brought down when slaves were sent to the beach.' Furthermore, the gold, ivory, wax, hides and tea which Conneau had imagined would be traded to the coastal tribes of Cape Mount by those further inland never came: the trade between them was in slaves, and slaves only. He had not yet given up on the farmer's life, but was adding to it another business, finding, he said enigmatically, that 'it was easier to plow the ocean than the land'. The handiest slaves were taken off the farm and with '20 large boys', Conneau laid out a shipyard, sawpit and blacksmith's shop. Three Monrovians were employed to run these three departments. One was a man reported to have Cherokee Indian as well as African blood, who went by the name of Curtis.

The first temptation came in 1844, in the shape of another American vessel. This one had come not to suppress the slave trade, but to participate in it. The *Atalanta* was carrying tobacco, powder, rum and cotton goods and her captain 'not understanding the mode of trade or the Spanish language', Conneau explained, 'engaged me to transact his business in Gallinas'. Conneau sailed, disposed of the goods on credit in the time-honoured fashion and was approached by a Spanish factor who wanted to buy the vessel. The agreement was made. The American would sell the craft to Conneau, thus not implicating himself in her sale to a slaver, and Conneau would sell her on to the Spaniard. Conneau knew he was 'directly aiding the traffic' and breaking his promise to Commander Seagram. But Lord Stanley's dismissal of his request for 'apprentices' rankled, and he reasoned to himself that 'in taking the agency of his vessel and covering her with my name till delivered to the Spaniard, I was no more amenable to a rebuke than many respectable merchants in Sierra Leone, Acora or Anamaboo who daily sold all sorts of English manufactured goods to noted slavers'. The Spaniard took possession of the ship at New Florence and ran seven hundred slaves through the British blockade when the cruiser was away getting supplies. Learning of this, and suspecting Conneau's involvement in other scams, the Squadron 'sent messages to question me on the subject. As I refused to give satisfaction or any information on the subject, a coolness was the result, and the British armed vessels deserted my establishment . . . our intercourse was from that moment allowed to diminish into a perfect *éloignement*.'

About this time King Fana-Toro of Cape Mount, Conneau's landlord, also defaulted on his anti-slave-trade agreement with the British, signed when Conneau was still a British protégé, urging abolition on his African partners. Fana-Toro, through Conneau, now begged to inform the British, that as that agreement 'was signed and stipulated in conjunction with others whom Her Majesty's Government pleases not to sanction' – he meant the refusal to consider Cape Mount British territory –

and that the fair spoken promises of Captain Tucker RN of a yearly present, not having been attended to . . . Fana-Toro having on his part, strictly kept his promise not to allow the shipment of slaves out of his territory, cannot consider himself bound to adhere to either of them, therefore he will consider all those agreements entered into between himself and Lieutenant Seagram, Captains Tucker and Denman RN as null and void.

It was not, of course, the full story. The internal wars of Cape Mount which had frustrated Conneau's hoped-for caravans of produce were also caused by Fana-Toro's attempt to abandon slaving and all its profits. 'I could not remain neutral', Conneau excused himself, inasmuch as New Florence was situated on the same side of the river with Toso, the King's town, while the enemy held the other border. The failure of my petition to the British government and the coolness of the men of war towards me was well known to both parties; therefore to protect myself and not give umbrage to Fana-Toro, I took his part . . . Several engagements took place, and many prisoners were made by both parties. The King insisted on my purchasing his share, a thing I had determined not to do . . . but such were [his] solicitations that I agreed that a factor from Gallinas should send one of his Clerks within my limits with slave goods to purchase the King's prisoners.

There were slaves again in his barracoons, but he had no ship to run the blockade and take them off except the *Atalanta*'s longboat, 23 feet long, 5 feet across and 3 feet deep. Needs must: re-rigged and fitted, she provided slave accommodation of extraordinarily awful dimensions. Thirty-three children were loaded aboard one dark night and away she went. By chance, Conneau bumped into the captain some time later in Bahia and learnt that all had survived their thirty-eight-day trip. 'Her Captain told me they would have perished of thirst but for the fortunate rencontre of a vessel who supplied them with water.' Conneau described the exploit as 'astounding daring'.

'Here we are', wrote a British officer home in 1845,

on the most miserable station in the wide world, nigger hunting – attempting an impossibility – the suppression of the Slave Trade.
We look upon the whole affair out here as a complete humbug. You may make treaties in London, and send the whole combined squadrons of England and France to this coast, and then you will not have gained your object. So long as a slave, worth only a few dollars here, fetches 80*l* or 100*l* in America, men and means will be found to evade the strictest blockade. The absurdity of blockading a coast 2,000 miles in extent must be obvious to the meanest capacity. Even if successful you must be prepared to continue the force forever and a day, or your labour is lost; for the moment the ships are removed, the business recommences.[14]

That disillusioned man was aboard the latest British flagship, the *Penelope*, which visited New Florence on her first tour of the coast just after Théophile Conneau resumed slaving. Conneau was invited aboard to speak with the new commodore. 'I saw at once,' he said, that Commodore Jones's 'temper had been soured by some injurious report against me.' What, asked Jones peremptorily, was his participation in the case of the *Atalanta*? 'Had I known such questions were to be put to me,' replied Conneau indignantly, 'I would certainly have declined your invitation. You cannot think me a gentleman if you consider me capable of divulging the secrets of men who were on friendly terms with me and who every day break bread under my roof . . . An incredulous smile played on [his] lip, and turning to one of his officers, he presented me as the Machiavelli of Africa.' Conneau 'made a grand salaam and left the ship, convinced that all intercourse was at an end with the English cruisers'.[15]

From Cape Mount, the *Penelope* steamed on to the Gallinas, where many treaties had been abandoned: some after the Attorney-General's criticism of Denman's attacks; others, since made, set aside when malcontents gathered round some rival to a chief who had palavered with the Squadron; others discarded when the factors' presents outvalued those of the British. Another opportunity for weary negotiation had just presented itself, for HMS *Growler* had found a Cuban slaver here with three Liberated Africans aboard her who had been kidnapped in Sierra Leone and sold back into slavery. Denman had had Fry Norman. Commodore Jones had these three men, proved to have been held in the barracoons of the Rogers brothers, slaver-tenants of the same Prince Manna whose men had taken Mrs Norman. In January, the *Penelope*, *Growler* and *Larne* sailed to demand redress for this assault on British citizens. Luisini Rogers asked for a day to reflect on their demands, a day more, a week as the ships waited. Later, Commodore Jones learnt it was to give him time 'to place an ambuscade for me as I should ascend the river':

This was to be effected by Manna bringing down from Guindamar, (his town further upriver) into the mangrove bushes which bordered the stream, the body of fighting men with whom he had just returned from carrying on a slave war up the country. In all these designs and perverseness they acted under the counsel of Don Angel Jimenes, the Spanish

244

slave agent at Dombocorro, who comforted them with assurances 'that I should not dare to molest them, and that they would be protected in London'.[16]

Commodore Jones proceeded with thoughts of the Attorney-General in mind; even more of the court case hanging over Captain Denman, badly stung in this wasps' nest. All goods were removed from the Spaniard's warehouse 'and placed in safety' before his barracoons were burnt to the ground. Upriver, the Rogers brothers' towns, tucked away behind the mangroves, were also destroyed by the marines. It being too late to do the same to Guindamar, Jones wrote warning Prince Manna of 'what he might expect if he did not within three days comply with my just demands'.

At palaver, Commodore Jones spoke carefully. The injuries on British subjects were 'grievous and intolerable and must be redressed' and 'we naturally looked to the Chiefs, as the Sovereigns of that country' for that redress: 'they must see the equity of this course, as they would naturally object to our exercising a jurisdiction ourselves within their territories.' After much prevarication, he brought them to the point, asking them '1st, Whether they considered Captain Denman's treaty binding upon them? 2nd, Whether they were prepared to send away the Spanish slave dealers, according to that Treaty? They answered distinctly in the negative.'

So Commodore Jones informed them that in that case he was obliged to remain where he was for as long as it took them to reconsider 'how much longer the Slave Trade could be carried on when it ceased to be gainful'.

Here it had virtually ceased; no vessel could carry away slaves, nor should any while I held the keys of Gallinas in my pocket. I adjured them, as Chiefs who ought to be the fathers of their people, to look before them, and consider whether it would not be well for them to provide for the time when the Slave Trade, by which they now subsisted, should cease to exist. Would it not be well to work out resources from the natural advantages of their fine country? England had set her face against the Slave Trade, and was acting against it with a power which would be found invincible, and must prevail at last. Finally, would they themselves suggest any thing in reason which could be considered a fair equivalent for giving up Slave Trade?

Twenty years ago, some commanders still spoke in hopeful terms of persuasion and appeal. No one used that language now. Commodore Jones found the men with whom he was dealing contemptible. 'I should have no hope from such [men],' he wrote to the Admiralty, 'if I had not ascertained their relative weakness, and that we can always act upon their fears. At least we have evidently impressed these people with a very wholesome terror, and they begin to think resistance to our power is useless.'

Captain Conneau was weary of his African life. The wars of the Cape Mount hinterland continued, villages were depopulated, the New Florence plantations refused to flourish and, returning from a trip to the Liberian villages to buy cattle and rice, he found Cherokee Curtis had deserted, throwing in his lot with the enemies of King Fana-Toro. 'To put the climax to my growing disgust, my cutter *Termagant* went on shore [i.e. grounded] on the bar, losing vessel and cargo.'[17]

It was time to leave Africa. One small boat remained to him, the *Poor Devil*, and she was but a hull, lacking planking, spars, sails, rigging, chain and anchors. He could not buy these items at Monrovia for Governor Buchanan knew he was slaving again. Conneau therefore sailed for New York to procure them. He returned to Africa in August 1846, a 'short and agreeable' passage blighted by the news of renewed war which met him at New Florence. King Fana-Toro had been attacked by a distant relative called George Cain, going now by the name Prince George. His collaborator was the blacksmith Cherokee Curtis, married to Prince George's sister. Conneau found their army camped on the beach below New Florence for, knowing that Conneau's own honeymoon with the British had ended, Cain and Curtis had embarked on one of their own.

Deals with the foreign squadrons had been added to war and intertribal palaver as a means for coastal peoples to settle domestic disputes. The British were again landing for hospitality and information at Cape Mount, but now their host was Curtis, no longer making his living at the anvil, but by trading Liberian gin and cloth for African rice and palm oil. Conneau's version of the events was naturally twisted. A stream of misinformation from Cain and Curtis, in his view, was accepted by British commanders who knew it was untrue but chose to believe it for their own ends. 'The astute and defaming communications of my two enemies', he wrote, still smarting ten years later, 'were not only believed but sought for. No crime but I was guilty of . . . a thousand absurdities were poured with the gall, bitter and malignant animosity of a native character when spurred by the aid of an obliged and civilized villain into the willing but not ignorant ears of the British officers.'

On 15 March 1847, British officers landed at New Florence, said they had reason to search his property and took away what Conneau said were 'two bars de justice, the same as used on board all men-of-war to secure disobedient sailors' but which they 'chose to believe' were meant for slaves. The following day, a party of marines and sailors landed and 'without provocation or giving notice, [the] Commanders ordered the premises on fire, my man in charge not being allowed even to save his wearing apparel'. Conneau was not there, but his Monrovian clerk later swore that 'the marines and Kroomen . . . helped themselves without scruple of whatever was not destroyed'. It is 'painful', Conneau continued, 'for me to chronicle the conflagration of Cape Mount and the destruction of my property. . . . Even today I am ignorant what authorised such unheard-of despotism. Not a word was left me wherewith I could trace a justification to exculpate the authors of my ruin.' An anti-slave-trade treaty was swiftly signed with Prince George Cain, Mr Curtis and the other local rulers whom Cain induced to join the pledge in return for British support.

The destruction of New Florence was not quite the end of slaving at Cape Mount, however, for Prince George broke his word – not to the British, but to his fellow-rulers. When the first year passed without slaving, the promised 'present' arrived from Britain but rather than distributing it, as agreed, among all signatories, 'Cain kept it', Lieutenant Forbes of the *Bonetta* was told; 'we [the chiefs] would not believe it; time passed, and as we received none of it, we called a meeting.' It took place at an inland town. 'When Cain arrived there he was asked if he had received that present, on his acknowledging it, we killed him.' Canoe-men brought a note to Forbes when the *Bonetta* arrived in the bay, hastily written, signed by Curtis.

A revolution has taken place; King Cain is murdered, my house is robbed, and everything belonging either to myself or the king, has been seized. From the urgent demands of the insurgents for the copy of the anti slave trade treaty, known to be in my possession, I infer that this revolution is in favour of the slave trade. All your washed clothes are taken.[18]

The 'insurgents', as Forbes called them, had headed for the beach to attack Curtis, too, and when they had destroyed Beach Town, they held a palaver to elect a new king. 'One chief, Tom Levan, argued in favour of the Slave Trade, declared that neither Fana-Toro, Cain, nor himself, had known what they were about when they signed the treaty, and ended by saying, that what their ancestors had done must be right, and they would sell slaves.'

Lieutenant Forbes, writing in 1848, thought 'the murder of Cain was a death-blow to the treaties at the North. . . . The entire stop that had been put to the trade, had in no way altered the minds of the people, for one simple reason, that a most lucrative traffic had been denied them, an ancient, and consequently to them a sacred, custom had been stopped, and nothing had been substituted.' It was a logical assumption for a tired commander who had seen too many treaties made and broken, too many quarrels over 'presents', too many petty, greedy rulers wedded to the easy profit of a trade he found abhorrent but even this intelligent man was mistaken.

Captain Conneau knew what Lieutenant Forbes did not: that the slave trade might make fitful efforts to return to its glorious old haunts, but it would never be the solid, lucrative business it had been. It was the trade of the old generation, not the new. A new wind was blowing in Cuba, as well as down the West African coast. Madrid was sending out Captains-General who occasionally upheld the law over the interests of the plantations, refusing their 'rouleaux' and acting on reports of incoming slave-ships. And a new fear was being discussed in the dizzy salons of Havana as it had been in the more sober ones of Baltimore and Philadelphia thirty years ago: a fear not of too few Africans, but of too many. 'Only imagine six hundred thousand slaves kept in subjection by a force not exceeding nine thousand men,' wrote a British naval officer patrolling there in 1842. 'Surely when by some accident those slaves find out their strength the whirlwind will be not less irresistible in its course, and then, alas for the glory of Havanah!'[19] And if slave-ships were less welcome in the Cuban ports of arrival, so also in the African ports of departure: if

London held its nerve, then however many times the treaties were broken, one British officer or another would come back and force a new one, and those who took the side of British guns and British trade would, in the end, be winners of their own domestic disputes and rivalries. A year or so after New Florence was destroyed, Conneau left for America. He never returned.

Despite the setbacks, the reneging on treaties or refusals to renew, and the constant, contrary pressure of the old ways and customs, blockade and treaty were beginning to have their effect. The coast was changing under a little more pressure here, a larger present there; the death of an old king or the unexpected success of palm oil in a rival's harbour. As ship after ship north of the Line went doggedly about its task, the agreements were beginning to stick; but it was brutally hard and tedious work for the men who had to make them.

16

Habits Not Ornamental to the Navy

'The time which precedes, and immediately follows, a change of [commodore]', warned the Sierra Leone Commissioners, 'is always a season of comparative inactivity.' This was especially true of the bleak months of 1845. Commodore Jones left Africa in April, for he and many of the *Penelope*'s company had gone down with fever. The steamer touched at Madeira to fuel, but the island's authorities were fearful of contagion and armed boats circled to prevent anyone coming off to the shore. They fell in with a brig from Gibraltar a couple of days later, which obliged with 130 tons of coal, ferried laboriously between the two vessels at open sea. On the last of this fuel, the *Penelope* came into Spithead on 8 May and Commodore Jones was carried to the Haslar Hospital. He died on 24 May, aged fifty-four.

On the coast, the Squadron waited to know which new broom would arrive next, bringing instructions manufactured in Whitehall and modified in the courts. A new impetus was badly needed, for the Squadron was growing slovenly. Some first lieutenants continued to keep a pristine ship, the decks scrubbed milky-white each morning, the hammocks aired, the 'tween decks cleared of cockroaches and the galley of rats, the men respectful and happy. Others no longer did. When the Squadron had first mustered to meet Commodore Jones, the officers of the newly arrived *Penelope* had not been impressed. 'The loss of life and demoralising effect to our service are very great', one wrote home, 'the climate and service being of that nature to prevent the proper exercise of discipline, and ships are anything but men of

war; many officers acquire habits neither beneficial to themselves nor orna-
mental to the navy.'[1]

With the Squadron in a 'very relaxed state',[2] the reputation of West African
service had changed. When Lieutenant Matson of the *Waterwitch* had gone
out in the '30s, the coast had been seen as a place for derring-do and bounty,
gallant action to raise midshipman to lieutenant and lieutenant to commander.
Now it was seen as one of monotony, and a dull trudging of officers among
ships depleted by fever, commanded by time-serving captains whose hearts
were not in the job; its despatches put at the bottom of the pile by administrators who wished they could be shot of the whole business.

When the *Penelope* returned to Sierra Leone under her next captain, there
were thirty 'Tower Hill volunteers' aboard her – men who accepted naval service
instead of gaol or transportation to Australia – for not enough regular seamen
would sign up for West Africa. When the newly built *Contest* was commissioned
by Commander McMurdo the following year, 'as many as 400 lieutenants applied
for appointments to her', reported *The Times*.

> It is well known she was manned in a few hours. Well, the usual
> number of officers were appointed to her, among them three lieu-
> tenants, the complement for vessels carrying commanders. All these
> officers left the *Contest*. Why? She was ordered to the Coast of Africa
> and the vessel, after shipping her mails and Admiralty despatches, was
> detained at Spithead for more than a week, because she could get no
> lieutenants to join her. She has at last gone to sea with only one officer
> of that class . . . and he has been for years past engaged in the coast
> guard service.[3]

When that year's 'slave trade statistics' were published, *The Times* was scornful.

> Such a hideous and anomalous proportion between killed and wounded,
> between deaths and recoveries, we never before remember to have
> seen . . . of those smitten on the West Coast of Africa scarcely one in
> three survives. In the black lottery of this mortal service escape is hope-
> less and invaliding is a prize against each one of which there are two
> deadly blanks. . . . Is it possible to feel any surprise at . . . hesitation [to
> go there]? To lie for months off the mouth of a steaming river, whose
> turbid waters roll down, day after day, the deadly vapours of corruption,

cribbed and cabined, under a scorching sun, in a narrow vessel, which the work of death soon converts into a charnel, without a chance or opportunity of . . . escaping the attacks of a far more ruthless foe than the tempest or the cannon;- to do all this in a thankless task, with the credit of the service as little as the peril is great.[4]

One officer would entertain his mess, later in his career, with an anecdote of West African service of this time, when he was still a scapegrace midshipman. 'The captain of his brig', he recalled, 'was much disliked by his officers

and being ill with yellow fever and likely to die, the first lieutenant used to drill the marines in the Burial Service on the deck over the captain's cabin, by way of cheering him up, the corporal giving his orders in a loud voice thus, 'The corpse is now a-coming up the 'atchway – reverse harms!'[5]

This was an extreme example of disrespect, but other records sketch a similar picture: sullen crews, sloppy discipline and dirty ships. Some of these were present in any large fleet, but there seems to have been almost a culture of them off West Africa in the depressed years of the mid-1840s.

Commodore Jones himself had been an irascible man: 'excessively savage since leaving England', one of his officers wrote just after arriving at Freetown. 'I am perhaps the only one in our mess except the youngsters whom he has not bullied.'[6] Captain Mansel of the *Actaeon* was even more troubled, or so he appears in the memoirs of his signalman, William Petty Ashcroft. Frequently savage – 'a regular fire-eater', Ashcroft said – he combined temper with suspicion of his own ship's company. As the *Actaeon* left for Africa, 'the Captain called me one day to his cabin'

and showed me where the signal books were stowed; they were kept in a box with lead at the bottom and holes in it in case of being captured by an enemy when they would be hove overboard with all the secret papers. To begin with, when he had a signal to make I would give him the slate to write the signal flags down but then sometimes I could not read one of his letters or figures; so then I was allowed to write the letters down myself but even then there were sometimes mistakes and so finally he would tell me what he wanted to signal and

I was allowed to look it up in the book, but neither officer nor man was allowed to know the meaning of the signals I was making.[7]

Cruising off Cabinda, they found dozens of captains plying their horrible trade under the Brazilian flag. One night, the young officer of the watch was informed a sail had been seen. He 'ordered the Bosun's mate to pipe *Watch make sail*' but 'we were so close that the pipe roused the men in the slaver', which got away, although the *Actaeon* managed to shoot away her maintopmast as she went. The crew asked the captain to man the boats to chase but 'he refused as so many had been killed lately on such operations. We crowded on every bit of canvas we could and wetted the sails with the fire engine. Every time the breeze freshened we would gain on her and the slaver would start heaving niggers overboard, some very close to us as they passed. The third evening we lost her.' Some slaver-captains were no tenderer to their own crew. The *Actaeon* came along-side one whose mate 'was standing over the man at the wheel with a gun. Apparently they had already shot the mastheadman for not sighting us earlier.' Captain Mansel was restrained from such measures, although he was vindictive enough. The young officer of the watch was 'relieved of duty and sent in exchange to the first man of war we fell in with'. He was not the only officer summarily booted off the ship; all three of the *Actaeon*'s midshipmen were disrated on the captain's orders during the voyage.

Two good prizes taken off Cabinda did not improve Captain Mansel's temper. Until Commodore Jones's successor arrived, Mansel was Senior Officer and the power did him no good. The *Actaeon* was at Ascension to rest and provision when a stand-off with an insolent marine set him on a course of folly. The man had in some way insulted a wife of one of the island's Kroomen. He was tried by Mansel and the captain of marines, the officer in charge of the Ascension garrison, found guilty and ordered drummed out of the corps. Here arose the first difficulty: Mansel wanted a drummer to drum the man from court to water's edge but the captain of marines 'would not allow any drumming on shore as it was the turtle breeding season and drums or gunfire would disturb them'. '"All right but I am the captain on the water", said Captain Mansel'; and the marine was towed out in a jolly-boat, drummer perched in the bow with his drum. Aboard ship, the marine was ordered to strip. '"All right", the man said, "but remember you are not punishing a marine private but a civilian and every lash you put on my back you shall pay for.'" He was given four dozen, refused to return to duty when told and, threatened with the cat again, 'said he would take "as many as the Captain liked" – at which the latter began to have doubts and took counsel with the Captain of Marines and the NCO's on shore.'

After this episode things really went sour aboard the *Actaeon*. One man was sentenced to have

six-water grog (one part grog to six parts water) for some trifling offence and, as the man came on to the lower deck after drinking it, he said 'this is the first sixes I have drunk in Her Majesty's service' and threw the basin under the fore ladder. This started a general smash-up of mess-traps. I got hold of a broomstick to defend our Top mess-shelf as it was the best in the ship, with basins and plates we had brought from England.

Alarmed by the fracas, Captain Mansel enquired, and when told by his officers that the men were unhappy, he mustered them and asked, 'Have you ever come on the quarterdeck and asked me for privileges which I have not granted?'

Have any other ships on the station greater privileges than you? If you had complained in a proper manner I would have seen you justified but as you have taken the law into your own hands you must abide by the consequences. You have got my monkey up and you won't get him down again in a hurry. Instead of being your friend as I always have been, in future I shall be your enemy.

From then, 'he kept us at it with nothing but drill': make sail, shorten sail, make sail, shorten sail, bring ship to anchor, up anchor, make sail, shorten sail . . . Even this did not assuage his resentment; sometimes he kept them hungry and even rationed their water to half a pint a day, a true penance in that climate. Once, he ordered all lights put out for he said he could smell a slaver to windward. It was a pathetically clumsy ruse. 'He wanted to hear what the men were saying about him as he put on an old coat and cap and went and sat down near where the watch were lying around on the main deck; but someone spotted him and raised the cry "Goose"; he never tried it again.' Perhaps knowing the captain had forfeited the men's respect, the first lieutenant, master and purser 'went on the lower deck to try and persuade the men to co-operate but they told the First Lieutenant to his face that the state of affairs was all his fault. . . . The next day the Captain had the crew aft; he was like a madman.'

But even punitive discipline could not satisfy the captain's itch nor entirely repress the men. First they made his pet geese drunk and set them staggering around the deck when another captain came to visit. Then a few men were selected to row his whaleboat ashore on Fernando Po and adjured to behave themselves while they waited for his return. As soon as he had gone, they entered a church and insulted the preacher, then they tied a cat to a horse's tail and 'the whole place was in an uproar' by the time he came haring back and caught them. The following day, Mansel and John Beecroft, the elderly Englishman recently made Her Majesty's Consul to the Bights, constituted a court between them and fined the young men £5 each. The *Actaeon*'s officers had a whip-round and paid it, and when Captain Mansel prepared to give the offenders three dozen lashes, 'requested him to desist as the men had already been punished under civil law'. He did so with bad grace. Towards the end of the *Actaeon*'s commission, they sailed to meet the new commodore at Ascension, who complimented Captain Mansel, by letter, on his crew's good behaviour.

'When we got to sea the Captain had the crew aft and read them the letter, then he said, "Now, suppose we turn over a new leaf and start again with a clean sheet." But some fool in the crew said "Stick to the same old dirty one!" "So be it," said the Captain' and the spiteful round of drill and jeers resumed.

The unhappy *Actaeon* was not the only ship to witness wanton cruelty under a Brazilian flag that year.

HMS *Albatross* was also wearily patrolling the Angolan coast. In September 1844, her boats took the Brazilian *Bolladero*, which vessel, it emerged before the Mixed Commission, had already made twenty-three successful voyages, been condemned three times and each time bought back by slavers. A couple of months later, her boats routed another Brazilian slaver, the *Albanez*, from her hiding place in a bay, surrounded by casks, rafts and barrels on which her slaves had been floated out from the beach for embarkation. When Mate Francis

Meynell went aboard, 'I had enough to do clearing the cabin of the niggers who were cramming their maws with Rhubarb', he wrote to his father.

About 200 slaves were actually aboard and not a drop of water for them. I never saw such a savage scene in my life, 2 died at noon but the brig [i.e. the *Albanez*, now under a British crew] came in to help as when we embarked the poor devils in the water casks and rafts in which they were floating 750 in all and gave them water they had been afloat all the day before waiting for the Brig and the ravenous way in which they tore each other from the water to get a drink was fearful and gave a very unenticing specimen of the trouble the prize-crew might expect.[8]

The *Albanez'* log told a common story:

We found she had cleared out of Loando about 12 days previously, bound to Pernambuco; but that after stretching off for a week to the westward, articles had been signed for a slave voyage, and she stood in for the Congo river, to embark her cargo. Of course the clearance for Pernambuco was nothing but a blind, as every arrangement must have been previously made to purchase her cargo and to provide her slave fitments. We have since heard that the merchants of Loando had entered into a bond of 16,000 dollars to guarantee that the vessel was actually going to Pernambuco, which they will probably have to pay as her captain and crew deserted her in such haste that he had not time to destroy his papers and log, which will be brought forward on the vessel's trial.

Nearly two decades previously, Brazil had declared the slave trade to be piracy. It had had no effect. Palmerston's Act of 1839 had brought Brazilian imports tumbling from about forty-five thousand slaves in 1838 to ten thousand in 1842, for most of them had been carried under the Portuguese flag which was now subject to the British patrol. Two years later, however, the number had risen again to fifty thousand for the Brazilian flag had stepped in to fill the gap. Lieutenant – now Commander – Matson of the *Waterwitch* was a clever man, his knowledge of conditions south of the Line second to none. He knew that when the British government had doubted and faltered in 1842, the closely watching Brazilian and African slavers had interpreted its timorousness as the collapse of its anti-slave-trade campaign.

British prestige had been dealt a great blow on the West African coast by the back-pedalling of 1842. When London 'first adopted the policy of increasing the blockade service', a Brazilian coffee merchant explained,[9] 'the Brazilian slave traders were very much alarmed [because] it was supposed that whatever England attempted to do, she was able to carry out; but we had not the impudence to suppose that she would not carry it out most efficiently; and therefore the Slave trade died away for some time'. But when Britain lost confidence in her own campaign, there had been first astonishment, then contempt. In May 1842, Commander Matson had expelled the slavers from the lands of 'Principe Jack' of Cabinda. When he visited a year later, they were back in residence. 'One time,' Jack told him, 'we think Englishmen be almost same as God Almighty; now we think he be same as other white man – all same as we.'[10] Contempt in Cabinda was hatred in Rio and Bahia where slaving had become patriotism: fighting one's corner against the arrogant British. The Brazilians, wrote home one British officer stationed there, 'have only one redeeming point, which is, that they all agree in cordially hating the English'.

In August 1844, Matson was in London and was asked, in consulation with Captain Denman and a senior judge of the Court of Admiralty, to advise on naval strategy. Matson agreed with Denman that 'capture of slave vessels must be secondary to preventing the embarkation of slaves', but said the strategy on which Denman insisted of 'never leaving open a slave-port' simply did not work in the south. 'No general rule can be laid down for adoption along the whole coast', he said. 'Different places require different modes of proceeding' and inshore coastal patrolling, rather than blockade, was vital south of the Line where there were many anchorages to shelter slavers. His advice was ignored. Not only had Commodore Jones been told to extend blockade along the whole beat, but he had also been ill-advisedly directed to leave 'the greater part' of the Angolan coast 'to the care of the Portuguese authorities, and consequently', Matson said, 'the [Brazilian] slavers had a very pretty time of it. They don't care how many doors you shut so that you leave one open.'

Frank Meynell was still waiting for the case of the *Albanez* to come before the Brazilian Mixed Commission when details of a brutal episode reached Freetown. HMS *Wasp* had taken the Brazilian *Felicidade* off Lagos, equipped for several hundred slaves. Her captain had surrendered without a struggle and the *Wasp*'s Lieutenant Stupart went aboard with a prize-crew and orders to chase another suspected slaver glimpsed on the horizon. The second slaver was the *Echo*, and the *Wasp* prize-crew took her triumphantly the following day and released 434 suffering blacks. With two ships to manage, the prize-crew had to split. Second in seniority to Stupart was fifteen-year-old Midshipman Thomas Palmer, whom Stupart instructed to take the *Felicidade* into Lagos and wait until the *Wasp* and the *Echo* came in, to sail in company to Sierra Leone. Four seamen, one marine and the *Wasp*'s ageing quarter-master were left under the midshipman's command. Within the hour, all seven were dead. Stabbed with his own bayonet, the marine was the first to be heaved over the side. Beaten about the head before he could draw his sword, Thomas Palmer was next, stunned into an easy death; then the old quartermaster, gurgling blood through a cutlass gash in his throat. The other four were hunted down in shrouds and lockers, and fingers that clung to the rails and gunwales were hacked away.

HMS *Star* was also patrolling these violent waters, however, and fell in with the *Felicidade* only hours later. Again the Brazilian slaver-crew heard the warning shot across their bow, hove-to and received another suspicious British lieutenant. There were no slaves, no irons, no tell-tale planks or caul-drons; but there were bloodstains not yet scrubbed from the deck and cuts and fresh bruises on the men standing sullenly at a distance, watching the Englishman interrogate their captain. They were called over. At first they said they had been injured by falling spars, but when they were questioned separately two made their bargain and turned queen's evidence. The *Felicidade* turned north under a second prize-crew, this time heading in the wake of the *Albanez* for Freetown and the courts.

To avoid the delaying winds of the Bights, the prize-crew took the *Felicidade* well out to sea, and were 200 miles from land when a squall dropped from nowhere and upended the vessel. Only the bow-rail remained clear of the sea and those not swept overboard clung desperately to it, the wind suddenly howling about them so dense with spray that none could see if his neighbour was still there, or he was left alone. When the squall passed, they counted heads, called names and looked in bewilderment at their bare and ruined vessel. A few men dived to see if boxes of food floated just below the surface but they found nothing and the sharks were already circling. They had three knives between them. With these, they hacked at the main boom and gaff to make timber for a raft, fashioned a small sail from the shredded canvas and hauled up what they could of the drowned ropes to rig it. On this primitive craft, ten men – English, Brazilian and Kroo – headed for the coast without rudder, oars, compass, food or water; almost naked, scoured and soaked by waves washing over the raft and burnt by the sun from which they had no shelter. Sharks bumped and nosed the planks beneath them. Four were lassooed, dragged aboard and eaten raw. A little fresh water was caught in the sail. Only five survived to sight land twenty days later.

Even by the brutal standards of the slave trade, the death of Midshipman Palmer was shocking. In July 1845, when the Brazilian crew of the *Felicidade* was brought before a British Admiralty court, charged with piracy, and Lieutenant Stupart stood to give evidence against them, the case was given much publicity. Were there slaves aboard the *Felicidade*, the court asked Stupart, when he detained her? There were not, he said, although she was equipped for slaving – but was that the important point, when British seamen had been killed in cold blood? Unfortunately, it was. There was no 'Equipment Clause' in Britain's treaty with Brazil. No Brazilian ship could be detained without slaves aboard, and if she were, her men were entitled to wrest her back by whatever means necessary. Not guilty.

Remember the Felicidade! This was the battle-cry of bluejackets boarding Brazilian vessels for years to come. An unknown number of Brazilian seamen took a bullet in the head in revenge for the deaths of Midshipman Palmer and his men, denied justice, at least in the view of the navy, by the courts of their own country.

Whatever the men hating their service on the African coast thought, government had not abandoned the Squadron. Though a chorus of dissatisfaction was never off-stage in the 1840s, and demands for the navy's withdrawal from the abolition campaign were always loud, both Lord Palmerston and Lord Aberdeen were firm in their resolve against the vile trade, and believed the Squadron to be an essential weapon in the fight.

It had begun to seem that the tide was turning against the Cuban traffic. The Brazilian trade, however, was booming. The Anglo–Brazilian treaty of 1826, regulating relations between the Squadron and slavers flying the Brazilian flag, would expire in March 1845. It had never been very effective but it was better than nothing and Lord Aberdeen had sent a British deputation to negotiate its renewal. It was a hopeless task. 'The slave trade', Aberdeen's envoy wrote home, 'is carried on more actively than it ever was; there is not the semblance on the part of the Executive Government, of a wish to repress it . . . the leading men here are too deeply implicated in it to allow the treaty to be fairly executed.'[11] What Aberdeen had in mind was to persuade Brazil to sign up to the same terms forced on Portugal in 1839, followed, he wrote to his envoy, 'with an intimation that if [the Brazilians] refuse to concur in effectual measures for the abolition of the trade, they will be treated in the same manner as Portugal'. A milder man than Palmerston, Aberdeen would nonetheless follow the precedent of the latter's 1839 Act despite its having been, as he admitted, 'a great stretch of power, and open to many objections in principle; but having been once sanctioned by parliament, the difficulty of applying it in a similar case is in great measure removed. We are terribly hampered by this Slave Trade', he continued,

> the questions about which meet us in every quarter and estrange from us our best friends. France, the United States, Spain, Portugal and Brazil all furnish matter for angry discussions every day. Never [has] a people made such a sacrifice as we have done to attain our object, and the payment of the money is the least part of it. We must not relax, but our progress has not been hitherto very encouraging.

The constant tension between the competing needs of abolition and commerce bedevilled negotiations in Rio. The Sugar Duty Act was dividing Britain almost as much as the Abolition Act four decades before. In it, one great nineteenth-century debate – Free Trade – came up against another – Abolition – and Free Trade won. Previously, sugar from British colonies had paid no tariff, whereas sugar from Brazil and Cuba had. The Free Traders held that such protectionism was wrong, and that all tariffs must be abolished; the abolitionists held that if they were, the boost given to slave-grown sugar would render any effort to counter the slave trade useless. One had to be balanced against the other at the negotiating table in Rio: the next treaty must mesh the desire of Brazil to sell its sugar with the desire of Britain both to buy it, cheap, and also to suppress its means of production. For months, suggestions were made, refused, countered with alternative proposals in a diplomatic to and fro; but what no British representative at that table expected was what happened on 12 March 1845, the day before the treaty expired. A short note was sent to the British mission that day stating simply that from 13 March, Royal Naval ships might no longer stop Brazilian vessels in any circumstances. No treaty would be signed to replace that about to expire. None was necessary, the Brazilian government blandly explained, for the slave trade had been extinct for fifteen years. There was nothing else: none of the alternative measures for suppression which the British had been led to believe would be employed by the Brazilian government itself; no suggestions, however sketchy, for some new mode of collaboration. The news reached Brazil as the men of the *Felicidade* were being tried. With this, 'Brazil', wrote *The Times*, 'may be said to have dropped the last pretence of co-operating with us'.[12]

The law officers of the Crown were consulted; might Brazil be still bound by the 1817 treaty with Portugal? She was not, and that avenue closed. However, those officers said, the clause in the 1826 treaty by which Brazilian slavers were declared pirates still held – and if they are pirates, they are international outlaws and may be seized by Royal Naval vessels. This was the background to the next 'great stretch of power' which Lord Aberdeen pushed through Parliament. Under a new British law, the Royal Navy would be empowered not by treaty, but by British legislation, to regard Brazilian vessels suspected of slaving as pirates and bring them to trial before courts of the British Admiralty. There was protest, of course: could Brazilian slaving be declared piracy because it was defined as such in a lapsed treaty with the British, rather than by Brazil's own law? Britain, one Member of Parliament pointed out, 'had no more right to make a law binding on the subjects of Brazil, than they did on the subjects of China, or of any other nation'.[13] The bill passed anyway. The Treasury tightened its belt and promised the Squadron would be raised from twenty-one to thirty ships by 1846. In Brazil, there was such an outcry that it was not safe for British sailors to set foot ashore and the British envoy was given an armed guard around his house.

It was Sir Charles Hotham, new commodore on the West African coast, who would have to make the new instructions effective. Hotham had just come from three years' service in South America, that continent of infinite, and infinitely bloody, tangles, whose peoples, having fought off their colonial masters, were bitterly fighting each other. He had commanded a flotilla of paddle-steamers up the winding, ill-dredged waters of the rivers Plate and Paraná, helping Buenos Aires defeat riverborne insurgents from the Argentine interior. He was, wrote one of his flagship lieutenants there, 'a first-rate officer, and in every sense of the word a gentleman . . . not a scientific man, but decidedly a clever man, a good linguist, very well informed in history and politics, and I imagine for a naval man a very good diplomatist'.[14]

Speaking fluent Spanish, able to work with the French – who were on the same side as the British in the Paraná campaign – and a hardened steamship commander, Hotham, for the Admiralty, was a natural choice to take command of the West African fleet. Some officers on the coast felt differently.

Instead of putting the Squadron, Commander Matson pointed out,

> under the command of an officer who had sufficient amount of local knowledge . . . the Admiralty selected one, who, although a very good officer, knew nothing about Africa, to which place, I believe, he was sent, merely because he happened to command a steam frigate which was found to be unfit for any other part of the world. It was to be expected that he would do more mischief during the first year of his command than he could repair during the two last. . . . Never were two more unsatisfactory years than those of 1846–7.[15]

He wrote these damning words in 1848, when a 'succession of untoward events' had brought his beloved Squadron to the brink of being disbanded by a Parliamentary Committee convinced it had failed.

Some of Hotham's difficulties were the normal consequence of a handover. Captain Mansel of the *Actaeon* did not bequeath a happy squadron and the admiring lieutenant from the South American station had put his finger on another significant problem. Hotham, he said, was 'a captain peculiarly careful about the health of his men, and one, who, being a single man with a good income, does not care about capturing slavers when it is attended with risking of the men's lives and health up the rivers'.[16] He was backed in this zealousness by the fact that blockade had fallen out of favour at the Admiralty. Patrol was back in, as Matson and others had wished; but orders from Hotham himself reduced the effect of this welcome change and frustrated those required to obey them. The close inshore work by ships' boats which Matson thought essential was vetoed as too damaging to men's health: 'patrol' was restricted to offshore sailing, which enraged those for whom 'detached service', however dangerous, was the only break in monotony, the only route to promotion and, they knew, the best method to flush out slavers. Under the regime of offshore patrol, men and officers confined for months in dull, steamy-hot quarters became as restless as they did during blockade; discipline suffered similarly and quarrels flared. Some officers sneaked through the mangrove to fight duels. Others insulted their captains and were dismissed. A spate of courts martial took place on quarterdecks off Angola and the Congo.

Second of the new commodore's unwelcome introductions was a rigid and unnecessary confidentiality by which his senior officers, more experienced than he, found their command strictly curtailed. 'When the orders came out of Commodore Hotham', wrote one,

> to keep off the coast, they were so stringent, that although as an officer I had three years' experience on the coast at that time, the order tied me up as if I had none ... it was not only tying us up from obtaining information on shore, but it actually tied us up from communicating with the cruisers which were stationed next or near us. I met with three Commanders and each officer said 'where are your orders?' The answer was 'mine are confidential'. The consequence was, that instead of gaining information from each other, and assisting each other to intercept slavers, or planning mutual efforts to bear upon a point, there could be no mutual aid or concert.[17]

Enterprising commanders had previously been left largely to their own devices by superior officers. Despairing of ever being sent a complete complement of adequate ships by the Admiralty, they had routinely undertaken what modifications they could on the spot: piling on huge spreads of canvas, changing the rigging, landing all unnecessary stores at Ascension to make the vessel lighter and swifter. All this was now vetoed. 'The cruisers were once efficient', Commander Matson said. 'Now they are not. Their wings are not only crippled but their talons are cut.'[18] So strongly did he feel about the Squadron's predicament that he was prepared to jeopardise his future career by pointing it out to the Lords of the Admiralty. The Squadron's instructions, he said bluntly, were defective. 'Parts', indeed, were 'calculated to perplex and mislead officers in the execution of their duty ... as the duties of officers are in these instructions so very minutely defined, every possible case being apparently provided for, there is little left for an officer but to obey them to the very letter; but to do so, in many cases, would be highly mischievous, and in some cases, physically impossible' and as 'they could not be strictly obeyed . . . they therefore, in some cases, became a dead letter'.

Hotham was not disliked by the men under his command, for by and large they understood that the restrictions he imposed on them sprang from care for the Squadron rather than indifference to or dislike of its work. They just thought those restrictions badly calculated to the purpose. There was a gulf between hardened commanders who had dealt with too many brutes and seen too many black bodies thrown overboard, and Charles Hotham, the softly spoken gentleman who abided by the rules. In June 1848, Commander George Sprigg, now of HMS *Ferret*, took the Brazilian schooner *Castro III*. One *Ferret* prize-crew was already absent, and the eternal fever had depleted the ship's remaining strength. 'The captain of the foretop had charge of one watch', Captain Sprigg would say, 'and the ship's cook of another.'[19] It was a dangerous situation into which to bring eleven ruthless prisoners who hated their captors, and no one had forgotten the *Felicidade*. The Brazilians were put in a small boat, given oars and some water, pointed at the coast and told to row. No one aboard the *Ferret* thought anything of it, but when Commodore Hotham learnt of the event, Captain Sprigg was brought before a court martial, charged with behaving 'in a cruel and oppressive manner, unbecoming the character of an officer in Her Majesty's navy'. Those who appeared in his defence – the acting bosun, the acting gunner, the master, several seamen, Commander Matson and Commander Butterfield – all thought he had done nothing wrong. Yet the case was part-proved. Captain Sprigg was 'reprimanded and admonished to be more circumspect in future'. Circumspection, it seemed, was the new and unwelcome watchword.

Despite these restrictions, these were still three years of furious naval activity, for there was no reduction in the number of Brazilian ships sailing in defiance of Britain's new law, nor of prizes taken along the southern coast. One steamer, HMS *Styx*, took twenty-nine in two years and more cases went before Admiralty courts than had ever gone before the Brazilian Mixed Commissions. This brought its own dangers, as Captain Sprigg had found, and done his best to circumvent. 'We have taken 12 prizes', wrote an officer of HMS *Prometheus*, 'since we have been upon the coast but in consequence of having to divide our crew so often to put on board the prizes hands to navigate them, we have been often left in a very helpless condition. We have had the fever on board, which has carried off six of our men a day.'[20] There seemed no breakthrough in the war with Brazilian slaving; only an endless parry and thrust. Each ship taken by the

British off Africa was replaced by several leaving Brazil. Each bay scoured clean of slaving filth – for not every commander obeyed Hotham's ban on detached service – was replaced by others the British knew nothing of. Nearly sixty thousand slaves entered Brazil in 1847, and in 1848 the first slave-steamer brought 1,200 from Angola in a space designed for 400.

In 1848, Lieutenant Frederick Forbes of the *Bonetta* returned from Africa to give his evidence to the latest of many Parliamentary Select Committees convened over the years to discuss the Squadron's future. Pressure had built, again, to exploding point in the British press and Parliament. Too many schools of thought had reached the same conclusion: the Squadron must be withdrawn, and the campaign either abandoned as hopeless, or pursued in some new way. Captain Matson summed up the prevailing mood. 'We have become wearied and disgusted', he wrote,

> with our repeated failures, and public opinion now runs high in favour of withdrawing our squadron, and permitting the Slave Trade to take its natural course . . . naval officers, generally, recommend the adoption of stringent coercive measures; Liverpool merchants tell us to withdraw our squadron, allow commerce to take its natural course, and carry out the principle of free trade in its most unlimited sense. West Indian proprietors and ship-owners tell us to throw a floating bridge across the Atlantic for the convenience of the quasi 'free emigrants' from Africa to America. Judges, Missionaries, Physicians, Slave-Traders &c. each have their own specific remedy.[21]

Everyone had seen the enormous sheaves of papers showing figures of slaves exported, to where and when; how many saved, from where and when; and, working into these the vagaries of changes of foreign governments more or less favourable to suppression, the arrival or withdrawal of foreign naval squadrons, the rise or fall in the price of slaves in foreign markets, ditto that of sugar, numbers of steam as opposed to sail, the use of blockade rather than patrol, concentration on the northern beat or the southern – from all these, public, press and Parliament had reached their conflicting conclusions that the Squadron was essential, helpful or useless.

Lord John Russell, who had backed the Niger Expedition in 1841, was now gloomy. 'The whole British navy', he wrote to the Treasury, 'would not be sufficient to stop the illegal slave trade because of the profit they derive . . . From 1845 on the strength and efficiency of the British Preventive Squadron has been raised to the highest point ever and supported by France and the United States, but still only [saved] four percent of slaves carried off from Africa in those years.' Further, he believed the cost of this fruitless exercise was at least £650,000 each year which, added to the estimated £20 million cost of emancipating slaves throughout the British Empire, was a massive burden. Commodore Hotham was similarly uncompromising in his pessimism when he came to give evidence to the Select Committee of 1848.

'Did you succeed in stopping the Slave Trade?' he was asked. He answered, 'No.'

> Did you cripple it to such an extent as in your opinion is calculated to give it a permanent check?
> No.
> In your opinion, is the effective blockade of the coast practicable?
> Certainly not.
> Are you acquainted with any modification of our present measures which would effect our object?
> I am not.
> Can you look forward to any definite period when the extinction of the trade will be thus effected?
> I cannot.[22]

Frederick Forbes agreed. Neither blockade nor treaty, he said, had any effect.

> There is only one real cure for the Slave Trade, and that is the introduction of a cheap and useful system of Trade under Government superintendence, assisted by a reduction of prices at first, but no presents. . . . Treaties might then be enforced if they were broken; while now, to expect an African king to keep a treaty, and offer him nothing but a dazzling present – to do this is idle. It is only placing him at the tender mercies of his subjects, who, assisted by Slave-merchants, would assuredly murder him.[23]

Captain Matson furiously demurred, as did Captain Denman. Both published fighting pamphlets in the Squadron's defence, for they agreed with the calculation implicit in Captain Conneau's departure from Africa: the slave trade was suppressible, and the Squadron could do the job if it were given the right tools and leadership. Other officers, past and present, weighed in: 'I am persuaded', wrote Captain Henry Dundas Trotter to *The Times*,

> that the probability of any improvement taking place in the condition of Africa, by the various means now in operation, entirely depends on the maintenance of the squadron; that the effects hitherto produced in the interior by our efforts on the coast have been altogether beneficial; and that the suppression of the Slave Trade may be effected if the system now in force be followed out with due vigour and perseverance.[24]

If Parliament abandoned the campaign and the Squadron now, decades of deaths from bullet and fever, loss of ships, hostility from other nations and huge expense – all this would be for nothing and the slave-marts closed at such great cost would reopen. President Roberts of Liberia agreed: 'the withdrawal of the squadron, thereby throwing open the traffic, would be most disastrous to the future welfare of Africa . . . so long as a market remains, and persons will resort to the coast for slaves, the natives will sell each other; and trading factories, model farms, or moral suasion, will have but little influence in restraining the natives from slave trading.'[25] But despite all the pamphlets, letters and speeches in its defence, the Squadron was unpopular. Too many people had lost faith in its campaign and its senior officers. The crusading fervour of the abolitionists was an outmoded cause: the obsession of one's grandfather or a great-aunt's passion. As the Select Committee sat through 1848, it seemed more and more certain that the Squadron would be recalled.

Already suggestions had been made as to what should replace it. Charles Hotham thought Britain should consent to slavery continuing in Brazil, 'for a fixed period and under certain conditions and checks'. Captain William Allen suggested the British 'superintend ourselves the traffic which we cannot suppress . . . that officers of a new mixed commission should supervise slave marts, where all slaves will be bonded labourers to that commission for a certain period.' *The Times* backed this idea:

> were we to apply our money and ships in buying, on the African coast, 50,000 head of negroes a year, and landing them free in our West Indian

ports, it would tend far more to the prosperity of our islands, and to the suppression of the Slave Trade, than all that our settlements and cruisers have done, with the balance of expense very much in our favour.[26]

Earlier that year, however, one blow had been struck in the Squadron's favour. The claim for damages following Captain Denman's destruction of the Gallinas factories in 1842 had been disallowed. Six years' discussion had brought the court to its decision: not only was the Spanish factor Tomás Burón found to be a criminal under Spanish law but it was decided that the British government's *post facto* approval of Denman's actions absolved the captain of personal liability: had there been any, it would have been borne by the Crown and not by the officer. Charles Hotham, returned to the African coast after advising the Select Committee, knew the judgment gave him personal protection. He made the most of it by preparing a final onslaught on the Gallinas before handing over to a new commodore. Backed by the decision of one British judge and the long perseverance of two British Foreign Ministers, seven ships anchored off the bar of that most notorious of slaving havens on 2 February 1849. Three hundred men in ships' boats landed and destroyed every barracoon and factory they could find in one day's destructive orgy. They returned aboard their ships with not a single British life lost. This time, the chiefs did not fight back and the slavers who begged their passage out with the departing Squadron did not return to resurrect their businesses. The long game seemed to be over in Gallinas, as it was in Sester.

The surrender of the Gallinas closed a great gap in the treaty network: forty-eight agreements, some still fragile but others of several years' duration, stretched from Cape Verde down to the equator: the Gallinas, Sherbro, Cape Mount, Sester, the Bonny and the Calabars. The dirtiest of all exit routes through which Africa had sold her children were closed. These were tremendous achievements, yet still the Select Committee in London debated. The Squadron's future, and that of West African slaving, hung in the balance when news came from Ouidah.

Francisco Felix de Souza was dead, and the landscape of slaving along the lower Guinea coast had changed for ever. He died on 8 May 1849, as the rains were setting in, aged eighty-two, with his three hundred wives and innumerable progeny squatting about the sodden compound where he had held court since anyone could remember, waiting. It was the end of an era. *Carpe diem*: into this moment of doubt and hesitation the envoys of abolition must step again.

17

Persevering Offenders

When Charles Hotham shut down the Gallinas, only 'two persevering offenders',[1] Lord Palmerston wrote, remained north of the Line. Still sending vast numbers of slaves to the ports and factors of the Bights were 'the King of Dahomey and the Chief of Lagos, who still refuse to yield to persuasion and who continue to thwart and to frustrate the measures of Her Majesty's Government'.

Even here in the Bights, however, there was a creeping sense that the last days were coming. The British were implacable, blockading and patrolling at sea, insinuating themselves inland, detaching old customers from the business and sending warships to cruise the coasts of Brazil and Cuba. In these days of steam, photographic testimony and officialdom, a feeling of anachronism was gathering, very slowly, like a mist far out at sea. The slavers felt it. All, now, invested a part of their fortunes in palm-oil plantations, and cut down on the vice-regal magnificence in which they used to live. De Souza himself had already ceased to be a major player. The intricacies of slave-credit had become too much for his ageing wits and his once-vast fortune had dwindled. The ships bearing trade goods from Bahia and Pernambuco now crossed the lagoon to younger merchants in Lagos and Porto Novo although there, too, there were fewer great displays of wealth and power: the vast distribution of presents to the mob; the weeks of rum, dance and death which for generations had kept appetite for the trade alive. The kings of Lagos and Porto Novo still reviled the British and lived closeted and blinkered with their Portuguese cabals but King Guezo of Dahomey had received British envoys at his inland capital of Abomey and heard their honeyed talk of subsidy and friendship. Recently, as well, other new groups had jostled disturbingly against the slave-hunting grounds of Yorubaland and built defiant settlements on their borders.

Strong new threads of Christianity and legitimate trade were snaking out across country from Sierra Leone to Yorubaland, replacing the slaving networks which had previously connected communities. Liberated Africans were no longer confined to Sierra Leone and Liberia. A first wave of émigrés had pushed out the borders of colonial territory, British and American, settling in the 1830s in the trading villages which John Kizell's generation had pioneered. A next wave went further, returning to where they, or their parents, had been enslaved. By the time of de Souza's death, a great trek south was under way to what would become Nigeria. The Sierra Leone pioneers had been joined by a different group: not men and women who had been freed by naval patrols, but 'Repatriates' who had bought their own freedom overseas, and returned from Brazil, the Caribbean and the United States. The Sunday streets of Ouidah and Porto Novo, names so long associated with slaving excess, were full now of former slaves, praising the God they had brought back with them.

Badagry, where Richard Lander had found Portuguese factories full of slaves twenty years ago, housed the fastest-growing Repatriate community. Most of the town's merchants were supplied from the hill-town of Abeokuta, 80 miles upriver, seat of another Christian Mission and Repatriate group. Here was a textbook example of the British vision: legitimate trade and faith spread by African effort alone, without need of British death and expense. Two obstacles hindered its development. First, the Repatriates' scattered communities were in the slave-hunting hinterlands of many marauding peoples. Second, goods could not be shipped from inland towns to Badagry because the slave traders would not open the river to them. For some time, Repatriates and missionaries had been sending appeals for intervention to London.

John Duncan was London's man on the spot. He was as remarkable a person as Richard Lander: a huge Scottish farm-labourer's son turned soldier then explorer. He had been aboard the steamer *Albert* as it shuddered and grated up the River Niger in 1841, broiling in his Lifeguards uniform at the head of treaty-parties sent to impress the chiefs along the way. He had returned to Scotland with shattered health and a leg whose sores would not dry, but in love with Africa. Since then, the Royal Geographical Society had – with distaste, for it would have preferred a gentleman for the job – funded him to seek the legendary Kong Mountains which turned out not to exist. Duncan had been presented to de Souza at Ouidah, and it had been de Souza's capricious pleasure to sponsor the explorer's journey into the interior, lending him bearers, guides, horses and hammocks. Duncan had been one of the first whites ever to enter King Guezo's capital, Abomey, 'City of Blood', and see the walls inlaid with human skulls, the rotten bodies hanging upside-down from crucifixes in the streets and the prisoners of war being decapitated for the enjoyment of the crowd. He had met the shockingly gentle monarch himself, of handsome early middle age, soft-voiced, his feet propped on a footstool of skulls as he discussed the new ideas of dash, trade and abolition. Together they had reviewed the famed and feared Amazon army of six thousand women and toasted the king's enemies from drinking-cups made from skulls.

Other white men had since visited Guezo and made their offer: a British pension in return for suppressing the slave trade. Each time he had refused. 'He begs the Queen of England to put a stop to the Slave Trade everywhere else, and allow him to continue it', wrote home one. He could not see, another reported, 'that he and his people can do without it. It is from the Slave Trade that he derives his principal revenue',[2] which he said was about £60,000 each year, although some observers thought it lower. Palm oil was already produced in Dahomey, and it was this the enemies of slaving wished to see promoted, but its revenue was paltry and where status came from war, who would turn to agriculture? Besides, palm oil brought its own problems: could the Queen of England, Guezo asked, prevent merchant ships calling near his territory 'as by means of trading vessels the people are getting rich, and withstanding his authority' and could she also oblige all local palm-oil factories to relocate to Ouidah, as then they would have to pay him duty. 'In the event of his attacking these places,' she was assured, 'he would not run the risk of injuring Englishmen or their property.' Lastly, would she 'send him some good Tower guns and blunderbusses, and plenty of them, to enable him to make war'.

Guezo's position had changed since he made these disingenuous or sly requests in November 1848. His oldest slaving partner, de Souza, was dead and there was defiance on his borders. He knew that where the towns of freedom in the north had at first been hemmed in by slavers, they had grown, slowly, to hem the slavers in. He knew, too, that the British, advised of de Souza's death, would be turning this latest opportunity of palaver about and seeking its most penetrable side. When John Duncan asked to visit again, he replied that an envoy and a naval officer might come, then turned to a more important matter. De Souza's glory days might be past but he had been a great man in Dahomey: he had helped put Guezo on the throne thirty years ago and been friend, colleague, advisor and broker since. Many ceremonies in his honour must be performed.

The officer selected to accompany John Duncan was Lieutenant Forbes of the *Bonetta*, who arrived in the usual undignified manner of Her Majesty's officers on this coast: in a hired canoe hurled by surf upon the beach, to be hauled above the waterline by shouting Africans and catch his breath. Forbes and Duncan awaited Guezo's stick in the old British fort at Ouidah. The gold-headed Malacca cane, carried before them, would ensure safe passage to Abomey. When they walked in the square and the markets, the Portuguese watched them in hostile silence. The supercargo of a Portuguese slave-ship came to town and the Caboceers gathered under huge painted umbrellas to receive him. Five hundred soldiers discharged muskets in salute. There was a band, a forest of flags, assurances of friendship. Don Domingo Martinez of Porto Novo, the largest slave-trader on the lagoons, came to dispense presents to his followers. 'The public square', Forbes wrote, 'ran with rum from three pipes started for the mob to wallow in. Thirty-five pipes of rum besides silk and cowries were sent to [King Guezo]. The Viceroy and all Caboceers were large receivers.'[3] Only Don Domingo, the watchers had reported, was able to make such gestures now.

It was a four-day journey to Abomey. Every African threw himself face down and piled dirt on his head as the king's stick passed at the front of the cavalcade. There were thirty-six bearers carrying hammocks, cowries, rum and baggage; then the young Englishman and the older, grimacing Scot, in pain from his wounded leg, who noted the fine agricultural land through which they passed and the wealth of its inhabitants. Ten miles from Abomey, they waited for Guezo's permission to enter his capital. When it came, Lieutenant Forbes put on his dress uniform, Mr Duncan his frock coat and they mounted again. The walls of the city became distinct across the land. When they could distinguish the human skulls atop the great gate, they halted, and awaited the Caboceers who would escort them to the king's presence.

It was Frederick Forbes's turn to pass through the narrow streets amid the pressing, shouting crowd, see the high red walls of the palace, the thousands of richly dressed royal wives, the ranks of Amazons and in their midst Guezo, now forty-eight and still, wrote Duncan, 'the frank, unassuming but intelligent man I had found him in 1845'.[4] The first encounter was a clashing chaos of review, colour, musket-fire, healths drunk, all the ceremonies familiar to both visitors from other visits to African royalty, but here on the grandest scale. At length the two men left for the quarters allotted them in the Prime Minister's compound, 'the King accompanying us across the square, where all now was animation: the thousands of armed men and women rushing round their Monarch, brandishing aloft their clubs and muskets, and yelling and shouting in a most fearful manner'.

The next day was taken up with the laborious, grafting ceremonial which marked any contact between African chiefs and the representatives of Britain: letters of introduction were presented, translated, approved; presents were asked for and given; champagne was drunk, a screen wafting down before the king each time he raised his glass, for it was taboo to see him eat or drink. Among the presents for Guezo were scarlet uniforms, which pleased him greatly. 'He was also pleased', Duncan wrote to Lord Palmerston, 'with a spinning-wheel sent by my mother from Scotland, and also with a small model weaving-loom I had made for him. He requested me to show him how to spin, which placed me in rather an awkward position. However, I acquitted myself to his satisfaction.' Guezo would not directly address the question of suppressing the slave trade, saying only that this could not be decided until after the 'Custom'. He admitted, Duncan wrote, 'the injustice of slave-trading, but remarked that we were a long time finding it out to be wrong'. His presents to his guests were '1 fine young cow, 3 goats, 6 fowls, 3 bags of native flour, 3 kegs of palm-oil for cooking, 3 measures of pepper, and 3 kegs of rum, besides 3 fine native cloths'.

Back in the quiet, cool rooms set aside for them across the square, Lieutenant Forbes added to his notes.

> Besides minor there is one annual festival known as the Customs, which takes place on the appearance of the third moon and lasts six weeks. To this festival the whole of his subjects are invited, also all foreigners, traders and others, sojourners in his kingdom, and all are assembled at the expense of the King. In order to defray this enormous expense, the King makes war on one or the other neighbouring countries and performs what is termed a 'slave-hunt'.[5]

One such slave-hunt was under preparation for 'the country of Anagoo', west of Abomey. 'The King thus states his reasons': the Anagoos had besieged

Abomey in the time of his grandfather and although since subjugated, 'he did not consider them as yet sufficiently punished; that he must have money (slaves for the ensuing Customs) and he thought of all his hereditary enemies, the Anagoos most deserved the chastisement'. Live by the Custom, die by the Custom: Guezo was trapped. If he did not go to war he would not have slaves; if he did not have slaves, he could not propitiate his people; if his people went unpropitiated, he would be deposed and killed.

Duncan and Forbes left Abomey with Guezo's letter to Lord Palmerston. It was full of flowers. The king begged to thank his distant friend 'for his good advice respecting the trade of this country',[6] assured him the Caboceers would be consulted as to suppressing the slave trade at the first opportunity and promised to give Duncan his decision at the next Custom.

> I have always a strong desire to cultivate a friendship with the people of England, and to establish and increase a trade with that country. Englishmen were my father's best friends, and he always told me to respect Englishmen, and look upon them in my heart as sincere in their promises and friendship. An Englishman's heart is big, like a large calabash that overflows with palm-wine for those who are thirsty.

John Duncan would never receive the decision. He already had dysentery when they left Abomey, a miserable journey ahead. A courteous message waited from Domingo Martinez at Ouidah: would they care to use his canoe to re-embark their ship? It took Lieutenant Forbes to rejoin the *Bonetta* and brought a ship's surgeon back to examine John Duncan, wrung dry and delirious. He died in November 1849, aged forty-four.

Dahomean troops fanned out across the countryside from the city the British envoys had just left, destroying villages and enslaving their people as they had every year for generations. 'The slave-hunts', wrote an observer,

> are something like the fashionable European 'battues'. They are attended by the King in person. He goes forth with his army and he pursues the sport for two or three months in every year. His wretched prey are the detached and feeble tribes living on the borders of his dominion. He works in detail; he assaults and captures each tribe one by one, and when he has thus sacked the hamlets contiguous to his State of their human treasure his feats of spoliation will be extended

to distances varying between 12 and 24 days' march from his capital of Abomey . . .

Traders, who are blacks, are sent out to act as spies. The spies bear their petty merchandise upon their heads to the Crooms* in the midst of the jungle. They make their observations and they scan and muster the means of defence possessed by each Croom. After a lapse of some months the spies return to the King, report by word of mouth the gleanings of their journey, and assume the guidance of the army. They instruct the chiefs, who are generally the elders, how the unsuspecting Crooms can be surrounded and how the inhabitants can be surprised. These military devices are usually matured and put into practice under favour of the night; and a whole gang of men, women, and children will find themselves in captivity on opening their eyes at the first crimson blush of day. Resistance entails death.[7]

The Portuguese waited to fill their barracoons and Lord Palmerston wrote to the man appointed to succeed John Duncan, Consul Beecroft of Fernando Po. He was to

represent to [Guezo] that the people who dwell in the Yoruba and Popo countries are the friends of England, and that the British Government takes a great interest in their welfare, and would see with much concern and displeasure any acts of violence or oppression committed against them; that, moreover, there are dwelling among those tribes many liberated Africans and British-born subjects whom Her Majesty's Government are bound to protect from injury.[8]

Beecroft arrived at Ouidah in March 1850 to carry out Palmerston's instructions. He was to visit Abeokuta and seek the 'actual wants, and wishes, and disposition of the Yoruba people' asking British protection for their trade and themselves, and to warn Guezo to leave them alone. He found interesting reports and unsettlement ashore. The annual Custom at Abomey had been unexpectedly postponed to May. No visitors would be received before then. 'The King has been unsuccessful in his last marauding expedition', he was told. 'Three or four of his principal chiefs have been captured by the enemy;

---

* i.e. villages.

which misfortune has no doubt perplexed a man of such an unconquerable spirit.'[9]

On the first day of the delayed Custom, public receptions were held for Consul Beecroft and Lieutenant Forbes. Isidoro de Souza, the sullen new Chacha (chief slave-broker), was there, dwarfed by the ghost of his father. Queen Victoria's latest letter to Guezo was read aloud and presents given. On the second day, the visitors were banned from the streets, for Guezo was sacrificing to his ancestors. When Forbes emerged, the heads were on display and the prisoners who would be tomorrow's sacrifices were being paraded. On the fourth day, eleven slaves were beheaded; three more would have been killed with them had Forbes and Beecroft not bought them for $100. Among them was an orphaned infant princess from one of the villages annihilated in the slave-hunts. They were not permitted to buy the rest. On the fifth day, 6,800 male and female troops were endlessly reviewed in broiling heat; on the seventh, more slaves were offered to the mob for death. And so it continued; parade, drink, death; parade, drink, death. Domingo Martinez called on the king with presents. The Custom dragged endlessly on. A woman came to find them: Mrs McCarthy, rescued years since by the Squadron and come south from Sierra Leone to settle near Abeokuta. Her husband John was being held in Abomey as a prisoner of war.

It took nearly three weeks of heat and delay before a palaver with Guezo was arranged. The king had a letter ready for his visitors to take to Victoria.

> Being desirous that the Slave Trade should be stopped in the minor ports prior to my entering into a Treaty, I have to request that you will endeavour to blockade the slave ports between Quitta and Lagos, and then I will endeavour to enter into an agreement for the stoppage of the Slave Trade in my own country.[10]

His people would not allow him to give up the trade entirely, he told Beecroft, but if the British queen would allow the ships of five named agents to pass, then he would suppress the trade of all other merchants. 'We gave them the short negative',[11] Forbes wrote. Then would she allow the ships of just three to pass unmolested? She would not.

> At this moment the king's countenance was almost blanched, his head down, his right hand rubbed his forehead, while his veins swelled, and

in a tremulous voice he added, 'Write to the queen and ask her to direct her men of war to allow one ship to pass in my name to the Brazils, to carry a cargo of slaves, and bring back goods for me.'

No.

Mr Beecroft broached the subject of Abeokuta but Guezo had had enough of the British and answered that 'he intended making war on Abeokuta and Mr Beecroft had better warn the white men to leave'. When the subject of John McCarthy was raised, Guezo dismissed them. 'Thus ended the palaver', wrote Lieutenant Forbes:

> and I am of opinion that future attempts unless by force, will fail in causing Guezo to give up the Slave Trade, or his pride admitting him to accept a subsidy. ... In everything he said he simply illustrated a desire to enrich himself at the expense of his neighbours. If his trade be stopped, his power is done. At the head of a military nation surrounded by enemies, he must have money, and would then treat for any trade. In a word, nothing but coercive measures will cause Guezo and his Ministers to give up the Slave Trade.

Mrs McCarthy was taken away 'to identify her husband' and did not come back. As he prepared to leave, Forbes asked the Caboceers about the McCarthys: they 'evaded the palaver and said it was a small question'. The frustration which had been building in Lieutenant Forbes spilt forth: 'I then addressed them thus: "I am going to England, and shall acquaint Her Majesty that the King of Dahomey holds a British subject prisoner: you know the consequences to your trade." The shock was electrical and they begged of me not to be angry. I then threw myself into a passion; dashed a book upon the table and told them I should act as I had told them. They looked much disconcerted.' On the far side of Cana, in the late afternoon, the McCarthys caught up with the British cavalcade. There were marks on Mrs McCarthy's flesh from where she had been held in chains.

When Lieutenant Forbes sailed for England, the orphaned girl – now baptised Sarah Forbes Bonetta – went with him, and the commodore again wrote to Guezo to warn him that war on British citizens in Abeokuta was war on Britain. If any were hurt, the Squadron would impose a blockade on his ports. It was, however, not the threatened blockade of African but an actual blockade of Brazilian ones which would crush the slave trade of the Bights.

Lord Aberdeen's Act for 'the Regulation and Final Abolition of the African Slave Trade' had been passed five years earlier, in 1845, when Brazil refused to renew any anti-slave-trade treaty with Britain on the specious grounds that there was no slave trade to abolish. The Act had authorised British warships to bring Brazilian slavers before British Admiralty courts but even this 'great stretch of power', as Aberdeen himself called it, had hardly affected the volume of Brazilian trade. Several naval officers called before the Parliamentary Select Committee which was still deliberating the Squadron's future said the best way to suppress Brazilian slaving was to take the naval campaign to Brazil. Some thought an island should be annexed to provide a British base and others thought an anti-slave-trade squadron should patrol the Brazilian coast as it did the West African one. A British South American fleet already existed, but had had little time for chasing slavers. Seven vessels not only had to cruise the vast coast from Callao to Pernambuco but had been engaged in the endless wars of the River Plata. Just as pressure on Brazilian suppliers in West Africa was mounting, however, those wars paused and a man of declared abolitionist passion was appointed to command of the South American station.

Any idea of slavers as gentlemen opponents had died an early death here. By the time slavers arrived in Brazil, conditions aboard were worse even than those which shocked prize-crews off West Africa. Both British and American capital were deeply implicated in the Brazilian trade and the American government, badgered for years by reports from its consul in Rio, had sent a warship or two to suppress overt American participation. In 1849, Lord Palmerston decided Britain must do the same. Spies were recruited on the Brazilian coast as they had been on the West African, with lavish use of Secret Service money. The captain of the Port of Rio was suborned into passing on information about slavers' movements; so was at least one formerly large-scale slave-trader, the editors of a couple of Brazilian newspapers and the handful of home-grown anti-slavery societies which, to everyone's surprise, were beginning to push their way to the surface. Africanisation; humanity; the feeling that it was better for Brazil to reform herself than be forcibly reformed by other nations, particularly the hated British; the emperor's personal distaste for the trade – all these thoughts were cohering in little groups which lobbied for Brazilian abolition, shouted down and derided at first but in existence, and now in receipt of British funds and support.

Admiral Barrington Reynolds, who took command of the station in October 1849, was delighted to commend muscular action to his commanders. In January, the steamer HMS *Cormorant* was informed that four ships flying Portuguese flags in the harbour of Rio were slavers. Commander Schomberg took the legal way first, requesting the four be detained and examined by Brazilian officials. The local chief of police did so, and 'acquitted the ships of any design to infringe the law'.[12] Schomberg seized the slavers nonetheless and sent them for adjudication at the British Vice-Admiralty court on St Helena. There was outrage, for they had been seized not at sea, but in Brazil's sovereign waters and this was an act of war.

In London, news of the *Cormorant's* actions was received just as the Parliamentary Select Committee concluded, after two years' discussion, that the Preventive Squadron could never suppress the slave trade completely and must be withdrawn. Partial measures such as the deployment of a squadron, the committee said, only prolonged and increased the trade's miseries. But the recommendation to withdraw coincided with Lord Palmerston's momentous decision that the same summary, unilateral action had to be taken against the Brazilian trade as he had taken against the Portuguese in 1839. He seized the moment, informing the Admiralty that Aberdeen's Act of 1845 had been misinterpreted. Henceforth, under his new, unilateral interpretation, there were to be 'no restrictions on the limits within which the search, detention and capture of slave traders . . . are to take place . . . in Brazilian waters as well as on the high seas'.[13] It was a complete *post-facto* approval of the *Cormorant's* actions, and was enthusiastically received by Admiral Reynolds in Brazil.

With only the authorisation of a British minister, ship after Brazilian ship was seized in Brazil's own waters, cut out of Brazil's own harbours and used as target practice if ill-found or sent to British courts if not. It was like shooting rats in a barrel. There were riots in the ports and Soares de Souza, Brazilian Foreign Minister, called in the British envoy. Soares de Souza knew the end was coming, but it was his desperately delicate task to bring abolition about with at least a semblance of popular support, and the appearance that he had not been cowed by Britain into doing so. The speed with which he succeeded was totally unexpected. In July, his abolition bill was adopted by the Chamber of Deputies. In September it was signed.

The sudden death of the Brazilian trade took everyone utterly by surprise. Slaving had seemed an unshakeable institution here, and a business so rooted in profit, custom and national honour as to seem immortal. Different causes were then, and have since been, ascribed. An outbreak of yellow fever brought by a slave-ship in 1849? The determination of Soares de Souza and the small band which argued the abolitionist case in the Chamber of Deputies? American measures to rein in the participation of American citizens? 'The achievement which I look back on with the greatest and purest pleasure', Lord Palmerston would say when he lay dying fifteen years later, 'was forcing the Brazilians to give up their slave trade.'[14] He firmly believed it was the result of the British South American fleet's battering of the slave-ports, and did not give a damn whether that was legal or not.

News of Brazil's capitulation reached King Guezo at the end of a disastrous year. In February, as the slave-hunting season approached, the British had warned him again to leave Abeokuta alone. 'It is not my intention to make war on Abeokuta', he replied. 'All British subjects in my dominions shall be held sacred.'[15] Five days later, his army approached Abeokuta at the run, women foremost. The defenders could not hold them back, and retreated within the city walls to seek terrified refuge in the mission compound. But the first of the feared women warriors to be seen was a live captive; then came the hand and foot of a female corpse and the news that no one had expected. The battle had turned. The defenders were on the attack, and taking trophies. Under cover of darkness Guezo fled, his army retreating behind him, attacked on all sides. Over one thousand Dahomean corpses were counted on the field the next morning. In various houses of Abeokuta, prisoners were being warily fed. A deserter from Guezo's army – a man taken into Dahomean slavery many years ago – brought news that Guezo had lost many thousand warriors and feared the reaction of the Abomey mob when it heard of the royal army's defeat. When the British learnt – as they must – that he had not only been beaten, but had lied when he told them no war was planned on Abeokuta, Guezo knew they would come for him.

Commodore Henry Bruce, who had replaced Charles Hotham, received the expected letter in June: 'To Her Most Gracious Majesty Victoria, Queen of England, Defender of the Faith, etc.':

The King of Dahomey sends his compliments to her Majesty, greeting, and wishes she would send him a soldier with a good head to hear some palaver from his mouth at the town of Abomey, so that he may report the same to Her Majesty.[16]

Frederick Forbes was back in Windsor with his family and little African protégée. This time the soldier with a good head would be Commander Wilmot of HMS *Harlequin*. 'It may be', Commodore Bruce instructed him, 'that the King's object is merely to have some influential mediator between him and the people of Yoruba' but 'advantage may be taken of his request' to press again the demand for both abolition and the 'termination of a war that involves the personal security of the British residents, missionaries and others located at Abeokuta'.[17] Wilmot was to put it to him 'whether a liberal and certain stipend from Great Britain, for three years, in addition to the revenue which he might obtain from the productions of his rich country and the establishment of legal commerce, would not be more advantageous to him, than obstinately clinging to a course which will ultimately leave him in poverty, and without a friend'. This was not exaggeration: since the defeat in Abeokuta, and news of the changes in Brazil, the slave trade in the Bights had almost come to a stop. 'Within the last two months,' one captain reported, '135 slaves were marched down from Abbeokuta to Lagos . . . but they were unable to find a purchaser [and] marched back into the interior; a circumstance hitherto unheard of by any of the residents . . . many of the slave-dealers are ruined, and at Lagos some of them are actually selling the furniture out of their houses to procure provisions for their slaves.'[18] That captain had recently spoken to a Frenchman bound for London with a cargo of Domingo Martinez's oil. 'Martinez asserted', the Frenchman had said, 'that if the British took or destroyed Lagos, Slavery would be done away with in the Bights.'

But Guezo was not the only slave-dealing chief in the delta who stood in the way of abolition. While Commodore Bruce waited to hear the results of his palaver with Commander Wilmot, his attention was turned to the other of Palmerston's 'persevering offenders': King Kosoko of Lagos.

'It is difficult,' Commander Heath of HMS *Niger* wrote to his new commodore, 'to unravel all the intricacies of an African quarrel', but his synthesis was this.

About six years ago, Akitoye, the King of Lagos, was expelled from his throne by Kosoko, the present King. Akitoye, with his followers, took refuge in Badagry which was then inhabited by a race called Popos. Jealousy and party spirit soon arose, and a feud commenced between Akitoye's followers and the Popos, who sided with Kosoko. The principal cause of this was, as far as I can understand, that the Popos had been accustomed to have an uninterrupted canoe-communication all along the lagoon from Porto Novo to Lagos, which Akitoye's party, being hostile to Lagos, wished to intercept at Badagry.[19]

The *Niger* was stationed off Badagry, partly in routine blockade but more urgently as protection to the British Mission, the Repatriate community and the town's merchants. The 'African quarrel' had just erupted into fighting: 'a large body' of Lagos people had come to Badagry to trade with the Popos; insults in the market-place had become a brawl, a brawl had become a battle, 'the fight commenced and the town was burnt to the ground'. The Lagos people had been repelled, but Badagry was bracing itself for renewed attack. King Kosoko had offered a reward for Akitoye's head and Akitoye had fled to the protection of the British consulate on Fernando Po. British merchants were demanding that the Squadron land men to protect their property and Abeokuta, newly bold from defeating Guezo, was sending two thousand men to join the Badagrians against Kosoko's expected army.

The Squadron's officers agreed. This was, reported Commodore Bruce, a quarrel 'purely of a domestic nature, and not one which warrants a neutral Power to interfere in a hostile manner'.[20] But there were intricacies here, for Akitoye was sheltering under the British flag and his supporters in Badagry were in no doubt that they were owed British protection. British missionaries there had been besieged by 'Akitoye's people . . . saying, Now Akitoye is gone we look to you as our head, he left us to your care when he went'.[21]

The usual letter was sent to Kosoko, warning of consequences if British persons or property were attacked and Domingo Martinez offered to forward a similar warning to the King of Porto Novo: 'the English do not wish to take any part in the quarrels of the country; let the natives fight as much as they choose, but let them beware if an Englishman suffers.'[22] This was not enough for the merchants or the insistent emissaries of Akitoye: they wanted the active, armed protection of the Squadron. It seems, wrote Reverend Townsend from the Abeokutan mission, that its officers 'regard the war . . . as having no reference to the English or the acts of the British Government' whereas in his view 'these wars result from the acts of her Majesty's cruisers, and from the efforts of

Englishmen towards establishing lawful trade'.[23] The reverend had a clearer view of cause and effect on the coast than London, still obstinately refusing to understand or accept the consequences of palaver and presents. In late June, still waiting for Kosoko to make his move, Abeokutan commanders boarded the *Niger* to give Commander Heath their 'earnest request that Akitoye might be brought back from Fernando Po, and set up by [the British] as King of Lagos'.[24]

Through the summer of 1851 everyone waited for Kosoko to make his move. Steamships hovered watchfully off Badagry. On 3 September, Commander Wilmot was in talks with the commander of the Abeokutan army. 'If you could only grant our desire to destroy Lagos', he was told,

> secure that wicked man Kosoko, and bring back Akitoye to Lagos, then we fear not, the whole country will enjoy peace, and if the Slave Trade is put down at Lagos, there will not be much more war in the country. But the particular word I mention to you this morning, is, that I and all the chiefs and people of Abbeokuta are most anxious to make friendship with you and all the English. We bow before your Queen and Government, and pray you to make a treaty with us. We promise to keep the law you give us by your help, for if we have English trade we do not want Slave Trade.[25]

John Beecroft was on Fernando Po with King Akitoye so it was Vice-Consul Fraser, John Duncan's successor, who next visited Abomey, and found Guezo 'anxious for presents, such as muskets, bayonets, powder, shot and shell, to annihilate the Abeokutians'. He was also desperate for time for if he could hold the British off until the rivers became fordable in March, then his armies might cross, reverse their defeat, burn Abeokuta, capture, kill or enslave the interfering foreign bodies on his borders and meet the envoys of Britain with renewed power. Could Commander Wilmot visit him again and talk? Commander Wilmot could not: he had visited once, and 'found whatever [Guezo] had to state relative to signing treaties was all twaddle'.[26]

In London, Lord Palmerston's position was shifting with each report of defiance and duplicity from Africa, success from Brazil and hesitation from a parliament due to debate whether to adopt the Select Committee's recommendation to disband the Squadron. Missionaries – black and white – consuls, merchants, officers and now the Abeokutan commanders were all urging him towards one course of action. Here, perhaps, was another wasps' nest for the smoking.

In August, the House finally debated the Select Committee's findings and the Squadron's supporters braced themselves for the expected vote for withdrawal. Instead, to everyone's intense surprise, a majority voted to save it. The determined, impassioned opposition to the Select Committee of a handful of men had swayed opinion at the last moment. 'If we give up this high and holy work', said Lord John Russell at the end of the long debate

> and proclaim ourselves to be no longer fitted to lead in the championship against the curse and crime of slavery, we have no longer a right to expect a continuance of those blessings which, by God's favour, we have so long enjoyed. I think . . . that the high, the moral and the Christian character of this nation is the main source and secret of its strength.[27]

The House of Commons had turned the Select Committee's conclusion on its head. If the Squadron, as that committee had proved, was not strong enough to carry out its task, then it must be not disbanded, but strengthened.

'It is not consistent,' a triumphant Lord Palmerston informed the Admiralty a month after the crucial vote to save the Squadron, 'with the honour and dignity of the British Government, that a warning deliberately given by a British Commodore, in entire conformity with the policy of Her Majesty's Government, and as deliberately set at nought, should be thus disregarded with impunity.'[28] Guezo had promised he would not attack British citizens, and he had broken his word. Ouidah, Palmerston ordered, 'and the rest of the Dahomian coast' must be blockaded until Guezo

> shall have concluded and signed an agreement, by which he shall bind himself to give up totally and entirely the Slave Trade, to prevent his subjects from practising that crime, and to expel all foreign slave-traders from his territory; to abandon the practice of human sacrifices; and to protect all missionaries who may come to reside within the range of his authority. Of course no money-compensation can now be given him for any pecuniary loss which he may incur by abandoning the Slave-trade.

As for Kosoko, that 'barbarous savage who has been put up and is supported by a set of slave-traders who have established themselves on the Island of Lagos', Commodore Bruce was to 'consider the practicability [of] sending into Lagos the small force which would be sufficient for the purpose of expelling [them] and for re-establishing in his stead the former chief, Akitoye'.[29] The essential condition was still attached. Bruce was directed 'not to keep possession of Lagos, nor to remain there beyond what is absolutely necessary'.[30]

Now things moved fast. Frederick Forbes was ordered back to Africa on 'special service': his mission this time was to organise the Abeokutan resistance to Guezo's expected attack. On the coast, Commodore Bruce sent notice to merchant houses and trading stations of the forthcoming blockade, orders to his commanders enjoining 'not to give occasion to foreign Governments to complain of any undue severity or annoyance in the accomplishment of this service'.[31] He also wrote to Consul Beecroft requesting he attend a meeting in Ouidah on 15 December to discuss how best to proceed. Then he sailed for Sierra Leone to fetch arms for the Abeokutans and 'as many of the liberated Africans' from there 'as might volunteer to join the cause of the Abeokutians'.[32] None would go without payment. 'Under this circumstance', he wrote in disgust, 'I declined to receive them.' At Ouidah, Guezo's viceroy forbade Vice-Consul Fraser to leave his house. Why? He could not say. For how long? At King Guezo's pleasure.

A last attempt was made to compel Kosoko to submit without a fight. Heading for his meeting with the Commodore, Consul Beecroft brought muskets, flints and Akitoye from Fernando Po to Badagry, where the king was met with 'demonstrations of unbounded joy'.[33] On 20 November, Beecroft steamed under flag of truce upriver to Lagos Island, where Kosoko and his Portuguese allies lived. A last-ditch meeting ended when Kosoko 'distinctly stated . . . that he would not enter into any treaty with the English, and did not wish their friendship'. As the British returned downriver, musket-fire from the shore began and the steamer *Bloodhound*, supposed to cover the boats, ran aground. Some British seamen landed and set fire to a part of Lagos Town, but still 'the mud-walls and very narrow streets afforded so great an advantage to the enemy, who were swarming in vast numbers, and proved themselves such good marksmen, that it was thought advisable to recall the people to their boats, as our people suffered much'. Convinced any further talks with Kosoko were futile, Beecroft wrote to Commander Thomas Forbes (no relation to Frederick), commander of HMS *Philomel* and, during the commodore's absence at Sierra Leone, senior officer in the Bights. 'I have no alternative but to apply to you for a sufficient force to compel [Kosoko] to make a treaty, or dethrone him and replace the rightful heir, Akitoye.'[34]

When Commander Thomas Forbes gathered his division off Lagos, he and the other commanders were hesitant. Should they not wait for Commodore Bruce, due shortly to arrive for the meeting of 15 December? Did a consul's request give them the authorisation to attack? Beecroft had no doubts and laid three of Palmerston's despatches on the table to make his point. The first, to the Lords of the Admiralty, advised 'it might be advisable to dethrone Kosoko . . . and set up his rival Akitoye'. The second authorised Beecroft to give 'certain supports' to Abeokuta. The third, on which the consul most rested his case, authorised him to require from the Squadron 'such force as would ensure his personal safety' if a first attempt at treaty-making failed, and with that force 'to obtain another interview with Kosoko'.[35] To lead a hostile force upriver in attack represented an extreme interpretation of these instructions but if the attack were successful, would anyone care? So they steamed back upriver on 25 November, the *Bloodhound* in front with another flag of truce. The expected musketry from the banks started as soon as they crossed the bar, the *Bloodhound* grounded again and fire from her boats was no match for the estimated five thousand men firing back. When they limped back over the bar that evening, no conference had been held and two men were dead and ten wounded. The expedition had been a disaster and the Squadron had been humiliated.

Commodore Bruce arrived off Ouidah, as expected, in mid-December. No eye-witness testimony of the meeting with his commanders survives to tell us just how he expressed himself to them. By the time he came to write his cold report to London, he was able to emphasise the gallantry of individuals, but his fury with John Beecroft still lifts off the page. 'There are circumstances connected with this transaction to which I am reluctantly compelled to draw [your] attention',[36] he wrote. Beecroft should have attempted no further 'negotiation' after the failed talks of 20 November. He should not 'without consulting me, have requested an officer under my orders to place himself in a position where hostilities were almost inevitable'. The instructions Beecroft had cited from Lord Palmerston were clearly designed to be used only after consultation with the commodore and he should have waited until the appointed meeting of 15 December before taking action. The failure of the expedition carried out under his orders had left Bruce in an invidious position, one which 'now leaves', he told the Admiralty, 'but one course of action open to me, which is, to inflict a summary and retributive punishment upon the chiefs of Lagos'. On 23 December, that punishment began.

At dawn, the steamer *Sampson* anchored at the back of the surf, where she could throw her shells across the lagoon to cover the boats as they advanced. Captain Jones went down into his gig to command the boats across the bar. With them into the river went the *Bloodhound* and John Beecroft's own small iron boat on which rockets had been mounted. They anchored just inside for the night and the captain addressed his men: they could expect no quarter when they ascended the river tomorrow.

On the hot morning of Christmas Eve, Mr Beecroft, Akitoye and six hundred-odd volunteers from Abeokuta arrived on the western bank and hailed the British boats. They were given white neck-ties to distinguish them from Kosoko's men in fighting. That afternoon, the Sampsons raided a downriver slave-station and took nine canoes under cover of the *Bloodhound*'s guns. Later, the *Bloodhound* dropped upriver on the incoming tide, her officers' task to work out the channel for tomorrow's flotilla and reconnoitre the defences of Lagos Island.

Kosoko and his Portuguese allies had done their work well. The entire west coast of the island had been fortified with an embankment and ditch to shelter Kosoko's musketry. Those creeks and bays deep enough for British boats to enter had been blocked off with double rows of vicious bamboo stakes. Where they must pass some narrow, shallow or otherwise troublesome point, batteries had been built, protected by strong coconut-tree stockades, to bombard them as they went. Muskets were seen protruding. The *Bloodhound* did not go round the north-west corner of the island to see Lagos Town, site of Kosoko's palace and the slavers' mansions, but turned back to rejoin the boats inside the bar. Captain Lyster of the *Penelope* came aboard to decide with Captain Jones the plan of attack. Christmas Day came and went, for the senior officers thought hostile action inappropriate; the chaplains did their work and the men had extra rations, but not too many of rum. All day, Kosoko's batteries took pot shots at the British but they were far out of range.

Early on Boxing Day, the two steamers *Bloodhound* and *Teazer*, and a host of ships' boats were on the move, opposed by musket-fire first from the banks of the river, then from those of Lagos Island. The *Bloodhound* reached the north-west corner where she had turned back on Christmas Eve and there her pilot discovered that since he had last entered Lagos Town, the channel had silted up. Stuck, yet again, in the sand and mud, the *Bloodhound* could only aim one of her guns at the shore. Worse, she was within range of one of the batteries. While her seamen threw out anchors, a constant fire was directed ashore from their eighteen-pounder, which silenced the great guns of the stockade but not the musket bullets which fell about them in showers. Until the tide lifted the *Bloodhound* from her temporary grave and brought the rest of the British boats to help her, she was a sitting target. It was vital to prevent other large guns being brought into position. All day, ships' boats scurried back and forth, firing into the banks wherever they saw movement.

Word came that the propellers of the *Teazer* had struck and that she, too, was grounded on a downriver shoal, within range of Kosoko's batteries, fixed into the gluey bottom with her own guns pointing in the wrong direction. There were two options: evacuate her men and leave the ship to her destruction; or land, under fire, and spike the enemies' guns. This was the first, desperate landing of the day: two hundred men rowed for shore under a storm of musket-balls and raced up the beach. A handful were left to guard the boats, and crouch, run and bring in the screaming wounded where they were felled, bind their dirty wounds and splash water on their faces. As the British advanced, Kosoko's men retreated to a second line of defence 60 yards inland. A brave lieutenant disabled the cannon. So far, so successful and very few casualties: but when the lieutenant ordered the retreat, the Lagos men came out of the bushes and attacked. If their musket-fire had been inaccurate, their hand-to-hand fighting was not: fourteen seamen died, and sixty-two were wounded, getting back to the boats.

The Bloodhounds, too, had decided the battery on the bank opposite them must be destroyed. Their huge carpenter stood neck-deep in water at the river's edge, 'axe in hand, hewing away at the stakes to make a passage for the boats to land', and the guns were duly spiked. Hours crawled past, full of shot and shell, everyone on the alert for movement on the bank, the boats flitting about the great body of the steamer, inert and helpless in the silt. A cloud of smoke rose from the bombardment of the British boats, spread and claimed both banks of the river. Beneath it, the two sides kept killing until the sudden night dropped between them like a curtain and brought silence. A few vessels slipped downriver in the night to transfer the British wounded to the ships outside the bar. North of Lagos Island, canoes evacuated families from their homes.

At first light, the boom and flare of guns began again and the *Teazer* lifted herself free of the imprisoning mud; twenty minutes later, she had groped for and found a channel through rising water and was steaming towards the *Bloodhound*. Within an hour, her rocket-boat had passed the *Bloodhound* and begun firing into Lagos Town. At eleven o'clock there was a mighty explosion and a cheer from the grimy British. They had hit Kosoko's magazine and the flames were spreading: licking, then devouring, thatched roofs with a sea-breeze blowing them on towards the market-place and beyond. Back came the rocket-boat to her station between the two steamers and a general hail of ship-to-shore fire began. Another lucky rocket struck the battery, another huge explosion rocked the boats and the battle was over. Two hours' work at full force had destroyed the town.

A message was sent ashore. Kosoko must present himself to the British within forty-eight hours. The next day was Sunday, a day of rest. While the officers planned an assault should Kosoko not come to terms, the men lay in the heat and watched the flames ashore, and the endless laden canoes which crossed from the burning town to other islands in the river. Captain Jones would not fire on them. 'I conceived', he said, 'that it was no part of the grand design with which England sent her forces here, to care whether a bed and table, and private property of any kind, were on one side of the river or the other . . . it was . . . desirable to show that we did not come for pillage, but that our sole object was to stop Slave Trade.'[37] When it was confirmed that Kosoko and his entourage had also left the burning town, a message was sent to the islands: 'they were told, and told to spread it far and wide, "never fear an attack from the English, but always come forward and meet them as friends; that we never fired first, but that if people assailed, we 'hit hard''''.

Akitoye was sent for. It was deemed politic that he be installed in his old palace by Abeokutian and Badagran forces, but fearing the landing would degenerate into looting, Commander Wilmot went with them to ensure the decencies of both pomp and restraint. 'I made him put on his kingly robes,' Wilmot reported, 'mount his horse, assemble all his warriors, and ride completely round the town; I went with him and made his people stop every ten minutes and call out "Hurrah for Akitoye!"; this pleased him very much and has had a good effect.'[38] Their route was strewn with reminders of the old regime. 'Skulls and bones were found by us in vast numbers', Wilmot said. Hundreds had been sacrificed in an effort to secure the intervention of the ancestors against the blockading British force; two had been impaled alive outside Kosoko's palace. On 1 January, Akitoye came back aboard the *Penelope* and signed a treaty abolishing the slave trade in his lands for ever.

When news that Lagos was destroyed and Akitoye reinstated reached Abomey, King Guezo acted fast and pragmatically. His stick was received at Vice-Consul Fraser's house the same day, and house arrest withdrawn. 'Express messengers' were sent to Commander Thomas Forbes. The de Souza brothers, the chiefs of Ouidah, Domingo Martinez – all received the summons to witness the signing of Dahomey's anti-slave-trade treaty. By the end of the month, the signatures of both 'persevering offenders' had joined those of their brother-rulers as far as Cape Verde. Within three months of Kosoko's expulsion, twelve more anti-slave-trade treaties had been signed with other rulers in the Bights. In 1850, twenty-three thousand slaves were imported into Brazil; in 1851, three thousand; in 1852, seven hundred.

It was, of course, a triumph; but Commodore Bruce knew just how fragile these triumphs could be. 'The Slave Trade requires no organised system for its supports', he wrote. 'It might cease for a century and be renewed in a week; remove the blockading squadron, and to-morrow, if the Spaniards or Brazilians were willing to buy slaves, the chiefs would be ready to sell them, notwithstanding their pledges to the contrary.'[39] The slaving flame could be reignited by the slightest spark blown across the ocean from Cuba or Brazil. Attack, deterrent, enforcement: these were the tasks which the navy could carry out, given the right tools; but to change a culture was not a task for which it was designed or prepared. Now the Squadron had cleared the ground, Bruce knew other agencies must plant their seeds.

There are, in my opinion, means, by the adoption of which, the squadron might, to effect all that is required of it on this point, be reduced to a number only sufficient to watch over the interests of legitimate traders, namely, by establishing Consuls and Agents at different places, whose duty it should be to ascertain whether or not the native chiefs to whom they are accredited, faithfully observe their engagements. [They should be] strictly forbidden to interfere in the political concerns of the countries in which they are residing, and prohibited from entering into commercial speculations.

Frederick Forbes left Abeokuta in March, sick with fever and dysentery, and was sent to Ascension to recover his health. He died there on 25 March, aged thirty-four, leaving a widow, four children of his own and his adopted African daughter, Sarah.

18

To an End, Immediately and Forever

Théophile Conneau was living modestly among friends in Baltimore, now in his late forties and suffering rather from rheumatism. Funds were low, and when a journalist suggested he publish his memoirs, he seized upon the idea. By March 1854, he had sent his last draft for editing. He took leave of his teenage American bride (Rosalie had been left in Africa) and sailed for France to arrange publication in Paris and see his brother, '*Médécin en Chef de l'Empereur*' no less. The reunion was affectionate. 'I soon informed my brother', Conneau wrote to his American editor, 'of the shattered circumstances of my affairs [and] dubious prospects.'[1] Impressed by seeing Théophile in scintillating form at a party, entertaining the guests with stories of Esther, Ama-de-Bella, whips, brands and shackles, the doctor 'informed the Emperor while at breakfast with his Empress' of his brother's presence in Paris. The imperial couple was intrigued, for France was in need of a 'colonial agent' for New Caledonia, the island she had just annexed north of Australia. The emperor's interest in his new subjects *outremer* was less than paternal: he considered a former slaver perfect for the job. An audience with the lovely Creole empress sealed the deal. As his old adversaries on the coast of Africa continued their weary regime of patrol and visit, Captain and Mrs Conneau took passage from the States to New Caledonia, an intrepid but respectable colonial official and his lady wife. He wrote to his editor 'at sea, coast of Peru', complaining of conditions aboard.

The *Empire City* is a very slow boat and very neglectfully kept. Her dining saloon being in the lower deck, passengers are deprived of light, air and ventilation during meal times. The berths are well enough, but full of insects and vermin. The table is certainly the worst served I have ever seen on board of any packets. The servants (Black Devils) are the greatest sauciest rascals in creation, and as their Chief is also a damned mustachio'd Negro, things are conducted with filthiness, impertinence and neglect. Such is the imprudence of those demons that if a passenger calls for a drop of water during the day and does not place a shilling in their greasy hands, he is sure not to get it.

No remorseful recollection of the *Areostatico* or the *Atalanta* leavened his annoyance. M. Conneau was not one to chuckle at the irony of things. 'Having trespassed on your patience and time with my troubles and advice', he concluded, 'permit me to close these most insignificant lines, with a kind adieu and my best wishes.'

'Now that the excitement of chasing and capturing slavers is almost at an end', came the report from the Preventive Squadron in late 1852, 'the monotony of the station is much complained of.'[2] Chase and capture were now rare above the Line, and routine consisted of patrol, patrol, patrol with occasional visits to ports to reprovision, fuel and check that the treaties were being observed. Cruising between Sierra Leone and Liberia drove one lieutenant to an almost hysterical fatigue.

21 Mar: Bilious. Calm and hot. Anchored off Isles de Los. Heavy tornado.
11 Apr: Rain, rain, rain. Nothing in sight but French barque standing to south east.
16 Apr: Troubled with the liver.
19 Apr: Rain in plenty.
20 Apr: Heavy rain.
23 Apr: Liver worse. Had myself cupped. Rain. Rain.
26 Apr: Heavy rain.
29 Apr: Dirty rainy day. Boats sent upriver returned having seen nothing.
2 May: Squall from west with rains.

8 May: Continual rain all day and night. Caught half a ton of rainwater.[3]

The monotony continued into June, then July, with rare breaks. President Roberts of Liberia came for dinner – 'a hale, ungainly looking man with a slight tinge of darkness' – and gave them thirty-four slaves to take to Sierra Leone. There was an occasional rumour of slave-ships, but nothing came of it. Tornadoes struck most days. The cutlass men were drilled; the small-arms men were drilled; boats rowed out with targets for practice with the great guns; '1st Class Boy fell awkward from the Main Futtock Shrouds was picked up having sustained a few bruises', more exercise, more musket drill, more targets, more rain, rain, rain.

Ships returning from northern commissions in 1852 and 1853 brought back the same story: that 'the Slave Trade is, so to speak, abolished'.[4] One reported 'vessels having the appearance of slavers are boarded, but though they are furnished with ring bolts and other equipments for the purpose of slaving, yet their papers are correct and it is evident that they are not engaged in the hateful traffic; indeed, the merchants on the coast, who were formerly so occupied, have now abandoned the trade'. Even in the Bights, the trade seemed dead. The occasional Spanish schooner or Brazilian steamer dashed in when the British cruisers turned away, for there were still small, semi-clandestine markets across the oceans although in Brazil, as one officer pointed out, slavers now required 'as much tact to get [their slaves] landed as was displayed in shipping them'.[5]

In Lagos, the palm-oilers were arriving in droves: first off the mark, a canny Piedmontese, was trading within six weeks of Akitoye's accession. Missionaries, too, had moved in, with Repatriates behind them, Sierra Leoneans arriving 'almost by every mail' and others returning from Brazil. A steamer was making regular mail-runs between Lagos and Liverpool and in June 1853, a British consul took up permanent residence. There were troubles, for Akitoye was not an inspiring ruler. Commander Wilmot, not a man to pull his punches, thought him 'an imbecile; totally without any character, save that of an idiot and drunkard. He began the day by drinking, and ended it by being carried to bed drunk and helpless.' Under his wavering rule, a few of the old traders opened communications with Kosoko and suggested he reverse the coup of 1851. He did so in August 1853, was repelled by British steamers and signed a temporising treaty. Recognised as chief of two inland towns and given a British pension, Kosoko renounced, he said, both the foreign slave trade and any claim on the throne of Lagos. For the moment, the lagoon, too, was quiet.

Commander Wilmot repeated Commodore Bruce's warning that prevention should not be relaxed too soon. He thought the four cruisers of the Southern Division, patrolling the Congo and Angola, were insufficient. 'The Slave Dealers will make a set at this part of the Coast now they find themselves pushed away from the Bights of Benin', he predicted, and 'so long as [there is] the remotest chance of [the local chiefs] being able to get rid of their Slaves at the high prices which they will naturally fetch, now that their scarcity is felt, and their value enhanced, so long will they turn a deaf ear to our promises and threats'.[6] Britain must hold firm, he wrote. If the Squadron were prematurely reduced, 'the whole of the western shores will again be alive with vessels carrying their living cargo across the "Big Water" . . . One or two years more, with an efficient Squadron, must complete the work in hand. A few thousands now will save millions hereafter, beside the sacrifice of many valuable lives.'

Nonetheless, it seemed the Preventive Squadron's long job was almost done. Soon the West African station could take on the status of others: a handful of vessels to keep a protective eye on British trade and citizens, ensure crime committed on and between Britons was punished and make the six-monthly visits thought necessary to ensure the treaties were not broken. When storms broke over the heads of half Europe in 1854, it seemed harmless to re-deploy much of the Preventive Squadron in the Crimean Sea.

It was one of the most bizarre *casi belli* in history – a quarrel between monks in Jerusalem over who had the right to polish which holy trinket – and it snowballed into a threat to the national and imperial interests of four states: Britain, France, Russia and Turkey. With Britain's peacetime navy insufficient to meet the Russian threat, overseas stations had to be raided and between May and August, five ships of the Preventive Squadron brought home their men for redeployment to the Crimea. France, too, was withdrawing vessels from round the world, and as ships left West Africa for eastern Europe, slaving burst again through the thin membrane of patrol. When the Treaty of Paris formally ended the Crimean War in March 1856 and released British ships from its horrors, the returning Squadron found itself facing a revived trade.

As the slave trade to Brazil had suddenly died, that to Cuba had risen from its grave. The old traders, Domingo Martinez chief among them, had led a brief revival in the Bights but the new Cuban trade, and the new breed of trader, were concentrated around the Congo. Here, the old, settled pattern of supplier, broker and customer was breaking up. The new men did not settle, like the Afro-Brazilians of the Bights or the Spaniards of the Gallinas. They were buccaneers, opportunists and nomads, of every nationality but sailing almost exclusively under the American flag. It was a new twist on an old and infuriating story.

'Vessels come out here from the Havannahs, Baltimore, New Orleans &c., with American colours, American papers, American captain and crews', wrote Commander Wilmot.

Very few bring cargoes out. They are destined for the Slave Trade and avowedly confess the fact when they arrive upon this coast . . . We are not allowed to search or detain these vessels, although we know, for they tell us so, that they are to be sold, and actually name the price expected, still we can do nothing so long as the American Flag waves over their heads, and the American papers exhibited to us, are in due form.

Everything is preserved in this order until the last moment. When they think the time has arrived for exchanging owners, the cruisers being out of sight, and not likely to interfere with their movements, the bargain is struck, the new captain and crews step on board, the American Flag is hauled down, and with the papers, destroyed. The vessel no longer claims American protection. She probably has no colours at all, but starts with her living cargo, trusting to chance for arriving safe where the Slaves are consigned to. The American captain laughs at us, and dares us to touch him. Here is a Slaver under our very guns, but we cannot detain him, not even lift his hatches.

The American Squadron had been in operation since 1843 and its record was unimpressive. There had been a rapid turnover of commodores, some completely uninterested, others only moderately so, but all hampered by circumstances out of their control. Commodore Isaac Mayo, patrolling the Congo in 1853, was only the latest of several American officers to make the obvious and vital points to the Naval Department: too few vessels made joint cruising and effective patrol impossible; the African coast was too far from their base at the Cape Verde Islands and the mutual right of search, or even visit, was still denied. The consequences were all around him. 'The Slave trade is reviving on this Southern Coast', he had written to Washington even before British and French ships were withdrawn to the Crimea, and American flags were 'extensively used' in its prosecution.

> Several cargoes of Slaves have been recently carried off in American Vessels, which having regular papers, defy the English cruisers, and hope to elude the vigilance of our Squadron, knowing it consists of only Three Vessels, serving on a coast of great extent, and dependent for provisions upon our depot at Porto Praya, in going to and from which much time is unavoidably consumed.[7]

'The Slave Trade', reported the *New York Times* in September 1856, 'is still going on in New York and Baltimore' and 'no one familiar with the details of the shipping business in this city is ignorant of it'.[8] The *New York Tribune* calculated in January 1857 that 'between 25 and 30 slavers left New York within the last three years'.[9] The *American Journal of Commerce* agreed: one or more slavers, that paper claimed, 'was always to be found fitting out at the New York docks'.[10] Some 'in Government', it continued, 'wish the law to be changed so that vessels engaged in the African trade shall take only American crews who could not easily be induced to engage in slave trading, except under false representations, and their deceivers would be liable to suffer for their temerity before a tribunal of justice'. Others said bonds should be required for the return of the ship so it could not be burnt in Cuba and that those implicated in the building, fitting out and supplying of slavers should also be punished. They were operating within forty-year-old blinkers. As Pedro Juan Zulueta and George Clevering could have told them, such measures were more easily demanded than devised and as those working on the African coast had known for years, only the mutual right of visit between British and American squadrons would bring the trade to an end. That, however, seemed no nearer than ever before.

The institution of slavery, associated as it was with the distinct identity of the South, was taking centre stage in American domestic politics. The African slave trade, however, had always been seen as a separate issue, arousing popular debate only when it coincided with the issue of right of search. Theoretically, the penalties for Americans caught slaving were severe, for it had been equated with piracy in 1820. This, too, was an old story: legislation without enforcement had no meaning and there was little enforcement within a culture of indifference. No sentence of death had been passed in four decades. Some judges and juries had sided openly with the accused; others had done their best but been foxed by the complexity of federal, state and 'international' law, in particular the lack of any equipment clause in American legislation. The crashing echoes of the early Mixed Commissions went unheard, or unremarked, across the Atlantic: not until 1840 did the Supreme Court overturn the decision of a New York judge that only ships detained with slaves actually aboard could be condemned as slavers. Since then, a slim majority of ships brought before courts had been confiscated but the individuals involved in their voyages had gone largely unpunished – acquittal by supportive juries for most; perhaps a small fine, a bail easily jumped or even a cell door left ajar for others; and, as those Mixed Commission echoes might also have told anyone interested in listening, confiscation of a slave-ship was ineffective when the profits of one successful voyage outweighed the failure of half a dozen.

One type of feral new slaver trading in the late 1850s would have been recognised by the Squadron captains of twenty years before: then he was an adventurous young Spaniard of good family; now he was a southern buck, bursting with secessionist bravado. Sportsmen, or those who regarded themselves as such, were among those dashing across to the Congo in uninsured, unregistered, sometimes ill-found vessels, careering thence to Cuba, pocketing the profits, burning the vessel and returning to their country clubs, confident no jury would convict them even if evidence of their activities could be found. Sometimes they paid for their slaves. Sometimes, never intending to return to Africa, they did not. Captain Corrie of the *Wanderer* was one of these.

The *Wanderer*, built in 1857 for a member of the New York Yacht Club – which was a very grand affair – was reputed to be the fastest and most luxurious yacht on Long Island. In 1858, her owner sold her to 'Captain' Corrie, a South Carolina gentleman. The club did not know – probably – that Corrie was an associate of Charles Lamar, Savannah businessman, Republican-hater and experienced facilitator of slaving voyages. On 25 June, Corrie brought his new yacht into Charleston, where she flew the club pennant and received society while cargo and fittings were loaded – wooden spoons, according to a newspaper report, '12,000 gallons of water, 30 six-quart pans, 20 five-quart ditto, and 50 one-pint ditto – along with '12 persons as "crew"' besides several others 'called "travelling companions of Captain Corrie" yet who appear to have received certain sums of money from him'. He had before him, Corrie said, a voyage of leisure and sport. At Port Spain, Trinidad, he received more admiring visitors, took on more water and left, ostensibly for St Helena and in fact for the Congo. Here he spent ten days dispensing more hospitality. The officers of the British frigate HMS *Medusa* dined happily aboard, and returned the invitation, for the presence of an entertaining American gentleman was a boon in that dull place. There was champagne and liquor, the *Medusa*'s master recalled, and when Corrie asked whether his new friends were not going to search the beautiful *Wanderer* for slaves, much appreciative laughter and slaps on the droll captain's back. Then he left for Benguela and took on 705 captive adolescents. When he offloaded them in Georgia, 625 were alive. The *Wanderer* was seized by federal officials and confiscated. Captain Corrie, Charles Lamar and several members of the crew were tried. They were acquitted.

Other, less flamboyant, slavers were working what a Boston paper called 'the mutual-aid dodge'. A 'regular fleet of vessels clear from different ports of the United States at the same time [with] distributed among them stores and water to fit out two or three of them for slavers'.

> When the coast is clear they all combine to aid the selected vessels in receiving stores and slaves with the greatest possible dispatch. By these means seven or eight vessels may be all engaged in the Slave Trade without having on board sufficient slave material to convict any one of them. . . . It rarely happens that there is more than one cruiser near a noted slave mart, and if she should succeed in making a prize, she generally leaves the place with it and proceeds to St Helena or Sierra Leone. Aware of her absence, the 'mutual aid' slavers despatch as many of their number as possible and generally run clear.[11]

These voyages left a paper trail of such complexity, spreading guilt among so many persons of so many nationalities, all operating under different conditions, laws and degrees of awareness, that it was practically impossible to bring anyone to justice even had that justice seemed desirable to those charged with seeing it done.

Prices in Cuba had risen to unheard-of levels – partly because slave-ships were now often burnt at the end of their voyages – and only the richest colonists could afford to buy. When a slave cost £3 8s in Africa and sold for £150 in Havana, packing in more than could survive the voyage was again sound business. Again came the terrible sights and reports of Negroes thrown overboard, or abandoned to drown in ships run aground, or dying in their dozens on stinking slave-decks. Again came the debate: was not the Squadron only worsening the fate of those it was supposed to save? Either 'leave the trade to itself', demanded *The Times*, as it had done at intervals for the past forty years, 'in which case it would be carried on with at least a mitigation of barbarity'; or 'thoroughly blockade' Cuba. 'The present position is of moderate and hesitating imbecility which will do nothing.'[12] One slaver captain taken in 1857 told his captors that he had 'run nine successful cargoes and been captured six times, and that he has lost £6,000 by this trip, but that he does not mind it, as, if he had succeeded in landing the cargo, he would have received £37,000 for the adventure'. This was the temptation, and although that figure of six captures to nine successful voyages shows the success of the post-war naval patrols in detecting and detaining, it also shows how little slavers were deterred from re-entering the trade.

As more American slavers – or slavers flying the American flag – appeared, more British officers brought them to in order – illegally – to ascertain nationality and more incidents of British 'abuse' were reported in Washington. On Christmas Eve 1857, the British minister Lord Lyons, bombarded with complaints about British officers exceeding their orders, confronted the American Secretary of State Lewis Cass, a man who revelled in his Anglophobia. Cuba, said Lord Lyons, was the last remaining slave-market in the world and if only America would honour its commitments, then joint British–American action could shut it down. The first part of Cass's response was predictable: complaints about British actions. The second was new. As the 'joint blockade' (a fiction he continued to employ) of the African coast had not worked, why did the British not force Spain to 'shut the ports of Cuba'[13] and station her ships there instead?

To Cass's surprise, Britain agreed. A Cuban blockade was already being promoted in London: it had worked in Brazil, went the thinking, so it could work in the West Indies too. It would have, had Cuban waters not straddled the highway of American commerce, full of American merchant shipping. When the British West Indian fleet was reinforced in 1858, complaints of

British abuse only multiplied, more stories of discourtesy and interference surfaced in the American press and hostility between the two countries was suddenly approaching the level of 1812, when war was actually declared, and 1842, when it was threatened. Northerners and southerners, Democrats and Republicans, put aside differences to join in condemning the British. Either British captains were pirates, they pointed out, or the actions they were carrying out on government orders were tantamount to acts of war. American warships were sent to the Gulf of Mexico 'to protect all vessels of the United States on the high seas from search or detention by the vessels of war of any other nation'.[14]

The Cuban blockade was initiated by Palmerston, but inherited by the government which replaced him in the general election of 1858. The new government reined in the West Indian fleet but found itself nonetheless caught up in yet another bout of negotiation with Washington over rights of search and visit. 'I have put it as strongly as possible', said Foreign Secretary Malmesbury, 'to the American government that if it is known that the American flag covers every iniquity, every pirate or slaver on earth will carry it and no other.'[15] It was the same reasoning that had been 'put to the American government' by many other Foreign Secretaries and it had as little effect. In June, Malmesbury accepted what his predecessors had not: that there was no right of visit under international law. War was averted and there was an orgy of self-congratulation in the American press that this last 'remnant of tutelage' was gone, the last of the hated apron-strings cut. It was calculated in 1859 that more slaving vessels left the ports of Cuba and the United States than at any time since 1830.

However, in return for Malmesbury's acknowledgement that British officers had no right to visit American ships in peacetime, the American government had to take some responsibility for policing its own shipping. The American squadron's base was finally moved from Cape Verde to the Angolan coast and four additional steamers were sent out. With another four stationed off Cuba, the results were striking: whereas previously they had managed an average of one per year, between August 1859 and April 1861 American warships caught twenty-eight slavers.[16] One of them was Captain Nathaniel Gordon, who had the great misfortune to be the only American slaver-captain ever to die for his crime: stopped off the Congo in August 1860 with 893 slaves, no papers, a crew of Spaniards, American and Frenchmen, he was taken back to the States, convicted and hanged. It was an isolated, if famous, case. When other, equally guilty, captains were caught that year and the following, courts reverted to their old, hesitant, lenient ways.

The influx of Recaptives brought to America and liberated by courts there posed a novel problem for American authorities. After a flurry of worried correspondence between Washington and local officials guarding unwanted groups of sick and hungry blacks, funds were provided to repatriate them to Liberia and orders sent out that they were henceforth to be taken directly there, rather than brought with the captured ships to the United States. This legislation passed smoothly, although the provision of a stipend to support them in their first months in Liberia was criticised by some: it was, said one southern Congressman, 'carrying sympathy, humanity or whatever it may be called, to an extreme. . . . I have no right to tax our people in order that we may support and educate the barbarians of Africa.'[17]

One of several ships commissioned to carry Recaptives to Liberia was the *Rebecca*, a beautiful Baltimore-built vessel owned – it appeared – by a company of New Orleans, which city she left in 1859 with forty Liberated Africans, an American crew and two Spanish gentlemen aboard. The *Rebecca* was well known on the West African coast. HMS *Viper* over-hauled her on sight and Lieutenant Hodgkinson was perplexed to find her employed on such a worthy errand. Having landed her sick and weary emigrants, the *Rebecca* headed south and the Spaniards who were her real owners congratulated themselves on giving the British this witty slip. The Congo, their destination, was full of warships – British, American and Portuguese. It was too risky to take on slaves here and they let the commander of HMS *Tigris* know the *Rebecca* had been after a slave-cargo, it was true; but was returning empty to the States, beaten by the patrols. Out to sea, the ship was repainted, rerigged, stripped of any identifying mark and turned back to shore. South of the Congo estuary, they took on 1,200 slaves. The *Vixen* puffed into view just as the last were loaded, but had no hope of catching her. The *Rebecca* was scuttled on the Cuban coast, netting her Spanish owners – and those who had covered her fictitious sale in New Orleans – a vast profit.

Cuba was not, in fact, the only remaining slave-market. For a frightening period in the late 1850s, it looked as though Britain was going to connive in reopening the old trade under a new name. Cruising off the Congo in late 1857, the USS *Dale* had boarded – also illegally – a French steamer and been told she was not a slaver, despite the shackles, casks, wooden spoons, gratings and all other slaving equipment aboard, but a transport taking 'free emigrants' to the French West Indies.

Britain, France, Spain, America: all these depended on the wealth of their plantations. The former two had emancipated their slaves, if only into the dubious status of 'apprentice'. The latter two had not and the disadvantage was clear. Britain and France had to populate their colonies with 'free' labour. Britain was able to import coolies from India and China (the conditions in which they were supplied and lived bringing their own scandals, campaigns and legislation). France had fewer sources and had turned to recruiting 'free emigrants' from West Africa. When Akitoye was reinstalled in Lagos, the old Marseilles house of Régis Aîné had opened its premises on the waterfront there. Slavers when that trade was legal, Régis Aîné now had a government contract to supply 'contract labour' to the French West Indies.

British and Dutch governments had both experimented with 'free emigration' from West Africa in the 1840s but given up the scheme. It had been seized on then by French and American observers as proof that Britain's aims were not philanthropic but directed only to the betterment of her commerce.[18]

One Old Calabar chief had been contacted by a consortium of Liverpool merchants ostensibly to know if any of his people would 'engage themselves as free labourers'.

I received your kind letter by the Magistrate, through Captain Todd, and by your wish I now write you to say, we be glad for supply you with slaves. I have spoken with King Archibury and all Calabar gentleman and be very glad to do the same. Regard to free emigration man no will go for himself. We shall buy them alsam [i.e. in the same way as] we do that time slave trade bin. We be very glad for them man to come back again to Calabar, but I fear that time they go for West Indies he no will com back here. We have all agree to charges four boxes of brass and copper rod for man, woman and children but shall not be able to supply the quantity you mention. I think we shall be able to get 400 or 500 for one vessel . . . the ship will have to pay convey to me and Archibury but no other

gentleman say, 10,000 copper for each town in cloth or any other
article of trade . . .[19]

It was signed, 'my dear Sir, your humble servant, Eyo Honesty King', signa-
tory to an anti-slave-trade treaty he would clearly tear up as soon as it was
outpriced. Lord Brougham, elderly but still trenchant, denounced the
scheme. Arguments put forward by the French government in its defence,
he said, such as 'bettering Negro conditions',[20] were identical to those used
decades ago to justify the slave trade.

The French emigration scheme had started in the Niger Delta, but its
influence spread swiftly. The superintendents of emigration ships, some of
them French officers left unemployed at the end of the Crimean War,
privately confirmed to the British who overhauled them that the Negroes
aboard had been bought as slaves in the interior, brought to the coast and
'liberated' so they could be put on board under indenture. Around Monrovia,
'no sooner was it known that apprentices would be bought than the chiefs
in different places began to make war on their weaker neighbours [with]
famishing sieges and bloody battles to supply the French ships with
emigrants'. HMS *Childers* investigated reports of a revived trade in the
Gallinas, where 'the messengers of Prince Mannah', Commander Fitzroy
reported, 'mistaking her for an American brig, told him 750 slaves were
ready for shipment'.

> The horrors attendant on slave-hunting are in full force. Prince Mannah
> and Prince Saltfish having barricaded their towns and made war on
> those in their neighbourhood, villages are deserted, and, in many cases
> the natives, in their haste to escape the miseries of slavery, have aban-
> doned their property, cattle &c.
>
> I regret to think that the revival of this infamous traffic and its
> consequent amount of human misery may be with justice attributed to
> the French Emigration scheme, and the trade carried on by American-
> built vessels, polluting the flag of the United States.

Until Britain would allow France to dip into the vast pool of coolie labour
in India, France would buy it in West Africa. If Britain condoned the French
scheme, asked some, thereby retaining a monopoly over Indian coolies, was
she not undermining, again, her own campaign on the West African coast?

Others posed a different question: if France were doing it, why not Britain too? Blockade, pointed out *The Times*, either of West Africa or of Cuba, might stop the import of slaves for a time but as soon as it were lifted, the trade would start again. On the other hand, 'slave labour and therefore the Slave Trade, may be driven out of the field by labour of a more lawful description . . . even if the importation of blacks into the West Indies be an evil, it is far the smaller of the two'.[21] The fountain of abolition was still putting forth its bitter water: in the last years of the decade, a few British 'emigrant' ships also left Sierra Leone with unprotected 'free' labour aboard for the West Indies.

French and British flirtation with 'free emigration' from West Africa was, however, brief. An agreement in 1861 formalised, and to some extent regulated, the provision of cheap labour from India for French colonies. But if the slave-marts which had eagerly popped up north of the equator to serve the new version of the trade were almost as easily closed, there still seemed no end to the slave trade proper: that continuing in full force and at enormous profit to Cuba, still carried in ships flying American flags which British officers molested at their peril and even the enlarged American Squadron could not suppress.

With the Bights again full of slavers servicing the continued demand from Cuba, damaging waves lapped at the shores of Lagos, where European and Repatriate communities had fallen into the same bitter infighting which had bedevilled Sierra Leone. Missionaries distrusted the consul; the consul distrusted the traders; no one liked the French, who loathed the British, and there was a very nasty squabble over the distribution of land along the coveted riverbank, with Squadron officers brought in to measure and remeasure each plot in an attempt to keep the peace. Akitoye had died and his son, King Dosunmu, was weaker even than his father. From Porto Novo, Badagry, Ouidah and Abomey came constant intelligence of treaty-breaking: slave-hunting, slave-trading and human sacrifice.

The latest British consul, Mr Brand, and the Lagos traders opened every letter from upcountry correspondents with foreboding. Abeokuta was again the declared target of Dahomey's slave-hunts, the threat only postponed by King Guezo's death in 1858. His son, King Glele, was no less warlike, no less dedicated to Custom than his father. In April, Consul Brand wrote to London that many on the coast were demanding that Ouidah, centre of the renewed slave trade in the Bights, be occupied by the British and that Lagos be transformed from consulship to colony. Occupation of Ouidah would wound Glele of Abomey, for his vast income came principally from slave-shipments through Ouidah: $20,000 each year from Domingo Martinez alone. Colonising Lagos would give Britain freedom of movement in her relations with neighbouring states and, alone, render the European trading presence secure. Consul Brand was dead of the fever when an 'informant' reported to the *West African Herald* later that year that a 'large screw steamer' had just left Ouidah 'with 1,200 slaves and got clear off'.

> While embarking these unfortunates 25 were drowned in their chains in the surf by the upsetting of the canoes. The greater part of these slaves were the produce of the King of Dahomey's late excursions. Since Gezo [the late king] died, [Glele] has made 14 slave-hunting expeditions. When I was at Whydah all the paths were closed and legal trade had quite stopped on account of these wars. At this very moment while I am writing all the whites and headmen of Whydah are in Dahomey, whither they have gone in obedience to [Glele's] orders to do honour to his 'custom' which is being carried on in tremendous style. Thousands of people are being sacrificed, and thousands are kept for the slavers.[22]

Abeokuta braced itself and the old questions were brought out for debate in Britain: prevention versus cure; patrol versus blockade; colony versus patrol. Could not, the *Herald* asked, its question relayed to the British public in the pages of *The Times*, some 'man of eloquence and influence'

> point out to the people of England the comparative uselessness of their expensive squadron out here, and the enormous benefits which must result to this country, and ultimately to England herself, morally and materially, if she would extend her establishments on this coast. Take away two-thirds of your squadron, and spend one-half its cost creating more stations on shore and greatly strengthening your old stations.[23]

The multiple, overlapping, bitterly contested reasons for which Lagos finally became a British colony cohered in 1860: the constant threat to communities owed British protection, disrupting legitimate trade in the delta and encouraging that in slaves; the weakness of King Dosunmu of Lagos and the strength of those who opposed him and the presence of a determined British consul, Henry Foote.

The event which seems to have clinched the matter for the Colonial Office was the arrival at Lagos in January 1861 of a French steamer whose commander went immediately to meet the former king, Kosoko. When intelligence of this reached London, where Lord Palmerston's party was again in government and the anti-slave-trade campaign back in forceful hands, the various kites flown by Palmerston, the Lagos consulate and the press caught fire. 'We may find ourselves in difficulty,' Palmerston said, 'if we don't take time by the forelock'[24] and the Foreign Secretary agreed. 'We cannot', he wrote, allow Lagos 'to fall again into the hands of the slavers' or to become 'a Depot for Negroes to be exported as Labourers to the French Colonies'. The talks which would result in France's 'coolie convention' began and a letter went to Consul Foote advising that the matter of cession had been 'decided in the affirmative'. Foote, too, was dead of the fever when it arrived, but his successor took the instructions to Commander Bedingfield, who brought HMS *Prometheus* across the bar to hasten Dosunmu's acceptance. On 6 August 1861, Lagos was ceded to the British.

Within a year, the slave trade to Cuba would be all but stopped: gone with a suddenness and completeness which mirrored its demise in Brazil a decade before. Britain would be left with a colony which would prove of great value in the future (although still described by the Colonial Office in 1864 as 'a deadly gift'). This is one reason for later accusations that the annexation of Lagos was 'a mere pretext for seeking economic and political domination', rather than a battle in the war against the slave trade. It did not look that way at the time. When Dosunmu signed his treaty, closing down the Cuban market seemed as distant a prospect as it had ever been.

The British annexation of Lagos did not end the transatlantic slave trade. It was war which finally shut it down, but not one in which the Preventive, or any other British squadron, fought.

In November 1860, Abraham Lincoln was elected President of the United

States. In April 1861, Confederate guns opened fire on the Union garrison at Fort Sumter and the American squadron was recalled from the West African coast. As the terrible conflict between Union and Confederacy consumed America, there were as few restraints on slave-ships flying the American flag as there had ever been, and a last-minute bonanza: brief in the trade's history but long for the estimated 20,000 Negroes sold out of Africa during the fourteen months it lasted.

The demands of the Civil War brought with them the unexpected reversal of Britain's and America's old roles: now Washington's ships were stopping and searching those of other nations to ensure they were not breaking the blockade of Confederate ports, British merchant captains were complaining of abuse and molestation and President Lincoln's administration was regarding old questions in a new light. In May 1861, Lincoln made it known to Lord Lyons, British minister in Washington, that he 'would have none of the squeamishness about allowing American vessels to be boarded and searched which had characterized [his] predecessors'.[25] A secret memorandum to this effect was signed but Lord John Russell, now prime minister, saw the opportunity finally to settle this question and demanded something more substantial than a gentleman's agreement. Negotiations began, with old actors tentatively voicing their new roles, but were held up for months when an American captain stopped a British vessel carrying Confederate representatives to London and Paris, and seized the men. Such was the outrage this caused that it seemed for a couple of months that Britain would not only recognise the Confederacy but even declare war on the Union.

Lincoln's government prudently backed down and disavowed the captain's action. When Britain followed this up by presenting for signature an anti-slave-trade treaty containing the mutual right of search, it was agreed with one condition: it must seem as if the treaty had originated in America, in order not to antagonise public opinion. Secretary of State Seward and Lord Lyons cooked up a story between them, one requesting amendments he knew would be acceptable, the other publicly demurring, then giving in. It was signed in April 1862 and would, Seward wrote, 'bring the African slave trade to an end immediately and forever'.[26] The instructions that British warships could 'overhaul any vessels which gave reasonable grounds for suspicion' arrived on the African coast in November, and the result was immediate. In 1861, fourteen thousand slaves arrived in Cuba; in 1862, ten thousand; in 1863, fewer than four thousand; thereafter, a trickle. In 1865, the Thirteenth Amendment emancipated the slaves of the United States and in 1869, they were joined by those of Cuba, the last slave-worked colony. The transatlantic slave trade had ended.

'We have spent 20,000,000*l* to abolish slavery', wrote a British merchant in 1845, 'and 20,000,000*l* more to repress the Slave Trade; yet does no one nation under Heaven give us credit for disinterested sincerity in this large expenditure of money and philanthropy. Whether the calm verdict of posterity will redress this injustice, time alone can show.'[27]

Over the sixty years of its existence, the Preventive Squadron freed about a hundred and sixty thousand slaves and lost seventeen thousand British seamen to death by disease, battle or accident. In 1869, the Preventive and Cape Squadrons merged. The slave trade was suppressed on the West African coast. Slavery was abolished in North America and Cuba. The trade continued from East Africa; it continued to and between the Arab states; it continued among the West African kingdoms. It continued, in different, semi-legalised forms, in the importation of coolie labour; it continues now in the trafficking of humans all over the globe for foul and exploitative purposes: Anti-Slavery International estimates there are about twelve million slaves living today. But the horrors of the Middle Passage had ended and binding statements of disgust and determination had been made. Thousands whose parents and grandparents had been indifferent to the slave trade now regarded it as indefensible.

It was often said that if the Squadron had been given full rein, it could have brought the slave trade to an end far earlier. But at what price? *A nation is not justified* . . . the words of William Scott were, largely, observed. Britain, largely, stayed on the right side of the law, with a few 'great stretches' afterwards legitimised by treaty, and honouring international law strengthened it slowly but immeasurably. The mutual right of search in a humanitarian cause; international courts to punish international crime and international policing to detect it: these arose from placing armed intervention, whatever its benevolent intentions, second to due process. They were advances won at the cost of tragic thousands sold to slaving but to the benefit of the far larger number they have since protected from other violent fates.

Notes

When a sequence of quotations from the same source occurs in the text, only the first of them is annotated. A new note indicates a change of source.

Prologue

1 Ali Eisami's story, dictated to a missionary, is reproduced in Philip Curtin, *Africa Remembered: Narratives by West Africans from the Era of the Slave Trade* (1967).

1 Black Bounty

1. Captain Hugh Crow, *Memoirs of the Late Captain Hugh Crow of Liverpool* (1830).
2. Frederick Charnier, *The Life of a Sailor, by a Captain in the Navy* (1832).
3. *Sierra Leone Gazette* (cited hereafter as SLG), April 1808.
4. Goree is now Dakar, capital of Senegal.
5. The Gallinas estuary was near the present-day town of Sulima, close to the Liberia–Sierra Leone border.
6. Cape Mount is now Robertsport, northern Liberia.
7. SLG, January 1808.
8. SLG, March 1808.
9. SLG, January 1808.
10. SLG, August 1809.
11. Charnier, *Life of a Sailor*, op. cit.
12. Frederick Hoffman, A. Beckford-Bevan and H. B. Wolryche-Whitmore (eds), *A Sailor of King George: The Journals of Captain Frederick Hoffman, RN, 1793–1814* (1901).
13. I refer here and later to the 'Colonial Office' for brevity. Between 1801 and 1854, responsibility for the colonies resided with the Secretary of State for War and the Colonies.

14. Governor Maxwell to Colonial Office, National Archive (NA) CO 267/38.

15. NA ADM 1/4221, quoted in Tara Helfman, 'The Court of Vice Admiralty at Sierra Leone and the Abolition of the West African Slave Trade' (2006).

16. SLG, November 1809.

17. SLG, 26 August 1809.

18. SLG, 20 August 1808.

19. His words were quoted in Samuel Samo, *The Trials of the Slave Traders* (1813).

20. SLG, November 1809.

21. The case was written up in the *Sierra Leone Gazette* of June 1820.

22. The case was written up in the *Sierra Leone Gazette* of November 1809.

2 Unlawful Force

1. The debate was reported in *The Times* of 29 December 1809.

2. Paola de Loando is now Luanda, capital of Angola.

3. Ouidah was known to the British as 'Whydah'.

4. There is a headstone in a graveyard in Hampshire bearing the following inscription: 'A male negro infant supposed to be nine or ten years of age, a native of Poppoe near Whidal [Whydah] on the coast of Africa and who had been stolen while playing in the bushes with another boy, was this day Baptised by the name of Irby Amelia Frederic, in grateful testimony of the humanity and intrepidity of his gallant deliverer, the humble Frederic Paul Irby, Captain of H.M. Ship the *Amelia*, who rescued this youth from bondage and from barbarism on the 6th January 1812, as he was on his passage with many other hapless children to the Brazils.'

5. NA CO 267/35.

6. Kizell's correspondence with Governor Columbine is reproduced in Sir George Ralph Collier, *West African Sketches compiled from the reports of Sir G R Collier, Sir Charles Maccarthy and other official sources* (1824).

7. Sixth Report of the Directors of the African Institution.

8. SLG, 17 August 1819.

9. Lords of the Admiralty to Sir James Lucas Yeo, captain of HM ship *Inconstant*, 20 March 1816, quoted in W. E. F. Ward, *The Royal Navy and the Slavers* (1969).

10. Surgeon Peter Leonard, *Records of a voyage to the western coast of Africa, and of the service on that station for the suppression of the Slave Trade, in the years 1830, 1831 and 1832* (1833).

11. W. P. Ashcroft, 'Reminiscences' (1964).

12. Quoted in Thomas Clarkson, *The History of the Rise, Progress and Accomplishment of the Abolition of the African Slave-Trade by the British Parliament* (1808).

13. From the log of HMS *Bann*, NA ADM 51/2180.

14. Letter printed in *The Times* of 25 April 1816.
15. Log of HMS *Bann*, op. cit.
16. Quoted in Ward, *The Royal Navy and the Slavers*, op. cit.
17. *The Times*, 31 December 1816.
18. *A view of the present state of the African slave trade* (Philadelphia 1824) from *From Slavery to Freedom: The African-American Pamphlet Collection, 1822–1909*, Rare Book and Special Collections Division, Library of Congress.
19. *The Times*, 13 June 1818.
20. SLG, 30 May 1818.
21. *The Times*, 13 June 1818.
22. SLG, 4 April 1818.
23. SLG, 25 October 1817.
24. SLG, 26 June 1819.
25. SLG, 7 August 1819.
26. SLG, 26 June 1819.
27. SLG, 19 February 1820.
28. Quoted in David Eltis, *Economic Growth and the Ending of the Transatlantic Slave Trade* (1981).
29. *Dodson's Admiralty Reports* 210.
30. SLG, 19 December 1818.
31. According to naval historian Christopher Lloyd, the Lists of Ships in Commission for the years between 1814 and 1820 are lost. These would have given us the exact date in late 1818 or early 1819 at which the station was created.

3 False Papers and Mongrel Vessels

1. SLG, 8 March 1820.
2. SLG, 21 August 1819.
3. SLG, 3 March 1821.
4. SLG, 3 March 1821.
5. Despatch from Commodore Collier to the Admiralty, 10 January 1821, reproduced in Parliamentary Papers XXII.
6. SLG, 23 March 1822.
7. SLG, 30 December 1820.
8. SLG, 17 June 1820.
9 SLG, 29 September 1821.
10. SLG, 16 February 1822.
11. SLG, 8 March 1820.
12. Letter from M'Carthy to the Colonial Office, 14 January 1822, reproduced in Parliamentary Papers XXII.

4 Bad Blood

1. Daniel Coker, *Journal of Daniel Coker: A Descendant of Africa, from the Time of Leaving New York, in the Ship* Elizabeth, *Capt. Sebor, on a Voyage to Sherbro, in Africa* . . . (1820).

2. Isaac V. Brown, *Biography of the Reverend Robert Finley, of Basking Ridge, N.J.* (1857).

3. *Journal of Daniel Coker*, op. cit.

4. Parliamentary Papers XXII.

5. ibid.

6. Letter from Captain Edward Trenchard, of USS *Cyane*, 10 April 1820, reproduced in A *view of the present state of the African slave trade* (1824).

7. A *view of the present state of the African slave trade*, op. cit.

8. Quoted in Benjamin Brawley, *A Social History of the American Negro, being a History of the Negro Problem in the United States. Including a History and Study of the Republic of Liberia* (1921).

9. The Americans initially knew it as 'Montserado' rather than 'Mesurado'.

10. A *view of the present state of the African slave trade*, op. cit.

11. Quoted in Donald L. Canney, *Africa Squadron: The US Navy and the Slave Trade 1842–1861* (2006).

12. A *view of the present state of the African slave trade*, op. cit.

13. Letter from Lieutenant Stockton of USS *Alligator* to the US Navy Department, 27 May 1821, quoted in A *view of the present state of the African slave trade*, op. cit.

14. Quoted in Ward, *The Royal Navy and the Slavers*, op. cit.

5 The Fever, the Deys and the Ashanti

1. Surgeon Alexander Bryson, *Report on the Climate and Principal Diseases of the African Station, compiled from Documents in the Office of the Director-General of the Medical Department* (1847).

2. Diary of Midshipman Cheesman Henry Binstead, Royal Naval Museum (RNM) 2005/76(1).

3. ibid., 2005/76(2).

4. Surgeon David James of HMS *Barracouta*, quoted in E.H. Burrows, *Captain Owen of the African Survey* (1979).

5. A South American root often used as a laxative.

6. RNM 2005/6(2).

7. *The Times*, 15 July 1823.

8. SLG, 15 November 1823

9. Dr James Hall, 'Abolition of the Slave Trade of Gallinas' (1850).

10. SLG, 4 December 1824.

11. Letter from George Woollcombe III to his uncle Henry Woollcombe III, 3 February 1824, Plymouth and West Devon Record Office (PWDRO) 710/578.

12. Letter from Lieutenant George Woollcombe to his uncle Henry Woollcombe III, 22 February 1824, PWDRO 710/579.

13. SLG, 16 April 1824.

14. Letter from Lieutenant George Woollcombe to his uncle Henry Woollcombe III, not dated but presumed to be mid-April 1824, PWDRO 710/580.

15. Letter from Lieutenant George Woollcombe to his uncle Henry Woollcombe III, 3 May 1824, PWDRO 710/581.

16. SLG, 21 August 1824.

17. *The Times*, 26 November 1825.

18. Letter from Lieutenant George Woollcombe to Commodore Bullen, 12 September 1824, reproduced in *The Times* of 7 May 1825.

19. Letter from Commodore Bullen to the Admiralty, 12 September 1824, reproduced in *The Times*, 7 May 1825.

20. SLG, 18 December 1824.

21. SLG, 21 August 1824.

22. Letter from Lieutenant George Woollcombe to his uncle Henry Woollcombe III, 22 September 1824, PWDRO 710/582.

6 Two Captains

1. SLG, 20 September 1823.

2. Robert Huish, *Travels of Richard and John Lander into the interior of Africa, for the discovery of the course and termination of the Niger* (1836).

3. William Fawkner's Narrative.

4. A letter from Thomas Hutton to his uncle, Mr Hutton of Ouidah, 7 August 1850 reproduced in Tim Coates, *King Guezo of Dahomey 1850–1852* (2001).

5. He is the subject of Bruce Chatwin's *Viceroy of Ouidah*.

6. Sir Henry Huntley, *Seven Years' Service on the Slave Coast of West Africa* (1850).

7. Commander C. A. Montresor, *Leaves from Memory's Log-Book and Jottings from Old Journals* (1887).

8. Théophile Conneau, *A Slaver's Log Book or Twenty Years' Residence in Africa* (1854).

9. Hugh Clapperton, *Journal of a Second Expedition into the Interior of Africa, from the Bight of Benin to Soccatoo . . .* (1829).

10. Huish, *Travels of Richard and John Lander*, op. cit.

7 Two Lieutenants

1. Sir Percy Moreton Scott, Bart, *Fifty Years in the Royal Navy* (1919).
2. Quoted in Basil Lubbock, *Cruisers, Corsairs and Slavers* (1993).
3. No relation to Commodore George Collier who had commanded the squadron 1819–22.
4. James Holman, *A Voyage round the World, including Travels in Africa, Asia, Australasia, America, etc, etc, from 1827 to 1832* (1834).
5. *The Times*, 14 February 1829.

8 A Costly Grave

1. Quoted in Burrows, *Captain Owen*, op. cit.
2. Now Quelimane, capital of Zambezia province in Mozambique.
3. *Narrative of Voyages to Explore the Shores of Africa, Afribia and Madagascar, performed in HM ships* Leven *and* Barracouta, *under the direction of Captain W. F. W. Owen* (1833).
4. Quoted in Burrows, *Captain Owen*, op. cit.
5. *The Times*, 15 May 1827.
6. *The Times*, 17 November 1827.
7. Governor Turner's report to the Colonial Office, 25 January 1826, reported in *The Times* of 21 July 1826.
8. Leonard, *Records of a voyage*, op. cit.
9. Thomas Boteler, *Narrative of a Voyage of Discovery* (1835).
10. Bryson, *Report*, op. cit.
11. Fernando Po is now Bioko.
12. Quoted in Burrows, *Captain Owen*, op. cit.
13. Quoted in Robert T. Brown, 'Fernando Po and the Anti-Sierra Leonean Campaign: 1826–1834' (1973).
14. Anyone who still believes the British Empire, in Africa or elsewhere, was the result of a careful, and carefully executed, strategy, need only take a short trip through the papers of the Colonial Office to realise how much it was born of muddle, incompetence and indecision.
15. Clarence is now Malabo.
16. Holman, *A Voyage round the World*, op. cit.
17. Sir James Edward Alexander, *Narrative of a Voyage of Observation among the Colonies of Western Africa in the Flag-ship* Thalia (1837).
18. Holman, *A Voyage round the World*, op. cit.

19. Richard Rush, American Minister in Britain in 1818, told Lord Castlereagh, Foreign Secretary, that impressments were 'more afflicting to humanity' than the African slave trade.
20. Holman, *A Voyage round the World*, op. cit.
21. *The Times*, 26 October 1829.
22. Quoted in Lubbock, *Cruisers, Corsairs & Slavers*, op. cit.
23. Alexander, op. cit. (1837).

9 Cuban Customs, Brazilian Buccaneers

1. Conneau, *A Slaver's Log Book*, op. cit.
2. Robert Walsh, *Notices of Brazil in 1828 and 1829* (1831).
3. *The Times*, 25 January 1831.
4. Broughton's report is quoted in Lubbock, *Cruisers, Corsairs & Slavers*, op. cit.
5. *The Times*, 24 November 1830.

10 Black Jokes And High Jinks

1. Letter of 1 August 1829, HIN/1 National Maritime Museum (NMM).
2. Officer's letter reproduced in *The Times*, 21 June 1830.
3. Case reported in *The Times*, 13 July 1831.
4. Letter of 2 March 1830, HIN/1 NMM.
5. Officer's letter reproduced in *The Times*, 21 June 1830.
6. Letter of 7 July 1830, HIN/1 NMM.
7. Letter of 6 June 1830, HIN/1 NMM.
8. Letter of 7 July 1830, HIN/1 NMM.
9. Letter of 7 September 1830, HIN/1 NMM.
10. Quoted in Lubbock, *Cruisers, Corsairs & Slavers*, op. cit.
11. Huntley, *Seven Years' Service*, op. cit.
12. Montresor, *Leaves and Jottings*, op. cit.
13. Letter of 7 September 1830, HIN/1 NMM.
14. Sir Henry Keppel, *A Sailor's Life under Four Sovereigns* (1899).
15. Huntley, *Seven Years' Service*, op. cit.
16. Keppel, *A Sailor's Life*, op. cit.
17. Huntley, *Seven Years' Service*, op. cit.
18. Madden's report was quoted in *The Times* of 22 October 1842.
19. *The Times*, 22 October 1842.
20. Montresor, *Leaves and Jottings*, op. cit.
21. ibid.
22. Keppel, *A Sailor's Life*, op. cit.

11 The First Great Blows

1. Leonard, *Records*, op. cit.
2. Letter of 28 May 1831, HIN/1 NMM.
3. Leonard, *Records*, op. cit.
4. Huntley, *Seven Years' Service*, op. cit.
5. Leonard, *Records*, op. cit.
6. Quoted in Lubbock, *Cruisers, Corsairs & Slavers*, op. cit.
7. *The Times*, 14 July 1835.
8. *The Times*, 13 September 1836.
9. Or 1833; he does not specify in his memoir.
10. Conneau, *A Slaver's Log Book*, op. cit.
11. Leonard, *Records*, op. cit.
12. Keppel, *A Sailor's Life*, op. cit.
13. Ibid.
14. Leonard, *Records*, op. cit.
15. Quoted in Leslie Bethell, 'The Origins of Lord Palmerston's Act of 1839' (1965).
16. *The Times*, 15 October 1839.
17. *The Times*, 17 April 1840.
18. Reports from the Select Committee on the Slave Trade, 1847–8, Henry James Matson's evidence.
19. Reports from the Select Committee on the Slave Trade, 1847–8, Joseph Denman's evidence.
20. Reports from the Select Committee on the Slave Trade, 1847–8, Edward Butterfield's evidence.

12 Willing Promoters And Partial Remedies

1. Conneau, *A Slaver's Log Book*, op. cit.
2. Quoted in *New York Commercial Advertiser*, 4 September 1838, reproduced in: http://amistad.mysticseaport.org/library/news/nyca/1839.09.04.consulinhavana.html
3. David Turnbull, *Travels in the West: Cuba, with notices of Porto Rico and the Slave Trade* (1840).
4. Quoted in *New York Commercial Advertiser*, 4 September 1838.
5. Commander Andrew H. Foote, *Africa and the American Flag* (1854).
6. *New York Morning Herald*, 8 October 1839.
7. Quoted in Hugh Soulsby, *The Right of Search and the Slave Trade in Anglo-American Relations, 1814–1862* (1933).

8. Conneau, *A Slaver's Log Book*, op. cit.
9. Enclosure to Charles H. Bell, letter of 2 October 1840, US National Archives (RG45) in C. Herbert Gilliland, '"Some More Wine, Captain Bell?": An Abolitionist Naval Officer and Theodore Canot on the African Coast' (2004).
10. Conneau, *A Slaver's Log Book*, op. cit.
11. Ephraim Douglass Adams, 'Lord Ashburton and the Treaty of Washington' (1912).

13 Blockade

1. Reports from the Select Committee on the Slave Trade, 1847–1848.
2. Bryson, *Report*, op. cit.
3. Reports from the Select Committee on the Slave Trade, 1847–1848.
4. ibid.
5. Conneau, *A Slaver's Log Book*, op. cit.
6. The Hon. Mrs Caroline Norton, *A Residence at Sierra Leone, described from a Journal kept on the spot, and from letters written to friends at home by a Lady* (1849).
7. Henry James Matson, *Remarks on the Slave Trade and the African Squadron* (1848).
8. Conneau, *A Slaver's Log Book*, op. cit.
9. Quoted in Ward, *The Royal Navy and the Slavers*, op. cit.
10. Sierra Leone Commissioners' Report to Lord Palmerston, 31 December 1840.
11. Conneau, *A Slaver's Log Book*, op. cit.
12. Commander Tucker to the Chief or Head Man of Corisco, 7 November 1840, Parliamentary Papers XLII.
13. Conneau, *A Slaver's Log Book*, op. cit.
14. Joseph Denman, *Instructions for the guidance of Her Majesty's Naval Officers employed in the suppression of the slave trade* (1844).

14 Commerce, Christianity and Civilisation

1. Thomas Fowell Buxton, *The African Slave Trade and its Remedy* (1839).
2. Richard and John Lander, *Journal of an Expedition to explore the course and termination of the Niger* (1832).
3. Instructions of Lord John Russell, British Colonial Secretary, to Her Majesty's Niger Commissioners (30 January 1841), *British Parliamentary Papers* (1843), vol. xlviii (472).
4. Quoted in *The Times* of 19 January 1842.
5. Reports from the Select Committee on the Slave Trade, 1847–1848.

6. SLG, 6 December 1823.
7. Quoted in Adam Jones, 'Little Popo and Agoue at the End of the Atlantic Slave Trade' in *Ports of the Slave Trade (Bights of Benin and Biafra)*, ed. Robin Law and Silke Strickrodt (1997).
8. Matson, *Remarks on the Slave Trade and the African Squadron*, op. cit.
9. Quoted in Ward, *The Royal Navy and the Slavers*, op. cit.
10. *The Times*, 4 October 1842.
11. *The Times*, 5 October 1842.
12. *The Times*, 28 October 1842.
13. *The Times*, 30 October 1842.
14. *The Times*, 19 October 1842.
15. Matson, *Remarks*, op. cit.
16. F. Deaville Walker, *The Story of the Church Missionary Society Nigeria Mission* (1930).

15 Palaver and Presents

1. Letter printed in *The Times* of 22 May 1846.
2. Lieutenant Frederick Forbes, *Six Months' Service in the African Blockade* (1849).
3. Lieutenant J. Pasco commanding HMS *Kite* to Senior Naval Officer, Cape of Good Hope, 6 June 1843, NA ADM 1/5547.
4. Ashcroft, 'Reminiscences', op. cit.
5. Matson, *Remarks*, op. cit.
6. Quoted in Jones, 'Little Popo and Agoue', op. cit.
7. Chief of Ambriz to Captain Foote of HMS *Madagascar*, 17 August 1843, NA ADM 1/5541.
8. Conneau, *A Slaver's Log Book*, op. cit.
9. Quoted in Christopher Lloyd, *The Navy and the Slave Trade* (1949).
10. Horatio Bridge, *Journal of an African Cruiser* (1845).
11. Letter printed in *The Times* of 22 May 1846.
12. *The Times*, 3 August 1844.
13. Conneau, *A Slaver's Log Book*, op. cit.
14. Letter printed in *The Times* of 8 October 1845.
15. Conneau, *A Slaver's Log Book*, op. cit.
16. Commodore Jones's report to Governor Fergusson, 24 February 1845, reproduced in: http://www.pdavis.nl/Jones_3.htm
17. Conneau, *A Slaver's Log Book*, op. cit.
18. Forbes, *Six Months' Service*, op. cit.
19. Montresor, *Leaves and Jottings*, op. cit.

16 Habits Not Ornamental to the Navy

1. Letter printed in *The Times* of 8 October 1845.
2. Matson, *Remarks*, op. cit.
3. *The Times*, 17 August 1846.
4. *The Times*, 28 August 1846.
5. Ashcroft, *Reminiscences*, op. cit.
6. Letter from Mate (later Lieutenant) Francis Meynell to his father, 7 July 1844, MEY/5 NMM.
7. Ashcroft, *Reminiscences*, op. cit.
8. Letter from Francis Meynell to his father, 2 May 1845, MEY/5 NMM.
9. Reports from the Select Committee on the Slave Trade, 1847–8, Jose Cliffe's evidence.
10. Matson, *Remarks*, op. cit.
11. Quoted in W. D. Jones, 'The Origins and Passage of Lord Aberdeen's Act' (1962): xlii.
12. *The Times*, 14 July 1845.
13. Quoted in Jones, 'Origins and Passage', op. cit.
14. Vice-Admiral Colomb, *Memoirs of Lieutenant Astley Cooper Key* (1898).
15. Matson, *Remarks*, op. cit.
16. Colomb, *Memoirs*, op. cit.
17. Reports from the Select Committee on the Slave Trade, 1847–8.
18. Matson, *Remarks*, op. cit.
19. *The Times*, 26 January 1849.
20. Letter printed in *The Times* of 3 June 1846.
21. Matson, *Remarks*, op. cit.
22. Reports from the Select Committee on the Slave Trade, 1847–8.
23. Forbes, *Six Months' Service*, op. cit.
24. *The Times*, 24 January 1849.
25. *The Times*, 9 October 1849.
26. *The Times*, 5 February 1848.

17 Persevering Offenders

1. Letter from Palmerston to the Lords Commissioners of the Admiralty, 27 September 1851, reproduced in Coates, *King Guezo of Dahomey*, op. cit.
2. Letter from the King of Dahomey to Queen Victoria, 3 November 1848, reproduced in ibid.

3. Lieutenant Frederick Forbes to Commodore Fanshawe, 1 November 1849, reproduced in ibid.

4. John Duncan to Lord Palmerston, 22 September 1849, reproduced in ibid.

5. Lieutenant Forbes to Commodore Fanshawe, 1 November 1849, reproduced in ibid.

6. The King of Dahomey to Lord Palmerston, 7 September 1849, reproduced in ibid.

7. Letter printed in *The Times*, 10 September 1863.

8. Lord Palmerston to Consul Beecroft, 25 February 1850 reproduced in Coates, *King Guezo*, op. cit.

9. Consul Beecroft to Viscount Palmerston, 8 April 1850, reproduced in ibid.

10 From King Guezo of Dahomey to Queen Victoria of Britain, 4 July 1850, reproduced in ibid.

11. Journal of Lieutenant Forbes on his mission to Dahomey, reproduced in ibid.

12. *The Times*, 15 March 1851.

13. Foreign Office to Admiralty, April 1850, quoted in Leslie Bethell, *The Abolition of the Brazilian Slave Trade: Britain, Brazil and the Slave Trade Question, 1807–1869*(1971).

14. Quoted in Hugh Thomas, *The Slave Trade: The History of the Atlantic Slave Trade 1440–1870* (1997).

15. Lieutenant Dew to Captain Adams, 27 February 1851, reproduced in Coates, *King Guezo*, op. cit.

16. The King of Dahomey to Queen Victoria, undated but written in May or early June 1851, reproduced in ibid.

17. Commodore Bruce to Commander Wilmot, 28 June 1851, reproduced in ibid.

18. Captain Adams to Commodore Fanshawe, 24 March 1851, reproduced in ibid.

19. Commander Heath to Commodore Bruce, 20 June 1851, reproduced in ibid.

20. Commodore Bruce to the Secretary of the Admiralty, 31 July 1851, reproduced in ibid.

21. Commander Heath to Commodore Bruce, 20 June 1851, reproduced in ibid.

22. Commander Heath to the King of Porto Novo, 29 June 1851, reproduced in ibid.

23. Rev. H. Townsend to Commander Wilmot, 5 August 1851, reproduced in ibid.

24. Commander Heath to Commodore Bruce, 17 July 1851, reproduced in ibid.

25. Obba Sharon to Commander Wilmot, 3 September 1851, reproduced in ibid.

26. Consul Beecroft to Lord Palmerston, 4 October 1851, reproduced in ibid.

27. Quoted in Thomas, *The Slave Trade*, op. cit.

28. Lord Palmerston to the Lords of the Admiralty, 27 September 1851, reproduced in Coates, *King Guezo*, op. cit.

29. Lord Palmerston to the Lords Commissioners of the Admiralty, 27 September 1851, reproduced in ibid.

30. Admiralty instructions to Commodore Bruce, 14 October 1851, reproduced in ibid.

31. General memo from Commodore Bruce, 6 December 1851, reproduced in ibid.
32. Commodore Bruce to the Admiralty, 6 December 1851, reproduced in ibid.
33. Consul Beecroft to Lord Palmerston, 26 November 1851, reproduced in ibid.
34. Consul Beecroft to Commander T. G. Forbes, 22 November 1851, reproduced in ibid.
35. Commander Heath to the Admiralty, 17 December 1851, reproduced in ibid.
36. Commodore Bruce to the Admiralty, 18 December 1851, reproduced in ibid.
37. Captain Jones to Commodore Bruce, 29 December 1851, reproduced in ibid.
38. Quoted in Robert Smith, 'The Lagos Consulate 1851–1861, an Outline' (1974).
39. Commodore Bruce to the Admiralty, 17 January 1852, reproduced in Coates, *King Guezo*, op. cit.

18 To an End, Immediately and Forever

1. Conneau, *A Slaver's Log Book*, op. cit.
2. Letter printed in *The Times* of 7 August 1852.
3. Journal of Lieutenant Thomas Davies, JOD/42, NMM.
4. Letter printed in *The Times* of 5 December 1851.
5. Letter printed in *The Times* of 24 September 1851.
6. Arthur Eardley Wilmot, Commander HMS *Harlequin*, *A letter to the Right Hon. Viscount Palmerston MP on the Present State of the African Slave Trade and the necessity of increasing the African Squadron*, 19 January 1853.
7. Commodore Mayo to US Secretary of the Navy, 10 November 1853, quoted in Donald L. Canney, *Africa Squadron: The U.S. Navy and the Slave Trade, 1842–1861* (2006).
8. Cited in *The Times*, 3 September 1856.
9. Cited in *The Times*, 14 January 1857.
10. Cited in *The Times*, 10 December 1856.
11. *New York Times*, 27 July 1860.
12. *The Times*, 21 May 1857.
13. Secretary Cass to Lord Napier, 10 April 1858, quoted in Don E. Fehrenbacher, *The Slaveholding Republic: An Account of the United States Government's Relations to Slavery* (2001).
14. Quoted in ibid.
15. *New-York Daily Tribune*, 2 July 1858.
16. Quoted in Fehrenbacher, *The Slaveholding Republic*, op. cit.
17. Quoted in ibid.
18. To this day, it continues contentious: Professor Johnson Asiegbu claims the Attorney-General's decision that Denman's attack on the Gallinas was illegal was part of a conspiracy to allow factories to be reinstated and provide more

captives for free emigration; as was the 'abandonment to the Portuguese Squadron of the hottest slave trading spots on the coast'.

19. Letter of 5 June 1850, reproduced in *The Times* of 18 July 1857.
20. *The Times*, 18 July 1857.
21. *The Times*, 29 June 1857.
22. Reproduced in *The Times* of 12 November 1860.
23. Letter reproduced in *The Times* of 13 August 1860.
24. Quoted in Robert Smith, 'The Lagos Consulate', op. cit.
25. Quoted in Fehrenbacher, *The Slaveholding Republic*, op. cit.
26. Quoted in ibid.
27. Letter to *The Times* of 29 March 1845.

SELECT BIBLIOGRAPHY

Anonymous Works

A view of the present state of the African slave trade, Philadelphia 1824

From Slavery to Freedom: The African-American Pamphlet Collection, 1822–1909, Rare Book and Special Collections Division, Library of Congress, available online at: http://lcweb2.loc.gov/ammem/aapchtml/aapchome.html

Narrative of Voyages to Explore the Shores of Africa, Afribia and Madagascar, performed in HM ships Leven and Barracouta, under the direction of Captain W. F. W. Owen, By Command of the Lords Commissioners of the Admiralty, London 1833

Works by Named Authors

Adams, Ephraim Douglass, 'Lord Ashburton and the Treaty of Washington', American Historical Review 17, 4 (July 1912): 764–82

Alexander, Archibald, A History of Colonization on the Western Coast of Africa, 1846, available online at: http://books.google.com/books

Alexander, Captain Sir James Edward, Narrative of a Voyage of Observation among the Colonies of West Africa and of a campaign in Kaffir-Land in 1835, London 1837

Ashcroft, W. P., 'Reminiscences', Naval Review (October 1964: 443 and January 1965: 62)

Ashmun, Rev. Jehudi, A History of the American Republic of Liberia, 1826, available online at: http://books.google.com/books

Asiegbu, J. U. J., 'The Dynamics of Freedom: A Study of Liberated African Emigration and British Antislavery Policy', Journal of Black Studies 7, 1 (September 1976): 95–106

Beecham, John, Ashanti and the Gold Coast, London 1841

Bethell, Leslie, 'The Mixed Commissions for the Suppression of the Transatlantic Slave Trade in the Nineteenth Century', Journal of African History 79 (1966): 79–89

——,'Britain, Portugal and the Suppression of the Slave Trade: The Origins of Lord Palmerston's Act of 1839', *English Historical Review* 80 (October 1965): 761–84

——, *The Abolition of the Brazilian Slave Trade: Britain, Brazil and the Slave Trade Question, 1807–1869*, Cambridge University Press, Cambridge 1970

Booth, Alan R., 'The United States African Squadron, 1843–1861', *Boston University Papers in African History*, ed. Jeffrey Butler, vol. 1, Boston University Press, Boston 1964.

Boteler, Captain Thomas, *Narrative of a Voyage of Discovery to Africa and Arabia, Performed in His Majesty's Ships* Leven *and* Barracouta, *from 1821 to 1826, under the Command of Capt. R. W. Owen, R.N.*, London 1835

Braidwood, Stephen J., *Black Poor and White Philanthropists*, Liverpool University Press, Liverpool 1994

Brawley, Benjamin, *A Social History of the American Negro, being a History of the Negro Problem in the United States. Including a History and Study of the Republic of Liberia*, New York 1921, available online at: www.Gutenberg.org

Bridge, Horatio, ed. Nathaniel Hawthorne, *Journal of an African Cruiser, comprising sketches of the Canaries, the Cape de Verds and other places on the west Coast of Africa. By an Officer of the US Navy*, London 1845

Brown, Isaac V., *Biography of the Reverend Robert Finley, of Basking Ridge, N. J.*, Philadelphia 1857

Brown, Robert T., 'Fernando Po and the Anti-Sierra Leonean Campaign: 1826–1834,' *The International Journal of African Historical Studies* 6, 2 (1973): 249–64

Bryson, Dr Alexander, *Report on the Climate and Principal Diseases of the African Station, compiled from Documents in the Office of the Director-General of the Medical Department*, London 1847

Burrows, E. H., *Captain Owen of the African Survey*, Rotterdam: Balkema 1979

Burton, Richard, *Two Trips to Gorilla Land and the Cataracts of the Congo*, London 1876, available online at: http://www.gutenberg.org/etext/8821

Buxton, Thomas Fowell, *The African Slave Trade and its Remedy*, London 1838

Campbell, Penelope, 'Maryland in Africa: the Maryland State Colonization Society, 1831–1857', *Journal of African History* 12, 4 (1971): 671–2

Canney, Donald L., *Africa Squadron: The US Navy and the Slave Trade, 1842–1861*, Potomac Books, Dulles, Virginia 2006

Canot, Theodore, *see* Conneau, Captain Théophile

Chamier, Frederick, *The Life of a Sailor, by a Captain in the Navy*, London 1832

Christopher, Emma, *Slave Ship Sailors and Their Captive Cargoes, 1730–1807*, Cambridge University Press, Cambridge 2006

Clapperton, Hugh, *Journal of a Second Expedition into the Interior of Africa, from the Bight of Benin to Soccatoo . . . to which is added, the Journal of Richard Lander from Kano to the sea-coast*, London 1829

Select Bibliography

Claridge, W. W., *History of the Gold Coast and Ashanti*, London 1915

Clarkson, Thomas, *The History of the Rise, Progress and Accomplishment of the Abolition of the African Slave-Trade by the British Parliament*, London 1808

Claude, George, *The Rise of British West Africa, Comprising the Early History of the Colony of Sierra Leone, the Gambia, Lagos, Gold Coast, etc.*, London 1904

Clowes, William Laird, *The Royal Navy: a history from the earliest times to the death of Queen Victoria*, London 1897–1903

Coates, Tim, *King Guezo of Dahomey 1850–52*, Uncovered Editions, London 2001

Coker, Rev. Daniel, *Journal of Daniel Coker: A Descendant of Africa, from the Time of Leaving New York, in the Ship* Elizabeth, *Capt. Sebor, on a Voyage to Sherbro, in Africa . . . 1820*, available online at: http://www.inmotionaame.org/texts/index.cfm

Collier, Sir George Ralph, *West African Sketches compiled from the reports of Sir G. R. Collier, Sir Charles Maccarthy and other official sources*, London 1824

Colomb, P.H., *Memoirs of Admiral Sir Astley Cooper Key*, Methuen, London 1898

Conneau, Captain Théophile: ['Canot, Theodore'], *A Slaver's Log Book, or Twenty Years' Residence in Africa*, Avon Books, New York 1976

Crow, Captain Hugh, *Memoirs of the late Captain Hugh Crow of Liverpool*, London 1830

Cruickshank, Brodie, *Eighteen Years on the Gold Coast of Africa*, London 1853

Curtin, Philip, ed., *Africa Remembered: Narratives by West Africans from the Era of the Slave Trade*, University of Wisconsin Press, Madison, Wisconsin 1968

Curtin, Philip D., ed. Paul E. Lovejoy, *Africans in Bondage: Studies in Slavery and the Slave Trade: Essays in honor of Philip D. Curtin on the occasion of the twenty-fifth anniversary of African Studies at the University of Wisconsin*, Madison, WI: African Studies Program, University of Wisconsin-Madison c. 1986

Daget, Serge, *La Repression de la traite des Noirs au XIXe siècle*, Paris: Karthala 1997

Deaville Walker, F., *The Story of the Church Missionary Society Nigeria Mission*, London 1930

Denman, Captain Joseph, *The African Squadron and Mr Hutt's Committee*, London 1850

——, *Instructions for the guidance of the captains and commanding officers of Her Majesty's ships of war employed in the suppression of the slave trade*, London 1844

Dorsey, Joseph C., *Slave Traffic in the Age of Abolition: Puerto Rico, West Africa and the non-Hispanic Caribbean, 1815–1859*, University Press of Florida, Gainsville 2003

Dubois, W. E. B., *The Suppression of the Slave-Trade to the United States of America, 1638–1870*, New York 1896

Du Chaillu, Paul B., *Exploration and Adventures in Equatorial Africa*, Paris 1861

Duncan, John, *Travels in West Africa in 1845 & 1846, comprising a Journey from Whydah, through the kingdom of Dahomey to Adofoodia, in the Interior*, London 1847

Eltis, David, *Economic Growth and the Ending of the Transatlantic Slave Trade*, Oxford University Press 1987

Eltis, David and James Walvin, eds, *The Abolition of the Atlantic Slave Trade: Origins and Effects in Europe, Africa, and the Americas*, University of Wisconsin Press, Madison, Wisconsin 1981

Fehrenbacher, Don E., *The Slaveholding Republic: An Account of the United States Government's Relations to Slavery*, New York: Oxford University Press 2001

Foote, Commander Andrew H., *Africa and the American Flag*, New York 1854

Forbes, Lieutenant Frederick, *Six Months' Service in the African Blockade*, London 1849

Fyfe, Christopher, *A History of Sierra Leone*, Oxford University Press, London 1962

Gilliland, C. Herbert, '"Some More Wine, Captain Bell?": An Abolitionist Naval Officer and Theodore Canot on the African Coast', Conference Papers of Historic Naval Ships Association, Annapolis, Maryland 2004

Hall, Basil, *Fragments of Voyages and Travels*, London 1832, available online at: http://books.google.com/books

Hall, Dr James, 'Abolition of the Slave Trade of Gallinas', *Annual Report, The American Colonization Society* 33 (1850): 33–6

Helfman, Tara, 'The Court of Vice Admiralty at Sierra Leone and the Abolition of the West African Slave Trade', *Yale Law Journal* 115, 5 (March) 2006

Hill, Pascoe Grenfell, *50 days on board a slave vessel: in the Mozambique Channel April and May 1843*, London 1844, available online at: http://books.google.com/books

Hoffman, Frederick, A. Beckford-Bevan and H. B. Wolryche-Whitmore (eds), *A Sailor of King George: the Journals of Captain Frederick Hoffman, RN, 1793–1814*, Chatham 1999

Hogg, Peter C., *The African Slave Trade and Its Suppression: A Classified and Annotated Bibliography of Books*, Frank Cass Publishers, London 1973

Holman, James, *A Voyage round the World, including Travels in Africa, Asia, Australasia, America, etc., etc., from 1827 to 1832*, London 1834

Hopkins, Antony G., 'Property Rights and Empire Building: Britain's Annexation of Lagos, 1861', *The Journal of Economic History* 40, 4 (December 1980): 777–798

Howard, Warren S., *American Slavers and the Federal Law, 1837–1862*, University of California Press, Berkeley, California 1963

Huish, Robert, *The travels of Richard and John Lander into the interior of Africa, for the discovery of the course and termination of the Niger*, London 1836

Huntley, Sir Henry, *Seven Years' Service on the Slave Coast of West Africa*, London 1850

Jennings, Lawrence C., 'France, Great Britain, and the Repression of the Slave Trade, 1841–1845', *French Historical Studies* 10, 1 (Spring, 1977): 101–25

Jones, Adam, 'Little Popo and Agoue at the End of the Atlantic Slave Trade' in *Ports of the Slave Trade (Bights of Benin and Biafra): papers from a conference at the Centre of Commonwealth Studies, University of Stirling*, ed. Robin Law and Silke Strickrodt, University of Stirling 1997

Select Bibliography

——, 'Théophile Conneau at Galinhas and New Sestos, 1838–1841: A Comparison of the Sources', *History in Africa* 8 (1981): 89–106

Jones, W. D. 'The Origins and Passage of Lord Aberdeen's Act', *Hispanic American Historical Review* 42,4: 502–520

Keppel, H., *A Sailor's Life under Four Sovereigns*, London 1899

Lander, Richard and Lander, John, *Journal of an Expedition to explore the course and termination of the Niger*, London 1832

Law, Robin and Strickrodt, Silke, eds, *Ports of the Slave Trade (Bights of Benin and Biafra): papers from a conference of the Centre of Commonwealth Studies, University of Stirling*, University of Stirling 1999

Leonard, Peter, *Records of a voyage to the western coast of Africa, and of the service in that station for the suppression of the Slave Trade, in the years 1830, 1831 and 1832*, Edinburgh 1833

Lynn, Martin, *Commerce and Economic Change in West Africa: The Palm Oil Trade in the Nineteenth Century*, Cambridge University Press, Cambridge 1997

Lloyd, Christopher, *The Navy and the Slave Trade: The Suppression of the African Slave Trade in the Nineteenth Century*, Longmans, Green 1949

Lovejoy, Paul, *Slavery, Commerce and Production in the Sokoto Caliphate of West Africa*, Trenton, NJ 2005

Lubbock, Basil, *Cruisers, Corsairs & Slavers. An Account of the Suppression of the Picaroon, Pirate & Slaver by the Royal Navy during the 19th Century*, Brown, Son & Ferguson, Glasgow 1993

Martínez-Fernández, Luis, *Fighting Slavery in the Caribbean: the Life and Times of a British Family in Nineteenth-Century Havana*, M. E. Sharpe, New York 1998

Mathieson, W. L., *Great Britain and the Slave Trade, 1839–1865*, Longmans 1929

Matson, Henry James, *Remarks on the Slave Trade and the African Squadron*, London 1848

Miers, Suzanne, *Britain and the Ending of the Slave Trade*, Longman, London 1975

Montresor, Commander C.J., *Leaves from Memory's Log-Book and Jottings from Old Journals*, London 1887

Norton, the Hon. Mrs Caroline, *A Residence at Sierra Leone, described from a Journal kept on the spot, and from letters written to friends at home by a Lady*, London 1849

Padfield, Peter, *Rule Britannia: the Victorian and Edwardian Navy*, Pimlico, London 2002

Peterson, John, *Province of Freedom: a history of Sierra Leone 1787–1870*, Faber, London 1969

Rankin, E. H., *The White Man's Grave: A Visit to Sierra Leone in 1834*, London 1836

Ross, David A., 'The Career of Domingo Martinez in the Bight of Benin 1833–64', *The Journal of African History* 6, 1 (1965): 79–90

Samo, Samuel, *The Trials of the Slave Traders*, London 1813

Schama, Simon, *Rough Crossings*, BBC Books, London 2005

Scott, Sir Percy Moreton, Bart, *Fifty Years in the Royal Navy*, London 1919

Sherwood, Marika, 'Britain, the Slave Trade and Slavery, 1808–1843', *Race & Class* 46 (2004): 54–77

Smith, Rev. George, *The Case of our West African Cruizers and West African Settlements fairly considered*, London 1848

Smith, Robert, 'The Lagos Consulate 1851–1861, an Outline', *Journal of African History* 15, 3 (1974)

Soulsby, Hugh, *The Right of Search and the Slave Trade in Anglo-American Relations, 1814–1862*, Johns Hopkins University Press, Baltimore, MD 1933

Southam, Brian, *Jane Austen and the Navy*, Hambledon and London 2000

Stockwell, G. S., *The Republic of Liberia: its geography, climate, soil and productions, with a history of its early settlement*, New York 1868

Sundiata, Ibrahim K., *From Slaving to Neoslavery: The Bight of Biafra and Fernando Po in the Era of Abolition 1827–1930*, University of Wisconsin Press, Madison, Wisconsin 1996

Thomas, Hugh, *The Slave Trade: The History of the Atlantic Slave Trade 1440–1870*, Picador, London 1997

Thompson, Thomas, *A Narrative of Facts connected with the Colony of Sierra Leone, addressed to the Friends of the Abolition of the Slave Trade and to the West Indian Planters*, London 1811

Thorpe, Robert, *Letter to William Wilberforce containing remarks on the reports of the Sierra Leone Company, and African Institution*, London 1815, available online at: http://books.google.com/books

Turnbull, David, *Travels in the West: Cuba, with notices of Porto Rico and the Slave Trade*, London 1840

Turner, Michael J., 'The Limits of Abolition: Government, Saints and the "African Question", c. 1780–1820', *English Historical Review* 112, 446 (April 1997): 319–57

Walsh, Rev. Robert, *Notices of Brazil in 1828 and 1829*, London 1830

Ward, W. E. F., *The Royal Navy and the Slavers*, Allen & Unwin, London 1969

Wilmot, Commander Sir Arthur Parry Eardley, *A letter to the Right Hon. Viscount Palmerston MP on the Present State of the African Slave Trade and the necessity of increasing the African Squadron*, London 1853

Yule, Lieutenant Henry, *The African Squadron Vindicated*, London 1850

Index

Index

Index